THE

COMPLETE WORKS

OF

ROBERT BURNS

(SELF-INTERPRETING)

ILLUSTRATED WITH SIXTY ETCHINGS
AND WOOD CUTS, MAPS AND FACSIMILES

VOLUME III

PHILADELPHIA
GEBBIE & CO., PUBLISHERS

POEMS AND SONGS.

INTRODUCTORY NOTE.

THE poetry and prose in the second volume brought us to the end of the Edinburgh period and to the eve of Burns's settlement at Ellisland. This present volume treats entirely of the Ellisland period.

Comment from us in this introduction would be superfluous, inasmuch as our notes run throughout the volume. Burns is now a married man, which event he celebrates in his most jovial manner :

> "I hae a wife o' my ain;
> I'll partake wi' naebody."

(*See* page 6, *infra.*)

G. G.

CONTENTS OF VOLUME III.

POETRY.

	PAGE
Epistle to Hugh Parker	1
Song—Of a' the Airts the Wind can Blaw	3
Song—I hae a Wife o' my Ain	6
Verses in Friars' Carse Hermitage	7
To Alex. Cunningham, Esq., Writer, Edinburgh	9
Song—Anna, thy Charms	11
The Fetê Champêtre	12
Epistle to Robert Graham, Esq., of Fintry, requesting a Favor	15
Song—The Day Returns	18
A Mother's Lament for her Son's Death	19
Song—O were I on Parnassus Hill	20
Song—The Fall of the Leaf	22
Song—I Reign in Jeanie's Bosom	23
Song—It is na, Jean, thy Bonie Face	23
Song—Auld Lang Syne	24
Song—The Silver Tassie	26
Verses on a Parting Kiss	28
Written in Friars' Carse Hermitage (later version)	29
The Poet's Progress	31
Elegy on the Year 1788	35
The Henpecked Husband	37
Versicles on Sign-Posts	38
Song—Robin Shure in Hairst	38
Ode, sacred to the Memory of Mrs. Oswald of Auchencruive	40
Pegasus at Wanlockhead	42
Sappho Rediviva—A Fragment	43
Song—She's Fair and Fause	45
Impromptu Lines to Captain Riddell	47
Lines to John M'Murdo of Drumlanrig	48
Rhyming Reply to a Note from Captain Riddell	49
Verses to Miss Cruikshank—"The Rosebud"	49
Song—Beware o' Bonie Ann	51

PAGE

Ode on the Departed Regency Bill 52
Epistle to James Tennant of Glenconner 55
A New Psalm for the Chapel of Kilmarnock 58
Sketch in Verse, inscribed to the Right Hon. C. J. Fox . 61
The Wounded Hare 64
Delia, an Ode 66
Song—The Gardener wi' his Paidle 67
Song—On a Bank of Flowers 68
Song—Young Jockie was the Blythest Lad 69
Song—The Banks of Nith 70
Song—Jamie Come Try Me 71
Song—I Love my Love in Secret 72
Song—Sweet Tibbie Dunbar 72
Song—The Captain's Lady 73
Song—John Anderson, My Jo 74
Song—My Love she's but a Lassie yet 75
Song—Tam Glen 76
Song—Carle, an' the King come 78
Song—The Laddie's dear sel 79
Song—Whistle o'er the Lave o't 80
Song—My Eppie Adair 80
Epigram on Francis Grose the Antiquary 81
On the late Captain Grose's Peregrinations 82
The Kirk of Scotland's Alarm—A Ballad 85
Sonnet to R. Graham, Esq., on Receiving a Favor 93
Extemporaneous Effusion on being appointed to an Excise
     Division 94
Caledonia—A Ballad 95
Song—Willie brew'd a Peck o' Maut 97
Song—Ca' the Yowes to the Knowes 101
Song—I Gaed a Waefu' Gate Yestreen 102
Song—Ay sae bonie, blythe and gay 103
Song—Highland Harry back again 104
Song—The Battle of Sherramuir 106
Song—The Braes o' Killiecrankie 108
Song—Awa', Whigs, Awa' 110
Song—A Waukrife Minnie 111
Song—The Captive Ribband 112
Song—Farewell to the Highlands 113
The Whistle—A Ballad 114
Address—"To Mary in Heaven" 119
Epistle to Dr. Blacklock 122
Address to the Toothache 126

PAGE

The Five Carlins—An Election Ballad 127
Election Ballad for Westerha' 132
Prologue spoken at the Theatre of Dumfries 133
Sketch—New Year's Day 1790 135
Scots Prologue for Mr. Sutherland 137
Lines to a Friend who Supplied a Newspaper 140
Elegy on Willie Nicol's Mare 142
Song—The Gowden Locks of Anna 143
Song—I murder hate 146
Song—Gudewife, count the lawin 147
Election Ballad at close of contest for representing the Dum-
    fries Burghs, 1790 149
Elegy on Captain Matthew Henderson 155
The Epitaph on   do.   do.   159
Verses on Captain Grose 161

PROSE.

Letter (5) to Richard Brown, Greenock—March 26 163
Letter (2) to Robert Cleghorn, Saughton Mills—March 31 . 164
Letter (5) to Gavin Hamilton, Mauchline—April 166
Letter (2) to William Dunbar, W.S.—April 7 166
Letter (10) to Miss Margt. Chalmers—April 7 168

THE POET'S MARRIAGE.

Letter (5) to James Smith, Linlithgow—April 28 170
Letter (10) to Mrs. Dunlop of Dunlop—April 28 172
Letter (1) to Prof. Dugald Stewart—May 3 173
Letter (11) to Mrs. Dunlop of Dunlop—May 4 174
Letter (1) to Samuel Brown, Kirkoswald—May 4 175
Letter (2) to James Johnson. Music Engraver—May 25 . . 176
Letter (6) to Robert Ainslie, Edinburgh—May 26 177
Letter (12) to Mrs. Dunlop of Dunlop—May 27 177

THE ELLISLAND PERIOD.

Letter (13) to Mrs. Dunlop, Haddington—June 14 179
Letter (7) to Robert Ainslie, Edinburgh—June 15 180
Letter (8) to Robert Ainslie. Edinburgh—June 23 182
Letter (9) to Robert Ainslie, Edinburgh—June 30 183
Letter (14) to Mrs. Dunlop of Dunlop—July 10 185
Letter (3) to Peter Hill, Bookseller, Edinburgh—July 18 . . 188

PAGE

Letter (1) to George Lockhart, Merchant—July 18 190
Letter (1) to Alexander Cunningham, Writer—July 27 . . . 191
Letter (15) to Mrs. Dunlop of Dunlop, Aug. 2 192
Burns's marriage confirmed by Daddie Auld—Aug. 5 . . . 195
Letter (1) to Robert M'Indoe, Mercht., Glasgow—Aug. 5 . 196
Letter (16) to Mrs. Dunlop of Dunlop—Aug. 16 197
Letter (10) to Robert Ainslie, Writer, Edinburgh—Aug. 23 . 199
Letter (2) to John Beugo, Engraver, Edinburgh—Sep. 9 . . 201
Letter (2) to Robert Graham, Esq., of Fintry—Sep. 10 . . 203
Letter (1) to Mrs. Robert Burns, Mauchline—Sep. 12 . . . 205
Letter (11) to Miss Margaret Chalmers—Sep. 16 (last of the
    series) 206
Some account of Peggy Chalmers 210
Letter (1) to Mr. Morison, Wright, Mauchline—Sep. 22 . . 211
Letter (3) to Robert Graham, Esq., of Fintry—Sep. 23 . . 211
Letter (17) to Mrs. Dunlop, of Dunlop—Sep. 27 213
Letter (4) to Peter Hill, Bookseller—Oct. 1 214
Centenary of the Revolution of 1688—Nov. 5 218
Letter (2) to the Editor of "The Star," London—Nov. 8 . 218
Letter (18) to Mrs. Dunlop of Dunlop—Nov. 13 221
Letter (3) to James Johnson, Engraver—Nov. 15 223
Letter (1) to Dr. Blacklock, Edinburgh—Nov. 15 224
Letter (1) to John M'Murdo, Esq., of Drumlanrig—Nov. 26 . 226
Mrs. Burns joins her husband at Ellisland—Dec. 227
Letter (19) to Mrs. Dunlop of Dunlop—Dec. 17 227
Letter (3) to Wm. Cruikshank, Edinburgh—Dec. 229
Letter (1) to John Tennant, Auchenbey—Dec. 22 230

1789.

Letter (20) to Mrs. Dunlop of Dunlop—Jan. 1 233
Letter (1) Gilbert Burns to Robert Burns—Jan. 1 235
Letter (5) to Dr. John Moore, London—Jan. 4 236
Letter (11) to Robert Ainslie, Edinburgh—Jan. 6 239
Letter (2) to John M'Murdo, Esq., of Drumlanrig—Jan. 9 . . 240
Letter (2) to Prof. Dugald Stewart—Jan. 20 242
Letter (2) to the Hon. Henry Erskine—Jan. 22 243
Letter (4) to James Johnson, Music Engraver—Jan. 23 . . 245
Letter (3) to Robt. Cleghorn. Saughton Mills—Jan. 23 . . 245
Letter (1) to Mr. David Blair, Birmingham—Jan. 23 246
Burns's Pocket Pistols—their history 247
Letter (2) to Alexander Cunningham, Esq.—Jan. 24 . . . 248
Letter (1) to Robert Riddell, Esq., of Glenriddell—Feb. . . 250
Letter (1) to the Right Rev. Dr. John Geddes—Feb. 3 . . 251

                                                    PAGE
Bishop Geddes, some account of him 253
Letter to the Right Hon. William Pitt—Feb. 255
Letter (9) to James Burness, Montrose—Feb. 9 259
Letter (1) William Burns to Robert Burns—Feb. 15 261
Letter (1) to William Burns, Longtown—March 2 263
Letter (21) to Mrs. Dunlop of Dunlop—March 4 264
Letter (1) to the Rev. Peter Carfrae—March 266
Letter (2) to William Burns, Longtown—March 10 268
Letter (6) to Dr. John Moore, London—March 23 269
Letter (3) to William Burns, Longtown—March 25 270
Letter (5) to Peter Hill, Bookseller—April 2 271
Letter (4) to William Burns, Longtown—April 15 274
Letter (5) to James Johnson, Music Engraver—April 24 . . 275
Letter (1) to Mrs. M'Murdo, Drumlanrig—May 2 275
Letter (22) to Mrs. Dunlop of Dunlop—May 4 277
Letter (3) to Alex. Cunningham, Esq., Edinburgh—May 4 . 278
Letter (5) to William Burns, Newcastle-on-Tyne—May 5 . 280
Letter (4) to Robert Graham, Esq., of Fintry—May 13 . . 281
Letter (6) to Richard Brown, Port-Glasgow—May 21 . . . 283
Letter (1) to James Hamilton, Grocer, Glasgow—May 26 . 283
Letter (4) to Mr. Wm. Creech. Ellisland. May 30 284
Letter (7) to Gavin Hamilton, Esq., Mauchline—June . . 285
Letter (1) to John M'Auley, Town Clerk, Dumbarton—
    June 4 286
Letter (12) to Robert Ainslie, Writer, Edinburgh—June 8 . 288
Letter (23) to Mrs. Dunlop of Dunlop—June 21 290
Letter (1) to Miss Helen M. Williams. London—July . . 291
Helen Maria Williams, some account of her 296
Letter (5) to Robert Graham, Esq., of Fintry—July 31 . 297
Letter (1) to David Sillar, Merchant, Irvine—Aug. 5 . . . 300
The Irvine Burns' Club. some account of it 300
Letter (5) to Robert Aiken, Esq., Ayr—Aug. 301
Letter (2) to John Logan, Esq., of Knockshinnoch—Aug. 7 302
Dr. M'Gill and the "Kirk's Alarm," some account of . . 303
Sonnet to Mr. Graham, of Fintry—Aug. 10 304
Letter (3) to Mr. Peter Stuart, London—Aug. 305
Peter Stuart's notes regarding Fergusson the poet . . . 306
Letter (6) to William Burns. Newcastle-on-Tyne—Aug. 14 . 307
Birth of the Poet's second son, Francis Wallace—Aug. 18 . 307
Letter (24) to Mrs. Dunlop of Dunlop—Sep. 6 307
Willie, Rob. and Allan. over "a peck o' maut" 310
The Contest for the Scandinavian Whistle 311
Letter (2) to Capt. Riddell of Glenriddell—Oct. 16 311
The third anniversary of Highland Mary's Death . . . 313

PAGE

Letter (13) to Robert Ainslie, Writer, Edinburgh—Nov. 1 . 313
Letter (7) to Richard Brown, Port-Glasgow—Nov. 4 . . . 315
Letter (7) to William Burns, Morpeth—Nov. 10 317
Letter (6) to Robert Graham, Esq., of Fintry—Dec. 9 . . . 318
The great Election contest for the Dumfries Boroughs . . 320
Letter (25) to Mrs. Dunlop of Dunlop—Dec. 13 322
Letter (1) to the Countess-Dowager Glencairn—Dec. . . . 325
Letter (1) to Lady W. M. Constable—Dec. 16 327
Letter (1) to Provost Maxwell, Lochmaben—Dec. 20 329
Letter (1) to George S. Sutherland, Player—Dec. 31 330

1790.

Letter (2) to Gilbert Burns, Mossgiel—Jan. 11 331
Letter (3) to William Dunbar, W.S.—Jan. 14 332
Letter (26) to Mrs. Dunlop of Dunlop—Jan. 25 334
Johnson's Preface to Museum, 3d Vol., published—Feb. 2 . 336
Letter (2) to George S. Sutherland, Dumfries Theatre—
    Feb. 1 337
Letter (6) to Peter Hill, Bookseller—Feb. 2 337
Mademoiselle Burns, some account of her 340
Letter (5) to Wm. Nicol, High School, Edinburgh—Feb. 9 . 341
Letter (2) William Burns to Robert Burns—Jan. 24 344
Letter (8) to Wm. Burns, Newcastle-on-Tyne—Feb. 10 . . . 345
Letter (1) to Dr. Mundell, Dumfries—Feb. 346
Letter (4) to Mr. Cunningham, Esq., Edinburgh—Feb. 13 . 347
Letter (7) to Peter Hill, Bookseller, Edinburgh—March 2 . . 350
Letter (3) William Burns to Robert Burns—March 21 . . . 352
Letter (27) to Mrs. Dunlop of Dunlop—April 10 354
Letter (1) to Alex. Findlater, Supervisor, Dumfries—May . 357
Letter (7) to Dr. John Moore, London—July 14 358
Letter (2) to John Murdoch, Teacher, London—July 16 . . 360
Death of William Burns in London—July 24 361
Letter (1) From John Murdoch to Robert Burns—Sep. 14 . 361
Letter (4) to Robert Cleghorn. Saughton Mills—July 23 . . 362
Letter (3) to John M'Murdo, Esq., Drumlanrig—Aug. 2 . 363
Letter (28) to Mrs. Dunlop of Dunlop—Aug. 8 364
Letter (5) to Alex. Cunningham, Esq., Edinburgh—Aug. 8 364
Letter (1) To Dr. James Anderson, Edinburgh—Sep. . . . 366
Letter (1) to Miss Craik, Arbiegland—Aug. 366
Letter (1) to David Newall, Writer, Dumfries—Sep. 3 . . 368
Letter (7) to Robert Graham. Esq.. of Fintry—Sep. 4 . . . 368
Letter (1) to Alex. Ferguson, Esq. of Craigdarroch—Sep. 3 . 371
Excise Prosecution—Burns as Counsel for the Crown . . . 372

PAGE

Letter (1) to Collector Mitchell. Dumfries—Sep. 374
Ramsay of Auchtertyre visits Ellisland 375
Excise Anecdotes 376
Letter (1) to Crauford Tait, Esq., W.S.—Oct. 15 378
Letter (3) to Prof. Dugald Stewart—Oct.   380
Letter (1) to Captain Grose, F.S.A.—Oct. 381
List of Captain Grose's Publications 382
Letter (6) [to Gavin Hamilton?]—14th June 1788 383

LIST OF ILLUSTRATIONS.

PAINTED BY   ENGRAVED BY   PAGE

Burns and Bonnie Jean (married). J. M. Wright . W. W. Dunbar (Frntp.)
Auld Lang Syne—"And there's a
   hand, my trusty fiere!" . . . H. Faber . . . H. Faber . . .   24
The Banks of the Nith . . . . D. O. Hill . . J. McGoffin . .   70
John Anderson, my jo . . . . . H. Faber . . . H. Faber . . .   74
Willie Brew'd a peck o' Maut . M. Rosenthal. M. Rosenthal .   97
Address to the Toothache . . . W. Small . . J. F. Sabin . . 126
Ellisland . . . . J. Ramage . . A. Willmore . . 163
Mrs. Lewis Hay (Margaret Chal-
   mers) . . . . H. Cook 206
Auld Lang Syne—"We twa hae
   paidl't i' the burn" . . . . . W. Small . . Teyssonnieres . 228
To Mary in Heaven . . . . . . S. Baugh . . . J. S. King . . . 313

WOOD CUT ILLUSTRATION.

PAGE

Fac-simile of Original Manuscript, "Beauteous Rosebud" (To
   Miss Cruickshank) 49

POEMS AND SONGS.

EPISTLE TO HUGH PARKER.

(Cunningham, 1834.)

In this strange land, this uncouth clime,
A land unknown to prose or rhyme ;
Where words ne'er cros't the Muse's heckles,*
Nor limpet in poetic shackles :
A land that Prose did never view it,
Except when drunk he *stacher't* thro' it,   staggered
Here, ambush'd by the *chimla* cheek,   chimney
Hid in an atmosphere of *reek*,   smoke
I hear a wheel thrum i' the *neuk*,   nook
I hear it—for in vain I *leuk*.   look
The red *peat* gleams, a fiery kernel,   turf
Enhuskèd by a fog infernal :
Here, for my wonted rhyming raptures,
I sit and count my sins by chapters ;
For life and *spunk* like ither Christians,   mettle
I'm dwindled down to mere existence,
Wi' nae converse but Gallowa' bodies, †
Wi' nae kenn'd face but "Jenny Geddes." ‡

---

* Heckles or Hackles—an instrument for dressing flax.
  † Ellisland is near the eastern border of the Stewartry of Kirkcudbright, a portion of the district popularly known as Galloway.—J. H.
  ‡ The poet's favorite mare named (in admiration real or mock) after that heroine of Presbyterianism, who, when the Dean of Edinburgh was about to read

III.   A

Jenny, my Pegasean pride!
Dowie she saunters down Nithside, *   spiritless
And ay a westlin leuk she throws,
While tears *hap* o'er her auld brown nose!   hóp
Was it for this, wi' *canny* care,   cautious
Thou *bure* the Bard through many a shire?†   bore
At *howes* or hillocks never stumbled,   hollows
And late or early never grumbled?—
O had I power like inclination,
I'd *heeze* thee up a constellation,   hoist
To canter with the Sagitarre,
Or *loup* the ecliptic like a bar;   leap
Or turn the pole like any arrow;
Or, when auld Phœbus bids good-morrow,
Down the zodiac urge the race,
And cast dirt on his godship's face;
For I could *lay* my bread and *kail*   wager   broth
He'd ne'er cast *saut* upo' thy tail.—‡   salt
Wi' a' this care and a' this grief,
And sma', sma' prospect of relief,
And nought but *peat-reek*§ i' my head,
How can I write what ye can read?—

Tarbolton, twenty-fourth o' June,
Ye'll find me in a better tune ; *
But till we meet and *weet* our whistle,   wet
Tak this excuse for nae epistle.

ROBERT BURNS.

[The foregoing appears to be the earliest result of the bard's
poetic musings, after taking possession of his farm in Dumfries-
shire. He arrived at Ellisland on 12th June, as we learn from
his correspondence, and until a new house could be built for him,
he had to put up with the wretched accommodation so humorously
described in the text.

Sometime during the preceding month of May, the poet, after
having privately adopted Jean Armour as his mate for life, went
through some legal formula in the office of Mr. Gavin Hamilton,
by which she obtained a title to be publicly designated "Mrs.
Burns." Accordingly, to this month of June, 1788, the poet after-
wards referred as his "honeymoon" period, although some ten
days thereof were spent in solitude by the banks of the Nith
at Ellisland.

The gentlemen to whom the preceding Epistle was addressed is
referred to in one of the poet's letters to Mr. Robert Muir of
Kilmarnock. On 26th August 1787, he sends his compliments to
Messrs. W. & H. Parker, and adds, "I hope Hughoc is going on
and prospering with God and Miss M'Causlin." We have no means
of ascertaining what degree of success attended his courtship of
that lady: his brother William, to whom the masonic song given
at p. 39 vol. II, is addressed, succeeded to the estate of Assloss, on the
death of his mother's brother, in 1802. According to Allan Cun-
ningham, Hugh Parker died about 1824, and the poem in the
text was then found among his papers.]

OF A' THE AIRTS THE WIND CAN BLAW.

Tune—"Miss Admiral Gordon's Strathspey."

(JOHNSON'S MUSEUM, 1790.)

OF a' the *airts* the wind can blaw,   points
    I dearly like the west,
For there the bonie lassie lives,
    The lassie I lo'e best :

---

* Tarbolton fair-day.—J. H.

There's wild-woods grow, and rivers *row*,*   roll
And mony a hill between :
But day and night my fancy's flight
Is ever wi' my Jean.

I see her in the dewy flowers,
I see her sweet and fair :
I hear her in the tunefu' birds,
I hear her charm the air :
There's not a bonie flower that springs
By fountain, *shaw*, or green ;   woodland
There's not a bonie bird that sings,
But minds me o' my Jean.

[This is a universal favorite among the lyrics of the author.
His note concerning it is simply this :—"The air is by Marshall,
the song I composed out of compliment to Mrs. Burns. *N.B.*—It
was during the honey-moon." The germ of the song, as we noted
before, is found in the fragment at page 123, vol. I.

"Tho' mountains rise, and deserts howl,
    And oceans roar between, &c."

We must now imagine the poet in his solitude at Ellisland,
betwixt the 12th and 22d of June, while his Jean is at Moss-

---

* Many have stumbled at this line. In Johnson's *Museum* it reads :—

"There wild-woods grow, &c."

In Wood's *Songs of Scotland :*—

"Though wild woods grow ;"

both of the proposed emendations being designed to improve the logic and
grammar of the verse. Robert Chambers says :—"It appears that both (of these
proposed improved) readings are wrong. for in the original manuscript of
Burns's contributions to Johnson, in the possession of (the late) Alexander
Hastie Esq., the line is written :—

"There's wild woods grow, &c.,"

as in our text. It is an example of a kind of syllogism occasionally employed
by Burns, in which the major proposition is merely expletive." It is only neces-
sary to add to this that the expression is idiomatic Scotch, though, like many
other ancient terms of speech, becoming obsolescent even in Scotland.—J. H.

giel—to quote his own words—"regularly, and constantly apprenticed to my mother and sisters in their dairy and other rural business." In the immediately preceding poem, he represents even "Jenny Geddes" as being homesick—

> "And ay a westlin leuk she throws,
>   While tears hap o'er her auld brown nose!"

and in this little song, Jenny's master follows her example.

> "Of a' the airts the wind can blaw.
>   I dearly like the west," &c.

Although Ayrshire is not directly west from Ellisland, but north-west, it is the Dumfries-shire custom always to speak of Ayrshire as "the West." The couplet,

> "There's wild-woods grow, and rivers row,
>   And mony a hill between"

would naturally give an American the idea that a considerable distance separated Ellisland from Mauchline. The distance is exactly 46 miles.

The briefness of the song has tempted some versifiers to make additions to it, for the sixteen lines of the text just go once through the melody. In particular Mr. John Hamilton, music-seller, Edinburgh, made a comparatively successful continuation, in two double stanzas, beginning,

> "O blaw, ye westlin winds blaw saft."

These verses by Hamilton are very musical and expressive, but were unfortunately composed under the mistaken idea, that the absence of Jean referred to in Burns's song, was that of Spring 1786, when she was removed to Paisley to avoid him. On the poet's own authority, however, the date and the occasion of the song are rendered certain, and at that time, instead of imploring the west winds to "bring the lassie back" to him, he had only to return to *her;* and moreover, she could not come "back" to Ellisland, where she had never yet been.

Notwithstanding these anachronisms, it is no small compliment to Mr. Hamilton, that Burns's own sixteen lines are now seldom dissociated from his imitator's supplementary ones. Cunningham, indeed, indicates that the whole thirty-two lines are by Burns; Lockhart, too, quotes the added lines as the poet's own; and

Professor Wilson, in his famous "Essay," adopts Hamilton's addendum as an authentic part of the song. In these circumstances, it seems right to record here the supplementary stanzas :—

> "O blaw, ye westlin winds, blaw saft, amang the leafy trees ;
> Wi' gentle gale, frae muir and dale, bring hame the laden bees :
> And bring the lassie back to me, that's ay sae neat and clean :
> Ae blink o' her wad banish care, sae charming is my Jean.

> "What sighs and vows, amang the knowes, hae pass'd atween us twa !
> How fain to meet, how wae to part, that day she gaed awa !
> The Powers aboon can only ken (to whom the heart is seen)
> That nane can be sae dear to me as my sweet, lovely Jean." *

John Hamilton, the author of these lines, was born in 1761, and died in 1814. He was much respected in Edinburgh society ; and Sir Walter Scott acknowledges his indebtedness to him as a contributor to his "Minstrelsy of the Scottish Border." The *Scots Magazine* thus announces his death :—"Sept. 23, 1814. In the 53rd year of his age, after a lingering and painful illness, John Hamilton, late music-seller in this city, author of many favorite Scots songs, and composer of several melodies of considerable merit."]

SONG—I HAE A WIFE O' MY AIN.

(JOHNSON'S MUSEUM, 1792.)

I HAE a wife o' my ain,
    I'll partake wi' naebody ;
I'll take Cuckold frae nane,
    I'll *gie* Cuckold to naebody.   give

I *hae* a penny to spend,   have
    There—thanks to naebody .
I hae naething to lend,
    I'll borrow frae naebody.

---

* Burns's own parallel couplet, in this connection, runs thus :—

    "That, dearer than my deathless soul, I still would love my Jean."

I am naebody's lord,
　I'll be slave to naebody ;
I hae a gude *braid* sword,　　　　broad
　I'll tak *dunts* frae naebody.　　　blows

I'll be merry and free,
　I'll be sad for naebody ;
Naebody cares for me,
　I care for naebody.

[This off-hand but characteristic effusion appears to have been produced at Ellisland, about the same time as the preceding song. The original MS. is in the British Museum. Burns wrote to Dr. Blacklock, and others of his friends (according to his own phrase) "from the field of Matrimony in June," and these verses, in imitation of an old ballad, were in all likelihood dashed off impromptu in one of those letters. Currie's observations in connection with this production are as follows :— "Pleased with surveying the grounds he was about to cultivate, and with rearing a building that should give shelter to his wife and children, and (as he fondly hoped) to his own grey hairs, sentiments of independence buoyed up his mind, pictures of domestic content and peace rose on his imagination ; and a few days passed away, as he himself informs us, the most tranquil, if not the happiest, which he ever experienced."]

(This "canty" little effusion is just the natural outburst of a newly married man, rejoicing that he *is* married, and resolved to be happy. The piece is an imitation of an old ballad, and, like most of these old-world productions, not remarkable for delicacy. The two first lines are from an old song.—J. H.)

VERSES IN FRIARS' CARSE HERMITAGE.

(CURRIE, 1800.)

THOU whom chance may hither lead,
Be thou clad in russet weed,
Be thou deckt in silken stole,
Grave these maxims on thy soul.

Life is but a day at most,
Sprung from night in darkness lost;[1]
Hope not sunshine every hour,
Fear not clouds will always lour.

Happiness is but a name,
Make content and ease thy aim,
Ambition is a meteor-gleam;
Fame a restless idle dream;
Peace, th' tend'rest flow'r of spring;
Pleasures, insects on the wing;
Those that sip the dew alone—
Make the butterflies thy own;
Those that would the bloom devour—
Crush the locusts, save the flower.

For the future be prepar'd,
Guard wherever thou can'st guard;
But thy utmost duly done,
Welcome what thou can'st not shun.
Follies past, give thou to air,
Make their *consequence* thy care:
Keep the name of Man in mind,
And dishonor not thy kind.
Reverence with lowly heart
Him, whose wondrous work thou art;
Keep His Goodness still in view,
Thy trust, and thy example, too.

Stranger, go! Heaven be thy guide!
Quod the Beadsman * of *Nidside*.   Nithside

---

*Beadsman or bedesman means literally a man whose specialty it is to pray, and hence it is a very appropriate appellation for the inhabitant of a hermitage, bound to pray for those by whose bounty he is sheltered and fed. The word is from Anglo-Saxon *bead*, a prayer, and the little ornaments known as *beads* are so called because they were first used to count prayers by, each one dropped indicating one prayer said, the prayer thus giving name to the ornaments, not they to the prayers.—J. H.

[Several manuscript copies of this piece are in existence. One of these bearing date, 28th June, 1788, the author transcribed in a letter to Mrs. Dunlop of 10th August, in which he tells her that the lines are "almost the only favors the Muses have conferred" since he came to that neighborhood. In the same letter, he also transcribes fourteen lines of one of his Epistles to Mr. Graham of Fintry : it therefore seems evident that he was now trying to act on the advice which Dr. Moore had given him a twelvemonth before. A letter from that gentleman, dated 23rd May 1787, has this passage :— "You ought to deal more sparingly for the future in the provincial dialect : why should you, by using that, limit the number of your admirers to those who understand the Scottish, when you can extend it to all persons of taste who understand the English language?" *

The visit which the poet paid to Ayrshire about 22nd June was a very short one, for he was back to Ellisland within a week. His next neighbor, at less than a mile's distance up the Nith, was the proprietor of Friars Carse — Mr. Robert Riddell (styled, of Glenriddell)—a gentleman of antiquarian and literary tastes, who kindly welcomed him, and gave him a key to admit him to his grounds at pleasure. In a little hermitage erected there, the poet was fond of spending an occasional musing hour, and the verses in the text are understood to have been composed under its shelter.]

¹ Two lines are here introduced in some of the copies :—
Day, how rapid in its flight,
Day, how few may see the night !

TO ALEX. CUNNINGHAM, ESQ., WRITER, EDINBURGH.

(DOUGLAS, 1877.)

ELLISLAND, NITHSDALE, *July 27th,* 1788.

My godlike friend—nay, do not stare,
  You think the phrase is odd-like ;
But 'God is Love,' the saints declare,
  Then surely thou art god-like.

---

* This edition of Burns fulfills Dr. Moore's suggestion by extending the number of the poet's admirers "to all persons of taste who understand the English language." Strange that it should have taken 100 years to make the publishing world aware of "this long-felt want !"—J. H.

And is thy ardor still the same?
And kindled still at ANNA?
Others may boast a partial flame,
But thou art a volcano!

Ev'n Wedlock asks not love beyond
Death's tie-dissolving portal;
But thou, omnipotently fond,
May'st promise love immortal!

Thy wounds such healing powers defy,
Such symptoms dire attend them,
That last great antihectic try—
MARRIAGE perhaps may mend them.

Sweet Anna has an air—a grace,
Divine, magnetic, touching;
She talks, she charms—but who can trace
The process of bewitching?

    *   *   *   *

My spurr-galled, spavined Pegasus makes so hobbling a progress over the course of *Extempore*, that I must here alight, and try the footpath of plain prose.

[The above lines form the introduction to a letter which will appear in its proper place, among the bard's correspondence. The original MS. is in possession of Mr. Cunningham's son—James Cunningham, Esq., W. S., Edinburgh. Several other manuscripts of the poet, in his possession, will be made use of as we progress. In the letter referred to, Burns says, with respect to his own marriage,—"This was a step of which I had no idea when you and I were together. . . . . When I tell you that Mrs. Burns was once 'my Jean,' you will know the rest. . . . She does not come from Ayrshire till my new house be ready, so I am eight or ten days at Mauchline and this place alternately."

The "Anna" referred to in the verses, of whom Cunningham was so much enamored, was a celebrated Edinburgh beauty, described by Burns as "an amiable and accomplished young lady with whom I fancy I have the honor of being a little acquainted." She was Miss Anne Stewart, daughter of John Stewart, Esq., of

East Craigs. The "omnipotently fond" lover, however, soon learned that his affections had been misplaced: for within six months after the date of Burns's letter recommending "marriage" to his friend, as the grand cure for the wounds from Cupid's shaft, she became the wife of his rival, Mr. Forrest Dewar, Surgeon. We find the name of this gentleman on the list of Town Councillors of Edinburgh who were elected in October 1788, William Creech being then one of the Bailies.]

SONG—ANNA, THY CHARMS.

(EDINBURGH ED., 1793.)

ANNA, thy charms my bosom fire,
   And waste my soul with care ;
But ah ! how bootless to admire,
   When fated to despair !

Yet in thy presence, lovely Fair,
   To hope may be forgiven ;
For sure 'twere impious to despair
   So much in sight of Heaven.

[This little epigrammatic song has hitherto been a puzzle among the productions of Burns. It occupies a whole page in his editions of 1793 and 1794, and no annotator has ever ventured to throw any light upon it. In short, had the song not appeared under the author's own authority, its authenticity might well have been questioned; for the language does not seem to flow naturally from his lips. and there is no known incident in his life to which it might refer.

The note attached to the preceding piece clears up the mystery satisfactorily. The song in the text is simply a vicarious effusion, intended to proceed from the lips of the author's forlorn friend Cunningham.]

THE FÊTE CHAMPÊTRE.

Tune—" Killicrankie."

(GILBERT BURNS'S ED., 1820.)

O WHA will to Saint Stephen's House,*
   To do our errands there, man?
O wha will to Saint Stephen's House
   O' th' merry lads of Ayr, man?
Or will we send a man o' law?
   Or will we send a sodger?
Or him wha led o'er Scotland a'
   The meikle Ursa-Major? †

Come, will ye court a noble lord,
   Or buy a score o' lairds, man?
For worth and honor pawn their word,
   Their vote shall be Glencaird's, ‡ man.
Ane *gies* them coin, ane gies them wine,   *gives*
   Anither gies them clatter;
Annbank, § wha guess'd the ladies' taste,
   He gies a Fête Champêtre.

When Love and Beauty heard the news,
   The gay green-woods amang, man;
Where, gathering flowers, and busking bowers,
   They heard the blackbird's sang, man:

---

* Saint Stephen's House :—the British Parliament is so named from its having originally held its sittings in a chapel dedicated to St. Stephen.—J. H.
† James Boswell, who accompanied Dr. Johnson on his Scottish tour. The gruff old lexicographer was contemptuously designated *Ursa-Major* by old Boswell of Auchinleck, in reply to his son's boast that he was " a great luminary, quite a constellation."—J. H.
‡ Sir John Whitefoord, then residing at Cloncaird or " Glencaird."
§ William Cunninghame, Esq., of Annbank and Enterkin.

A vow, they seal'd it with a kiss,
　　Sir Politics to fetter ;
As their's alone, the patent bliss,
　　To hold a Fête Champêtre.

Then mounted Mirth on gleesome wing,
　　O'er hill and dale she flew, man ;
Ilk wimpling burn, ilk crystal spring,　each purling brook
　　Ilk glen and *shaw* she knew, man :　　wood
She summon'd every social sprite,
　　That sports by wood or water,
On th' bonie banks of Ayr to meet,
　　And keep this Fête Champêtre.

Cauld Boreas, wi' his boisterous crew,
　　Were bound to stakes like *kye*, man ;　　cows
And Cynthia's car, o' silver fu',
　　Clamb up the starry sky, man :
Reflected beams dwell in the streams,
　　Or down the current shatter ;
The western breeze steals thro' the trees,
　　To view this Fête Champêtre.

How many a robe sae gaily floats !
　　What sparkling jewels glance, man !
To Harmony's enchanting notes,
　　As moves the mazy dance, man.
The echoing wood, the winding flood,
　　Like Paradise did glitter,
When angels met, at Adam's *yett*,　　gate
　　To hold their Fête Champêtre.

When Politics came there, to mix
　　And make his ether-stane,* man !

---

* Adder-stone :—in allusion to a superstition that the little round, streaked globules occasionally found in waste places were formed from the slime of adders, and operated as charms. They are really beads fashioned and worn by the early Britons.—J. H.

He circled round the magic ground,
  But entrance found he nane, man :
He blush'd for shame, he quat his name,
  Forswore it, every letter,
Wi' humble prayer to join and share
  This festive Fête Champêtre.

[Writing to an Edinburgh correspondent in September 1788, the
poet says—"I am generally about half my time in Ayrshire, with
my 'darling Jean,' and then, at lucid intervals, I throw my horny
fist across my be-cobwebbed lyre, much in the same manner as an
old wife throws her hands across the spokes of her spinning-wheel."
It is pleasing to hear him admit that his "lucid intervals" of
devotion to the Muse occurred while he was enjoying the society
of his wife; and accordingly we may be certain that the above
poem was the result of one of those visits. The incident thus
celebrated occurred during the summer or autumn of 1788 ; but
Gilbert Burns, in his account of the transaction, does not say how
his brother was led to interest himself so much in this local affair.
The "Fête Champetre" was an entertainment given by William
Cunninghame, Esq., of Annbank and Enterkin, to the gentry of
Ayrshire, on the occasion of his attaining his majority and enter-
ing on possession of his grandfather's estates. He wished to in-
troduce himself with *éclat* to the county, and hit upon the novelty
of an open air festival within his grounds on the banks of the
Ayr. The peasantry believed that the real object of the gathering
was a political one, with a view to arrange about the candidature
at the next parliamentary election. The poet, however, explains
that Love and Beauty conspired to exclude politics from the
charmed circle.

The entertainer, Mr. Cunninghame, was some years afterwards
(June 18, 1794) married to Miss Catherine Stewart, eldest daughter
of Major General Alexander Stewart of Afton. The only issue of
that marriage, William Allason Cunninghame, Esq., of Logan and
Afton, is still alive.]

EPISTLE TO ROBERT GRAHAM, Esq. OF FINTRY,

REQUESTING A FAVOR.*

(CURRIE, 1800.)

WHEN Nature her great master-piece design'd,
And fram'd her last, best work, the human mind,
Her eye intent on all the mazy plan,
She form'd of various parts the various Man.

Then first she calls the useful many forth ;
Plain plodding Industry, and sober Worth :
Thence peasants, farmers, native sons of earth,
And merchandise' whole genus take their birth :
Each prudent cit a warm existence finds,
And all mechanics' many-apron'd kinds.
Some other rarer sorts are wanted yet,
The lead and buoy are needful to the net :
The *caput mortuum* of gross desires
Makes a material for mere knights and squires ;
The martial phosphorus is taught to flow,
She kneads the lumpish philosophic dough,
Then marks th' unyielding mass with grave designs,
Law, physic, politics, and deep divines ;
Last, she sublimes th' Aurora of the poles,
The flashing elements of female souls.

The order'd system fair before her stood,
Nature, well pleas'd, pronounc'd it very good ;

---

* " This is our poet's first epistle to Graham of Fintry. It is not equal to his later one—'Late crippled of an arm,' &c., but it contains too much of the characteristic vigor of its author to be suppressed. A little more knowledge of natural history, or of chemistry was wanted to enable him to execute the original conception correctly."—*Currie.*

But ere she gave creating labor o'er,
Half-jest, she tried one curious labor more.
Some spumy, fiery, *ignis fatuus* matter,
Such as the slightest breath of air might scatter ;
With arch-alacrity and conscious glee,
(Nature may have her whim as well as we,
Her Hogarth-art perhaps she meant to show it),
She forms the thing and christens it—a Poet :
Creature, tho' oft the prey of care and sorrow,
When blest to-day, unmindful of to-morrow ;
A being form'd t' amuse his graver friends,
Admir'd and prais'd—and there the homage ends ;
A mortal quite unfit for Fortune's strife,
Yet oft the sport of all the ills of life ;
Prone to enjoy each pleasure riches give,
Yet haply wanting wherewithal to live ;
Longing to wipe each tear, to heal each groan,
Yet frequent all unheeded in his own.
But honest Nature is not quite a Turk,
She laugh'd at first, then felt for her poor work :
Pitying the propless climber of mankind,
She cast about a *standard tree* to find ;
And, to support his helpless woodbine state,
Attach'd him to the generous, truly great :
A title, and the only one I claim,
To lay strong hold for help on bounteous Graham.

Pity the tuneful Muses' hapless train,
Weak, timid landsmen on life's stormy main !
Their hearts no selfish stern absorbent stuff,
That never gives—tho' humbly takes enough ;
The little fate allows, they share as soon,
Unlike sage proverb'd Wisdom's hard-wrung boon :
The world were blest did bliss on them depend,
Ah, that " the friendly e'er should want a friend!"
Let Prudence number o'er each sturdy son,
Who life and wisdom at one race begun,

Who feel by reason and who give by rule,
(Instinct's a brute, and sentiment a fool!)
Who make poor "will do" wait upon "I should"—
We own they're prudent, but who feels they're good?
Ye wise ones, hence! ye hurt the social eye!
God's image rudely etch'd on base alloy!
But come ye who the godlike pleasure know,
Heaven's attribute distinguish'd—to bestow!
Whose arms of love would grasp the human race:
Come *thou* who giv'st with all a courtier's grace;
FRIEND OF MY LIFE, true patron of my rhymes!
Prop of my dearest hopes for future times.
Why shrinks my soul half blushing, half afraid,
Backward, abash'd to ask thy friendly aid?
I know my need, I know thy giving hand,
I crave thy friendship at thy kind command;
But there are such who court the tuneful Nine—
Heavens! should the branded character be mine!
Whose *verse* in manhood's pride sublimely flows,
Yet vilest reptiles in their begging *prose*.

Mark, how their lofty independent spirit
Soars on the spurning wing of injur'd merit!
Seek you the proofs in private life to find?
Pity the best of words should be but wind!
So, to heaven's gates the lark's shrill song ascends,
But grovelling on the earth the carol ends.
In all the clam'rous cry of starving want,
They dun Benevolence with shameless front;
Oblige them, patronise their tinsel lays—
They persecute you all your future days!
Ere my poor soul such deep damnation stain,
My horny fist assume the plough again,
The pie-bald jacket let me patch once more,
On eighteenpence a week I've liv'd before.
Tho', thanks to Heaven, I dare even that last shift,
I trust, meantime, my boon is in thy gift:

III.   B

That, plac'd by thee upon the wish'd-for height,
Where, man and nature fairer in her sight,
My Muse may imp her wing for some sublimer flight.

[The date of this production is made certain by the poet's letter
to Miss Chalmers, written from Ellisland, 16th September, 1788.
He there says—"I very lately—namely, since harvest began—wrote
a poem, not in imitation, but in the manner, of Pope's *Moral
Epistles*. It is only a short essay, just to try the strength of my
Muse's pinion in that way." In the same letter he says, "You
will be pleased to hear that I have laid aside idle *éclat*, and bind
every day after my reapers. To save me from that horrid situa-
tion of at any time going down, in a losing bargain of a farm,
to misery, I have taken my excise instructions, and have my com-
mission in my pocket for any emergency of fortune. If I could
set all before your view, whatever disrespect, you, in common with
the world, have for this business, I know you would approve of
my idea."
The favor, therefore, that our poet requested from Mr. Graham
in a prose letter which accompanied his poetic epistle, was to
use his influence to have him appointed Excise officer of the dis-
trict in proximity to Ellisland. That desire of his was gratified
about one year after the date of the above Epistle.]

SONG—THE DAY RETURNS.

Tune—"Seventh of November."

(JOHNSON'S MUSEUM, 1790.)

I composed this song out of compliment to one of the hap-
piest and worthiest married couples in the world, Robert Rid-
dell. Esq., of Glenriddell. and his lady. At their fireside I
have enjoyed more pleasant evenings than at all the houses
of fashionable people in this country put together; and to
their kindness and hospitality I am indebted for many of the
happiest hours of my life.—*R. B.*, 1791.

THE day returns, my bosom burns,
  The blissful day we twa did meet :
Tho' winter wild in tempest toil'd,
  Ne'er summer-sun was half sae sweet

Than a' the pride that loads the tide,
　And crosses o'er the sultry line;
Than kingly robes, than crowns and globes,
　˙Heav'n gave me more—it made thee mine!

While day and night can bring delight,
　Or Nature aught of pleasure give;
While joys above my mind can move,
　For thee and thee alone I live.
When that grim foe of life below
　Comes in between to make us part,
The iron hand that breaks our band,
　It breaks my bliss—it breaks my heart!

[The date of this song is proved to be prior to 16th September 1788, by the poet's letter of that date to Miss Chalmers, in which the song is transcribed. He remarks thus :—"Johnson's Collection of Scots songs is going on in the third volume; and of consequence finds me a consumpt for a great deal of idle metre. One of the most tolerable things I have done in that way is two stanzas I made to an air a musical gentleman of my acquaintance composed for the anniversary of his wedding-day, which happens on the 7th of November."].

A MOTHER'S LAMENT

FOR THE DEATH OF HER SON.

(JOHNSON'S MUSEUM, 1790.)

FATE gave the word, the arrow sped,
　And pierc'd my darling's heart;
And with him all the joys are fled
　Life can to me impart.

By cruel hands the sapling drops,
　In dust dishonor'd laid;
So fell the pride of all my hopes,
　My age's future shade.

The mother-linnet in the brake
  Bewails her ravish'd young;
So I, for my lost darling's sake,
  Lament the live-day long.

Death, oft I've fear'd thy fatal blow,
  Now, fond, I bare my breast;
O, do thou kindly lay me low
  With him I love, at rest!

[The date of this pathetic lyric is proved by the poet's letter to Mrs. Dunlop of 27th September 1788, in which he says, "I am just arrived at Mauchline from Nithsdale, and will be here a fortnight. I was on horseback this morning by three o'clock; for between my wife and my farm is just forty-six miles. As I jogged on in the dark I was taken with a poetic fit as follows:"—The above is then transcribed with the explanation that it represents "Mrs. Fergusson of Craigdarroch's lamentation for the death of her son, an uncommonly promising youth of eighteen or nineteen years of age." A newspaper obituary gives the date of the youth's death—November 19, 1787. It seems that Mrs. Stewart of Stair, an early patron of the poet, lost her only son by death about the same time (5th December, 1787). Accordingly, it was but natural that Burns should enclose her a copy of this Lament, which applied as closely to her bereavement as to that suffered by Mrs. Fergusson.]

SONG—O WERE I ON PARNASSUS HILL.

(JOHNSON'S MUSEUM, 1790.)

O WERE I on Parnassus hill,
Or had o' Helicon my fill,
That I might catch poetic skill,
    To sing how dear I love thee!
But Nith *maun* be my Muses' well,   must
My Muse must be thy bonie sel',
On Corsincon I'll *glowr* and spell,   gaze
    And write how dear I love thee.*

---

* Byron imitates the rhyme and refrain of this song of Burns in his celebrated song "Maid of Athens."—J. H.

Then come, sweet Muse, inspire my lay !
For a' the *lee-lang* simmer's day   live-long
I couldna sing, I couldna say,
    How much, how dear, I love thee,
I see thee dancing o'er the green,
Thy waist sae *jimp*, thy limbs sae *clean*,   small }
                                               shapely }
Thy tempting lips, thy roguish een—
    By Heaven and Earth I love thee !

By night, by day, a-field, at hame,
The thoughts o' thee my breast inflame ;
And ay I muse and sing thy name—
    I only live to love thee.
Tho' I were doom'd to wander on,
Beyond the sea, beyond the sun,
Till my last weary sand was run ;
    Till then—and then I love thee !

[This song in honor · of Mrs. Burns was composed at Nithside
during the summer or autumn of 1788, while she still remained
in Ayrshire. It is perhaps the most luxuriantly rich of all his
amatory ballads, and has the fine distinction of being perfectly
legitimate. The "Corsincon" on which the eye of the bard was
fixed during his musings, is a high conical hill at the base of
which the infant Nith enters Dumfries-shire from New Cumnock
in Ayrshire. The latter half of the second stanza of this lyric has
been often instanced as the very perfection of personal description
in a love-song. Writing to Miss Chalmers regarding his Jean about
the date of this composition, he says :— "I have got the hand-
somest figure, the sweetest temper, the soundest constitution, and
the kindest heart in the country. . . . And she has (O the partial
lover ! you will cry) the finest 'wood-note wild' I ever heard."
The air in Johnson is by Oswald—"My Love is lost to me."]

THE FALL OF THE LEAF.

(JOHNSON'S MUSEUM, 1790.)

THE lazy mist hangs from the brow of the hill,
Concealing the course of the dark winding rill ;
How languid the scenes, late so sprightly, appear !
As Autumn to Winter resigns the pale year.

The forests are leafless, the meadows are brown,
And all the gay foppery of summer is flown :
Apart let me wander, apart let me muse,
How quick Time is flying, how keen Fate pursues !

How long I have liv'd—but how much liv'd in vain,
How little of life's scanty span may remain,
What aspects old Time in his progress has worn,
What ties cruel Fate, in my bosom has torn.

How foolish, or worse, till our summit is gain'd !
And downward, how weaken'd, how darken'd, how
      pain'd !
Life is not worth having with all it can give—
For something beyond it poor man sure must live.

[This grave production, apparently freshly composed, was sent
along with "The Mother's Lament" to Dr. Blacklock, in the
poet's letter to him, dated from Mauchline 15th November 1788.
He there says—"I have sent you two melancholy things, and I
tremble lest they should too well suit the tone of your present
feelings." He adds that he is "to move bag and baggage to Niths-
dale in a fortnight," and that he is "more and more pleased with
the step he took regarding Jean."]

I REIGN IN JEANIE'S BOSOM.

(JOHNSON'S MUSEUM, 1796.)

LOUIS,* what reck I by thee,
    Or Geordie † on his ocean?
Dyvor, beggar *louns* to me,   bankrupt   low fellows
    I reign in Jeanie's bosom.

Let her crown my love her law,
    And in her breast enthrone me,
Kings and nations—*swith awa!*   off with you
    Reif randies I disown ye !   thieving bullies

[Such were the poet's sentiments, and such his expressions when
he welcomed his wife to Nithsdale in the first week of December
1788. His house at Ellisland was not yet in a seasoned condition
for being used with comfort as a dwelling, and he had obtained
the temporary use of a picturesque lodging about a mile farther
down the Nith, at a place called "The Isle," from which locality
his letters were occasionally dated during that winter.

Cunningham has observed regarding the style of this little song:
—"It is one of Burns's happy efforts, although the language is
perhaps too peculiar to be fully felt by any, save Scotchmen; but
to them it comes with a compact vigor of expression not usual in
words fitted to music."]

IT IS NA, JEAN, THY BONIE FACE.

(JOHNSON'S MUSEUM, 1792.)

IT is na, Jean, thy bonie face,
    Nor shape that I admire ;
Altho' thy beauty and thy grace
    Might weel awake desire.

---

* King of France.
† George III., King of Britain.

Something, in ilka part o' thee,
  To praise, to love, I find,
But dear as is thy form to me,
  Still dearer is thy mind.

Nae mair ungenerous wish I hae,
  Nor stronger in my breast,
Than, if I canna mak thee sae,
  At least to see thee blest.

Content am I, if Heaven shall give
  But happiness to thee ;
And as wi' thee I'd wish to live,
  For thee I'd bear to die.

[These verses, which read like a calmly affectionate address by
Burns to his wife, he informs us himself " were originally English,
and that he gave them a Scotch dress." They are set in the
Museum to a tune by Oswald, called " The Maid's Complaint,"
which Stenhouse says is one of the finest Scottish airs that Oswald
ever composed.]

AULD LANG SYNE.

(JOHNSON'S MUSEUM, 1796.)

SHOULD auld acquaintance be forgot,
  And never brought to mind ?
Should auld acquaintance be forgot,
  And auld lang syne !

Chorus.—For auld lang syne, my dear,
      For auld lang syne,
    We'll tak a cup o' kindness yet,
      For auld lang syne.

And surely ye'll be your pint *stowp!*   flagon
  And surely I'll be mine !
And we'll tak a cup o' kindness yet,
  For auld lang syne.[1]
      For auld, &c.

H. FABER, PINX. & ETCH?

We twa hae run about the braes,
   And *pou'd* the *gowans* fine ;   pulled   daisies
But we've wander'd mony a weary *fitt*   foot
   Sin' auld lang syne.
        For auld, &c.

We twa hae *paidl'd* in the burn,   waded
   Frae morning sun till *dine ;*   dinner-time (*noon*)
But seas between us braid hae roar'd
   Sin' auld lang syne.
        For auld, &c.

And there's a hand, my trusty *fiere!*   comrade
   And gie's a hand o' thine !
And we'll tak a right *gude-willie*   mutually friendly
    waught, *   draught
   For auld lang syne.
        For auld, &c.

[Of the two versions of this song, we adapt for our text that supplied to Johnson in preference to the copy made for George Thomson. The arrangement of the verses is more natural : it wants the redundant syllable in the fourth line of stanza first : and the spelling of the Scotch words is more correct. The poet transcribed the song for Mrs. Dunlop in his letter to her, dated 17th December 1788, and it is unfortunate that Dr. Currie did not print a verbatim copy of it, along with that letter, instead of simply referring his reader to the Thomson correspondence for it. Thomson's closing verse stands second in Johnson, where it seems in its proper place, as having manifest reference to the earlier stages of the interview between the long separated friends. Many of our readers must have observed, that when a social company unites in singing the song before dispersing, it is the custom for the singers

---

* Gude-willie waught:—No expression of Burns has been more generally misunderstood than this. Hogg and Motherwell, Cunningham. Chambers and Waddell print it "*gude willie-waught*" as if "*willie-waught*" were a separate word. and Chambers even glosses the fabricated compound "draught." There is no such word. "*Gude-willie*" is a common Scotch adjective signifying with hearty good-will, friendly, and is the antonym or opposite of "*ill-willie*," signifying malicious (See Vol. I., p. 317, l. 2). "*Waught*" is a word in every-day use for a hearty drink. The expression, then, simply means a drink taken with hearty, mutual good-will.—J. H.

to join hands in a circle at the words, "And there's a hand," &c. This ought to conclude the song, with the chorus sung rapidly and emphatically thereafter. But how awkwardly, and out-of-place, does the slow singing of Thomson's closing verse come in after that excitement! "And surely ye'll be your pint stowp," &c—No, no! The play is over: no more pint stowps!

The poet pretended, both to Mrs. Dunlop and George Thomson, that this song is the work of some heaven-inspired minstrel of the olden time, and to Thomson he went the length of saying, "it was never in print, nor even in manuscript till I took it down from an old man's singing."] (This statement has given rise in some quarters to doubts as to the authorship. They are plainly groundless. Is it credible that a song of such unrivalled merit could have remained unknown to all Scotland, save one "old man?" No one ever heard of it till Burns sent it to Mrs. Dunlop and Johnson. Chambers well remarks, that Burns was prone to indulge in little mystifications regarding his songs.—J. H.)

[1] This stanza is shifted to the end, in the Thomson copy. It must be mentioned that there exists a MS. of the song in the poet's holograph — a kind of parody, intended apparently for "mighty Squireships of the quorum,"—in which the first verse runs thus :—

> Should auld acquaintance be forgot,
> And never thought upon!
> Let's hae a waught o' Malaga,
> For auld lang syne.

THE SILVER TASSIE.

(JOHNSON'S MUSEUM, 1790.)

Go, fetch to me a pint o' wine,
   And fill it in a silver *tassie;*   cup
That I may drink before I go,
   A service to my bonie lassie.
The boat rocks at the pier o' Leith;
   Fu' loud the wind blaws frae the Ferry;
The ship rides by the Berwick-law,*
   And I *maun* leave my bonie Mary.   must

* North Berwick-Law is a conical hill forming a conspicuous object from the pier of Leith. The word "Law" is one of the many Scotch synonyms for hill. —J. H.

The trumpets sound, the banners fly,
  The glittering spears are rankèd ready;
The shouts o' war are heard afar,
  The battle closes deep and bloody;
It's not the roar o' sea or shore,
  Wad mak me langer wish to tarry;   would
Nor shouts o' war that's heard afar—
  It's leaving thee, my bonie Mary!

[There are few of Burns's lyrics that are more admired than this, which was first communicated in December 1788 (to Mrs. Dunlop), along with his immortal "Auld Lang Syne." These "two old stanzas" as he termed them, he afterwards admitted were his own, with exception of the four opening lines.

It is said that this song was suggested to Burns on witnessing a love-parting at the pier of Leith, between a young lady and her lover, a military officer who was about to step into the boat which was to convey him to a ship, ready to sail abroad with his Regiment.

With respect to the melody intended by Burns for this song, we find from the original MS. in the British Museum that he directed the words to be set to a tune in Oswald's Collection, called "The Secret Kiss." The air given in Johnson is said by Stenhouse to have been recovered and communicated by the poet, and such being the case, it is a pity to see that air thrust aside to make way for such unsuitable tunes as the song is now usually sung to. We therefore reproduce the air from Johnson.

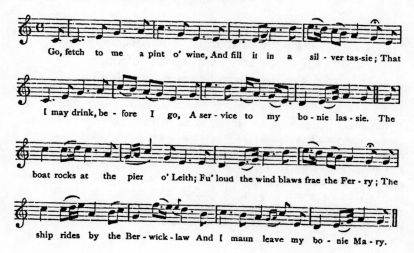

Go, fetch to me a pint o' wine, And fill it in a sil-ver tas-sie; That I may drink, be-fore I go, A ser-vice to my bo-nie las-sie. The boat rocks at the pier o' Leith; Fu' loud the wind blaws frae the Fer-ry; The ship rides by the Ber-wick-law And I maun leave my bo-nie Ma-ry.

(The four lines which Burns acknowledges having borrowed occur near the close of a ballad composed about 1636 by Lesley, the laird of Eden on Deveron-side, Banffshire, and grandfather of Archbishop Sharpe :—

> "Ye'll bring me here a pint of wine,
> A server and a siller tassie,
> That I may drink before I gang,
> A health to my ain bonny lassie."—J. H.)

THE PARTING KISS.

(CHAMBERS, 1838.)

HUMID seal of soft affections,
Tenderest pledge of future bliss,
Dearest tie of young connections,
Love's first snowdrop, virgin kiss!

Speaking silence, dumb confession,
Passion's birth, and infant's play,
Dove-like fondness, chaste concession,
Glowing dawn of future day!

Sorrowing joy, Adieu's last action,
(Lingering lips must now disjoin),
What words can ever speak affection
So thrilling and sincere as thine!

[No place appears better fitted to introduce this piece, than in connection with the immediately preceding song. All that is known regarding the production is that it appeared upwards of fifty years ago as a poem by Burns, in a periodical paper published at Liverpool, under the title of "The Kaleidoscope." Chambers remarks that "Burns's authorship of it cannot well be doubted;" but we should like to be told something regarding the manuscript of a piece so different from the alleged author's usual style of composition.]

WRITTEN IN FRIARS CARSE HERMITAGE, ON NITHSIDE.

LATER VERSION.

(EDINBURGH ED., 1793.)

THOU whom chance may hither lead,
Be thou clad in russet weed,
Be thou deckt in silken stole,
Grave these counsels on thy soul.

Life is but a day at most,
Sprung from night,—in darkness lost ;[1]
Hope not sunshine ev'ry hour,
Fear not clouds will always lour.

As Youth and Love with sprightly dance,
Beneath thy morning star advance,
Pleasure with her siren air
May delude the thoughtless pair ;
Let Prudence bless Enjoyment's cup,
Then raptur'd sip, and sip it up.

As thy day grows warm and high,
Life's meridian flaming nigh,
Dost thou spurn the humble vale?
Life's proud summits would'st thou scale?
Check thy climbing step, elate,
Evils lurk in felon wait :
Dangers, eagle-pinioned, bold,
Soar around each cliffy hold ;
While cheerful Peace, with linnet song,
Chants the lowly dells among.

As the shades of ev'ning close,
Beck'ning thee to long repose ;
As life itself becomes disease,
Seek the chimney-nook of ease :
There ruminate with sober thought,
On all thou'st seen, and heard, and wrought,
And teach the sportive younkers round,
Saws of experience, sage and sound :
Say, man's true, genuine estimate,[2]
The grand criterion of his fate,
Is not, art thou high or low?
Did thy fortune ebb or flow?[3]
Did many talents gild thy span?
Or frugal Nature grudge thee one?
Tell them, and press it on their mind,
As thou thyself must shortly find,
The smile or frown of awful Heav'n,
To Virtue or to Vice is giv'n ;
Say, to be just, and kind, and wise—
There solid self-enjoyment lies ;
That foolish, selfish, faithless ways
Lead to be wretched, vile, and base.

Thus resign'd and quiet, creep
To the bed of lasting sleep,—
Sleep, whence thou shall ne'er awake,
Night, where dawn shall never break,
Till future life, future no more,
To light and joy the good restore,
To light and joy unknown before.

Stranger, go ! Heav'n be thy guide !
Quod the Beadsman of Nithside.

[This altered version of a poem that seems to have cost the author
much pains was written in December 1788. He inscribed with his
diamond pen, on one of the panes of glass in the grotto, the

opening eight and the closing two lines of the poem, and when the hermitage was removed by the proprietor in 1835, an old lady bought the pane for five guineas. The mansion and grounds of Friars Carse have frequently changed owners since Captain Riddell's death in 1794, and they now belong to Thomas Nelson, Esq., by whom the hermitage has been tastefully rebuilt.

The following variations occur in collating manuscripts of this poem :—

[1] *The following couplet is here introduced :—*
Day how rapid in its flight !
Day, how few must see the night.

[2]   estimate,
Say the criterion of their fate,
The important query of their state,
Is not, &c.

[3]   flow ?
Wert thou cottager or king,
Peer or peasant ? no such thing
Tell them, &c.]

THE POET'S PROGRESS.

A POEM IN EMBRYO.

(DOUGLAS, 1877.)

THOU, Nature, partial Nature, I arraign ;
Of thy caprice maternal I complain.
    The peopled fold thy kindly care have found,
The horned bull, tremendous, spurns the ground ;
The lordly lion has enough and more,
The forest trembles at his very roar ;
Thou giv'st the ass his hide, the snail his shell,
The puny wasp, victorious, guards his cell.
Thy minions, kings defend, control, devour,
In all th' omnipotence of rule and power :
Foxes and statesmen subtile wiles ensure ;
The cit and polecat stink, and are secure :
Toads with their poison, doctors with their drug,
The priest and hedgehog, in their robes, are snug :
E'en silly women have defensive arts,
Their eyes, their tongues—and nameless other parts.

But O thou cruel stepmother and hard,
To thy poor fenceless, naked child, the Bard !
A thing unteachable in worldly skill,
And half an idiot too, more helpless still :
No heels to bear him from the op'ning dun,
No claws to dig, his hated sight to shun :
No horns, but those by luckless Hymen worn,
And those, alas ! not Amalthea's horn :
No nerves olfact'ry, true to Mammon's foot,
Or grunting, grub sagacious, evil's root :
The silly sheep that wanders wild astray,
Is not more friendless, is not more a prey ;
Vampyre-booksellers drain him to the heart,
And viper-critics cureless venom dart.

Critics ! appall'd I venture on the name,
Those cut-throat bandits in the paths of fame,
Bloody dissectors, worse than ten Monroes,*
He hacks to teach, they mangle to expose :
By blockhead's daring into madness stung,
His heart by wanton, causeless malice wrung,
His well-won bays—than life itself more dear—
By miscreants torn who ne'er one sprig must wear ;
Foil'd, bleeding, tortur'd in th' unequal strife,
The hapless Poet flounces on thro' life,
Till, fled each hope that once his bosom fired,
And fled each Muse that glorious once inspir'd,
Low-sunk in squalid, unprotected age,
Dead even resentment for his injur'd page,
He heeds no more the ruthless critics' rage.

So by some hedge the generous steed deceas'd,
For half-starv'd, snarling curs a dainty feast ;
By toil and famine worn to skin and bone,
Lies, senseless of each tugging bitch's son.

.   .   .   .   .   .

---

* An allusion to Dr. Monroe, then a distinguished Professor of Anatomy in the
University of Edinburgh.—J. H.

A little upright, pert, tart, tripping wight,
And still his precious self his dear delight ;
Who loves his own smart shadow in the streets,
Better than e'er the fairest she he meets ;
Much specious lore, but little understood,
(Veneering oft outshines the solid wood),
His solid sense, by inches you must tell,
But mete his cunning by the Scottish ell ! *
A man of fashion too, he made his tour,
Learn'd "vive la bagatelle et vive l'amour ; "
So travell'd monkies their grimace improve,
Polish their grin—nay, sigh for ladies' love !
His meddling vanity, a busy fiend,
Still making work his selfish craft must mend.

.   .   .   .   .   .

.   .   .   .   .   .

.   .   .   Crochallan came,
The old cock'd hat, the brown surtout—the same ;
His grisly beard just bristling in its might—
'Twas four long nights and days from shaving-night !
His uncomb'd, hoary locks, wild-staring, thatch'd
A head, for thought profound and clear, unmatch'd ;
Yet, tho' his caustic wit was biting-rude,
His heart was warm, benevolent and good.

.   .   .   .   .   .

O Dulness, portion of the truly blest !
Calm, shelter'd haven of eternal rest !
Thy sons ne'er madden in the fierce extremes
Of Fortune's polar frost, or torrid beams ;
If mantling high she fills the golden cup,
With sober, selfish ease they sip it up ;
Conscious the bounteous meed they well deserve,
They only wonder "some folks" do not starve !

---

* This couplet is supplied from another MS. : it may have been inadvertently
omitted by the poet in making the copy from which the text is taken. It seems
indispensable to the completeness of the passage.

III.   C

The grave, sage hern thus easy picks his frog,
And thinks the mallard a sad worthless dog.
When disappointment snaps the thread of Hope,
When, thro' disastrous night, they darkling grope,
With deaf endurance sluggishly they bear,
And just conclude that "fools are Fortune's care;"
So, heavy, passive to the tempest's shocks,
Strong on the sign-post stands the stupid ox.
    Not so the idle Muses' mad-cap train,
Not such the workings of their moon-struck brain;
In equanimity they never dwell,
By turns in soaring heaven, or vaulted hell !

[The concluding twenty lines of the preceding poem are in-
scribed in the poet's admired letter to Mrs. Dunlop of 1st Janu-
ary 1789, the original manuscript of which is now in possession
of Mr. Robert Clarke, Cincinnati, Ohio, U.S. The passage is thus
introduced :—" I am a very sincere believer in the Bible; but I
am drawn by the conviction of a man, not by the halter of an
ass.—Apropos to an ass; how do you like the following apostro-
phe to Dulness, which I intend to interweave in the *Poet's Pro-
gress?*—"O Dulness," &c.   He certainly had been engaged in
the composition of this piece when he penned the following sen-
tence to the same lady about a fortnight before :—" My small
scale of farming is exceedingly more simple than what you have
lately seen at Moreham Mains.   But, be that as it may, the heart
of *the man*, and the fancy of *the poet*, are the two grand con-
siderations for which I live. If miry ridges and dirty dunghills,
are to engross the best part of the functions of my soul immor-
tal, I had better been a rook or a magpie at once, and then I
should not have been plagued with any ideas superior to the
breaking of clods and picking up grubs; not to mention barn-
door cocks and mallards—creatures with which I could almost ex-
change lives at any time."
    The holograph copy from which the text is printed is in pos-
session of Mr. Paterson, Publisher, Edinburgh, and it seems to be
the identical MS. which the poet enclosed to Professor Dugald
Stewart, from Ellisland on 20th January 1789. His letter of that
date thus refers to the poem :—"These fragments, if my design
succeed, are but a small part of the intended whole.   I propose
it shall be the work of my utmost exertions, ripened by years :
of course I do not wish it much known.   The fragment beginning
"A little, upright, pert, tart," &c., I have not shown to man living

till I now send it to you. It forms the postulate, the axioms,
the definition of a character which, if it appear at all, shall be
placed in a variety of lights. This particular part I send you
merely as a sample of my hand at portrait-sketching; but lest
idle conjecture should pretend to point out the original, please
to let it be for your single, sole inspection." The reader, of
course, will understand that the portrait-sketch referred to was
intended to depict Mr. Creech.

In the poet's letter to Dr. Moore, of 4th January 1789, he says,
"I cannot boast of Mr. Creech's ingenuous fair-dealing to me.
He kept me hanging about Edinburgh from the 7th of August
1787, until the 13th April 1788, before he would condescend to
give me a statement of affairs : nor had I got it even then but for
an angry letter I wrote him which irritated his pride. 'I could'
—not 'a tale,' but a *detail* 'unfold'; but what am I that I should
speak against the Lord's anointed Bailie of Edinburgh? . . .
Perhaps I injure the man in the idea I am sometimes tempted
to have of him : God forbid I should!" It is pleasant to add,
that Burns wrote to the same correspondent on 23rd March 1789,
in this satisfactory manner regarding his publisher :—"I was at
Edinburgh lately, and settled finally with Mr. Creech ; and I must
own that at last he has been amicable and fair with me."

The bulk of the foregoing poem was afterwards moulded into
an Epistle to Mr. Graham of Fintry, which the poet has dated
"5th October, 1791," and as we shall print it in its proper place,
we do not here point out the variations.]

ELEGY ON THE YEAR 1788.

(STEWART, 1801.)

FOR lords or kings I *dinna* mourn,	do not
E'en let them die—for that they're born :	
But oh! prodigious to reflec'!	
A *Towmont*, sirs, is gane to wreck!	twelvemonth
O *Eighty-eight*, in thy sma' space,	
What dire events hae taken place!	
Of what enjoyments thou hast reft us!	
In what a pickle thou hast left us!	
The Spanish empire's *tint* a head,*	lost
And my auld teethless *Bawtie's* dead :	name of his dog

---

* Charles III. of Spain, died 13th December 1788.

The *tulyie's teugh* 'tween Pitt and Fox,   strife is tough
And 'tween our Maggie's twa wee cocks ;[1]
The *tane* is game, a bluidy devil,   one
But to the hen-birds unco civil ;
The tither's something *dour* o' treadin',[2]   backward
But better stuff ne'er claw'd a *midden*.   dunghill

Ye ministers, come mount the poupit,
An' cry till ye be hoarse an' *roupet*,*   nearly voiceless
For *Eighty-eight*, he wished you weel,
An' *gied* ye a' baith *gear* an' meal ;   gave   wealth
E'en mony a *plack*, and mony a peck,   coin
Ye ken yoursels, for little feck ! †

Ye bonie lasses, *dight* your *e'en*,   dry   eyes
For some o' you hae *tint* a frien' ;   lost
In *Eighty-eight*, ye ken, was *taen*   taken
What ye'll ne'er *hae* to *gie* again.   have   give

Observe the very *nowt* an' sheep,   nolt
How *dowff* an' *daviely*[3] .they creep ;   dull listlessly
Nay, even the *yirth* itsel does cry,   earth
For E'nburgh wells are grutten dry. ‡

O *Eighty-nine*, thou's but a *bairn*,   infant
An' no *owre auld*, I hope to learn !   too old
Thou beardless boy, I pray tak care,
Thou now has got thy Daddy's chair ;
Nae hand-cuff'd, *mizl'd*, hap-shackl'd   muzzled
        Regent, §

---

* See Vol. 1, p. 213.
† For little value rendered.—J. H.
‡ Edinburgh wells have wept themselves dry. The Edinburgh newspapers in December 1788 have many references to a scarcity of water in consequence of the wells being frozen up.—J. H.
§ In November 1788, the king shewed symptoms of mental disease, and proposals for a Regent were discussed.

But, like himsel, a full free agent,
Be sure ye follow out the plan
Nae *waur* than he did, honest man !   worse
As *muckle* better as you can.   much

January 1, 1789.

[This off-hand sketch found its way into the newspapers, not long after it was composed. Stewart, in 1801, published a version, either from the manuscript or other source, differing in some respects from the one given by Cromek in 1808. A collation of these exhibits the following, among other slight, variations :—

    ¹ our gudewife's wee birdie-cocks.
    ² dour, has nae sic breedin.   ³ dowie now.—J. H.]

THE HENPECKED HUSBAND.

(STEWART, 1801.)

CURS'D be the man, the poorest wretch in life,
The crouching vassal to a tyrant wife !
Who has no will but by her high permission,
Who has not sixpence but in her possession ;
Who must to her his dear friend's secrets tell,
Who dreads a curtain lecture worse than hell.
Were't such the wife had fallen to my part,
I'd. break her spirit or I'd break her heart ;
I'd charm her with the magic of a switch,
I'd kiss her maids, and kick the perverse b—h.

[Allan Cunningham says that a story went that the lady of a house where the poet had dined expressed herself somewhat uncivilly in regard to the deep potations and extravagant habits of her husband, and that her freedom of tongue was paid back by these verses.—J. H.]

VERSICLES ON SIGN-POSTS.

(ALEX. SMITH'S ED., 1867.)

"The everlasting surliness of a lion, Saracen's head, &c., or the unchanging blandness of the landlord welcoming a traveller, on some sign-posts, would be no bad similes of the constant affected fierceness of a Bully, or the eternal simper of a Frenchman or a Fiddler."—*R. B.*

His face with smile eternal drest,
Just like the landlord to his guest,
High as they hang with creaking din,
To index out the Country Inn.

He looked just as your sign-post Lions do,
With aspect fierce, and quite as harmless too.

A head, pure, sinless quite of brain and soul,
The very image of a barber's Poll ;
It shews a human face, and wears a wig,
And looks, when well preserv'd, amazing big.

[These scraps are found in the MS. Book presented by Burns to Mrs. Dunlop, about the year 1788. One of the entries under this heading is the couplet made use of in "The Poet's Progress," lines fifth and sixth from the close. Alexander Smith remarks concerning the present text—"The versicles themselves are of little worth, and are indebted entirely to their paternity for their appearance here."]

ROBIN SHURE IN HAIRST.

(JOHNSON'S MUSEUM, 1803.)

Chorus.—Robin *shure* in *hairst*,   reaped   harvest
         I shure wi' him ;
         Fient a heuk had I,   never a hook
         Yet I *stack* by him.   stuck

I *gaed* up to Dunse,   went
 To warp a *wab* o' plaiden,   web
At his daddie's *yett,*   gate
 Wha met me but Robin !
 Robin shure, &c.

Was na Robin bauld,
 Tho' I was a cotter,
Play'd me sic a trick,
 An' me the *Eller's dochter !*   Elder's daughter
 Robin shure, &c.

Robin promis'd me
 A' my winter *vittle ;*   provisions
Fient haet he had but three   Deuce a thing
 Guse-feathers and a *whittle !*   knife
 Robin shure, &c.

[This is a revision of an old song entitled "Robin Sheared in Hairst." The identity of the Robin for whom Burns adapted it has escaped most of his annotators. In a letter to Robert Ainslie, dated 6th January 1789, Burns says, "I am still catering for Johnson's publication ; and, among others, I have brushed up the following old favorite song a little, with a view to your worship." Ainslie's father was a rich farmer at Berriewell near Dunse. He, himself, was apprenticed to an Edinburgh writer to the Signet or lawyer, and was Burns's companion on his first tour—that, namely, to the Border counties. The allusions to Dunse and the three "guse-feathers and a whittle" (three goose feathers and a pen-knife—all the worldly goods owned by the lawyer's clerk) become thus clear. In a postscript to the poet's letter to Ainslie of 23rd August 1787, he thus specially refers to a child which Ainslie wished to name after Burns :—"Call your boy what you think proper, only interject 'Burns.' What do you say to a Scripture name ? for instance Zimri Burns Ainslie, or Ahitophel ? &c. Look your Bible for these two heroes," &c. The reader will understand that Robert Ainslie was then a single man. He became afterwards a respectable writer to the Signet, and Lockhart, writing in 1828, says of him :— "Among other changes 'which fleeting time procureth,' this amiable gentleman, whose youthful gaiety made him a chosen associate of Burns, is now chiefly known as the author of some Manuals of Devotion." He was married, 22nd December 1798, and died 11th April 1838.—J. H.]

ODE, SACRED TO THE MEMORY OF MRS. OSWALD OF AUCHENCRUIVE.

(EDINBURGH ED., 1793.)

DWELLER in yon dungeon dark,
Hangman of creation ! mark,
Who in widow-weeds appears,
Laden with unhonor'd years,
Noosing with care a bursting purse,
Baited with many a deadly curse?

STROPHE.

View the wither'd Beldam's face ;
Can thy keen inspection trace
Aught of Humanity's sweet, melting grace?
Note that eye, 'tis rheum o'erflows ;
Pity's flood *there* never rose,
See these hands, ne'er stretch'd to save,
Hands that took, but never gave :
Keeper of Mammon's iron chest,
Lo, there she goes, unpitied and unblest,
She goes, but not to realms of everlasting rest !

ANTISTROPHE.

Plunderer of Armies ! lift thine eyes,
(A while forbear, ye torturing fiends ;)
Seest thou whose step, unwilling, hither bends?
No fallen angel, hurl'd from upper skies ;
'Tis thy trusty quondam Mate,
Doom'd to share thy fiery fate ;
She, tardy, hell-ward plies.

EPODE.

And are they of no more avail,
Ten thousand glittering pounds a-year?
In other worlds can Mammon fail,
　Omnipotent as he is here!
O, bitter mockery of the pompous bier,
　While down the wretched Vital Part is driven!
The cave-lodg'd Beggar, with a conscience clear,
　Expires in rags, unknown, and goes to Heaven.

[Auchencruive, as the name indicates, is a holm situated on a remarkable crook of the river, about three miles from the mouth of the Ayr. Within the peninsula formed, by the bend, is "Leglen Wood," noted by Harry the minstrel as a favorite hiding place of Wallace the hero. Burns tells us in his autobiography, that while yet a boy, he made a Sabbath-day's journey from Mount Oliphant—a distance of six miles, to pay his respects to the spot where his heroic countryman found shelter. The lands of Auchencruive were purchased, about 1760, by Richard Oswald, husband of the lady held up to execration by Burns. He was a merchant in London, and was appointed a plenipotentiary to sign the Articles of Peace with the United States in 1782. At his death, without issue, the estate went to George Oswald, son of his brother James, whose eldest son, Richard Alexander Oswald (born in 1771) became M.P. for Ayrshire, and married the beautiful Lucy Johnston, celebrated by Burns in 1795. Thus we see that the dowager widow, who died "unpitied and unblest" on 6th December 1788, was no blood relation to the grand-nephew whose good-will the poet afterwards cultivated in Dumfries.

Burns enclosed the above Ode to Dr. Moore, in a letter where he thus narrates the occasion which caused him to write it,—"You probably knew the lady personally, an honor which I cannot boast; but I spent my early years in her neighborhood, and among her servants and tenants. I know that she was detested with the most heartfelt cordiality. However, in the particular part of her conduct which roused my poetic wrath, she was much less blameable. In January last, in my road to Ayrshire, I had put up at Bailie Whigham's, in Sanquhar, the only tolerable inn in the place. The frost was keen, and the grim evening and howling wind, were ushering in a night of snow and drift. My horse and I were both much fatigued with the labors of the day, and just as my friend the Bailie and I were bidding defiance to the storm over a smoking bowl, in wheels the funeral pageantry of the late great Mrs. Oswald, and poor I am forced to brave all the horrors of the tempestuous night, and jade my horse—my young favorite horse, whom I had just christened 'Pegasus'—twelve miles farther on, through the wildest moors and hills of Ayrshire, to New Cumnock, the next inn. The powers of poesy and prose sink under me when I would describe what I felt. Suffice it to say, that when a good fire at New Cumnock had so far recovered my frozen sinews, I sat down and wrote the enclosed Ode."

The poet's holograph transcript of this Ode is now in the possession of A. Ireland, Esq., Bowdon, Cheshire.]

PEGASUS AT WANLOCKHEAD.*

(CUNNINGHAM, 1835.)

WITH Pegasus † upon a day,
    Apollo weary flying,
Through frosty hills the journey lay,
    On foot the way was plying.

Poor slipshod giddy Pegasus
    Was but a sorry walker;
To Vulcan then Apollo goes,
    To get a frosty caulker.

Obliging Vulcan fell to work,
    Threw by his coat and bonnet,
And did Sol's business in a crack;
    Sol paid him with a sonnet.

Ye Vulcan's sons of Wanlockhead,
    Pity my sad disaster;
My Pegasus is poorly shod,
    I'll pay you like my master.

To John Taylor, Ramage's, 3 o'clock.

---

* A lead-mining village, on the mountain range of the Lowthers, which separate Dumfries-shire from the counties of Ayr and Lanark.—J. H.
† Pegasus was the name of the poet's riding horse, that succeeded " Jenny Geddes." See Note to last piece.—J. H.

[The explanation of this little production, as given by Allan Cunningham, is that Burns, in the course of one of his journeys as an exciseman, arrived one day at Wanlockhead when the roads were slippery with ice, and felt the necessity of having his horse's shoes sharpened. The Vulcan of the village, having a monopoly of trade, vowed he could not then spare time to attend to the poet's wants ; and from the inn Burns indited these verses to John Taylor, a person who had influence with the smith, and prevailed on him at once to frost the shoes of Pegasus. The poet was thereby enabled to resume his journey with some safety, after having paid Vulcan with the Muse's coin, and a dram at the inn.] (The smith lived for thirty years after accommodating the poet, and used to say that he had never been "weel paid but ance, and that was by a poet, who paid me in money, paid me in drink, and paid me in verse."—J. H.)

SAPPHO REDIVIVA—A FRAGMENT.

(DOUGLAS, 1877.)

ELLISLAND, 24th January 1789—My dear Cunningham. . . . I shall ask your opinion of some verses I have lately begun, on a theme of which you are the best judge I ever saw. It is Love, too, though not just warranted by the law of nations. A married lady of my acquaintance, whose *crim. con.* amour with a certain Captain has made some noise in the world, is supposed to write to him, now in the West Indies, as follows :—

By all I lov'd, neglected and forgot,
No friendly face e'er lights my squalid cot ;
Shunn'd, hated, wrong'd, unpitied, unredrest,
The mock'd quotation of the scorner's jest ! *

In vain would Prudence, with decorous sneer,
Point out a censuring world, and bid me fear ;
Above the world, on wings of Love, I rise—
I know its worst, and can that worst despise :

---

* These four lines and introduction are quoted verbatim from the poet's original letter addressed to his friend Alexander Cunningham, writer, Edinburgh, now in possession of that gentleman's son, James Cunningham, Esq., W. S. Unfortunately the latter two pages, containing the remainder of the verses transcribed, and the conclusion of the letter, have disappeared.

Let Prudence's direst bodements on me fall,
M . . . . . . y, rich reward, o'erpays them all ! *

Mild zephyrs waft thee to life's farthest shore,
Nor think of me and my distresses more,—
Falsehood accurst ! No ! still I beg a place,
Still near thy heart some little, little trace ;
For that dear trace the world I would resign :
O let me live, and die, and think it mine !

" I burn, I burn, as when thro' ripen'd corn
By driving winds the crackling flames are borne ; "†
Now raving-wild, I curse that fatal night,
Then bless the hour that charm'd my guilty sight :
In vain the laws their feeble force oppose,
Chain'd at Love's feet, they groan, his vanquish'd
          foes :
In vain Religion meets my shrinking eye,
I dare not combat, but I turn and fly :
Conscience in vain upbraids th' unhallow'd fire,
Love grasps her scorpions—stifled they expire !
Reason drops headlong from his sacred throne,
Your dear idea reigns, and reigns alone ;
Each thought intoxicated homage yields,
And riots wanton in forbidden fields.

By all on high adoring mortals know !
By all the conscious villain fears below !
By your dear self !—the last great oath I swear,
Not life, nor soul, were ever half so dear ! ‡

---

* These six lines, together with the two closing lines of the preceding frag-
ment, are found quoted by the poet in his letter to Mrs. M'Lehose (Clarinda)
dated 1794, apparently the last communication which passed between them.
  † Quoted from Pope's "Sappho to Phaon."
  ‡ These eighteen lines are preserved in the British Museum, written by Burns
on a separate sheet, with no heading or other explanation of their connection.
They were printed in the Aldine edition of Burns, 1839, as having been addressed
to "Clarinda" in 1788; but they are neither included, nor referred to, in the
authorised edition of that correspondence, 1843.

[The lines of which the text is composed have been surrounded with considerable mystery. Sundry scraps of the effusion found their way into the later portions of the Clarinda correspondence; but the poet's letter to Alex. Cunningham, partly quoted in our heading, not only fixes its date, but proves that Clarinda was not the subject of it. Indeed the circumstances in the intercommunion betwixt "Sylvander and Clarinda" were never such as to warrant language like that in the text to be used on either side, between the correspondents.

The verses were written in reference to a celebrated Court of Session case, which, in one of its stages, was discussed and decided on, while Burns was present in court, on 7th March 1787. On the following day, he thus wrote to his Ayrshire friend, Mr. Gavin Hamilton, concerning it :—"Poor Captain Montgomery is cast. Yesterday it was tried whether the husband could proceed against the unfortunate lover without first divorcing his wife; and their gravities on the bench were unanimously of opinion that M—— may prosecute for damages directly, and need not divorce his wife at all if he pleases. O all ye powers of love unfortunate, and friendless woe, pour the balm of sympathising pity on the grief-torn, tender heart of the hapless fair one!"

R. Chambers has given the explanation that the lady he referred to was heiress of S——, in Ayrshire, and that, after bearing two children to her husband, she deserted him in June 1783, and cohabited with Captain James Montgomery, of the 93rd regiment of foot. She bore a child to Montgomery in November 1784; but, judging from Burns's expressions, there would seem to have been extenuating circumstances in the conduct of the lady. The policy of the husband in abstaining from a process of divorce which would separate him from the lady's estate, was not generally admired.]

SONG—SHE'S FAIR AND FAUSE.

(JOHNSON'S MUSEUM, 1792.)

SHE'S fair and *fause* that causes my smart,	false
I lo'ed her *meikle* and lang ;	much
She's broken her vow, she's broken my heart,	
And I may e'en *gae* hang.	go
A coof cam in wi' routh o' gear,*	
And I hae *tint* my dearest dear ;	lost

---

* A blockhead came in with abundance of wealth.—J. H.

But Woman is but *warld's gear*,   world's goods
  Sae let the bonie lass gang.

Whae'er ye be that woman love,
  To this be never blind ;
Nae *ferlie* 'tis tho' fickle she prove,   wonder
  A woman has't by kind.
O Woman lovely, Woman fair !
An angel form's *faun* to thy share,   fallen
'Twad been o'er *meikle* to *gien* thee mair—   much }
  I mean an angel mind.   given }

[The occasion from which this powerful little song emanated
will be at once apparent by giving the following extract from the
record of Marriages in the Scots Magazine, and a quotation from
Burns's letter to his friend Cunningham, in relation thereto :—
"13*th January* 1789. At Edinburgh, Mr. Forrest Dewar, Surgeon,
to Miss Anne Stewart, daughter of John Stewart, Esq., of East
Craigs."

"*Ellisland, 24th January* 1789.—My dear Cunningham, when I
saw in my last newspaper that a surgeon in Edinburgh was mar-
ried to a certain amiable and accomplished young lady whose
name begins with ANNE; a lady with whom I fancy I have the
honor of being a little acquainted, I sincerely felt for a much es-
teemed friend of mine. As you are the single, only instance that
ever came within the sphere of my observation of human nature,
of a young fellow, dissipated but not debauched, a circumstance
that has ever given me the highest idea of the native qualities of
your heart, I am certain that a disappointment in the tender
passion must, to you, be a very serious matter. To the hopeful
youth, keen on the badger foot of Mammon, or listed under the
gaudy banners of ambition, a love-disappointment, as such, is an
easy business ; nay, perhaps he hugs himself on his escape ; but
to your scanty tribe of mankind, whose souls bear—on the richest
materials—the most elegant impress of the Great Creator, love
enters deeply into their existence : it is entwined with their very
thread of life. I myself can affirm, both from bachelor and wed-
lock experience, that love is the Alpha and Omega of human en-
joyment . . . . Without it, life, to the poor inmates of the cot-
tage would be a damning gift."

We began this note with an extract from the records of Mar-
riage, and shall bring it to a close in like manner :—"*April* 10,
1792.—At Edinburgh, Mr. Alexander Cunningham, writer, to Miss

Agnes Moir, youngest daughter of the late Rev. Henry Moir, minister at Auchertoul." This subject will be resumed when we arrive at another of Burns's songs connected with Cunningham's love-disappointment.—See page 174, Vol. IV.]

IMPROMPTU LINES TO CAPTAIN RIDDELL,

ON RETURNING A NEWSPAPER.

(CROMEK, 1808.)

YOUR News and Review, sir,
I've read through and through, sir,
With little admiring or blaming ;
The Papers are barren
Of home-news or foreign,
No murders or rapes worth the naming.

Our friends, the Reviewers,
Those chippers and hewers,
Are judges of mortar and stone, sir ;
But of *meet* or *unmeet*,
In a fabric complete,
I'll boldly pronounce they are none, sir.

My goose-quill too rude is
To tell all your goodness
Bestow'd on your servant, the Poet ;
Would to God I had one
Like a beam of the sun,
And then all the world, sir, should know it !

ELLISLAND, *Monday morning.*

[These lines tell somewhat of the kindly compliments and familiar intercourse that passed current between the poet and his neighbor at Friars Carse, even so early as this, the first year of their acquaintance. About the same date, a prose note addressed to that gentleman still farther exemplifies this intimacy, and shews when Burns began to transcribe for Mr. Riddell those poems which now form one volume of what are known as "Burns's Glenriddell MSS." in the Athenæum Library at Liverpool.

Chambers well observes, that the verses in the text "exhibit that wonderful facilty of diction which Burns possessed even under the greatest rhyming difficulties." It would seem that the Review sent by Mr. Riddell for the bard's perusal contained some strictures on his poetry].

LINES TO JOHN M'MURDO, ESQ., OF DRUM-LANRIG.

SENT WITH SOME OF THE AUTHOR'S POEMS.

(CUNNINGHAM'S ED., 1834.)

O COULD I give thee India's wealth,
  As I this trifle send ;
Because thy joy in both would be
  To share them with a friend.

But golden sands did never grace
  The 'Heliconian stream ;
Then take what gold could never buy—
  An honest Bard's esteem.

[On the 9th of January, 1789, Burns wrote to this gentleman enclosing what he termed "nearly my newest song, one that has cost me some pains, though that is but an equivocal mark of its excellence." And he adds—"two or three others I have by me, which shall do themselves the honor to wait on you at your leisure."

The poet's intimacy with the neighboring gentry, commenced shortly after his settlement at Ellisland, and the friendship of Mr. M'Murdo and his family he enjoyed till the close of his life.]

Miss Jeany Cruikshank, Edin—

Beauteous Rosebud, young & gay,
Blooming on the early day,
Never may'st thou, lovely Flower,
Chilly shrink in sleety shower!
Never Eurus' pois'nous breath,
Never Boreas' hoary path,
Never baneful stellar Lights
Taint thee with untimely blights!
Never, never reptile-thief
Riot in thy virgin leaf,
Nor even Sol too fiercely view
Thy bosom blushing still with dew!
But may'st thou long, sweet, crimson gem,
Grateful deck thy native Stem:
Till some evening, sober, calm,
Dropping dews & breathing balm,
While all around the woodland rings,
And every bird thy requiem sings;
Thou amid the dirgeful sound
Shed thy dying honors round,
And resign to parent earth
The loveliest Form she'er gave birth!

April 19th 1790   Robt. Burns——

RHYMING REPLY TO A NOTE FROM CAPTAIN RIDDELL.

(DOUGLAS, 1877.)

DEAR SIR, at ony time or tide,
I'd rather sit wi' you than ride,
   Though 'twere wi' royal Geordie:
And trowth, your kindness, soon and late,
Aft *gars* me to mysel look *blate*— makes   bashful
   The Lord in Heav'n reward ye!

ELLISLAND.   R. BURNS.

[The Laird of Friar's Carse had arranged to ride out with Burns; but the weather proving unpropitious, he despatched the following to the poet:

    " Dear Bard, to ride this day is vain,
      For it will be a steeping rain,
        So come and sit wi' me;
    We'll fill up twa-three leaves wi' scraps,
    And *whyles* fill up the time wi' cracks,   sometimes
      And spend the day wi' glee."—R. R.

Riddell's note apparently bears reference to the unpublished scraps of poetry which Burns had undertaken to insert in a bound volume of blank paper that Riddell had, in 1789, procured for the purpose.

The lines in the text are written, in the poet's usual bold hand, on the back of Captain Riddell's lines. The interesting document was in the possession of the late Sam Bough, Esq., R.S.A.]

TO MISS CRUICKSHANK,

A VERY YOUNG LADY.

WRITTEN ON THE BLANK LEAF OF A BOOK, PRESENTED TO HER BY THE AUTHOR.

(EDINBURGH ED.. 1793.)

BEAUTEOUS Rosebud, young and gay,
Blooming on thy early May,
Never may'st thou, lovely flower,
Chilly shrink in sleety shower!

III.   D

Never Boreas' hoary path,
Never Eurus' pois'nous breath,
Never baleful stellar lights,
Taint thee with untimely blights!
Never, never reptile thief
Riot on thy virgin leaf!
Nor even Sol too fiercely view
Thy bosom blushing still with dew!

May'st thou long, sweet crimson gem,
Richly deck thy native stem;
Till some ev'ning, sober, calm,
Dropping dews, and breathing balm,
While all around the woodland rings,
And ev'ry bird thy requiem sings;
Thou, amid the dirgeful sound,
Shed thy dying honors round,
And resign to parent Earth
The loveliest form she e'er gave birth.

[Burns paid a brief visit to Edinburgh towards the close of February 1789, his main object being to get a final settlement with Mr. Creech, in which he succeeded to his satisfaction. We suppose it was at this time that the above lines of compliment to his favorite little "Rosebud." were composed and inscribed. A copy is inserted near the beginning of the Glenriddell MS., in which the reading of the second line is—

"Blooming on the early day," *

The following announcement in the Scots Magazine refers to the marriage of the young lady to whom the lines were addressed: —"June 1st, 1804—At Jedburgh, James Henderson, writer there, to Miss Jane Cruickshank, daughter of the deceased William Cruickshank, High School, Edinburgh."] (We learn from Chambers, on the authority of a daughter-in-law of Mrs. Henderson, that a beau-

---

* A holograph of this poem is now in the possession of Mr. George W. Childs, of Philadelphia, to whom we are indebted for the privilege of presenting a facsimile of this beautiful piece. Mr. Childs's holograph corresponds exactly with the Glenriddell MS., except that it transposes the 5th and 6th lines.—J. H.

tiful portrait of her (then in the possession of her only surviving son) "justifies the appellation of the *Rosebud*, as, judging from the Hebe-like appearance of the picture, she must have been a strikingly beautiful girl." The same lady owns a china bowl broken by Burns on one of his "merry nights" with Cruickshanks at St. James's Square.—J. H.)

BEWARE O' BONIE ANN.

(JOHNSON'S MUSEUM, 1790.)

YE gallants bright, I *rede* you right,   advise
   Beware o' bonie Ann ;
Her comely face sae fu' o' grace,
   Your heart she will trepan :
Her *een* sae bright, like stars by **night**,   eyes
   Her skin is like the swan ;
Sae *jimply* lac'd, her *genty* waist,   tightly slender
   That sweetly ye might span.

Youth, Grace, and Love attendant move,
   And pleasure leads the van :
In a' their charms, and conquering arms,
   They wait on bonie Ann.
The captive bands may chain the hands,
   But love enslaves the man :
Ye gallants braw, I rede you a',
   Beware o' bonie Ann !

[This would appear to have been composed during the visit to Edinburgh, referred to in the preceding note. The father of the young lady was Allan Masterton, who professed to teach Music as well as Penmanship. He was appointed teacher of writing in the High School of Edinburgh, in August 1795 ; and, to enable him to attend his other engagements, his brother, Dugald Masterton, and also his nephew, Dugald Masterton, junior, were conjoined with him in the appointment. Allan died in 1799, and Dugald in 1800. The young woman whose charms are celebrated in the text became the wife of a medical man residing at Bath and afterwards in London, named Derbishire. From a Canadian Obituary, we copy the following :—" 27th March 1863. Died at Quebec, Mr. Stewart Derbishire, Her Majesty's printer there. He was the son of Dr. Derbishire of Bath, and his mother was Miss Ann Masterton, daughter of Allan Masterton, writing-master, High School, Edinburgh."]

ODE ON THE DEPARTED REGENCY BILL.

(BRIGHT'S GLENRIDDELL MSS. (PRIVATELY PRINTED), 1874.)

DAUGHTER of Chaos' doting years,
Nurse of ten thousand hopes and fears,
Whether thy airy, unsubstantial shade
(The rights of sepulture now duly paid)
Spread abroad its hideous form
On the roaring civil storm,
Deafening din and warring rage
Factions wild with factions wage ;
Or under ground, deep-sunk, profound,
  Among the demons of the earth,
With groans that make the mountains shake,
  Thou mourn thy ill-starr'd, blighted birth ;
Or in the uncreated Void,
  Where seeds of future being fight,
With lessen'd step thou wander wide,
  To greet thy Mother—Ancient Night,
And as each jarring, monster-mass is past,
Fond recollect what once thou wast :
In manner due, beneath this sacred oak,
Hear, Spirit, hear ! thy presence I invoke !
  By a Monarch's heaven-struck fate,
  By a disunited State,
  By a generous Prince's wrongs,
  By a Senate's strife of tongues,
  By a premier's sullen pride,
  Low'ring on the changing tide ;

By dread Thurlow's powers to awe—
Rhetoric, blasphemy and law ;
By the turbulent ocean—
A Nation's commotion,
By the harlot-caresses
Of borough addresses,
By days few and evil,
(Thy portion, poor devil !)
By Power, Wealth and Show,
   (The Gods by men adored,)
By nameless Poverty,
   (Their hell abhorred,)
By all they hope, by all they fear,
Hear ! and Appear !

Stare not on me, thou ghastly Power !
Nor, grim with chained defiance, low'r :
   No Babel-structure would *I* build
   Where, order exil'd from his native sway,
Confusion may the REGENT-sceptre wield,
   While all would rule and none obey :
Go, to the world of Man relate
The story of thy sad, eventful fate ;
And call presumptuous Hope to hear
And bid him check his blind career ;
And tell the sore-prest sons of Care,
   Never, never to despair !

Paint Charles's speed on wings of fire,
The object of his fond desire,
Beyond his boldest hopes, at hand :
Paint all the triumph of the Portland Band ;
Mark how they lift the joy-exulting voice,
And how their num'rous creditors rejoice ;
But just as hopes to warm enjoyment rise,
Cry CONVALESCENCE ! and the vision flies.

Then next portray a dark'ning twilight gloom,
    Eclipsing sad a gay, rejoicing morn,
While proud Ambition to th' untimely tomb
    By gnashing, grim, despairing fiends is borne :
Paint ruin, in the shape of high D[undas]
    Gaping with giddy terror o'er the brow ;
In vain he struggles, the fates behind him press,
    And clam'rous hell yawns for her prey below :
How fallen *That*, whose pride late scaled the skies !
And *This*, like Lucifer, no more to rise !
    Again pronounce the powerful word ;
See Day, triumphant from the night, restored.

Then know this truth, ye Sons of Men !
    (Thus ends thy moral tale,)
Your darkest terrors may be vain,
    Your brightest hopes may fail.

[In the "Elegy for the year 1788," some reference was made
to the King's illness, and consequent excitement regarding the
appointment of a Regent. From 17th October, 1788, when His
Majesty was taken ill (or more plainly speaking, when he became
apparently hopelessly insane), a daily report of his condition was
published. A form of public prayer for the King's recovery was
prepared by the Archbishop of Canterbury, and read in the churches
from and after 23d November. In the House of Commons on
8th December, Mr. Fox, in seconding the government motion
for appointing a committee to enquire and report on the consti-
tutional mode of continuing the executive government under
existing circumstances, declared his opinion that there could be
no suspension of executive government so long as there existed
an Heir-apparent of full age and capacity. The Prince of Wales,
he considered, "had as indisputable rights to assume the reins
of government, and exercise the powers of Sovereignty at pres-
ent, as in the case of his Majesty having undergone a natural
and perfect demise."

Mr. Pitt, in reply, said that the doctrine just laid down by
the Right Hon. Gentleman was, to the last degree, alarming, and
he held that his language was little short of treason to the con-
stitution. Indeed, he considered that the Prince of Wales was,
in the present emergency, "no more entitled by right to the
administration than any other subject in the kingdom. The right

lay with the Parliament alone to appoint a Regent, and if, in its discretion, the Prince of Wales should be selected as the most proper person to represent his Royal Father in the government, the parliament had a right to fetter the appointment with such limitations and restrictions as were necessary for the preservation of its allegiance to the sovereign, and of the people's interests." Out of these conflicting positions arose that "strife of tongues" in the senate, and "turbulent ocean of a nation's commotion" to which the poet refers in the foregoing Ode. The clamor, however, was suddenly checked, and the Regency Bill slaughtered by the king's "Convalescence" being declared about the close of the first week of March, 1789. This disappointed the hopes of the Whig party, which calculated on sailing into power during the Regency of the Prince. The "Charles" of the third paragraph is Mr. Fox, and the "Portland Band" is the Whig party.

The only known manuscript of this poem is that inscribed in Captain Riddell's volume now preserved at Liverpool, from which the text is taken.] (The reason for these lines being kept so long unpublished was the fear of the possessor that their publication would give offence to the Royal Family. Burns's special attack on "high Dundas" may be, at least partially, accounted for by reference to the note on his poem on the death of Robert Dundas, Esq., of Arniston, Vol. II, p. 138.—J. H.)

EPISTLE TO JAMES TENNANT OF GLEN-CONNER.

(CUNNINGHAM, 1834.)

AULD comrade dear, and brither sinner,
How's a' the folk about Glenconner?
How do you this *blae** eastlin wind,   chill
That's like to blaw a body blind?
For me, my faculties are frozen,
My dearest member nearly *dozen'd*.   benumbed
I've sent you here, by Johnie Simson,
Twa sage philosophers to glimpse on;
Smith, wi' his sympathetic feeling,
An' Reid, to common sense appealing.

---

* Blae means literally livid. It is often applied to a chilling wind from the wan color it gives to the face.—J. H.

Philosophers have fought and wrangled,
An' *meikle* Greek an' Latin mangled,   much
Till wi' their logic-jargon tir'd,
And in the depth of science mir'd,
To common sense they now appeal,
What wives and *wabsters* see and feel.   weavers
But, hark ye, friend! I charge you strictly,
Peruse them, an' return them quickly :
For now I'm grown sae cursed *douce*   decent
I pray and ponder *but the house;* *   in the kitchen
My *shins, my lane,* I there sit roastin,   ankles   alone
Perusing Bunyan, Brown an' Boston †
Till by an' by, if I *haud on,*   persevere
I'll grunt a real gospel groan :
Already I begin to try it,
To cast my e'en up like a *pyet,*   magpie
When by the gun she tumbles o'er
Flutt'ring an' gasping in her gore :
Sae shortly you shall see me bright,
A burning an' a shining light.

My heart-warm love to guid auld Glen, ‡
The ace an' *wale* of honest men :   pick
When bending down wi' auld grey hairs
Beneath the load of years and cares,
May He who made him still support him,
An' views beyond the grave comfòrt him ;
His worthy fam'ly far and near,
God bless them a' wi' grace and *gear!*   wealth

---

* See note, Vol. I., p. 47.

† Bunyan all know. Rev. John Brown of Haddington (ancestor of the genial and gifted author of " Rab and his Freens ") was editor of an annotated edition of the Bible very popular in Scotland. Boston was Minister of Ettrick, Selkirkshire, and author of a famous theological treatise called "The Fourfold State."—J. H.

‡ Glen is a contraction for Glenconner, the father of Burns's correspondent. It has already been explained that it is the custom in Scotland to address and speak of "lairds" after the name of their properties and farmers after that of their farms.—J. H.

My auld schoolfellow, preacher Willie,
The manly tar, my mason-billie,
And Auchenbay, I wish him joy;
If he's a parent, lass or boy,
May he be *dad*, and Meg the *mither*,
Just five-and-forty years thegither!
And no forgetting wabster Charlie,
I'm tauld he offers very fairly.
An' Lord, remember singing *Sannock*,   Alexander
Wi' *hale breeks*, saxpence, an' a *bannock!* * whole
And next, my auld acquaintance, Nancy,   breeches
Since she is fitted to her fancy,   cake
An' her kind stars hae *airted till* her   guided to
A guid *chiel* wi' a *pickle siller*.† fellow   some cash
My kindest, best respects, I sen' it,
To cousin Kate, an' sister Janet:
Tell them, frae me, wi' chiels be cautious,
For, faith, they'll *aiblins fin'* them   perhaps find
     fashious;   troublesome
To grant a heart is fairly civil,
But to grant a maidenhead 's the devil.
An' lastly, Jamie, for yoursel,
May guardian angels tak a spell,
An' steer you seven miles south o' hell:
But first, before you see heaven's glory,
May ye get mony a merry story,
Mony a laugh, and mony a drink,
And ay eneugh o' needfu' *clink*.   cash

Now *fare ye weel*, an' joy be wi' you: farewell
For my sake, this I beg it o' you,

---

* Sufficiency of clothing, moderate means, and enough to eat. Compare :—

   " Fortune, if thou'll but gie me still
      Hale breeks, a scone, and whisky gill." Scotch Drink.—J. H.

† Siller is, in Scotland, the generic term for money, and points back to a time
when gold coin was nearly unknown to the common people.—J. H.

Assist poor Simson a' ye can,
Ye'll fin' him just an honest man ;
Sae I conclude, and quat my chanter,
Your's, saint or sinner,
                    ROB THE RANTER.

[This Epistle seems to have been addressed to the son of
"guid auld Glen," to whom the poet refers in his letter to
Robert Muir, of 7th March 1788 :—"I took old Glenconner with
me to Mr. Miller's farm ; and he was so pleased with it that I
have wrote an offer to Mr. Miller which, if he accepts, shall make
me sit down a plain farmer—the happiest of lives when a man can
live by it."

Glenconner is in the parish of Ochiltree. "Auld Glen," whose
name was John, was twice married. His son, James, to whom this
epistle is addressed, was of the first family, while "Preacher Wil-
lie" and "Wabster Charlie" were by the second marriage. Willie
was subsequently known for his History of Hindostan, and Charlie
became the founder of the famous chemical works of St. Rollox,
Glasgow, in which he was succeeded by his son John, and later by
his grandson, Charles, proprietor of the Estate of the Glen, Peeble-
shire. The "manly tar, my mason-billie" was David Tennant, who
latterly lived in Swansea, Wales.

Mr. Tennant, of the Glen, possesses a book which was presented
by Burns to "guid auld Glen" on 20th Dec. 1786, with holograph
inscription, thus : "A paltry present from Robert Burns, the Scotch
Bard, to his own friend, and his father's friend, John Tennant, in
Glenconner."]

A NEW PSALM FOR THE CHAPEL OF KILMARNOCK,

ON THE THANKSGIVING-DAY FOR HIS MAJESTY'S RECOVERY.

(HATELY WADDELL'S ED., 1867.)

As I am not devoutly attached to a certain monarch, I
cannot say that my heart ran any risk of bursting, on
Thursday was se'ennight with the struggling emotions of grati-
tude. God forgive me for speaking evil of dignities ! but I must
say, that I look on the whole business as a solemn farce of

pageant mummery. The following are a few stanzas of new
Psalmody for that "joyful solemnity" which I sent to a
London newspaper, with the date and preface following :—
'Kilmarnock, 25th April. Mr. Printer, In a certain chapel,
not fifty leagues from the market cross of this good town, the
following stanzas of Psalmody, it is said, were composed for,
and devoutly sung on, the late joyful solemnity of the 23rd.'
Letter to Mrs. Dunlop, 4th May 1789.

O SING a new song to the Lord,
   Make, all and every one,
A joyful noise, even for the king
   His restoration.

The sons of Belial in the land
   Did set their heads together ;
Come, let us sweep them off, said they,
   Like an o'erflowing river.

They set their heads together, I say,
   They set their heads together ;
On right, on left, and every hand,
   We saw none to deliver.

Thou madest strong two chosen ones,
   To quell the Wicked's pride ;
That Young Man, great in Issachar,
   The burden-bearing tribe.

And him, among the Princes, chief
   In our Jerusalem,
The judge that's mighty in thy law,
   The man that fears thy name.

Yet they, even they, with all their strength,
   Began to faint and fail ;
Even as two howling, ravenous wolves
   To dogs do turn their tail.

Th' ungodly o'er the just prevail'd,
 For so thou hadst appointed ;
That thou might'st greater glory give
 Unto thine own anointed.

And now thou hast restored our State,
 Pity our Kirk also ;
For she by tribulations
 Is now brought very low.

Consume that high-place Patronage,
 From off thy holy hill ;
And in thy fury burn the book—
 Even of that man M'Gill.*

Now hear our prayer, accept our song,
 And fight thy chosen's battle :
We seek but little, Lord, from thee ;
 Thou kens we get as little.

[The letter to Mrs. Dunlop, from which the foregoing Psalm
and its heading are taken, was, by some mistake on the part of
Dr. Currie, or perhaps clerical error of the poet himself, set down
as "4th April," instead of 4th May 1789. The day of National
Thanksgiving for the King's recovery was not appointed till 8th
April, on which day His Majesty sent a message to both Houses
of Parliament announcing that he had appointed Thursday 23rd
April to be observed as a day of public thanksgiving to Almighty
God for the removal of his affliction. And for the greater sol-
emnity of that day, His Majesty had resolved to go to St. Paul's
Cathedral to return thanks to God for the great mercy which
had been extended to him. It was accordingly ordered that both
Houses of Parliament should attend His Majesty at St. Paul's
on said occasion.

Early in March appeared a series of favorable reports betok-
ening the convalescence of the King, and on the 12th of that
month his complete restoration was officially announced. In Lon-

---

* Dr. Wm. M'Gill of Ayr, who published in 1784 an essay on the death of Jesus
Christ, of a Socinian tendency, which was condemned by the evangelical party
as heretical.

don the Church bells were set a-ringing, the Park and Tower
guns were fired at noon, and there was a grand illumination at
night. In Edinburgh, the public rejoicing and illumination were
three days earlier.

The procession to and from St. Paul's Cathedral on 23rd
April, and the service there, were of the most magnificent de-
scription. From the reading of the accounts thereof, Burns was
led to indite the foregoing parody of one of the Scotch metrical
psalms. The "Young Man, great in Issachar" is undoubtedly the
Premier, William Pitt, and the "Judge that's mighty in the
law" must be the Lord Chancellor Thurlow, with his

> "—————— powers to awe.
> His rhetoric, blasphemy and law."

After transcribing the verses in the text, the poet adds in his
letter:—"You must know that the publisher of one of the most
blasphemous party London Newspapers is an acquaintance of
mine, and as I am a little tinctured with the 'Buff and Blue,'
myself, I now and then help him to a stanza."]

SKETCH IN VERSE,

INSCRIBED TO THE RIGHT HON. C. J. FOX.

(CURRIE, 1800.)

How Wisdom and Folly meet, mix, and unite,
How Virtue and Vice blend their black and their
    white,
How Genius, th' illustrious father of fiction,
Confounds rule and law, reconciles contradiction,
I sing: If these mortals, the critics, should bustle,
I care not, not I—let the critics go whistle.

But now for a Patron, whose name and whose glory,
At once may illustrate and honor my story.

Thou first of our orators, first of our wits;
Yet whose parts and acquirements seem just lucky hits;
With knowledge so vast, and with judgment so strong,
No man with the half of 'em e'er could go wrong;

With passions so potent, and fancies so bright,
No man with the half of 'em e'er could go right;
A sorry, poor, misbegot son of the Muses,
For using thy name, offers fifty excuses.

Good L—d, what is Man! for as simple he looks,
Do but try to develop his hooks and his crooks;
With his depths and his shallows, his good and his
    evil,
All in all he's a problem must puzzle the devil.

On his one ruling passion Sir Pope hugely labors,
That, like th' old Hebrew walking-switch eats up its
    neighbors;
Mankind are his show-box—a friend, would you know
    him?
Pull the string, Ruling passion the picture will shew
    him.
What pity, in rearing so beauteous a system,
One trifling particular, *Truth*, should have miss'd him;
For, spite of his fine theoretic positions,
Mankind is a science defies definitions.

Some sort all our qualities each to its tribe,
And think human nature they truly describe;
Have you found this, or t'other? There's more in the
    wind;
As by one drunken fellow his comrades you'll find.
But such is the flaw, or the depth of the plan,
In the make of that wonderful creature called Man;
No two virtues, whatever relation they claim,
Nor even two different shades of the same.
Though like as was ever twin brother to brother,
Possessing the one shall imply you've the other.

But truce with abstraction, and truce with a Muse
Whose rhymes you'll perhaps, Sir, ne'er deign to
    peruse:

Will you leave your *justings*, your jars, and   joustings
    your quarrels,
Contending with Billy for proud-nodding laurels?
My much-honor'd Patron, believe your poor poet,
Your courage, much more than your prudence, you
    show it :
In vain with Squire Billy for laurels you struggle ;
He'll have them by fair trade, if not, he will smuggle :
Not cabinets even of kings would conceal 'em,
He'd up the back-stairs, and by G— he would steal
    'em !
Then feats like Squire Billy's you ne'er can achieve
    'em ;
It is not, out-do him—the task is, out-thieve him !

[The foregoing " Essay on Man," not quite in the manner of
Pope, was partially transcribed to Mrs. Dunlop in the same letter
of 4th May 1789, in which he gave her the preceding " Stanzas
of new Psalmody." In reference to this poem he writes :—" I have
another poetic whim in my head, which I at present dedicate, or
rather inscribe, to the Right Hon. C. J. Fox ; but how long that
fancy may hold I cannot say."

The closing sixteen lines of this piece were first published from
the poet's MS. in the Aldine Edition 1839. This production seems
to exemplify the correctness of Professor Walker's opinion that
Burns was incapable of applying himself to any long-sustained ef-
fort on one subject ; otherwise we might have expected from him
a continuation of his " Poet's Progress," instead of the above dis-
cursive flight.

The London Newspaper referred to by the poet in connection
with this and the preceding piece, of which the Editor was his
own acquaintance, could be none other than " The Evening Star,"
edited by Peter Stuart, who had corresponded with Burns in 1787,
on the subject of his headstone to Fergusson the poet.]

THE WOUNDED HARE.

(EDINBURGH ED., 1793.)

"I have just put the last hand to a little poem, which I think will be something to your taste. One morning lately, as I was out pretty early in the fields, sowing some grass-seeds, I heard the burst of a shot from a neighboring plantation, and presently a poor little wounded hare came crippling by me. You will guess my indignation at the inhuman fellow who could shoot a hare at this season, when all of them have young ones. Indeed, there is something in this business of destroying, for our sport, individuals in the animal creation that do not injure us materially, which I could never reconcile to my ideas of virtue."—*Letter to Alex. Cunningham, 4th May* 1789.

INHUMAN man! curse on thy barb'rous art,
  And blasted· be thy murder-aiming eye;
  May never pity soothe thee with a sigh,
Nor never [1] pleasure glad thy cruel heart!

Go live, poor wand'rer of the wood and field!
  The bitter little that of life remains:
  No more the thickening brakes and [2] verdant plains
To thee a home, or food, or pastime yield.

Seek, mangled wretch, some place of wonted rest,
  No more of rest, but now thy dying bed!
  The sheltering rushes whistling o'er thy head,
The cold earth with thy bloody bosom prest. [3]

Perhaps a mother's anguish adds its woe;
  The playful pair crowd fondly by thy side;
  Ah! helpless nurslings, who will now provide
That life a mother only can bestow! [4]

Oft as by winding Nith I, musing, wait
The sober eve, or hail the cheerful dawn,
I'll miss thee sporting o'er the dewy lawn,
And curse the ruffian's arm,[5] and mourn thy hapless
    fate.

[The author submitted this little poem to the critical judgment of his friend Dr. Gregory of Edinburgh, and from the remarks of that accomplished scholar, he was induced to make a few emendations which will appear from the variations hereto subjoined. Dr. Currie has remarked that "the criticism is not more distinguished by its good sense, than by its freedom from ceremony." Burns was, however, rather "taken aback" by it, for in a letter he wrote soon after he says—"Dr. Gregory is a good man, but he crucifies me. I believe in his iron justice; but, like the devils, I believe and tremble."

One of the advices given by Gregory was to change the structure of the stanza, "as the measure does not flow well; the rhyme of the fourth line being almost lost by its distance from the first." Burns seems to have been of a different opinion in that respect; for he afterwards composed several pieces on the same model, in particular, the Sonnet on his own Birthday, 1793, and the Sonnet on the death of Riddell of Glenriddel, 1794. Tennyson has now made this form of stanza very popular.

The variations are as follow :—

[1] ever   [2] or   [3] *This whole stanza differs thus—*
Seek, mangl'd innocent, some wonted form;
That wonted form, alas! thy dying bed!
The sheltering rushes whistling o'er thy head,
The cold earth with thy blood-stain'd bosom warm.
[4] *This whole stanza was suppressed in the Author's edition, and perhaps it is the best in the poem.*   [5] ruthless wretch.]

(In the above, and kindred pieces, as the lines to the Mouse, to the Mountain Daisy, The Winter Night, &c., Burns shows at his best. Poetically this piece is far superior to the two political compositions preceding it. It is only when his emotions are moved that Burns appears in all his power, and then he moves the emotions of all mankind. Tenderness to animals is the feeling most conspicuous in his verses after the passion of love.—J. H.)

DELIA, AN ODE.

(LIVES OF SCOTTISH POETS, 1822.)

"To the Editor of *The Star*.*—Mr. Printer—If the productions of a simple ploughman can merit a place in the same paper with Sylvester Otway, and the other favorites of the Muses who illuminate the *Star* with the lustre of genius, your insertion of the enclosed trifle will be succeeded by future communications from—Yours, &c.,   R. BURNS.
Ellisland, near Dumfries, 18th May 1789."

FAIR the face of orient day,
   Fair the tints of op'ning rose;
But fairer still my Delia dawns,
   More lovely far her beauty shows.

Sweet the lark's wild warbled lay,
   Sweet the tinkling rill to hear;
But, Delia, more delightful still,
   Steal thine accents on mine ear.

The flower-enamor'd, busy bee
   The rosy banquet loves to sip;
Sweet the streamlet's limpid lapse,
   To the sun-brown'd Arab's lip.

But, Delia, on thy balmy lips
   Let me, no vagrant insect, rove;
O let me steal one liquid kiss,
   For, Oh! my soul is parch'd with love.

---

* The journal in which this piece appeared was the London *Star*, the first of the daily evening papers. The publisher was Mr. Peter Stuart, who had formed an acquaintance with Burns some years previously and corresponded with him in reference to Fergusson's grave.—J. H.

[In reference to the above poem we quote the following note by Robert Chambers :—"There is usually printed in Burns's works a little ode, entitled *Delia*, which from its deficiency of force and true feeling, some have suspected to be not his composition. Allan Cunningham tells a feasible enough looking story about it. 'One day when the Poet was at Brownhill, in Nithsdale, a friend read some verses composed after the pattern of Pope's song by a person of quality, and said : "Burns, this is beyond you. The Muse of Kyle cannot match the Muse of London City." The poet took the paper, hummed the verses over, and then recited *Delia, an Ode.*'" Brownhill was a noted Inn in the Parish of Closeburn, some four or five miles north of Ellisland, and a favorite resting-place of Burns. Many of its panes bore the impress of his diamond. Dalgarnock, where the heroine of "The Braw Wooer" went to the tryste, is an old parish incorporated in Closeburn.—J. H.]

THE GARD'NER WI' HIS PAIDLE.

Tune—"The Gardener's March."

(JOHNSON'S MUSEUM, 1790.)

WHEN rosy May comes in wi' flowers,
To deck her gay, green-spreading bowers,
Then busy, busy are his hours,
    The Gard'ner wi' his paidle.

The crystal waters gently fa',
The merry birds are lovers a',
The scented breezes round him blaw—
    The Gard'ner wi' his paidle.

When purple morning starts the hare
To steal upon her early fare ;
Then thro' the dew he *maun* repair—   must
    The Gard'ner wi' his paidle.

When day, expiring in the west,
The curtain draws o' Nature's rest,
He flies to her arms he lo'es best,
    The Gard'ner wi' his paidle.

[The engraving of the music-plates for volume third of the *Museum* was going on apace, and Burns never lost an opportunity of supplying the proposed airs with suitable words. A few years after this time, he deprived the Gardeners of the honor of this song by altering it to suit the air "Dainty Davie" for George Thomson's collection. This was done by adding a chorus, and changing the closing line of each stanza; but in other respects the two songs are nearly identical.]

ON A BANK OF FLOWERS.

(JOHNSON'S MUSEUM, 1790.)

ON a bank of flowers in a summer day,
   For summer lightly drest.
The youthful, blooming Nelly lay,
   With love and sleep opprest;
When Willie, wand'ring thro' the wood,
Who for her favor oft had sued;
     He gaz'd, he wish'd,
     He fear'd, he blush'd,
And trembled where he stood.

Her closèd eyes, like weapons sheath'd,
   Were seal'd in soft repose;
Her lip, still as she fragrant breath'd,
   It richer dyed the rose;
The springing lilies, sweetly prest,
Wild-wanton kiss'd her rival breast;
     He gaz'd, he wish'd,
     He fear'd, he blush'd,
His bosom ill at rest.

Her robes light-waving in the breeze,
   Her tender limbs embrace;
Her lovely form, her native ease,
   All harmony and grace;

Tumultuous tides his pulses roll,
A faltering, ardent kiss he stole ;
 He gaz'd, he wish'd,
 He fear'd, he blush'd,
And sigh'd his very soul.

As flies the partridge from the brake,
 On fear-inspirèd wings,
So Nelly starting, half-awake,
 Away affrighted springs ;
But Willie, follow'd—as he should,
He overtook her in the wood ;
 He vow'd, he pray'd,
 He found the maid
Forgiving all and good.

[This is merely a new versification of an old song by Mr.
Theobald, set to a beautiful air by a German musician (John E.
Gaillard) which became so popular in Scotland, as to find its way
into the list of Scotch tunes. Burns has compressed the older
version, and rendered the lyric much more modest. The original
may be found in Ramsay's "Tea-table Miscellany."]

YOUNG JOCKIE WAS THE BLYTHEST LAD.

(JOHNSON'S MUSEUM, 1790.)

YOUNG Jockie was the blythest lad,
 In a' our town* or *hereawa ;* hereabout
Fu' blythe he whistled at the *gaud,* † goad
 Fu' lightly danc'd he in the ha' :

He *roos'd* my een sae bonie blue, praised
 He roos'd my waist sae *genty sma*'; elegantly small
An' ay my heart cam to my *mou,* mouth
 When ne'er *a body* heard or saw. any one

---

* Town in Scotland often means the buildings on a farm. Hence the farm-
house with out-houses are called "a farm-town."—J. H.
† While driving the plough-horses.—J. H.

My Jockie toils upon the plain,
   Thro' wind and weet, thro' frost and snaw ;
And o'er the lea I *leuk fu' fain*,   look right longingly
   When Jockie's *owsen* hameward *ca'*.   oxen are driven}

An' ay the night comes round again,
   When in his arms he taks me a' ;
An' ay he vows he'll be my *ain*,   own
   As lang as he has breath to draw.

[This fine love-song was composed to suit an air in Oswald's
Pocket Companion, having the same title ; and Stenhouse informs
us that, with exception of three or four lines, the words in the
text are entirely by Burns.]

THE BANKS OF NITH.

(JOHNSON'S MUSEUM, 1790.)

THE Thames flows proudly to the sea,
   Where royal cities stately stand ;
But sweeter flows the Nith to me,
   Where Comyns *ance* had high command.   once
When shall I see that honor'd land,
   That winding stream I love so dear !
Must wayward Fortune's adverse hand
   For ever, ever keep me here !

How lovely, Nith, thy fruitful vales,
   Where bounding hawthorns gayly bloom ;
And sweetly spread thy sloping dales,
   Where lambkins wanton through the broom !
Tho' wandering now must be my doom,
   Far from thy bonie banks and braes,
May there my latest hours consume,
   Amang the friends of early days !

[This song, intended to depict the feelings of a native of Niths-
dale resident in London, reflecting on his youthful associations of
"Auld Langsyne," was composed to fit a melody by Captain Rid-
dell, in the measure of "Goodnight and joy be wi' ye a'"—"You
will see"—he afterwards wrote to his friend the Colonel of Cro-
challan—"by looking into the third volume of Johnson, that I
have contributed my mite there."]

JAMIE, COME TRY ME.

(JOHNSON'S MUSEUM, 1790.)

Chorus.—Jamie, come try me,
   Jamie, come try me,
  · If thou would win my love,
   Jamie, come try me.

If thou should ask my love,
  Could I deny thee?
If thou would win my love,
  Jamie, come try me!
   Jamie, come try me, &c.

If thou should kiss me, love,
  Wha could espy thee?
If thou wad be my love,
  Jamie, come try me!
   Jamie, come try me, &c.

[These simple stanzas are set in the Museum to a melody by
Oswald, which, when tested, is found to be merely a violin varia-
tion of the tender old Scottish air, "I'll never leave thee." It is
so much beyond the compass of ordinary voices, that we do not
wonder at this little song failing to become popular.]

I LOVE MY LOVE IN SECRET.

(JOHNSON'S MUSEUM, 1790.)

My Sandy *gied* to me a ring,   gave
Was a' beset wi' diamonds fine ;
But I gied him a far better thing,
I gied my heart in pledge o' his ring.

Chorus.—My Sandy O, my Sandy O,
     My bonie, bonie Sandy O ;
     Tho' the love that I owe
     To thee I dare na show,
     Yet I love my love in secret, my Sandy O.

My Sandy brak a piece o' *gowd*,   gold
While down his cheeks the *saut* tears *row'd ;*   salt}
He took a half, and gied it to me,   rolled}
And I'll keep it till the hour I die.
     My Sandy O, &c.

[Although this snatch reads little better than doggrel, the hand
of Burns is visible in it. The old words were very impure, and it
was necessary to preserve the sprightly air. The last stanza re-
cords a very interesting old custom between lovers when fated to
undergo a temporary separation—the breaking of a piece of gold
or silver, one half of which was retained by each party until
sundered hands and hearts could permanently join. The old song
of "Logie o' Buchan," refers to the same practice—

     "He had but ae saxpence, he brak it in twa,
       An' gae me the hauf o't when he gaed awa."]

SWEET TIBBIE DUNBAR.

(JOHNSON'S MUSEUM, 1790.)

O WILT thou go wi' me, sweet, *Tibbie* Dunbar? Isabella
O wilt thou go wi' me, sweet Tibbie Dunbar?
Wilt thou ride on a horse, or be drawn in a car,
Or walk by my side, O sweet Tibbie Dunbar?

I care na thy daddie, his lands and his money,
I care na thy kin, sae high and sae lordly ;
But say that thou'lt hae me for better or waur,
And come in thy coatie, sweet Tibbie Dunbar.

[This is entirely by Burns, written with a view to preserve an air
he much admired, called "Johnie M'Gill," after its supposed com-
poser, John M'Gill, a Girvan fiddler. Perhaps, however. it was so
named through some local fame it had acquired by his excellent
performance of it on the violin. It has been claimed as an Irish
air. Since Burns's days the melody has become widely known, in
consequence of Hector Macneill's words to it, " Come under my
plaidie, the night's gaun to fa'."]

THE CAPTAIN'S LADY.

(JOHNSON'S MUSEUM, 1790.)

Chorus.—O mount and go, mount and make you ready,
          O mount and go, and be the Captain's Lady.

WHEN the drums do beat, and the cannons rattle,
Thou shalt sit in state, and see thy love in battle :
When the drums do beat, and the cannons rattle,
Thou shalt sit in state, and see thy love in battle.
          O mount and go, &c.

When the vanquish'd foe sues for peace and quiet,
To the shades we'll go, and in love enjoy it :
When the vanquish'd foe sues for peace and quiet,
To the shades we'll go, and in love enjoy it.
          O mount and go, &c.

[Stenhouse, who had an opportunity of inspecting Johnson's
manuscripts, informs us that these words are by Burns, and we can
well believe it, for they evince his usual force. The following
will give an idea of the old words :—

Chorus.—I will away, and I will not tarry,
          I will away, and be a Captain's lady.

A Captain's lady fair, she is a dame of honor,
And she has got her maids ay to wait upon her:
Ay to wait upon her, and get a' things ready,
So I will away and be a Captain's lady.
        I will away, &c.

The song was very popular during the Duke of Marlborough's time, and the incessant warfare of that period.]

JOHN ANDERSON, MY JO.

(JOHNSON'S MUSEUM, 1790.)

JOHN Anderson, my jo, John,
    When we were first acquent ;
Your locks were like the raven,
    Your bonie brow was *brent ;*   clear and smooth
But now your brow is *beld,* John,   bald
    Your locks are like the snaw ;
But blessings on your frosty *pow,*   head
    John Anderson, my jo.

John Anderson, my jo, John,
    We *clamb* the hill thegither ;   climbed
And mony a *cantie* day, John,   happy
    We've had wi' ane anither :
Now we *maun* totter down, John,   must
    And hand in hand we'll go,
And sleep thegither at the foot,
    John Anderson, my jo.

[This perfect gem has been sadly abused by admiring versifiers, who, in the vain hope of rendering it more complete by adding stanzas of their own, have only set up a foil to increase the brightness of Burns's classic production. Dr. Currie. in 1800, raised his protest against a so-called "Improved" version of this song which had been given in the first volume of a collection entitled "Poetry, original and selected," printed by Brash and Reid, of Glasgow. With respect to the additional verses, he remarks that

" every reader of discernment will see they are by an inferior hand; and the real author of them ought neither to have given them, nor suffered them to be given to the world, as the production of Burns."

In the *Scots Magazine* for 1797, the version thus complained of by Currie, is given as "John Anderson, my Jo, Improved—by Robert Burns," and consists in all of eight double stanzas, including the two in our text, marred by unhappy alterations. Dr. Waddell mentions that the version in question was the production of Mr. William Reid, one of the partners of the publishing firm of Brash and Reid.]

MY LOVE, SHE'S BUT A LASSIE YET.

(JOHNSON'S MUSEUM, 1790.)

My love, she's but a lassie yet,　　
My love, she's but a lassie yet;　　
We'll let her stand a year or twa,　　
She'll no be half sae saucy yet;　　
I rue the day I sought her O!　　
I rue the day I sought her O!　　
Wha gets her need*na* say he's woo'd,　　　　not　　
But he may say he has bought her O.

Come draw a drap o' the best *o't* yet,　　　　of it　　
Come draw a drap o' the best o't yet;　　
Gae seek for pleasure whare ye will,　　　　go　　
But here I never miss'd it yet,　　
We're a' dry wi' drinkin o't,　　
We're a' dry wi' drinkin o't;　　
The minister kiss't the fiddler's wife;　　
He could na preach for thinkin o't.

[Stenhouse claims the title and the four concluding lines of this remarkable ditty as ancient; and the remainder, he assures us, is the composition of Burns. The melody is a favorite dancing-tune, and was anciently known as "Lady Badinscoth's Reel." It was, nevertheless, used as a song so early as 1641, in scorn of the

Lords of the congregation and the covenanters. A pamphlet of
that period gives the following sample of the words.

> Put up thy dagger, Jamie,
> It never was intended
> That Bishops fall, no, not at all,
> When Parliament is ended.
> 'Twas only for to *flam* thee   deceive
> That all things should be mended;
> But we've got the game, and we'll keep the same,
> When Parliament is ended.]

SONG—TAM GLEN.

(JOHNSON'S MUSEUM, 1790.)

My heart is a breaking, dear *Tittie*,   Sister
   Some counsel unto me come len',
To anger them a' is a pity,
   But what will I do wi' Tam Glen?

I'm thinking, wi' sic a braw fellow,
   In *poortith* I might mak a *fen';* *   poverty   shift
What care I in riches to wallow,
   If I *mauna* marry Tam Glen!   must not

There's Lowrie the *laird* o' Drumeller—   proprietor
   "Gude day to you"—brute! he comes *ben:*   in
He brags and he blaws o' his *siller*,   money
   But when will he dance like Tam Glen!

My *Minnie* does constantly *deave* me,   mother   deafen
   And bids me beware o' young men ;
They flatter, she says, to deceive me,
   But wha can think sae o' Tam Glen!

---

* The phrase "make a fen'" means to make a shift to get along.—J. H.

My daddie says, *gin* I'll forsake him,　　　　if
　He'd gie me gude hunder marks ten ;*
But, if it's ordain'd I maun take him,
　O wha will I get but Tam Glen !

Yestreen at the Valentine's dealing,
　My heart to my *mou gied* a *sten ;*　mouth gave　bound
For thrice I drew ane without failing,
　And thrice it was written "Tam Glen" !

The last Halloween I was *waukin*　waking (*watching*)
　My *droukit* sark-sleeve, as ye ken,　drenched
His likeness came up the house staukin,
　And the very grey breeks o' Tam Glen ! †

Come, counsel, dear Tittie, don't tarry ;
　I'll gie ye my bonie black hen,
Gif ye will advise me to marry　　　　It
　The lad I *lo'e* dearly, Tam Glen.　love

[This has, from the day of its first publication, been considered one of the happiest of its author's humorous songs. Dr. Waddell well observes that "feminine love and logic were never more admirably combined, and the *moral* elevated for ever above the base *commercial* idea of matrimony." It is recorded that when the lads and lasses of the period met after its publication, that they were wont with a slap on the thigh, to salute each other with "the very grey breeks o' Tam Glen."

In the *Museum*, it is set to an old tune, called "Tam Glen," consisting of one part only, which has some arch character in it; but that air has long been laid aside for the two-part melody, called "The muckin o' Geordie's byre," which suits it admirably.]

---

* The mark was thirteen shillings and fourpence Scotch, or one shilling and one and a third penny sterling.—J. H.
† Drenching the shirt-sleeve by putting it in water and watching it while it dries is one of the old Hallowe'en customs. Superstition says that the watcher's future mate will come and turn it.—J. H.

CARLE, AN THE KING COME.

(JOHNSON'S MUSEUM, 1790.)

Chorus.—*Carle*, an the King come,   comrade
            Carle, an the King come,
            Thou shalt dance and I will sing,
            Carle, an the King come.

An somebody were come again,   if
Then somebody *maun* cross the main,   must
And every man shall *hae* his *ain*,   have   own
      Carle, an the King come,
            Carle, an the King come, &c.

I trow we *swappet* for the *warse*,   bartered   worse
We gae the boot and better horse ;
· An that we'll tell them at the *corss*,   cross
      Carle, an the King come,
            Carle, an the King come, &c.

Coggie, an the King come,   drinking-cup
Coggie, an the King come,
I' se be *fou*, an' thou'se be *toom*,   I will   full   empty
      Coggie, an the King come,
            Coggie, an the King come, &c.

[This is an old song, dating from the period of the Cromwell
Interregnum, dressed up by Burns, whose improvements are very
apparent on comparing it with any version of the song printed be-
fore the year 1789. The last verse, addressed to the "Coggie" of
the singer, is very characteristic, *fou* being used in its double,
punning sense, just as *full* might be with us. The poet introduced
a similar stanza at the close of "Hey tuttie taitie," thus :—

> "Cog, an ye were ay fou,
>   Cog, an ye were ay fou,
>   I wad sit an' sing to you,
>   An ye were ay fou!"]

THE LADDIE'S DEAR SEL'.

(JOHNSON'S MUSEUM, 1790.)

THERE'S a youth in this city, it were a great pity
    That he from our lasses should wander awa' ;
For he's bonie and *braw*, weel-favor'd witha',   fine
    An' his hair has a natural *buckle* an' a'.   curl

His coat is the hue o' his bonnet sae blue,
    His *fecket* is white as the new-driven snaw ;   under-shirt
His hose they are *blae*, and his *shoon* like the   pale-blue
    slae,   shoes sloe
    And his clear *siller* buckles, they dazzle us a'.   silver

For beauty and fortune the laddie's been courtin ;
    Weel-featur'd, *weel-tocher'd*, weel-mounted   well-dowered
        and braw ;
But chiefly the siller that *gars* him *gang till* her,   makes
    The penny's the jewel that beautifies a'.   go to

There's Meg wi' the *mailen* that fain wad   small farm
    a haen him,   have had
    And Susie, wha's daddie was *laird* o' the Ha' ;   owner
There's *lang-tocher'd* Nancy maist fetters   largely dowered
    his fancy,
    But the laddie's dear sel, he loes dearest of a'.

[The poet's note to Glenriddell's copy says—"The first half-
stanza of the song is old, and the rest is mine. The air is
claimed by Neil Gow, who calls it the Lament for his brother."]

WHISTLE O'ER THE LAVE O'T.

(JOHNSON'S MUSEUM, 1790.)

FIRST when Maggie was my care,
Heav'n, I thought, was in her air,
Now we're married—*speir na mair*,   ask no more
    But whistle o'er the *lave o't!*   rest of it
Meg was meek, and Meg was mild,
Sweet and harmless as a child—(¹)
Wiser men than me's beguil'd ;
    Whistle o'er the lave o't !

How we live, my Meg and me,
How we love, and how we *gree*,   agree
I care na by how few may see—
    Whistle o'er the lave o't !
Wha I wish were maggot's meat,
Dish'd up in her winding-sheet,
I could write—but Meg may see't—
    Whistle o'er the lave o't !

[This favorite song was written by Burns as a substitute for some witty but indelicate verses preserved in Herd's Collection. The air, which is very popular, has been claimed as the composition of John Bruce, a musician who resided in Dumfries about 1720. There can be little doubt, however, that the air was known under the name of "Dance Katie Bairdie," long antecedent to that date. The following variation is found in some manuscripts :—

¹ Bonie Meg was Nature's child.]

MY *EPPIE* ADAIR.   Elspeth

(JOHNSON'S MUSEUM, 1790.)

Chorus.—AN' O my Eppie, my jewel, my Eppie,
    Wha wad na be happy wi' Eppie Adair !

By love, and by beauty, by law, and by duty,
I swear to be true to my Eppie Adair!
By love, and by beauty, by law, and by duty,
I swear to be true to my Eppie Adair!
　　And O my Eppie, &c.

A' pleasure exile me, dishonor defile me,
If e'er I beguile ye, my Eppie Adair!
A' pleasure exile me, dishonor defile me,
If e'er I beguile thee, my Eppie Adair!
　　And O my Eppie, &c.

[These words were supplied to fit a very beautiful melody by
Oswald.]

EPIGRAM ON FRANCIS GROSE THE ANTI-QUARY.

(STEWART, 1801.)

THE Devil got notice that Grose was a-dying,
So whip! at the summons, old Satan came flying;
But when he approach'd where poor Francis lay moan-
　　ing,
And saw each bed-post with its burthen a-groaning,
Astonish'd, confounded, cries Satan—'By G—,
I'll want him ere take such a damnable load!'

[This Epigram was published in the *Scots Magazine* for June
1791, in connection with a brief memoir of Grose, who died sud-
denly in Dublin on the 12th of the preceding month. He seems
to have been born in 1740, as his age at his death is stated to
have been fifty-one. His father was a wealthy jeweller, resident
at Richmond, near London, and died in 1769. In early life,
Grose held a commission as Captain in the Surrey Militia, of
which he became Adjutant and Paymaster. His personal extrav-
agance and careless bookkeeping caused him to resign that post,
and his pecuniary difficulties having roused his latent talents for

III.　　　　　　　　　　F

antiquarian research, his after-life was devoted to literature of that kind. He married, and had his headquarters at Canterbury, where he obtained a great reputation for wit and sociality; and it is pleasing to be told by his biographer, that "when he set the table in a roar, it was never at the expense of virtue or good manners."

Such was the gentleman who was introduced to Burns at the board of Mr. Riddell of Friar's Carse in the summer of 1789. It is stated in the magazine notice above referred to, that the Epigram in the text "was so much relished by Grose, that he made it serve as an excuse for prolonging the convivial occasion which gave it birth to a very late hour."]

ON THE

LATE CAPTAIN GROSE'S

PEREGRINATIONS THRO' SCOTLAND, COLLECTING THE ANTIQUITIES OF THAT KINGDOM.

(EDINBURGH ED., 1793.)

HEAR, Land o' Cakes, and brither Scots,
Frae Maidenkirk to Johnnie Groat's;*—
If there's a hole in a' your coats,
   I *rede* you *tent* it :† counsel attend
A *chield's* amang you takin notes,   fellow is
   And faith he'll prent it :

If in your bounds ye chance to light
Upon a fine, fat, *fodgel* wight,   jolly
O' stature short, but genius bright,
   That's he, mark weel ;
And wow ! he has an unco sleight
   O' cauk and keel.‡

---

* Maidenkirk is an inversion of Kirkmaiden, the most southerly parish in Scotland. Johnnie Groat's, or John o' Groat's, is in Caithness-shire, and is the most northerly point in Scotland.—J. H.

† Take care to keep it out of sight.—J. H.

‡ He has uncommon skill in painting with chalks—white and red.—J. H.

By ·some auld, *houlet*-haunted *biggin,** owl   building
Or kirk deserted by its *riggin,*   roof
It's ten to ane ye'll find him snug in
      Some *eldritch* part,   unholy
Wi' deils, they say, L—d save 's! *colleaguin* conspiring
      At some black art.

Ilk ghaist that haunts auld ha' or *chaumer,* every} chamber}
Ye gipsy-gang that deal in glamour, †
And you, deep-read in hell's black grammar,
      Warlocks and witches ;
Ye'll quake at his conjuring hammer,
      Ye midnight bitches.

It's tauld he was a sodger bred,
And ane wad rather *fa'n* than fled ;   fallen
But now he's *quat* the *spurtle*-blade,   quitted   sword
      And *dog-skin wallet,*   knapsack
And taen the—Antiquarian trade,
      I think they call it.

He has a *fouth* o' auld nick-nackets :   abundance
Rusty *airn* caps and jinglin jackets,‡   iron
Wad *haud* the Lothians three§ in *tackets,* keep} shoe-nails}
      A *towmont* gude ;   twelvemonth
And parritch-pats and auld *saut-backets,*   salt-boxes
      Before the Flood.

---

* *Vide* his Antiquities of Scotland. (*R. B.* 1793.)

† Glamour is deception by supernatural means. To "cast the glamour" over a person is to make him or her see things in a false, and commonly in too favorable, a light. Johnie Faa, the king of the gipsies, "cast the glamour" over the Countess of Cassilis so that she fell in love with him.—J. H.

‡ *Vide* his treatise on ancient armor and weapons.—*R. B.,* 1793.

§ The "Lothians three" are three counties in Scotland, namely Mid-Lothian or Edinburgh-shire, West-Lothian or Linlithgowshire, and East-Lothian or Haddingtonshire.—J. H.

Of Eve's first fire he has a cinder ;
Auld Tubalcain's fire-*shool* and fender ;   shovel
That which distinguishèd the gender
    O' Balaam's ass :
A broomstick o' the witch of Endor.
    Weel *shod* wi' brass.   mounted

Forbye, he'll shape you aff fu' *gleg* besides smartly
The cut of Adam's *philibeg ;*   kilt
The knife that *nicket* Abel's *craig* cut throat
    He'll prove you fully,
It was a *faulding jocteleg,** folding knife
    Or lang-kail *gullie.* large knife

But wad ye see him in his glee,
For *meikle* glee and fun has he, much
Then set him down, and twa or three
    Gude fellows wi' him :
And port, O port ! shine thou *a wee*, a short time
    And then ye'll see him !

Now, by the Pow'rs o' verse and prose !
Thou art a dainty chield, O Grose !—
Whae'er o' thee shall ill suppose,
    They sair *misca'* thee ; miscall
I'd take the rascal by the nose,
    Wad say, " Shame *fa'* thee." befall

[This poem, with a few verbal variations, and curtailed of one
stanza, appeared in the *Scots Magazine* for November, 1791. We
have also been assured that it had been printed so early as 4th
September, 1789, in the columns of the *Kelso Chronicle*, with the
signature " Thomas A. Linn " attached.

Grose's method of publishing his works was to issue them in
numbers, with four plates and letterpress in each, at 3*s.* 6*d.* ; and

---

* The etymology of this word was unknown till recently, when an old knife
was found with the cutler's name marked ' Jacques de Liege.' Thus it is in
exact analogy with, ' Andrea di Ferrara.'—*Lord Hailes.*

again in volumes as these were completed. His work on the "Antiquities of England and Wales" was commenced in 1773, and the fourth volume appeared in 1776. He supplemented these by two additional volumes embracing subjects in Guernsey and Jersey; and in 1787, the entire work was reprinted in eight volumes. He also produced several subsidiary works, such as his "Military Antiquities," and "A Treatise on Ancient Armor," prior to his labors in Scotland, from 1789 to 1791. He commenced his operations in Dumfries-shire, as is proved by the dates engraved upon his earlier plates. "Sweetheart Abbey" is marked "June 1789," and "Lincluden Abbey" is dated "August 1789." A young man travelled along with him who made himself very handy in many respects, and not least in etching the copperplates for his work. The Captain termed him his "Guinea-pig." His work on the "Antiquities of Scotland" was completed in 1791, in two volumes, comprising 190 views with letterpress. In May of that year, he arrived in Dublin with the object of executing a similar antiquarian work for Ireland; but, shortly after his arrival, he was seized with an apoplectic fit, which carried him off on the 12th of that month.]

THE KIRK OF SCOTLAND'S ALARM.

A BALLAD.

Tune—"Come rouse, Brother Sportsmen!"

(STEWART, 1801.)

ORTHODOX! orthodox, who believe in John Knox,
  Let me sound an alarm to your conscience:
A heretic blast has been blown in the West,
  That "what is no sense must be nonsense,"
Orthodox! That "what is no sense must be nonsense."

Doctor Mac! Doctor Mac, you should *streek*   stretch
            on a rack,
  To strike evil-doers wi' terror:
To join Faith and Sense, upon any pretence,
  Was heretic, damnable error,
Doctor Mac!* 'Twas heretic, damnable error.

---

* Dr. M'Gill, Ayr.—*R. B.*

Town of Ayr ! town of Ayr, it was rash, I declare,
  To meddle wi' mischief a-brewing,*
Provost John † is still deaf to the Church's relief,
  And Orator Bob ‡ is its ruin,   .
Town of Ayr ! Yes, Orator Bob is its ruin.

D'rymple mild ! D'rymple mild, tho' your heart's like
    a child's,
  And your life like the new-driven snaw,
Yet that winna save you, auld Satan must have you,
  For preaching that three's ane an' twa,
D'rymple mild ! § For preaching that three's ane an' twa.

Calvin's sons ! Calvin's sons, seize your spiritual guns,
  Ammunition you never can need ;
Your hearts are the stuff will be powder enough,
  And your skulls are a storehouse o' lead,
Calvin's sons ! Your skulls are a storehouse o' lead.

Rumble John ! rumble John, mount the steps with a
        groan,
    Cry, "the Book is with heresy cramm'd ; "
Then out wi' your ladle, deal brimstone like
        aidle,   liquid manure
  And roar ev'ry note of the D—'d,
Rumble John ! ‖ And roar ev'ry note of the D—'d.

Simper James ! simper James, leave your fair
      Killie dames,   Kilmarnock
  There's a holier chase in your view :

I'll lay on your head, that the pack you'll soon lead,
  For puppies like you there's but few,
Simper James ! * For puppies like you there's but few.

Singet Sawnie ! singet Sawnie, are ye   singed (*puny-looking*)
     huirdin the penny,   hoarding
Unconscious what danger awaits?
With a jump, yell, and howl, alarm ev'ry soul,
  For Hannibal's just at your gates,
Singet Sawnie ! † For Hannibal's just at your gates. ‡

Poet Willie ! poet Willie, gie the Doctor a volley,
  Wi' your "Liberty's Chain" and your wit ;
O'er Pegasus' side ye ne'er laid a stride,
  Ye but smelt, man, the place where he sh-t,
Poet Willie ! § Ye but smelt, man, the place where
  he sh-t.

Barr Steenie ! Barr Steenie, what mean ye? what
     mean ye?
  If ye meddle nae mair wi' the matter,
Ye may hae some pretence, man, to *havins*   manners
     and sense, man,
  Wi' people that ken ye nae better,
Barr Steenie ! ‖ Wi' people that ken ye nae better.

Jamie Goose ! Jamie Goose, ye made but toom roose, **
  In hunting the wicked Lieutenant ;

---

* James Mackinlay, Kilmarnock.—*R. B.*
† Alexander Moodie of Riccarton.—*R. B.*
‡ An allusion to Hannibal approaching the gates of Rome.—J. H.
§ William Peebles, in Newton-upon-Ayr, a poetaster, who, among many other things, published an ode on the Centenary of the Revolution, in which was the line,
     "And bound in Liberty's endearing chain."—*R. B.*

‖ Stephen Young, of Barr.—*R. B.*
** You gained but little glory.—J. H.

But the Doctor's your mark, for the L—d's holy ark,
 He has cooper'd an' *ca'd* a wrang pin in't, driven
Jamie Goose ! * He has cooper'd· an' ca'd a wrang
  pin in't.

Davie Bluster ! Davie Bluster, for a saint if ye muster,
 The *core* is *no* nice o' recruits ; party not
Yet to worth let's be just, royal blood ye might boast,
 If the Ass were the king o' the brutes,
Davie Bluster ! † If the Ass were the king o' the
  brutes.

Cessnock-side! Cessnock-side, wi' your turkey-cock pride,
 Of manhood but sma' is your share :
Ye've the figure, 'tis true, ev'n your foes maun allow,
 And your friends dare na say ye hae mair,
Cessnock-side ! ‡ And your friends dare na say ye
  hae mair.

Muirland Jock ! muirland Jock, when the L—d makes
  a rock,
 To crush common-sense for her sins ;
If ill-manners were wit, there's no mortal so fit
 To confound the poor Doctor at ance,
Muirland Jock ! § To confound the poor Doctor at
  ance.

Andro *Gowk !* Andro Gowk, ye may slander cuckoo (*fool*)
  the Book,
 An' the Book nought the *waur*, let me tell ye ; worse

---

* James Young, in New Cumnock, who had lately been foiled in an ecclesiastical prosecution against a Lieutenant Mitchel.—*R. B*

† David Grant, Ochiltree.—*R. B.*

‡ George Smith, Galston.—*R. B* Burns praises Dr. Smith in "The Holy Fair." His feeling towards him seems to have changed.—J. H.

§ John Shepherd, Muirkirk.—*R. B.*

Tho' ye're rich, an' look big, yet, lay by hat an' wig,
　　An' ye'll hae a calf's-head o' sma' value,
Andro Gowk ! *　Ye'll hae a calf's-head o' sma' value.

Daddy Auld ! daddie Auld, there's a *tod* in the　　fox
　　　　fauld,　　　　　　　　　　　　　　　　　fold
　　A tod *meikle waur* than the clerk ; †　　much worse
Tho' ye do little *skaith*, ye'll be in at the death,　hurt
　　For *gif* ye canna bite, ye may bark,　　　　　if
Daddy Auld ! ‡　Gif ye canna bite, ye may bark.

Holy Will ! holy Will, there was wit in your skull,
　　When ye pilfer'd the alms o' the poor ;
The *timmer* is scant when ye're taen for　timber (*material*)
　　　　a saunt,
　　Wha should swing in a *rape* for an hour,　　rope
Holy Will ! §　Ye should swing in a rape for an hour.

Poet Burns ! poet Burns, wi' your priest-*skelpin*　spanking
　　　　turns,
　　Why desert ye your auld native shire ?
Your muse is a gypsy, yet were she e'en tipsy,
　　She could ca' us *nae waur* than we are,　　no worse
Poet Burns !　She could ca' us nae waur than we are.

PRESENTATION STANZAS TO CORRESPONDENTS.

Factor John ! Factor John, whom the L—d made
　　　　alone,
　　And ne'er made anither, thy peer,

----

* Dr. Andrew Mitchel, Monkton.—*R. B.*
† Burns always liked to term Gavin Hamilton "The Clerk."
‡ William Auld, Mauchline : see "Holy Willie's Prayer."—*R. B.*
§ *Vide* the "Prayer" of this saint.—*R. B.* The "Saint" was Holy Willie. For "Prayer" see vol. i., p. 91.—*J. H.*

Thy poor servant, the Bard, in respectful regard,
  He presents thee this token sincere,
Factor John ! He presents thee this token sincere.

Afton's Laird ! Afton's Laird, when your pen can be
        spared,
  A copy of this I bequeath,
On the same *sicker* score as I mention'd before, secure
  To that trusty auld worthy, Clackleith, *
Afton's Laird ! To that trusty auld worthy, Clackleith.

[The history of the foregoing satire may be briefly stated thus :—
Dr. William M'Gill, one of the two ministers of the parochial
charge of Ayr, had published, in 1786, an Essay on the Death of
Christ, the doctrines of which were reckoned unscriptural by the
evangelical party in the church. It provoked much severe criti-
cism ; but its author remained silent, till a neighboring minister,
Dr. William Peebles, in preaching a centenary sermon on the Rev-
olution, on 5th November, 1788, denounced the essay as
heretical, and its author as one who received the privileges of the
church with one hand, and stabbed her with the other. M'Gill
published a defence ; but on 15th April, 1789, a complaint of his
non-orthodoxy was lodged with the Synod. The case came before
the General Assembly in May following ; and by a deliverance of
that Court, a remit was ordered to be made to a committee of fif-
teen ministers and ten elders to draw up an abstract of objection-
able passages from Dr. M'Gill's publication, and to lay the same
before the presbytery within two months. William Fisher—the
" Holy Willie " whom the poet had already so severely scourged—
was one of the elders chosen, and the ministers satirized in this
poem (commencing at stanza sixth) were all against the accused.
On 15th July, 1789, the committee was formed, and began its work ;
and at this stage Burns interposed by lending the aid of his pen in
favor of M'Gill.

We first hear of this satire in the poet's letter to Mr. John
Logan of Knockshinnoch, of date 7th August, 1789. He had
picked up acquaintance with that gentleman in course of his fre-

---

* Mr. Johnston of Clackleith, a neighbor of Mr. Logan of Knockshinnoch or
"laird of Afton." It has already been said that it is the custom in Scotland to
name lairds after their properties and farmers after their farms.—J. H.

quent journeys between Ellisland and Mauchline, during the previous twelve months.   He thus proceeds :—" I dare not write you a long letter, as I am going to intrude on your time with a long ballad.   I have, as you will shortly see, finished ' The Kirk's Alarm ;' but, now that it is done, and that I have laughed once or twice at the conceits in some of the stanzas, I am determined not to let it get into the public; so I send you this copy, the first that I have sent to Ayrshire, except some few of the stanzas which I wrote off in embryo for Gavin Hamilton, under the express provision and request that you will only read it to ' *a few of us,*' and do not on any account give, or permit to be taken, any copy of the ballad.   If I could be of any service to Dr. M'Gill, I would do it, though it should be at a much greater expense than irritating a few bigoted priests ; but I am afraid that serving him in his present *embarras* is a task too hard for me.   I have enemies enow, God knows, though I do not wantonly add to the number.   Still, as I think there is some merit in two or three of the thoughts, I send it to you as a small, but sincere testimony how much, and with what respectful esteem I am," &c.

Burns would seem to have gathered quite a little troop of friends in the vale of Afton, near New Cumnock.   From some inspiration connected with this district must have sprung the bard's exquisite pastoral song, "Afton Water," which we conjecture to have been composed in 1791.   Sanquhar, near the boundary line between Dumfries and Ayr shires, also was a favorite resting-place of the poet in his journeys between Ellisland and Ayrshire ; and a constant intercourse was kept up between "Crichton Peel" * and the vale of Afton.   A curious memorandum in Burns's handwriting addressed to Provost Edward Whigham of Sanquhar has recently turned up, which evinces that fact.   It is as follows : "Mem.—To get from John French his sets of the following old Scots airs—(1) The auld yowe jumpt o'er the tether.   (2) Nine nights awa, welcome hame my dearie.   (3) A' the nights o' the year, the chapman drinks nae water.   If Mr. Whigham will, either of himself, or through the medium of that hearty veteran of original wit, and social iniquity—Clackleith—procure these airs, it will be extremely obliging to—R. B."

One of the supplementary " presentation stanzas " in the text refers to Mr. Johnston of Clackleith, who was to have the privilege of a copy of this satire

"On the same sicker score as I mentioned before,"

---

* The burgh of Sanquhar is so called because an ancient castle or peel-house of the Crichtons stands close to it, in which "The Admirable Crichton" is said to have been born.   The close intercourse was between the Provost of Sanquhar, Mr. Whigham, and Mr. Logan and other friends in the vale of Afton.—J. H.

that is on the terms of the "express provision and request" embodied in the letter above quoted.

The "factor John" of the other "presentation stanza" was, in all likelihood, John Kennedy, factor to the last Earl of Dumfries, who is noticed at p. 256, vol. I., and to whom the "Mountain Daisy" was enclosed in April, 1786. The same expression is made use of here, which he adopted three years after this date, in the song "O saw ye bonie Lesley"—"Nature made her what she is, and never made anither."

Burns enclosed a copy of "The Kirk's Alarm" to Mr. Graham of Fintry some months after it was composed, and, in the letter which accompanied it, says, "I think you must have heard of Dr. M'Gill, one of the clergymen of Ayr, and his heretical book. God help him, poor man! Though he is one of the worthiest, as well as one of the ablest, of the whole priesthood of the Kirk of Scotland, in every sense of that ambiguous term, yet the poor Doctor and his numerous family are in imminent danger of being thrown out to the mercy of the winter winds." The issue of this prosecution was not very satisfactory to Burns, and other lovers of free enquiry; for M'Gill, after enduring the brow-beating of his censors for two years, was harassed into the humbling necessity of apologizing to the offended majority in the church courts, and of declaring his adherence to the Kirk's Confession of Faith in all points.

The poet's notes to his own text are chiefly taken from the Glenriddell MS. In farther explanation of verse third—"Town of Ayr," &c., it is necessary to state that when Dr. M'Gill's case first came before the Synod, the Magistrates of that town published an advertisement in the newspapers, bearing a warm testimony to the excellence of the defender's character, and their appreciation of his services as a pastor.

The manuscripts of this satire are very numerous, and very dissimilar in the arrangement of the stanzas. The copies having the fullest number of verses, contain eighteen, exclusive of a supplementary or presentation stanza.

A very fine holograph copy is preserved in the Poet's Monument at Edinburgh. It has seventeen verses, and the supplementary one, addressed to "Factor John." The stanza omitted is the one dedicated to "Holy Will;" and that concerning "Muirland Jock" differs very much from, but is no improvement on, the one in our text. Allan Cunningham gives a variation of this verse:— "Muirland George, whom the L—d made a scourge." This does not tally with the author's note which marks "John Shepherd, of Muirkirk" as the person hit at.

The Glenriddell version is headed, "A ballad on the heresy of Dr. M'Gill, Ayr," and contains fifteen stanzas, those omitted being "Holy Will," "Singet Sawnie," and "Town of Ayr;" and the verse on "Davie Bluster" is a new formation, beginning "Davie Rant." *

There are two holograph copies in the British Museum, from one of which we take our heading, while the name of the tune to which the ballad is to be sung is from the Edinburgh MS. There are eleven stanzas in one of the Museum copies, and only nine in the other. The latter is the one which was transcribed for Mr. Graham of Fintry, where, instead of "Orthodox," we have "Brother Scots" for the opening words. The other verses are (2) Dr. Mac, (3) Town of Ayr, (4) D'rymple mild, (5) Calvin's sons, (6) Rumble John, (7) Daddie Auld, (8) Singet Sawnie, (9) Poet Willie. The verses wanting in the other copy of eleven stanzas are "Holy Will," "Poet Burns," "Muirland Jock," "Cess-nock-side," "Barr Steenie," "Andro Gowk," and "Davie Bluster." In that copy, the stanza on "Jamie Goose" is changed to "Billy Goose."]

SONNET ON RECEIVING A FAVOR.

10 AUG., 1789.

Addressed to ROBERT GRAHAM, Esq. of Fintry.

(CURRIE, 1800.)

I CALL no Goddess to inspire my strains,
A fabled Muse may suit a bard that feigns:
Friend of my life! my ardent spirit burns,
And all the tribute of my heart returns,
For boons accorded, goodness ever new,
The gift still dearer, as the giver you.
Thou orb of day! thou other paler light!
And all ye many sparkling stars of night!
If aught that giver from my mind efface,
If I that giver's bounty e'er disgrace,

---

* The remodelled verse in the Glenriddell MS. reads thus:—

    Davie Rant, Davie Rant, in a face like a saunt,
       And a heart that would poison a hog,
    Raise an impudent roar, like a breaker lee-shore,
       Or the Kirk will be *tint* in a bog.

Then roll to me along your wand'ring spheres,
Only to number out a villain's years!
I lay my hand upon my swelling breast,
And grateful would, but cannot speak the rest.

[At page 15, *supra*, the reader has seen the poet's epistle, soliciting the favor which, now, after a year's waiting, had been granted. That favor consisted in a formal appointment to exercise the duties of an exciseman in the rural district where the poet's farm was situated. However, he does not appear to have entered upon these avocations till the month of November following. The earliest reference to this in his correspondence occurs on the first of that month, when he merely informs Ainslie of the appointment. Writing to Mr. Graham on 9th December, he says, "I have found the Excise business go on a great deal smoother with me than I expected, owing a good deal to the generous friendship of Mr. Mitchell, my collector, and the kind assistance of Mr. Findlater, my supervisor. I dare to be honest, and I fear no labor. Nor do I find my hurried life greatly inimical to my correspondence with the Muses. I take the liberty to enclose you a few bagatelles, all of them the productions of my leisure thoughts in my Excise rides."
The original MS. of the text, with postmark of date, is in the possession of James T. Gibson-Craig, Esq., Edinburgh, which contains the concluding couplet, omitted by Currie, and which does not usually form a part of the text of this poem.]

EXTEMPORANEOUS EFFUSION

ON BEING APPOINTED TO AN EXCISE DIVISION.

(CROMEK, 1808.)

SEARCHING auld wives' barrels,
    Ochon, the day!
That *clarty barm* should stain my laurels; dirty yeast
    But—what'll ye say?
These movin' things *ca'd* wives an'   called
    weans,   children
Wad move the very hearts o' stanes!

[Eight days after the preceding sonnet to Mr. Graham was composed, the poet's wife brought him a son who was named Francis Wallace, in compliment to the family name of his patron, Mrs. Dunlop. In his epistle to Dr. Blacklock in the following October, he refers to this subject in similar terms to those in the text:—

> "I'm turn'd a gauger—Peace be here!
> Parnassian queans, I fear, I fear,
>   Ye'd now disdain me,
> And then my fifty pounds a year
>   Will little gain me."

To his friend Ainslie he says, on 1st November:—"Without ever having been an expectant, as they call their journeymen excisemen, I was directly planted down to all intents and purposes an officer of Excise, there to flourish and bring forth fruits—worthy of repentance. I know how the word "exciseman," or still more opprobrious "gauger" will sound in your ears. I too have seen the day when my auditory nerves would have felt very delicately on this subject; but a wife and children are things that have a wonderful power in blunting these kind of sensations. Fifty pounds a year for life, and a provision for widows and orphans, you will allow, is no bad settlement for a *poet*."

But the best sentiment he uttered on the subject was to the mother of his patron Glencairn, " I would much rather have it said that my profession borrowed credit from me, than that I borrowed credit from my profession."]

CALEDONIA—A BALLAD.

Tune—"Caledonian Hunts' Delight" of Mr. Gow.

(CURRIE, 1800.)

THERE was once a time, but old Time was then
          young,
    That brave Caledonia, the chief of her line,
From some of your northern deities sprung,
    (Who knows not that brave Caledonia's divine?)
From Tweed to the *Orcades* was her domain,   Orkneys
    To hunt, or to pasture, or do what she would:
Her heav'nly relations there fixèd her reign,
    And pledg'd her their godheads to warrant it good.

A lambkin in peace, but a lion in war,
   The pride of her kindred, the heroine grew :
Her grandsire, old Odin,* triumphantly swore,—
   "Whoe'er shall provoke thee, th' encounter shall
       rue !"
With tillage or pasture at times she would sport,
   To feed her fair flocks by her green rustling corn ;
But chiefly the woods were her fav'rite resort,
   Her darling amusement, the hounds and the horn.

Long quiet she reigned ; till thitherward steers
   A flight of bold eagles from Adria's strand : †
Repeated, successive, for many long years,
   They darken'd the air, and they plunder'd the
      land :
Their pounces were murder, and terror their cry,
   They'd conquer'd and ruin'd a world beside ;
She took to her hills, and her arrows let fly,
   The daring invaders, they fled or they died.

The Cameleon-Savage disturb'd her repose,
   With tumult, disquiet, rebellion, and strife ;
Provok'd beyond bearing, at last she arose,
   And robb'd him at once of his hopes and his life :‡
The Anglian lion, the terror of France,
   Oft prowling, ensanguin'd the Tweed's silver flood ;
But, taught by the bright Caledonian lance,
   He learnèd to fear in his own native wood.

The fell Harpy-raven took wing from the north,
   The scourge of the seas, and the dread of the
      shore ; §
The wild Scandinavian boar issued forth
   To wanton in carnage and wallow in gore : ||

---

* Scandinavian god of war.—J. H.   † The Romans.
‡ The Picts; termed by the poet "Cameleon-like" from their habit of painting
themselves.—J. H.
§ The Angles and Saxons. || The Danes.

O'er countries and kingdoms their fury prevail'd,
  No arts could appease them, no arms could repel ;
But brave Caledonia in vain they assail'd,
  As Largs well can witness, and Loncartie tell.*

Thus bold, independent, unconquer'd, and free,
  Her bright course of glory for ever shall run :
For brave Caledonia immortal must be ;
  I'll prove it from Euclid as clear as the sun :
Rectangle-triangle, the figure we'll chuse :
  The upright is Chance, and old Time is the base ;
But brave Caledonia's the hypothenuse ;
  Then, ergo, she'll match them, and match them
      always.†

[The original MS. of this production, accompanied with a note
to Johnson, is in the possession of Mr. W. F. Watson of Edinburgh.
Our text has been collated with and corrected from the manuscript,
which is dated January 1789. The poet directs it to be united with
Gow's set of "The Caledonian Hunt's Delight."]

SONG—WILLIE BREW'D A PECK O' MAUT.

(JOHNSON'S MUSEUM. 1790.)

The air is Masterton's, the song mine. The occasion of it
was this : Mr. William Nicol, of the High School, Edinburgh,
during the Autumn vacation being at Moffat, honest Allan
(who was at that time on a visit to Dalswinton), and I went
to pay Nicol a visit. We had such a joyous meeting that
Mr. Masterton and I agreed, each in our own way, that we
should celebrate the business. (*R. B., Glenriddell notes.*)

O WILLIE brew'd a peck o' *maut*,   malt
  And Rob and Allan cam to see ;
Three blyther hearts, that *lee-lang* night,   live-long
  Ye wad na found in *Christendie.*   Christendom

---

* Two famous battles in which the Scandinavians were defeated.
  † This singular figure of poetry, taken from the mathematics, refers to the
famous proposition of Pythagoras, the 47th of Euclid. In a right-angled triangle,
the square of the hypothenuse is always equal to the squares of the two other
sides.—*Currie.*

III.   G

Chorus.—We are na *fou*, we're nae that fou, full *(tipsy)*
  But just a drappie in our e'e ;
  The cock may craw, the day may *daw*, dawn
  And ay we'll taste the *barley bree*. whisky

  Here are we met, three merry boys,
   Three merry boys I *trow* are we ;   aver
  And mony a night we've merry been,
   And mony mae we hope to be !
   We are na fou, &c.

  It is the moon, I ken her horn,
   That's blinkin' in the *lift* sae *hie ;* sky high
  She shines sae bright to *wyle* us hame, entice
   But, by my sooth, she'll wait *a wee !* a while
   We are nae fou, &c.

  Wha first shall rise to *gang awa,* go away
   A cuckold, coward *loun* is he ! low fellow
  Wha first* beside his chair shall fa',
   He is the King amang us three.
   We are na fou, &c.

[Some controversy has taken place as to the exact house in which this merry meeting occurred, Allan Cunningham disregarding Burns's statement that Nicol was at Moffat, and that Master-

---

*In Currie's Edition and Johnson's "Museum" this line reads as printed above Waddell. too. adopts and defends the reading "first." while Mr. Douglas follows Currie, with the remark that the earliest alteration in the text that he has observed is in the reprint of 1813, and that Gilbert Burns (1820) made the same change without remark. On the other hand, Cunningham, Hogg and Motherwell, Chambers, and Gilfillan have "last."
We believe the reading :—

  "Wha first beside his chair shall fa'"

to be the true, and much superior, one. The antithesis is stronger and clearer. The first to "rise to gang awa" is a "coward loon," but it is altogether different in the case of him who shall first fall in the cause. "He is the king amang us three."—J. H.

ton and himself went to pay Nicol a visit; lays the scene of the exploit at Laggan, a small property which Nicol purchased, but we are informed that Nicol did not effect the purchase of Laggan till 1790, however Cunningham says, the tradition in the vale of the Nith around Moffat runs that the three worthies met,

> " A wee before the sun gaed down."

The sun, however, rose on their carousal, if the tradition of the land may be trusted.

"We had such a joyous meeting," says Burns, "that Masterton and I agreed, each in our own way, to celebrate the business." Allan accordingly composed the air, and Robert wrote the verses. They became almost instantly popular. The punch was made, it is said, by the experienced hand of Nicol, a jovial man and no flincher; and more merry stories, and more queer tales were told on that night, as a person who waited on them asserted, "than wad hae made a book." It was the pleasure of Nicol, sometimes when at table, to assert that, as a punishment for keeping other than sober company, he was enduring a sort of hell upon earth—nay, he would declare that he was dead and condemned—suffering penal torments— and relate conversations which he had held with the Prince of Darkness concerning friends left behind. These strange sallies had generally an ironical meaning; and once, it is said, when glancing at the Poet's irregularities, the later exclaimed—

> " *Losh* man, hae mercy wi' your *knatch*—   Lord   grip
>   Your bodkin's *bauld*."   bold

The bowl in which Willie made the punch for this carousal is formed of Inverary marble, and was wrought for the Poet by his father-in-law, a skilful mason. On the death of Burns it was rimmed and bottomed with silver, and presented to Alexander Cunningham. On his death, after several vicissitudes of fortune, it fell into the hands of Archibald Hastie, of London, (1834,) who, sensible of the worth and use of a relic so precious, preserves it with proper care; and duly, on the 25th of January, sets it before a select company of Burnsites, full of the reeking liquor which its great owner loved. An Irish gentleman wished to know, it is said, if gold could buy it; but observing the owner shake his head, exclaimed, "it is very well where it is, but I wished to take it to Ireland with me, for Burns, to be a Scotchman, had more of the right Irish heart about him than any body that ever penned ballads."

As stated in the introductory quotation from Burns, the three participants in this jovial symposium were the poet himself and his friends William Nicol and Allan Masterton, both of Edinburgh High School. Allan was a musical composer.—G. G.]

The High School vacation-period extended from about the 12th of August to the close of September. Nicol's lodging, in the vicinity of Moffat, and on the road between that village and "Tibbie Shiel's" Inn, had been selected as the meeting-place. The name of the place is "Willie's Mill," and a drawing of it is now in the poet's monument, Edinburgh.

The rich and, we may add, comically caustic humor of this, the best of all convivial songs, is not perceived in all its fullness till we recognize the fact that it really was not the Moon that the solemnly drunk singer saw, but the Sun.* The identification of her by her "horn" becomes, thus, doubly ludicrous. The "horn" was in his own eye. Other people might not know her, but she could not deceive him. No wonder she shone "sæ bright." It was broad day. The fact that the luminary was "sæ hie" slyly indicates the length of the sitting. Viewed in this light, the drunken challenge to the cock to craw, and the day to daw becomes irresistibly humorous.

Dr. Currie, writing in 1799—just ten years after the incident narrated in the above song—says, "These three honest fellows—all men of uncommon talents—are now all under the turf." In 1821, John Struthers, author of some good verses, produced a telling sequel to this song, based on that remark of Dr. Currie. Its last stanza thus moralises,—

"Nae mair in learning Willie toils, nor Allan wakes the melting lay,
 Nor Rab, wi' fancy-witching wiles, beguiles the hour o' dawning day;
 For tho' they were na very fou, that wicked 'wee drap in the e'e'
 Has done its turn; untimely now the green grass waves o'er a' the three."

---

*The effect the convivial habits of the Scotland of those days was wont occasionally to produce on the visual organs is well illustrated by the following anecdote. Two good fellows were jogging homewards one morning after having made a night of it. "Willie," said one of them, "isna' the moon shining awfu bricht the nicht?" "Moon?" replied Willie, "man yon's no' the moon: yon's the sun." "Nonsense, do ye think I dinna' ken the moon when I see her? I'll lay ye a gill it's the moon." "Done," quoth Willie; "now how will we settle it?" At the moment a third party came in sight working his way over the brow of the hill. It was agreed to refer the matter to him and to make the bet half a mutchkin, that he too might have a share. He came up. "Honest man," said the first speaker, "Me and my neebor hæ a bit difference here and we want you to settle it. I say yon's the moon, and he threeps it's the sun. Now wha's richt?" The worthy appealed to, gazed at the luminary with earnest and drunken gravity. "Weel, freens, I couldna' just say precisely," was his cautious reply, "I'm a stranger in these parts."—G. G.

CA' THE YOWES TO THE KNOWES.

(JOHNSON'S MUSEUM, 1790.)

This beautiful song is in the true Scotch taste ; yet I do not know that either air or words were in print before.—*R. B.,— Glenriddell notes.*

Chorus.—*Ca'* the *yowes* to the *knowes,*   _{drive} _{ewes}
                                                uplands
    Ca' them where the heather grows,
    Ca' them where the burnie *rowes,*   rolls
    My bonie dearie.

As I *gaed* down the water-side,   went
There I met my shepherd lad :
He row'd me sweetly in his plaid,
    An *ca'd* me his dearie.   called
      Ca' the yowes, &c.

Will ye gang down the water-side,
And see the waves sae sweetly glide
Beneath the hazels spreading wide,
    The moon it shines fu' clearly.
      Ca' the yowes, &c.

Ye sall get gowns and ribbons meet,
Calf-leather *shoon* upon your feet,   shoes
And in my arms thou'lt lie and sleep,
    An' ay *sall* be my dearie.   shall
      Ca' the yowes, &c.

If ye'll but stand to what ye've said,
I'se gang wi' thee, my shepherd lad,
And ye may row me in your plaid,
    And I sall be your dearie.
      Ca' the yowes, &c.

While waters *wimple* to the sea,   meandei
While day *blinks* in the *lift sae hie,* shines}
                              sky so high}
Till clay-cauld death sall blin' my e'e,
  Ye sall be my dearie.
    Ca' the knowes, &c.

[We think that the above song was one of the fruits of the
poet's visit, at this period, to the pastoral district around Moffat.
Mrs. Burns used to point out that the second and also the
closing stanza of the song are entirely Burns's own, the re-
mainder having been only mended by him. He afterwards fur-
nished for George Thomson a highly finished lyric for the same
air, preserving the old chorus. The melody is wild and simple,
having only one part.]

I GAED A WAEFU' GATE YESTREEN.

(JOHNSON'S MUSEUM, 1790.)

I *GAED* a *waefu' gate* yestreen,   went   woful road
  A gate I fear I'll dearly rue;
I gat my death frae twa sweet *een*,   eyes
  Twa lovely een o' bonie blue.
'Twas not her golden ringlets bright,
  Her lips, like roses wat wi' dew,
Her heaving bosom, lily-white—
  It was her een sae bonie blue.

She talk'd, she smil'd, my heart she wiled;
  She charm'd my soul I *wist na* how;   knew not
And ay the stound, the deadly wound,
  Cam frae her een sae bonie blue.
But "spare to speak, and spare to speed;"*
  She'll *aiblins* listen to my vow;   perhaps
Should she refuse, I'll lay my *dead*   death
  To her twa een sae bonie blue.

[Miss Jeanie Jaffrey, a daughter of the Rev. Andrew Jaffrey,
minister of Lochmaben, was the blue-eyed charmer who inspired
this favorite little song. Dr. Currie refers to her, in 1800, as "Mrs.

---

* A proverbial expression, signifying unless you speak you cannot hope for
success.—J. H.

R . . . . of New York, lately of Liverpool." Her husband's name
was Renwick, and her position in the chief city of the United
States was one of distinguished respectability. Washington Irving
was proud of her friendship and society : and some years after her
death in October, 1850, her memoirs were published, along with a
collected volume of her writings. In the correspondence of Burns,
a letter addressed by him to Provost Maxwell of Lochmaben makes
special reference to her father as ' that worthy old veteran in re-
ligion and good-fellowship.' Mrs. Renwick, after perusing Allan
Cunningham's Life of the Poet, wrote to her sister in 1838, point-
ing out some errors in fact into which that biographer had fallen,
and explained that " It was after dining in company with the poet
at the house of Mr. Nicol who was then lodging at Moffat for the
benefit of his child's health, that Burns sent to me the two songs,
' Willie brewed a peck o' maut,' and ' The blue-eyed lassie.' 1 was
then only fifteen years old." Her son became Professor of Natural
Philosophy and Chemistry, in Columbia College, New York.

This same lady is also now generally credited with being the
inspirer of the following song :

SONG—AY SAE BONIE, BLYTHE AND GAY.

(NEW YORK MIRROR, 1840.)

WHEN first I saw my Jeanie's face, I could not tell
    what ail'd me,
My heart went flutt'ring pit-a-pat, my e'en they
    almost fail'd me ;
She's ay sae neat, sae trim, sae light, the Graces
    round her hover,
Ae look depriv'd me o' my heart, and I became a
    lover.
    She's ay, ay sae blythe, sae gay, she's ay sae blythe
        and cheerie,
    She's ay sae bonie, blythe and gay, O *gin*   would
        I were her dearie !

Had I Dundas's * whole estate, or Hopetoun's † wealth
    to shine in,
Did warlike laurels crown my brow, or humbler bays
    entwining,

---

* Earl of Melville.—J. H.   † Earl of Hopetoun.—J. H.

I'd lay them a' at Jeanie's feet, could I but hope to
move her,
And prouder than a belted knight, I'd be my Jeanie's
lover.
She's ay, ay sae blythe, sae gay, &c.

But sair I fear some happier swain has gain'd sweet
Jeanie's favor,
If so, may every bliss be hers, tho' I maun never have
her :
But gang she east, or gang she west, 'twixt Forth
and Tweed all over,
While men have eyes, or ears, or taste, she'll always
find a lover.
She's ay, ay sae blythe, sae gay, &c.

[Mr. Douglas in his Edinburgh edition 1877, consigns this song
to small type because he doubts Burns's connection with it. We
believe that Burns's hand can be seen in every line, and we are
further confirmed in this belief by reference to Alexander Smith's
edition, where Smith notes that he collates his text with the orig-
inal MS.—G. G.]

HIGHLAND HARRY BACK AGAIN.

(JOHNSON'S MUSEUM, 1790.)

The oldest title I ever heard to this air was, "The High-
land Watch's Farewell to Ireland." The chorus I picked up
from an old woman in Dunblane; the rest of the song is
mine.—R. B.—Glenriddell Notes.

My Harry was a gallant gay,
Fu' stately *strade* he on the plain ;   strode
But now he's banish'd far away,
I'll never see him back again.

Chorus.—O for him back again !
O for him back again !
I wad gie a' Knockhaspie's land *
For Highland Harry back again.

* The name Knockhaspie is after a part of the farm of Mossgiel.—J. H.

When a' the *lave* gae to their bed,   rest
. I wander *dowie* up the glen ;   sadly
I set me down and *greet* my fill,   weep
And ay I wish him back again.[1]
O for him, &c.

O were some villains *hangit* high,   hanged
And *ilka* body had their *ain !*   every   own
Then I might see the joyfu' sight,
My Highland Harry back again.[2]
O for him, &c.

[The copy of this song in the Hastie Collection at the British
Museum is not in Burns's handwriting, and contains two addi-
tional stanzas and some variations which we annex for what they
are worth.   Several Jacobite and Highland subjects are contained
in the third volume of Johnson (published on 2nd February 1790,)
and it is very probable that the presence of Nicol and Master-
ton in Nithsdale and Annandale at this period would set the
poet a-musing in that direction.
The additional verses referred to are as follow :—

> Sad was the day and sad the hour
> He left me on his native plain,
> An' rush'd, his sair-wrang'd Prince to join,
> But oh, he ne'er cam back again !
> O for him, &c.
>
> Strong was my Harry's arm in war.
> Unmatch'd on a' Culloden plain ;
> But Vengeance mark'd him for his ain:
> For oh, he ne'er cam back again !
> O for him back again !
> The auld Stuarts back again !
> I wad gie a' my father's land
> To see them a' come back again.
> VAR.—[1] An' sair I greet and aft I wish
> For Highland Harry back again.
>
> [2] That I wi' joy might welcome hame
> My Prince and Harry back again.]

THE BATTLE OF SHERRAMUIR.

Tune—" The Cameron Rant."

(JOHNSON'S MUSEUM, 1790.)

" O CAM ye here the fight to shun,
    Or herd the sheep wi' me man ?
Or were ye at the Sherra-muir,
    Or did the battle see, man ? "
I saw the battle, *sair* and *teugh*,   sore   tough
And *reekin*-red ran mony a *sheugh ;*   smoking ditch
My heart, for fear, gaed sough for sough,*
To hear the *thuds*, and see the *cluds*   blows clouds
O' clans frae woods, in tartan *duds*,   rags
    Wha *glaum'd* at kingdoms three, man. grasped
      La, la, la, la, &c.

The red-coat lads, wi' black cockades,
    To meet them were *na slaw*, man ;   not slow
They rush'd and push'd, and blude outgush'd,
    And mony a *bouk* did fa', man :   bulk (*carcass*)
The great Argyle led on his files,
I *wat* they glanc'd for twenty miles ;   wot
They *hough'd* the clans like nine-pin *kyles*, slashed }
skittles }
They hack'd and hash'd, while braid-swords clash'd,
And thro' they dash'd, and hew'd and smash'd,
    Till *fey* men died awa, man.   doomed
      La, la, la, la, &c.

But had ye seen the *philibegs*,   kilts
    And *skyrin* tartan *trews*, man ; checked trowsers
When in the teeth they dar'd our Whigs,
    And covenant Trueblues,† man :
In lines extended lang and large,

---

*My heart beat keeping time with the blows.—J. H.
† The color of the Covenanters' standard, in their struggle against their perse-
cutors under Charles II, was blue, hence *true-blue* came to signify a staunch
Covenanter or Presbyterian.—J. H.

When *baig'nets* overpower'd the *targe*,*　　　bayonets }
　　　　　　　　　　　　　　　　　　　　　shield }
And thousands hasten'd to the charge ;
Wi' Highland wrath they frae the sheath
Drew blades o' death, till, out o' breath,
　　They fled like frighted *dows*, man !　　　doves
　　　La, la, la, la, &c.

" O how deil, Tam, can that be true?
　　The chase *gaed* frae the north, man ;　　　went
I saw mysel, they did pursue
　　The horseman back to Forth, man ;
And at Dunblane,† in my ain sight,
They took the brig wi' a' their might,‡
And straught to Stirling wing'd their flight:
But, cursed lot ! the gates were shut ;
And mony a huntit poor red-coat,
　　For fear amaist did *swarf*, man !"　　　swoon
　　　La, la, la, la, &c.

My sister Kate cam up the gate
　　Wi' crowdie§ unto me, man ;
She swoor she saw some rebels run
　　To Perth and to Dundee,‖ man ;
Their left-hand general had nae skill ;
The Angus¶ lads had nae good will
That day their neibors' blude to spill ;
For fear, by foes, that they should lose
Their *cogs* o' brose ;** they scar'd at blows,　wooden }
　　　　　　　　　　　　　　　　　　　dishes }
　　And hameward fast did flee man.[3]
　　　La, la, la, la, &c.

---

* Shield or target worn on the arm by the Highlanders.—J. H.
† A village in Stirlingshire. close to, and south of, the field of battle.—J. H.
‡ Spurred over the bridge with all the speed they could.—J. H.
§ Crowdie is properly oatmeal with cold water poured over it, and stirred.　It
is sometimes used generically for any oatmeal diet, as brose or porridge.—J. H.
‖ Towns north of the field of battle.—J. H.
¶ A name for the county of Forfar.—J. H.
** Brose is made by pouring boiling water on oatmeal, and stirring.—J. H.

They've lost some gallant gentlemen,
   Amang the Highland clans, man !
I fear my Lord Panmure is slain,
   Or in his en'mies' hands, man.⁴
Now wad ye sing this double flight,
Some fell for wrang, and some for right ;
But mony bade the world gude-night ;
Say, pell and mell, wi' muskets' knell
How Tories * fell, and Whigs to hell
   Flew off in frighted bands, man !⁵
      La, la, la, la, &c.

[This song although but a paraphrase of the older ballad by
the Rev. John Barclay, who founded a religious sect in Edin-
burgh, called the "Bereans," is really so well-executed as to de-
serve to be regarded as an original production. The poet accord-
ingly has affixed his name to it in the *Museum.*

The battle of Dunblane, or Sheriff-muir, was fought on 13th
November 1715, between the Earl of Mar, for the Chevalier, and
the Duke of Argyle, for the Government ; both sides claimed
the victory, the left wing of either army being routed.
We mark the following variations :—

   ¹ (This line omitted).   ² bayonets opposed.
   ³ Their cogs o' brose ; all crying woes,
      And so it goes, you see, man.
   ⁴ Or fallen in Whiggish hands, man.
   ⁵ Then ye may tell, how pell and mell,
      By red claymores and muskets' knell,
   Wi' dying yell, the Tories fell,
      And Whigs to hell did flee, man.

In this closing passage there is a line too much for the music,
and the rhyme to "hands" in the fourth line of the stanza is
lost.]

THE BRAES O' KILLIECRANKIE.

(JOHNSON'S MUSEUM, 1790.)

WHARE hae ye been sae *braw*, lad?   smart
   Whare hae ye been sae *brankie*, O?   spruce

---

* Tories were the Jacobites or Highlandmen, Whigs were the Presbyterian
loyalists under Argyle. The words remain in British politics, though with
changed sense.—J. H.

Whare hae ye been sae braw, lad?
Cam ye by Killiecrankie, O?

Chorus.—An ye had been whare I hae been,
　　　Ye wad nae been sae *cantie*, O ;　　merry
　　An ye had seen what I hae seen,
　　　I' the Braes o' Killiecrankie, O.

I faught at land, I faught at sea,
　At hame I faught my Auntie, O ;
But I met the devil an' Dundee,
　On the Braes o' Killiecrankie, O.
　　An ye had been, &c.

The bauld Pitcur * fell in a *furr*,　　　furrow
　An' Clavers † gat a *clankie*, O !　　death-blow
Or I had fed an Athole *gled*,　　　　kite
　On the Braes o' Killiecrankie, O.
　　An ye had been, &c.

[This production speaks for itself, as being the undoubted com-
position of Burns. His note in the Glenriddell MS. is historical
only ; "The battle of Killiecrankie was the last stand made by
the Clans for James II, after his abdication. Here the gallant
Lord Dundee fell in the moment of victory, and with him fell
the hopes of the party. General M'Kay, when he found the
Highlanders did not pursue his flying army said, 'Dundee must
be killed, or he never would have overlooked this advantage.'
A great stone marks the spot where Dundee fell." The stone
here referred to is Druidical, and may have stood there thousands
of years before Dundee's time.] (Killiecrankie is a beautiful pass
in Athole, Perthshire, giving entrance to the Highlands. Here
the battle was fought, July 27, 1689, in which the loyalists were
defeated in a few minutes. One of Aytoun's finest ballads cele-
brates the death of Graham, Viscount Dundee.—J. H.)

---

* The laird of Pitcur.—J. H.
† Graham of Claverhouse, Viscount Dundee, leader of the Highlanders.—J. H.

AWA' WHIGS,* AWA'.

(JOHNSON'S MUSEUM, 1790.)

Chorus.—Awa' Whigs, awa' !
     Awa' Whigs, awa' !
       Ye're but a pack o' traitor *louns*,   knaves
       Ye'll do nae gude at a'.

Our *thrissles* flourish'd fresh and fair,   thistles
     And bonie bloom'd our roses ;
But Whigs cam' like a frost in June,
     An' wither'd a' our *posies.*   garlands
       Awa' Whigs, &c.

Our ancient crown's *fa'en* in the dust†—   fallen
     Deil blin' them wi' the *stoure o't !*   dust of it
An' write their names in his black beuk,
     Wha gae the Whigs the power o't.
       Awa' Whigs, &c.

Our sad decay in church and state
     Surpasses my *descriving :*   describing
The Whigs cam' o'er us for a curse,
     An' we hae done wi' thriving.
       Awa' Whigs, &c.

Grim vengeance lang has taen a nap,
     But we may see him waukin :
Gude help the day when Royal heads
     Are hunted like a *maukin !*   hare
       Awa' Whigs, &c.

[Chambers following Cunningham, says that this is based on
an old Jacobite song, the second and last stanzas only being by
Burns.

---

* Hanoverian dynasty and their supporters. See Note to last piece.—J. H.
† The crown of the Stuart line, who were anciently kings of Scotland.—J. H.

The melody to which this song is sung is very plaintive, bearing a strong resemblance to that of "My dearie an thou die."— J. H.]

A *WAUKRIFE MINNIE.*   wakeful mother

(JOHNSON'S MUSEUM. 1790.)

I picked up this old song and tune from a country girl in Nithsdale. I never met with it elsewhere in Scotland.— *R. B., Glenriddell Notes.*

WHARE are you *gaun*, my bonie lass,   going
    Whare are you gaun, my hiney?
She answered me right saucilie,
    An errand for my minnie.

O whare live ye, my bonie lass,
    O whare live ye, my hiney?
By yon burnside, *gin* ye *maun ken*,   since must know
    In a wee house wi' my minnie.

But I *foor* up the glen at e'en,   fared
    To see my bonie lassie ;
And lang before the grey morn cam,
    She was na half sae saucie.

O *weary fa'* the waukrife cock,   ill-luck to
    And the foumart lay his crawin ! *
He wauken'd the auld wife frae her sleep,
    A *wee blink or* the *dawin.*   little before dawn

An angry wife I *wat* she raise,   wot
    And o'er the bed she brocht her ;
And wi' a *meikle* hazle *rung*   large stick
    She made her a *weel-pay'd* dochter.   well-spanked

O fare thee weel, my bonie lass,
    O fare thee weel, my hiney !
Thou art a gay an' a bonie lass,
    But thou hast a waukrife minnie.

---

* And may the polecat stop his crowing.—J. H.

[Stenhouse assures us that this song is not to be found in any
collection prior to the Museum; so we may safely conclude that
only a very small portion, if any, was taken down from the
"country girl's" singing. The air may have been noted down by
Masterton, in the way Burns represents in the head-note.]

THE CAPTIVE RIBBAND.

(JOHNSON'S MUSEUM, 1790.)

DEAR Myra, the captive ribband's mine,
   'Twas all my faithful love could gain;
And would you ask me to resign
   The sole reward that crowns my pain?

Go, bid the hero who has run
   Thro' fields of death to gather fame,
Go, bid him lay his laurels down,
   And all his well-earn'd praise disclaim.

The ribband shall its freedom lose—
   Lose all the bliss it had with you,
And share the fate I would impose
   On thee, wert thou my captive too.

It shall upon my bosom live,
   Or clasp me in a close embrace;
And at its fortune if you grieve,
   Retrieve its doom, and take its place.

[Solely on the authority of Mr. Stenhouse, the able illustrator
of Johnson's Musical Museum, we give the above as a production
of Burns. It is not in the Hastie collection of the poet's songs
in the British Museum; but Stenhouse may have seen the poet's
manuscript. No remarks regarding Burns ever gave greater and
wider offence than some words of Sir Walter Scott in the *Quar-
terly Review*, when he spoke of his "plebeian" spirit, and char-
acterized our national poet as devoid of "that spirit of chivalry
which, since the feudal times, has pervaded the higher ranks
of European society." Sir Walter would surely have qualified his
expressions had the above song been placed in his hands as one
of the exciseman's performances.]

FAREWELL TO THE HIGHLANDS.

(JOHNSON'S MUSEUM, 1790.)

FAREWELL to the Highlands, farewell to the north,
The birth-place of Valor, the country of Worth ;
Wherever I wander, wherever I rove,
The hills of the Highlands for ever I love.

Chorus.—

My heart's in the Highlands, my heart is not here,
My heart's in the Highlands, a-chasing the deer ;
A-chasing the wild-deer, and following the roe,
My heart's in the Highlands wherever I go.

Farewell to the mountains, high-cover'd with snow,
Farewell to the *straths* and green vallies below ;   dales
Farewell to the forests and wild-hanging woods,
Farewell to the torrents and loud pouring floods.
My heart's in the Highlands, &c.

[The poet, in his Glenriddell notes, tells us that the words which
form the chorus of this song are old, and the rest his own compo-
sition. Mr. C. K. Sharpe, in his additional notes to the Museum,
gives what he terms the old words, taken from a stall copy, headed
"The Strong Walls of Derry," and he mentions that they were
much in favor with Sir Walter Scott, who used to sing a portion
of the ballad when called upon for a song. We can imagine how
the prudent Sir Walter would warble forth the following lines at
the festive board, when he found that "elder's hours" were ap-
proaching :—

> "There is many a word spoken, but few of the best,
> And he that speaks fairest, lives longest at rest ;
> I speak by experience—my mind serves me so,
> But my heart's in the Highlands wherever I go.

> *Chorus.*—We'll drink and gae hame, boys, we'll drink and gae hame,
> If we stay ony langer we'll get a bad name,
> We'll get a bad name, sirs! we'll fill oursels fou ;
> And the strong walls of Derry are ill to win through."

The melody to which Burns composed his verses is a Gaelic one,
called "Failte na miosg," or *The Musket Salute,* which seems to
go well with the sentiment of the song.]

III.   H

(The characteristic of Burns's revisions is that he reproduces by a few brief touches all the true poetry diffused through some old song. A main charm in many of these adaptations is their condensation and dramatic force, and this forms no exception.—J. H.)

THE WHISTLE—A BALLAD.

(JOHNSON'S MUSEUM, 1792.)

As the authentic *prose* history of the Whistle is curious. I shall here give it.—In the train of Anne of Denmark, when she came to Scotland with our James the Sixth, there came over also a Danish gentleman of gigantic stature and great prowess, and a matchless champion of Bacchus. He had a curious ebony ca' or Whistle, which, at the commencement of the orgies, he laid on the table ; and whoever was last able to blow it, every body else being disabled by the potency of the bottle, was to carry off the Whistle as a trophy of victory. The Dane produced credentials of his victories, without a single defeat, at the courts of Copenhagen, Stockholm, Moscow, Warsaw, and several of the petty courts in Germany ; and challenged the Scots Bacchanalians to the alternative of trying his prowess, or else acknowledging their inferiority.—After many overthrows on the part of the Scots, the Dane was encountered by Sir Robert Laurie of Maxwelton, ancestor of the present worthy baronet of that name, who, after three days and nights' hard contest, left the Scandinavian under the table,

And blew on the Whistle his Requiem shrill.

Sir Walter, son to Sir Robert before-mentioned, afterwards lost the Whistle to Walter Riddel of Glenriddell, who had married a sister of Sir Walter's.—On Friday, the 16th of October, 1790, at Friars-carse, the Whistle was once more contended for, as related in the ballad, by the present Sir Robert Laurie : Robert Riddel, Esq.. of Glenriddell. lineal descendant and representative of Walter Riddel, who won the Whistle, and in whose family it had continued ; and Alexander Ferguson, Esq. of Craigdarroch, likewise descended of the great Sir Robert ; which last gentleman carried off the hard-won honors of the field.—*R. B.*

I SING of a Whistle, a Whistle of worth,
I sing of a Whistle, the pride of the North,
Was brought to the court of our good Scottish King,
And long with this Whistle all Scotland shall ring.

Old Loda,* still rueing the arm of Fingal,
The god of the bottle sends down from his hall—
"This Whistle's your challenge, to Scotland get o'er,
And drink them to hell, Sir! or ne'er see me more!"

Old poets have sung, and old chronicles tell,
What champions ventur'd, what champions fell:
The son of great Loda was conqueror still,
And blew on the Whistle their requiem shrill.

Till Robert, the Lord of the Cairn and the Scaur,†
Unmatch'd at the bottle, unconquer'd in war,
He drank his poor god-ship as deep as the sea;
No tide of the Baltic e'er drunker than he.

Thus Robert, victorious, the trophy has gain'd;
Which now in his house has for ages remain'd;
Till three noble chieftains, and all of his blood,
The jovial contest again have renew'd.

Three joyous good fellows, with hearts clear of flaw;
Craigdarroch, so famous for wit, worth, and law;
And trusty Glenriddel, so skill'd in old coins;
And gallant Sir Robert, deep-read in old wines.

Craigdarroch began, with a tongue smooth as oil,
Desiring Glenriddel to yield up the spoil;
Or else he would muster the heads of the clan,
And once more, in claret, try which was the man.

"By the gods of the ancients!" Glenriddel replies,
"Before I surrender so glorious a prize,
I'll conjure the ghost of the great Rorie More,‡
And bumper his horn with him twenty times o'er."

---

* See Ossian's 'Caric-thura.'—R. B.
† Two streams in the Maxwelton estate.—J. H.
‡ See Johnson's "Tour in the Hebrides."—R. B.

Sir Robert, a soldier, no speech would pretend,
But he ne'er turn'd his back on his foe, or his friend;
Said, "Toss down the Whistle, the prize of the field,"
And, knee-deep in claret, he'd die ere he'd yield.

To the board of Glenriddel our heroes repair,
So noted for drowning of sorrow and care;
But, for wine and for welcome, not more known to
        fame,
Than the sense, wit, and taste, of a sweet lovely dame.

A bard was selected to witness the fray,
And tell future ages the feats of the day;
A Bard who detested all sadness and spleen,
And wish'd that Parnassus a vineyard had been.

The dinner being over, the claret they ply,
And ev'ry new cork is a new spring of joy;
In the bands of old friendship and kindred so set,
And the bands grew the tighter the more they were
        wet.

Gay Pleasure ran riot as bumpers ran o'er;
Bright Phœbus ne'er witness'd so joyous a core,
And vow'd that to leave them he was quite forlorn,
Till Cynthia hinted he'd see them next morn.

Six bottles a-piece had well wore out the night,
When gallant Sir Robert, to finish the fight,
Turn'd o'er in one bumper a bottle of red,
And swore 'twas the way that their ancestors did.

Then worthy Glenriddel, so cautious and sage,
No longer the warfare ungodly would wage;
A high Ruling Elder * to wallow in wine;
He left the foul business to folks less divine.

---

* An Elder in the Presbyterian Church.—J. H.

The gallant Sir Robert fought hard to the end ;
But who can with Fate and quart bumpers contend?
Though Fate said, a hero should perish in light ;
So uprose bright Phœbus—and down fell the knight.

Next up rose our Bard, like a prophet in drink :—
"Craigdarroch, thou'll soar when creation shall sink !
But if thou would flourish immortal in rhyme,
Come—one bottle more—and have at the sublime !

"Thy line, that have struggled for freedom with
        Bruce,
Shall heroes and patriots ever produce :
So thine be the laurel, and mine be the bay ;
The field thou hast won, by yon bright god of day !"

[Besides the explanation given by the Bard himself in his
copious headnote, the following interesting document, which had
been recovered by Cromek in 1807, and is now in possession of
his representatives, will throw light on the incident narrated in
the ballad. Captain Patrick Miller, younger of Dalswinton, had in
1793, made application to Mr. Ferguson of Craigdarroch (the victor
in the contest) for some information concerning the affair, and the
annexed memoranda, in the handwriting of Mr. M'Murdo, were
forwarded in reply :—

Doquet.

" The original Bett between Sir Robert Laurie and Craigdarroch, for the noted
Whistle, which is so much celebrated by Robert Burns's Poem—in which Bett I
was named Judge—1789.
The Bett decided at Carse—16th Oct. 1789.
Won by Craigdarroch—he drank upds. of 5 Bottles of Claret.

MEMORANDUM FOR THE WHISTLE.

The Whistle gained by Sir Robert Laurie, (now) in possession of Mr. Riddell
of Glenriddell, is to be ascertained to the heirs of the said Sir Robert now ex-
isting, being Sir R. L., Mr. R. of G., and Mr. F. of C.—to be settled under the
arbitration of Mr. Jn. M'Murdo: the business to be decided at Carse, the 16th
of October, 1789.   (Signed)   ALEX. FERGUSON.
                                        R. LAURIE.
                                        ROBT. RIDDELL.

COWHILL, 10*th October*, 1789.
Jno. M'Murdo accepts as Judge—
Geo. Johnston witness, to be present—
Patrick Miller witness to be pre. if possible.
Minute of Bett between Sir Robert Laurie and Craigdarroch. 1789."

A foolish controversy has been kept up in Scotland as to whether Burns was actually present at the contest for the whistle. It is really a matter of little interest to our readers, or indeed to anyone, but there seems no reason to question his presence. It is put beyond reasonable doubt by the discovery at Craigdarroch House, the residence of the victor, of a rhymed verse of four lines in Burns's handwriting accepting an invitation to be present. The versicle—mere doggerel—is as follows :—

> "The King's poor blackguard slave am I,
>   And scarce can spare a minute;
> But I'll be with you by and by,
>   Or else the devil's in it.—R. B."

On the back of the holograph of these lines is the following endorsement: "wrote by Mr. Burns, October, 1789, upon a card being sent him to come to Glenriddell's at Carse, to drink a cheerful glass with Sir Robert Laurie, Mr. Alexander Ferguson, and Glenriddell, upon the meeting of drinking for the Danes Whistle, and gained by Alexander Ferguson." Burns's presence at the compotation is even more firmly established by the direct testimony of the late William Hunter, Blacksmith, Closeburn, who made affidavit that he was a servant of Mr. Riddell's and on waiting on the occasion— "Burns" he depones "was present the whole evening. He was invited to attend the party . . to commemorate the day by a song. When the ladies had retired Burns withdrew from the dining table, and set down in a window looking down the river Nith : a small table was before him. During the evening Burns nearly emptied two bottles of spirits, the one of brandy, the other of rum, mixing them with warm water. He had pen, ink and paper before him and continued the whole evening to write. He seemed to have little conversation with the three gentlemen. I think he was composing the Whistle. About sunrise the two gentlemen were carried to bed. Craigdarroch walked himself up-stairs. Burns after he had assisted the two gentlemen to bed, walked to his own farm-house of Ellisland. He seemed a little the worse of drink, but he was quite able to walk." The writer of this note may say that in his youth he knew William Hunter, and that he was always regarded as a trustworthy man. Mr. Waddell adduces further satisfactory evidence of Burns's presence at the contest. Sir Robert Laurie, it may be added, was of the same family with "Annie Laurie," also famous in song.

The reader will observe that the poet, in his introductory note to this poem, has set down, "1790" for 1789—a mistake which he also made in his head-note to the poem on Captain Grose's peregrination, which he dates "1790."

W. F. Watson, Esq.. Edinburgh, possesses the author's first rough sketch of the six opening stanzas of "The Whistle," probably those he wrote on the night in question, showing, as might be expected, some curious readings. The holograph copies of the finished Ballad appear to have been liberally distributed by the poet. One now possessed by John Adam, Esq., Town Chamberlain, Greenock, and written on Excise paper, has the following presentation-stanza appended to it :—

> " But one sorry quill, and that worne to the core,
>   No paper—but such as I shew it ;
> But such as it is, will the good Laird of Torr,
>   Accept, and excuse the poor Poet ?"—J. H.]

TO MARY IN HEAVEN,

(JOHNSON'S MUSEUM. 1790.)

THOU ling'ring star, with less'ning ray,
　　That lov'st to greet the early morn,
Again thou usher'st in the day
　　My Mary from my soul was torn.
O Mary ! dear departed shade !
　　Where is thy place of blissful rest ?
See'st thou thy lover lowly laid ?
　　Hear'st thou the groans that rend his breast ?

That sacred hour can I forget,
　　Can I forget the hallow'd grove,
Where, by the winding Ayr, we met,
　　To live one day of parting love !
Eternity can not efface
　　Those records dear of transports past,
Thy image at our last embrace,
　　Ah ! little thought we 'twas our last !

Ayr, gurgling, kiss'd his pebbled shore,
　　O'erhung with wild-woods, thickening green ;
The fragrant birch and hawthorn hoar,
　　'Twin'd amorous round the raptur'd scene :

The flowers sprang wanton to be prest,
    The birds sang love on every spray ;
Till too, too soon, the glowing west,
    Proclaim'd the speed of wingèd day.

Still o'er these scenes my mem'ry wakes,
    And fondly broods with miser-care ;
Time but th' impression stronger makes,
    As streams their channels deeper wear,
My Mary ! dear departed shade !
Where is thy place of blissful rest ?
See'st thou thy lover lowly laid ?
Hear'st thou the groans that rend his breast ?

[In glancing over the correspondence of Burns, year after year
from 1786 onwards, it seems as if a cloud had settled down over his
soul about the end of each autumn. In his letter to Aiken of that
season in 1786, he says—"Even in the hour of social mirth, my
gaiety is the madness of an intoxicated criminal under the hands
of the executioner." Towards the close of 1787 he tells Miss
Chalmers that the tints of his mind are "vying with the livid
horror preceding a midnight thunder-storm : misfortune, bodily
constitution, hell, and myself, have formed a quadruple alliance to
guarantee" such horrors. About the same period in 1788, he is
gloomy again, and thus writes to Mrs. Dunlop after his first six
months' farming at Ellisland :—"If miry ridges and dirty dunghills
are to engross the best part of the functions of my soul immortal,
I had better been a rook or a magpie at once, and then I should
not have been plagued with any ideas superior to breaking clods
and picking up grubs ; not to mention barn-cocks and mallards—
creatures with which I could almost exchange lives at any time."
In the year following, just after the solemn verses in the text had
been composed, we find him in a letter, which quotes one of its
stanzas, complaining to Mrs. Dunlop that he is "groaning under
the miseries of a diseased nervous system . . . For now near
three weeks I have been obliged for a time to give up my Excise
books. being scarce able to lift my head. much less to ride once a
week over ten muir parishes." Finally, at the same season, three
years thereafter, when he had just composed his last saddening
reminiscence of *Highland Mary*, he thus writes to the same lady—
"Alas ! who would wish for many years ? What is it but to drag
existence until our joys gradually expire and leave us in a night
of misery, like the gloom which blots out the stars, one by one

from the face of heaven, and leaves us without a ray of comfort in the howling waste!"

The following details, communicated by Cromek, which refer to the parting interview between Burns and Mary, so fondly painted in the text, have since been strongly confirmed by recovery of the pocket-bible presented to her by the poet on the occasion :—"This adieu was performed with all those simple and striking ceremonials which rustic sentiment has devised to prolong tender emotions, and to inspire awe. The lovers stood on each side of a small purling brook; they laved their hands in its limpid stream, and holding a bible between them, pronounced their vows to be faithful to each other. They parted—never to meet again!"

The words are set in the *Museum* to a melody by Miss Johnson of Hilton, called "Captain Cooke's Death." We have heard these attempted to be sung to the tune of "Mary's Dream;" but it seems profanation to make them vocal to other melody than that of the poet's own words.]

(Regarding the circumstances in which this sublime and pathetic monologue was produced, Mr. Lockhart, on Mrs. Burns's own authority, states as follows :—"He spent that day, though laboring under cold, in the usual work of the harvest, and apparently in excellent spirits. But as the twilight deepened, he appeared to grow very sad about something, and at length wandered out to the barnyard, to which his wife, in her anxiety, followed him, entreating him to observe that frost had set in, and to return to the fireside. On being again and again requested to do so, he at length promised compliance. but still remained where he was, striding up and down slowly, and contemplating the sky, which was singularly clear and starry. At length Mrs. Burns found him stretched on a mass of straw, with his eyes fixed on a beautiful planet 'that shone like another moon,' and prevailed on him to come in. He, immediately on entering the house, called for his desk. and wrote exactly as they now stand, with all the ease of one copying from memory, these sublime and poetic verses.")

[Dr. Waddell feelingly and tritely says :—"By that accident of death, Mary herself entered on an immortality more beautiful than Beatrice' or Laura's, in which respect neither complaint as against Burns, nor sorrow as for her, should ever be obtruded on the world. It was enough for Mary and for mankind that Burns once loved her. Her name, her fame, her sweet bright womanly reputation, her existence itself, with all the honor and the glory, the tombstones. the statues. the monuments, the inscriptions. the pathetic paragraphs, the world of interest and inquiry connected with it, depend all absolutely and forever upon him. How then has she been injured by such abundant love, or insulted by an apotheosis of melody that would have satisfied half the women in the world? Gentle, good, and true she no doubt was; blue-eyed and yellow-haired, and comely, but never graceful; and born of such parents as Mr. Chambers describes, or educated apparently as she was, the probability is that she was not endowed with a tithe of the sweet indefinite attractions with which Burns alone has invested her. A lofty monument in Greenock churchyard, and an occasional paragraph of gallant tearful sympathy for her fate, are quite admissible in their place. But what did we know of her and of her virtues, except from Burns? All such monuments and paragraphs for her require to be countersigned by him. He is the sole responsible party; and on any other condition whatever they are sheer impertinences. On the whole, therefore, it may be found better to leave Highland Mary where she is, safe and beautiful, in the undivided custody of her immortal lover, who never sullied a hair of her head, or wronged her in the remotest degree by any indifference."—G. G.]

EPISTLE TO DR. BLACKLOCK.

(CURRIE, 1800.)

Ellisland, 21st Oct., 1789.

Wow, but your letter made me *vauntie!*   proud
And are ye hale, and weel and *cantie?*   cheerful
I ken'd it still, your *wee bit jauntie*   little jaunt
        Wad *bring ye to:*   restore you
Lord send you ay as weel's I want ye!
        And then ye'll do.

The ill thief blaw the Heron * south!
And never drink be near his drouth!
He tauld myself by word o' mouth,
        He'd tak my letter;
I *lippen'd* to the *chiel* in truth,   trusted   fellow
        And *bade* nae better.   asked

But *aiblins* honest Master Heron   perhaps
Had, at the time, some dainty fair one

---

* Robert Heron, author of a History of Scotland, and of a Life of Burns.

To *ware* his theologic care on,   spend
       And holy study ;
And tired o' sauls to waste his *lear* on,   learning
       E'en tried the body.

But what d'ye think, my trusty *fier*,   friend
I'm turn'd a gauger—Peace be here !
Parnassian *queans*, I fear, I fear,   nymphs
       Ye'll now disdain me !
And then my fifty pounds a year
       Will little gain me.

Ye *glaiket*, gleesome dainty *damies*,   giddy dames
Wha, by Castalia's *wimplin* streamies,   purling
Lowp, sing, and lave your pretty limbies, leap
       Ye ken, ye ken,
That strang necessity supreme is
       'Mang sons o' men.

I hae a wife and twa wee *laddies ;*   boys
They *maun hae* brose and *brats o'*   must have }
   duddies :   rags of clothing }
Ye ken yoursels my heart right proud is—
       I need na vaunt—
But I'll sned besoms, thraw saugh woodies,†
       Before they want.

Lord help me thro' this warld o' care !
I'm weary sick o't late and air !
Not but I hae a richer share
       Than mony ithers ;
But why should ae man better fare,
       And a' men brithers ?

Come, Firm Resolve, take thou the van,
Thou stalk o' carl-hemp ‡ in man !

---

* " He ventur'd the soul, and I risk'd the body."—*Jolly Beggars.*
† I'll cut brooms, or weave willow-baskets.—J. H.
‡ Male-hemp, or flax, or that which bears the seed, as being the stronger.
" You have a stalk of carl-hemp in you," is a Scotch proverbial expression,
meaning you have manly strength of character.—J. H.

And let us mind, faint heart ne'er wan
　　　　A lady fair ;
Wha does the utmost that he can,
　　　　Will *whyles* do mair.   sometimes

But to conclude my silly rhyme
(I'm *scant* o' verse and scant o' time),   scarce
To make a happy fireside clime
　　　　To *weans* and wife,   children
That's the true pathos and sublime
　　　　Of human life.

My compliments to sister Beckie,
And eke the same to honest Lucky ;
I wat she is a daintie *chuckie*,*   good wife or matron
　　　　As e'er tread clay ;
And gratefully, my gude auld cockie,
　　　　I'm yours for ay.
　　　　　　　　　ROBERT BURNS.

[Dr. Blacklock had addressed a versified epistle to Burns from
Edinburgh on the 24th August of this year, which the poet had
replied to, entrusting the conveyance of his letter to a private hand,
Mr. Robert Heron, a young licentiate of the Church, who proved
a faithless messenger. This fact is referred to in the second and
third stanzas of the text. The Rev. Thomas Blacklock, D.D., was
born in Annan, in 1721, of poor parents who came originally from
England. When about six months old, he lost his eyesight
through smallpox. His father dying when the son was nine-
teen years old. Dr. Stevenson of Edinburgh, who admired his
early genius, brought him to that city, where he was educated
for the Church at the University He published a small volume
of poetry so early as 1746, and in 1754 was brought into further
public notice by Prof. Joseph Spence of Oxford, who published a
memoir of him, and some fresh specimens of his poetry. He is
styled "the Rev. Mr. Blacklock" in a volume containing several
of his poems, produced in 1760 ; and in 1766 the degree of D.D.
was conferred on him. A situation within the University was pro-
vided for him, and the remainder of his life was spent in circum-

---

* A familiar term for a brood-hen, transferred endearingly to the mother of a
family.—J. H.

stances of comfort.   Dr. Johnson sought him out when he visited
Edinburgh in 1773, and "looked on him with reverence." The
same Robert Heron who is censured by Burns in the text, speaks
of Dr. Blacklock, as an "angel upon earth," and Lockhart in his
life of our poet finely remarks that although "the writings of
Blacklock are forgotten, the memory of his virtues will not pass
away till mankind shall have ceased to sympathise with the mis-
fortunes of genius, and to appreciate the poetry of Burns."
  Blacklock showed his filial piety by erecting in St. Michael's
Churchyard, Dumfries, a tombstone to the memory of his father,
there buried.   He was crushed to death in 1740, by the fall of a
malt-kiln, and the tablet bears a poetical inscription which is in-
cluded in Dr. Blacklock's works.   This friend and correspondent
of Burns died on 7th July 1791, and was buried in the ground at-
tached to the old chapel-of-ease in Buccleuch Street, Edinburgh.
The following is the letter sent by Blacklock :]

> " Dear Burns, thou brother of my heart,
>   Both for thy virtues and thy art ;
>   If art it may be called in thee,
>   Which nature's bounty, large and free,
>   With pleasure on thy breast diffuses,
>   And warms thy soul with all the Muses.
>   Whether to laugh with easy grace,
>   Thy numbers move the sage's face,
>   Or bid the softer passion rise,
>   And ruthless souls with grief surprise,
>   'Tis nature's voice distinctly felt,
>   Through thee her organ, thus to melt.
>
> " Most anxiously I wish to know,
>   With thee of late how matters go ;
>   How keeps thy much-loved Jean her health ?
>   What promises thy farm of wealth ?
>   Whether the muse persists to smile,
>   And all thy anxious cares beguile ?
>   Whether bright fancy keeps alive ?
>   And how thy darling infants thrive ?
>
> " For me, with grief and sickness spent,
>   Since I my journey homeward bent,
>   Spirits depress'd no more I mourn,
>   But vigor, life, and health return.
>   No more to gloomy thoughts a prey,
>   I sleep all night, and live all day ;
>   By turns my book and friend enjoy,
>   And thus my circling hours employ.
>   Happy while yet these hours remain,
>   If Burns could join the cheerful train,
>   With wonted zeal, sincere and fervent,
>   Salute once more his humble servant.
>
>   THOMAS BLACKLOCK."

ADDRESS TO THE TOOTHACHE.

(CURRIE, 1800.)

My curse upon your venom'd *stang*,   sting
'That shoots my tortur'd gums alang,
An' thro' my *lug* gies sic a twang,   ear
      Wi' gnawing vengeance,
Tearing my nerves wi' bitter pang,
      Like racking engines !

When fevers burn, or agues freeze us,
Rheumatics gnaw, or colics squeeze us,
Our neibors' sympathy can ease us,
      Wi' pitying moan ;
But thee—thou hell o' a' diseases—
      They mock our groan !

Adown my beard the slavers trickle,
I kick* the wee stools o'er the *mickle*,   large
While round the fire the *giglets keckle*,   young jades }
                         laugh }
      To see me *loup*,   leap
An', raving mad, I wish a *heckle*   flax-dressers' comb
      Were in their doup !

In a' the numerous human *dools*,   griefs
                     harvests fool- }
Ill *hairsts*, *daft* bargains, *cutty-stools*,   ish   pen- }
Or worthy frien's rak'd i' the *mools*,—   ance-stools }
                       mould
      Sad sights to see !
The trick o' knaves, or *fash* o' fools,   trouble
      Thou bear'st the *gree !* pre-eminence

Where'er that place be priests ca' hell,
Where a' the tones o' misery yell,

---

* Cunningham, followed by Chambers, has " kick " instead of " throw," other
editors using " throw."

An rankèt plagues their numbers tell,
        In dreadfu' raw,
Thou, TOOTHACHE, surely bear'st the bell,*
        Amang them a'!

O thou grim, mischief-making chiel,
That *gars* the notes o' discord squeel,   makes
Till *daft* mankind aft dance a reel   mad
        In gore, a shoe-thick,
Gie a' the faes o' SCOTLAND'S weal   twelve-⎫
        A *towmond's* toothache!   month's⎭

[Mr. Douglas, on the evidence of finding a copy of this piece
written in Burns's hand on the fly-leaf of a copy of the Kilmar-
nock edition, thinks that it must have been produced prior to April,
1787. This is by no means conclusive, so we leave it in the
chronological place where it has hitherto appeared :—viz. in 1789.
In a letter to Creech, supposed to have been written 30th May,
1789 (the year is wanting in the holograph), he speaks of "an
omnipotent toothache engrossing all his inner man," and this gives
probability at least that it was in 1789.—J. H.]

THE FIVE CARLINS,†

AN ELECTION BALLAD.

Tune—"Chevy Chase."

(LOCKHART'S LIFE OF BURNS, 1828.)

THERE was ‡ five *Carlins* in the South,   old women
    They fell upon a scheme,
To send a lad § to London town,
    To bring them tidings hame.

---

* A silver bell used to be the prize at horse-races in Scotland, and is yet at
Lanark. To "bear the bell" is to carry off the prize.—J. H.

† The Five Dumfries Boroughs. In Scotland it is the custom to group several
of the less populous burghs together so as to make up a constituency large
enough to be entitled to a representative in Parliament. The Dumfries group
consisted of the burghs of Dumfries, Annan, Kirkcudbright, Sanquhar, and
Lochmaben. From being on the South of Scotland it sometimes receives the
name of "the Southern group."—J. H.

‡ Lockhart and others print "were ;" but "was" is the author's word.

§ A member of Parliament.

Nor only bring them tidings hame,
  But do their errands there,
And *aiblins gowd* and honor baith   mayhap gold
  Might be that laddie's share.

There was Maggy by the banks o' Nith,*
  A dame wi' pride eneugh ;
And Marjory o' the mony Lochs,†
  A Carlin auld and *teugh.*   tough

And blinkin Bess of Annandale,
  That dwelt near Solway-side : ‡
And whisky Jean, that took her gill,
  In Galloway sae wide.§

And black Joan, frae Crichton Peel,‖
  O' gipsy kith an' kin ;
Five *wighter* Carlins were na found   weightier
  The South countrie within.

To send a lad to London town,
  They met upon a day ;
And *mony* a knight. and mony a *laird,*   many⎫
                                                  landowner⎬
  This errand fain *wad gae.*   would go

O mony a knight, and mony a laird,
  This errand fain wad gae ;
But nae ane could their fancy please,
  O ne'er a *ane* but *twae.*   one   two

The first ane was a belted Knight,
  Bred of a Border band ;**
And he wad gae to London town,
  Might nae man him withstand.

---

* Dumfries.
  † Lochmaben. There are nine "lochs" or natural lakes in the neighborhood
of Lochmaben.—J. H.
  ‡ Annan
  § Kirkcudbright, the only one of the burghs not in the county of Dumfries.
It is the county town of the Stewartry of Kirkcudbright, and is therefore in
Galloway.—J. H.
  ‖ Sanquhar. An ancient castle or peel-house of the Crichton family stands
here. It is called "black" from having coal mines in its neighborhood.—J. H.
  ** Sir James Johnston of Westerhall.

And he wad do their errands weel,
   And *meikle* he wad say ;   much
And *ilka* ane about the court   every
   Wad bid to him gude-day.*

The *neist* cam in a Soger youth,†   next
   Who spak wi' modest grace,
And he wad gae to London Town,
   If sae their pleasure was.

He wad nae *hecht* them courtly gifts,   promise
   Nor meikle speech pretend ;
But he wad hecht an honest heart,
   Wad ne'er desert his friend.

Then, *wham* to chuse, and wham refuse, whom
   At strife *thir* Carlins fell ;   these
For some had Gentlefolks to please,
   And some *wad* please themsel.   would

Then out spak *mim-mou'd* Meg o' Nith, prim-
   And she spak up wi' pride,   mouthed
And she wad send the Soger youth,
   Whatever might betide.

For the auld Gudeman o' London court ‡
   She didna care a pin ;
But she wad send the Soger youth,
   To greet his eldest son.§

Then up sprang Bess O' Annandale,
   And a deadly aith she's ta'en,
That she *wad* vote the Border Knight, would
   Though she should vote *her lane.*   alone

---

* Would salute and welcome him. He was a Tory and a supporter of King George, and opposed to the claims of the Prince of Wales on the regency bill, then being pressed by the Whig party, owing to the King's alarming malady.—J. H.
  † Captain Patrick Miller of Dalswinton.
  ‡ The King, George III.—J. H
  § The Prince of Wales, afterwards George IV.

  III.   I

For far-off fowls hae feathers fair,
    And fools o' change are fain ;
But I hae tried the Border Knight,
    And I'll try him yet again.

Says black Joan frae Crichton Peel,
    A Carlin *stoor* and grim,   *austere*
The auld Gudeman, and the young Gudeman,
    For me may sink or swim ;

For fools will prate o' right or wrang,
    While knaves laugh them to scorn ;
But the Soger's friends hae blawn the best,
    So he shall bear the horn.

Then whisky Jean spak *owre* her drink,   *over*
    Ye weel ken, *kimmers* a',   *gossips*
The auld Gudeman o' London court,
    His back's been at the wa' ; *

And mony a friend that kiss'd his *caup*   *cup*
    Is now a *fremit* wight ;   *estranged*
But it's ne'er be said o' whisky Jean,—
    We'll send the Border Knight.

Then slow raise Marjory o' the *Lochs*,   *Lakes*
    And wrinkled was her brow,
Her ancient weed was russet gray,
    Her auld Scots bluid was true ;

There's some great folk set light by me,†
    I set as light by them ;
But I will send to London town
    Wham I like best at hame.[2]   *whom*

Sae how this weighty plea may end,
    Nae mortal wight can tell ;
God grant the King and *ilka* man   *every*
    May look weel to himsel.

---

* George III. had become helpless from threatened lunacy.—J. H.
† Think lightly of me.

[A contest for the representation in Parliament of the Dumfries group of boroughs commenced in September 1789, which more or less commanded the interest of these districts until its close in the month of July following. The candidates were Sir James Johnston of Westerhall, the previous member, and Captain Patrick Miller, Younger of Dalswinton, son of the poet's landlord. The great bulk of Burns's friends and patrons belonged to the Whig party; but his detestation of the Duke of Queensberry seems to have biased his inclinations towards the Tory side in this election, although in the above ballad he affects neutrality. On 9th December 1789 he enclosed it to Mr. Graham of Fintry with the following remarks :—"I am too little a man to have any political attachments. I am deeply indebted to, and have the warmest veneration for, individuals of both parties ; but a man who has it in his power to be the father of a country, and who is only known to that country by the mischiefs he does in it, is a character that one cannot speak of with patience. Sir James Johnston does 'what man can do,' but yet I doubt his fate. Of the burgh of Annan he is secure; Kirkcudbright is dubious. He has the provost; but Lord Daer, who does the honors of great man to the place, makes every effort in his power for the opposite interest. Dumfries and Sanquhar are decidedly the Duke's, 'to let or sell;' so Lochmaben, a city containing upwards of fourscore living souls 'that cannot discern between their right hand and their left' (for drunkenness), has at present the balance of power in her hands.* The provost is devoted to Sir James ; but his Grace thinks he has a majority of the council, though I, who have the honor to be a burgess of the town, and know somewhat behind the curtain, could tell him a different story."

The version of this ballad given in Cunningham's edition was printed from a holograph copy in his possession. That copy is now in the British Museum, and its chief peculiarity is that it varies very considerably from that published by Lockhart, in the arrangement of its stanzas towards the close. We consider the latter more picturesque and effective, and what is of some importance, it was the version which Sir Walter Scott expressed his high admiration of; and the concluding stanzas where Marjory gives her dictum, he was fond of reciting for their characteristic force. On the occasion of Mr. Scott of Harden (afterwards Lord Polwarth) being for the third time elected Member for the county of Roxburgh, in 1830, Sir Walter made a telling speech at the dinner thereafter given to the electors at Jedburgh. His peroration closed with a quotation from this ballad, thus :—

> ' Far away fowls hae feathers fair,
> And fools o' change are fain ; "—

---

* A somewhat irreverent allusion to Jonah iv, ii.—J. H.

then pressing his hands upon the shoulder of Mr. Scott, he continued :—

> " But we hae tried the Border Knight,
> And we'll try him yet again."

A copy of the ballad which the poet sent to Mrs. Stewart of Afton Lodge, corresponds in arrangement with that of Lockhart. The only variations of importance are the following :—

> ¹ And swore a deadly aith,
> Says " I will send the border Knight
> Spite o' you Carlins baith."
> ² The London court set light by me,
> I set as light by them ;
> And I will send the Soger lad,
> To *shaw* that court the same.]   show

ELECTION BALLAD FOR WESTERHA'.

(CUNNINGHAM, 1834.)

THE *Laddies* by the banks o' Nith   boys
    Wad trust his Grace* wi' a', Jamie ;
But he'll *sair* them, as he sair'd the King—   serve
    Turn tail and rin awa, Jamie.

Chorus.—Up and *waur* them a', Jamie,   worst
    Up and waur them a' ;
    The Johnstones hae the guidin o't,†
    Ye turncoat Whigs awa !

The day he stood his country's friend,
    Or *gied* her faes a claw, Jamie,   gave
Or frae puir man a blessin *wan*,   won
    That day the Duke ne'er saw, Jamie.
    Up and waur them, &c.

But wha is he, his country's boast ?
    Like him there is na twa, Jamie ;
There's no a *callant tents* the kye,   boy herds
    But kens o' Westerha', Jamie.
    Up and waur them, &c.

---

* The Duke of Queensberry.—J. H.
† An old Annandale proverb or war-cry, where the clan Johnstone used to be all-powerful. Chambers reminds us that the Gordons were the subject of a similar saying in the North, which forms the title of a beautiful melody.—J. H.

To end the wark, here's Whistlebirk,
Lang may his whistle blaw, Jamie ;
And Maxwell true, o' sterling blue ;
And we'll be Johnstones a', Jamie.
Up and waur them, &c.

[Here the poet deliberately sides with the Tory candidate, and contrasts his character with that of the Duke of Queensberry. No mention is made of the opposite candidate, who is treated as a mere instrument in the Duke's hands. His Grace was considered as having proved something like a traitor to the king on the late occasion of the Regency Bill, when he led the minority who voted for the surrender of unrestricted royal power into the hands of the Prince of Wales. The poet thus remarks regarding the Whig candidate in his letter to Mr. Graham, partly quoted above :—" My landlord's son is, *entre nous*, a youth by no means above mediocrity in his abilities, and is said to have a huckster-lust for shillings, pence, and farthings."

The reference in the closing verse is to Alexander Birtwhistle, provost of Kirkcudbright, a wealthy merchant of much influence, and in politics a Tory.] (We give here a ballad generally classed as a production of 1789. The original MS. of the production, accompanied with a note to Johnson, is, however, in the possession of Mr. W. F. Watson of Edinburgh. and it bears date 23d January, 1789. We restore the piece, therefore, at least to the year of its production. The poet directs it to be united with the "Caledonian Hunts Delight" and hopes the words will be found to suit "the excellent air they are designed for." Johnson did not include the ballad in his collection.—J. H.)

PROLOGUE SPOKEN AT THE THEATRE OF DUMFRIES,

ON NEW YEAR'S DAY EVENING, 1790.

(CURRIE, 1800.)

"ELLISLAND, Thursday morning.—Sir, Jogging home yesternight, it occurred to me that as your next night is the first night of the New Year, a few lines allusive to the season, by way of Prologue, Interlude, or what you please. might take pretty well. The enclosed verses are very incor-

rect, because they are almost the first crude suggestions of
my Muse, by way of bearing me company in my darkling
journey . . . but if they can be of any service to Mr.
Sutherland and his friends, I shall kiss my hands to my
Lady Muse, and own myself much her debtor.—I am, &c.,
                              ROBERT BURNS."
Inedited letter to Mr. George Sutherland, Player, Dumfries.

No song nor dance I bring from yon great city,
That queens it o'er our taste—the more's the pity :
Tho' by the bye, abroad why will you roam ?
Good sense and taste are natives here at home :
But not for panegyric I appear,
I come to wish you all a good New Year !
Old Father Time deputes me here before ye,
Not for to preach, but tell his simple story :
The sage, grave Ancient cough'd, and bade me say,
" You're one year older this important day,"
If wiser too—he hinted some suggestion,
But 'twould be rude, you know, to ask the question ;
And with a would-be-roguish leer and wink,
Said—" Sutherland, in one word, bid them—Think ! " '

Ye sprightly youths, quite flush with hope and spirit,
Who think to storm the world by dint of merit,
To you the dotard has a deal to say,
In his sly, dry, sententious, proverb way !
He bids you mind, amid your thoughtless rattle,
That the first blow is ever half the battle ;
That tho' some by the skirt may try to snatch him,
Yet by the forelock is the hold to catch him ;
That whether doing, suffering, or forbearing,
You may do miracles by persevering.

Last, tho' not least in love, ye youthful fair,
Angelic forms, high Heaven's peculiar care !
To you old Bald-pate smoothes his wrinkled brow,
And humbly begs you'll mind the important—Now !
To crown your happiness he asks your leave,
And offers, bliss to give and to receive.

For our sincere, tho' haply weak endeavors,
With grateful pride we own your many favors ;
And howsoe'er our tongues may ill reveal it,
Believe our glowing bosoms truly feel it.

[A letter written by Burns to Lady Glencairn in December, 1789,
informs her that he had been turning his thoughts to the drama.
"I do not mean (he adds) the stately buskin of the Tragic Muse.
Does not your ladyship think that an Edinburgh theatre would be
more amused with affectation, folly, and whim of Scottish growth,
than manner, which by far the greatest part of the audience can
only know at second-hand ? "

To his brother Gilbert, he enclosed a copy of the above Prologue,
on 11th January, 1790, which he says was spouted by Mr. Suther-
land, on New Year's Day evening to his audience with applause.
He complains of his unfitness for exertion in writing, in his
present state of mind. " My nerves," he says, " are in a d——
state. I feel that horrid hypochondria pervading every atom of both
body and soul. This farm has undone my enjoyment of myself.
It is a ruinous affair on all hands. But let it go to ——! I'll
fight it out, and be off with it."

The original manuscript of this Prologue, as well as the letter
which enclosed it is now possessed by J. B. Greenshields, Esq., of
Kerse, Lesmahagow. The closing line of the first paragraph, in
Currie's copy reads,
         ¹ He bade me on you press this one word—" Think."]

SKETCH—NEW YEAR'S DAY [1790].

TO MRS. DUNLOP.

(CURRIE, 1800.)

THIS day, Time winds th' exhausted chain ;
To run the twelvemonths' length again :
I see the old, bald-pated fellow,
With ardent eyes, complexion sallow,
Adjust the unimpair'd machine,
To wheel the equal, dull routine.

The absent lover, minor heir,
In vain assail him with their prayer ;
Deaf as my friend, he sees them press,
Nor makes the hour one moment less.

Will you (the Major's with the hounds,
The happy tenants share his rounds;
Coila's fair Rachel's care to-day,
And blooming Keith's engaged with Gray)
From housewife cares a minute borrow,
(That grandchild's cap will do to-morrow,)
And join with me a-moralizing;
This day's propitious to be wise in.

First, what did yesternight deliver?
"Another year has gone for ever."
And what is this day's strong suggestion?
"The passing moment's all we rest on!"
Rest on—for what? what do we here?
Or why regard the passing year?
Will Time, amus'd with proverb'd lore,
Add to our date one minute more?
A few days may—a few years must—
Repose us in the silent dust.
Then, is it wise to damp our bliss?
Yes—all such reasonings are amiss!
The voice of Nature loudly cries,
And many a message from the skies,
That something in us never dies:
That on this frail, uncertain state,
Hang matters of eternal weight:
That future life in worlds unknown
Must take its hue from this alone;
Whether—as heavenly glory bright,
Or dark as Misery's woeful night.

Since then, my honor'd first of friends,
On this poor being all depends;
Let us th' important—Now—employ,
And live as those who never die.
Tho' you, with days and honors crown'd,
Witness that filial circle round,

(A sight life's sorrows to repulse,
A sight pale Envy to convulse),
Others now claim your chief regard ;
Yourself, you wait your bright reward.

[Burns seldom allowed a New-year's Day to pass without some-
thing from his pen being addressed to Mrs. Dunlop. We are not
expressly assured that 1790 is the proper date of these lines ; but
the family likeness between it and the Prologue to Sutherland,
just given, renders this almost certain. The "Major" referred to
in the second paragraph, may have been either Andrew, the fourth,
or James, the fifth son of Mrs. Dunlop, as both of them attained
that rank in the American War.

The "fair Rachel," and the "blooming Keith" of the text were
daughters respectively of the patroness of Burns, the one being
then engaged with a drawing, or piece of sampler-work, represent-
ing "Coila," from *The Vision*, and the other being similarly
occupied with a subject from Gray's *Elegy*. Mrs. Dunlop was
apparently a widow when Burns attracted her notice in 1786, and
survived, as Dowager Mrs. Dunlop of Dunlop to May 24th, 1815.]

SCOTS PROLOGUE FOR MR. SUTHERLAND,

ON HIS BENEFIT-NIGHT, AT THE THEATRE, DUMFRIES.

(STEWART, 1801.)

"I was much disappointed, my dear Sir, in wanting your
most agreeable company yesterday. However, I heartily pray
for good weather next Sunday ; and whatever aerial Being has
the guidance of the elements may take any other half dozen
of Sundays he pleases, and clothe them with 'vapors and
clouds and storms, until he terrify himself at the combustion
of his own raising'—I shall see you on Wednesday forenoon.
In the greatest hurry, &c.—*R. B.—Monday Morning.*"

WHAT needs this *din* about the town o' Lon'on,	noise
How this new play an' that new sang is comin ?	
Why is outlandish stuff sae *meikle* courted ?	much
Does nonsense mend, like brandy when imported ?	
Is there nae poet, burning keen for fame,	
Will try to *gie* us sangs and plays at hame ?	give

For Comedy abroad he need na toil,
A fool and knave are plants of every soil ;
Nor need he hunt as far as Rome or Greece,
To gather matter for a serious piece ;
There's themes enow in Caledonian story,
Would shew the Tragic Muse in a' her glory.—

　　Is there no daring Bard will rise and tell
How glorious Wallace stood, how—hapless fell?
Where are the Muses fled that could produce
A drama worthy o' the name o' Bruce?
How here, even here, he first unsheath'd the sword
'Gainst mighty England and her guilty Lord ;
And after mony a bloody, deathless doing,
Wrench'd his dear country from the jaws of Ruin !
O for a Shakespeare, or an Otway scene,
To draw the lovely, hapless Scottish Queen !
Vain all th' omnipotence of female charms
'Gainst headlong, ruthless, mad Rebellion's arms :
She fell but fell with spirit truly Roman,
To glut that direst foe—a vengeful woman ;
A woman, (tho' the phrase may seem uncivil,)
As able and as wicked as the Devil !
One Douglas lives in Home's immortal page,
But Douglasses were heroes every age :
And tho' your fathers, prodigal of life,
A Douglas followed to the martial strife,
Perhaps, if bowls row right, and Right succeeds,
Ye yet may follow where a Douglas leads !

　　As ye hae generous done, if a' the land
Would take the Muses' servants by the hand ;
Not only hear, but patronize, befriend them,
And where ye justly can commend, commend them ;
And *aiblins* when they winna stand the test,　perhaps
Wink hard, and say "The folks hae done their best!"

Would a' the land do this, then I'll be *caition*,   security
Ye'll soon hae Poets o' the Scottish nation
Will *gar* Fame blaw until her trumpet crack,   make
And *warsle* Time, an' lay him on his back !   wrestle

For us and for our Stage, should ony *spier*,   ask
"Whase aught thae chiels * maks a' this bustle
    here?"
My best leg foremost, I'll set up my bow—
We have the honor to belong to you !
We're your ain *bairns*, e'en guide us as ye like,   children
But like good mithers, *shore* before ye strike ;   warn
And gratefu' still, I trust ye'll ever find us,
For gen'rous patronage, and *meikle* kindness   much
We've got frae a' professions, sorts and ranks :
God help us ! we're but poor — *ye'se* get but   you will
    thanks.

[In a letter to Wm. Nicol, dated 9th Feb. 1789, the poet refers
to this Prologue, and its predecessor, thus :—"For these two or
three months, on an average, I have not ridden less than 200
miles per week. I have done little in the poetic way ; but I
have given Mr. Sutherland two Prologues, one of which was delivered
last week. Mr. Sutherland, the manager, was introduced to me
by a friend from Ayr ; and a worthier or cleverer fellow I have
rarely met with."

The sentiments, so well expressed in the text, correspond with
those contained in the poet's letter to the Countess of Glen-
cairn, already partly quoted, and if farther proof were wanting
that Burns was at this time really turning his thoughts on the
Drama, we need only point to his letter to Peter Hill, Book-
seller, of 2nd March 1790, in which he orders for his own use,
copies of "Otway's Plays, Ben Jonson's, Dryden's, Congreve's,
Wycherley's, Vanbrugh's, Cibber's, and the more modern dramatic
works of Macklin, Garrick, Foote, Colman and Sheridan."—At
same time he says, "A good copy of Molière in French, I also
much want. Any other good dramatic authors in that language
I want also ; but comic authors chiefly, though I should wish
to have Racine, Corneille. and Voltaire too."

The six concluding lines of the second paragraph of the text

---

* Who owns these fellows : i. e. whom do they serve?—J. H.

are wanting in the original MS. transmitted to Sutherland, and were afterwards added in a copy from which Cromek supplied these lines in the *Reliques*.]

LINES TO A GENTLEMAN,

WHO HAD SENT THE POET A NEWSPAPER, AND OFFERED TO CONTINUE IT FREE OF EXPENSE.

(CURRIE, 1800.)

KIND Sir, I've read your paper through,
And faith, to me, 'twas really new!
How guessed ye, Sir, what maist I wanted?
This mony a day I've *grain'd* and   groaned
    gaunted,   yawned
To ken what French mischief was brewin;
Or what the *drumlie* Dutch were doin;   muddy
That vile *doup-skelper*, Emperor Joseph,   bastinadoer
If Venus yet had got his nose off;
Or how the *collieshangie* works   contention
Atween the Russians and the Turks,
Or if the Swede, before he halt,
Would play anither Charles the *twalt;* *   twelfth
If Denmark, any body spak o't;
Or Poland, wha had now the *tack* o't; †   lease
How cut-throat Prussian blades were *hingin;*   hanging
How *libbet* Italy was singin;   castrated
If Spaniard, Portuguese, or Swiss,
Were sayin or takin aught amiss;
Or how our merry lads at hame,
In Britain's court kept up the game;
How royal George, the Lord leuk o'er him!
Was managing St. Stephens' quorum; ‡
If *sleekit* Chatham Will was livin,   sly
Or *glaikit* Charlie got his *nieve* in;   thoughtless   fist

---

* In 1789, Gustavus Adolphus of Sweden had, at this time, Chambers says, adopted vigorous measures against Russia. Several of his own nobles appear to have disapproved of his policy, and were arrested by him.—J. H.
† If any one spoke of Denmark, or who now owned Poland.—J. H.
‡ The British House of Parliament.—J. H.

How daddie Burke the plea was cookin,
If Warren Hastings' neck was *yeukin;* *　　　itching
How *cesses, stents*, and fees were *rax'd*, ᵗᵃˣᵉˢ burdens }
Or if bare a—— yet were tax'd ; †　　　stretched }
The news o' princes, dukes, and earls,
Pimps, sharpers, bawds, and opera-girls ;
If that *daft buckie*, Geordie Wales, .　　　wild buck
Was threshin still at *hizzies'* tails ;　　　wenches'
Or if he was grown *oughtlins douser*, anything decenter
And no a perfect *kintra cooser :*　　　country stallion
A' this and mair I never heard of ;
And, but for you, I might despair'd of.
So, gratefu', back your *news* I send you, newspaper
And pray a' gude things may attend you !

ELLISLAND, *Monday Morning*, 1790.

[It seems now to be held certain that Mr. Peter Stuart of the London " Star" was the kind friend to whom this good-humored and clever effusion was addressed. The contents manifest that Burns was not an inattentive reader of political news. About the year 1838, Mr. Daniel Stuart, surviving brother of the late editor of the *Star*, published some particulars, to the effect that Burns had been offered £50 per annum by Mr. Peter Stuart, for a small weekly contribution to the *Star*, either in prose or verse, which the poet did not see his way to accept.

It would appear that, from some cause or other, the delivery of the Star newspaper at Ellisland was irregular, and in order to check that irregularity the poet despatched the following remonstrance to headquarters :—

> " Dear Peter, dear Peter,
> We poor sons of metre
> Are often negleckit, ye ken :
> For instance, your sheet, man,
> (Tho' glad I'm to see't, man),
> I get it no ae day in ten.—*R. B.*]

---

* If he was in danger of being hanged.—J. H.
† Everything was being taxed at this time.—J. H.

ELEGY ON WILLIE NICOL'S MARE.

(CROMEK, 1808.)

PEG NICHOLSON was a good bay mare,
    As ever trod on iron ;
But now she's floating down the Nith,
    And past the mouth o' Cairn.*

Peg Nicholson was a good bay mare,
    An' rode thro' thick an' thin ;
But now she's floating down the Nith,
    And wanting even the skin.

Peg Nicholson was a good bay mare,
    And ance she bore a priest ;
But now she's floating down the Nith,
    For Solway fish a feast.

Peg Nicholson was a good bay mare,
    An' the priest he rode her sair ;
And much oppress'd, and bruis'd she was,
    As priest-rid cattle are,—&c. &c.

[These extempore ballad stanzas form the close of a letter from
Burns to Nicol, dated February 9th, 1790, announcing the death
of the dominie's mare which had been left at, or sent out to,
Ellisland in an unthriving condition, with a view to be recruited
a little before being offered for sale at some neighboring fair. The
poet says :—" I refused fifty-five shillings for her, which was the
highest bode I could squeeze for her. I fed her up, and had her
in fine order for Dumfries fair ; when, four or five days before
the fair, she was seized with an unaccountable disorder in the
sinews, or somewhere in the bones of the neck ; with a weakness,
or total want of power in her fillets ; and, in short, the whole
vertebrae of her spine seemed to be diseased and unhinged ;
and in eight-and-forty hours, in spite of the two best farriers
in the country, she died, and be d—— to her !"

* An affluent of the Nith, near Ellisland.—J. H.

The expressions "priest-rid," and "the priest he rode her sair," refer to the fact that Nicol, by education, was originally intended for the Church, and had been licensed to preach. The name of the mare was bestowed at Ellisland, in burlesque reference to the insane woman, Margaret Nicholson, who attempted to stab King George III. in 1786. The original manuscript of these verses and relative letter is now in possession of Mrs. Warrington, at Worsborough Hall, near Barnsley, the grand-daughter of R. H. Cromek.]

THE GOWDEN LOCKS OF ANNA.

(CROMEK'S SELECT SCOTTISH SONGS, 1810.)

YESTREEN I had a pint o' wine,
    A place where body saw na ;
Yestreen lay on this breast o' mine
    The *gowden* locks of Anna.   golden

The hungry Jew in wilderness,
    Rejoicing o'er his manna,
Was naething to my *hiney* bliss   honey
    Upon the lips of Anna.

Ye monarchs, take the East and West,
    Frae Indus to Savannah ;
Gie me, within my straining grasp,
    The melting form of Anna :

There I'll despise Imperial charms,
    An Empress or Sultana,
While dying raptures, in her arms,
    I give and take wi' Anna !

Awa, thou flaunting God of Day !
    Awa, thou pale Diana !
I'lk Star, gae hide thy twinkling ray,   Each
    When I'm to meet my Anna !

Come, in thy raven plumage, Night,
  (Sun, Moon, and Stars, withdrawn a' ;)
And bring an angel-pen to write
  My transports with my Anna !

POSTSCRIPT.

The Kirk an' State may join an' tell,
  To do sic things I *maunna:*   must not
The Kirk an' State may gae to h—,
  And I'll gae to my Anna.

She is the sunshine o' my e'e,
  To live *but* her I canna ;   without
Had I on earth but wishes three,
  The first should be my Anna.

[It seems to be an undisputed fact that the heroine of these
burning stanzas was Anne Park—a niece of Mrs. Hyslop, the land-
lady of the Globe Tavern, Dumfries. About the close of October
1789 Burns entered on his Excise duties, and the business he re-
quired to transact with Collector Mitchell in connection with that
work, led him frequently to Dumfries. The election canvas for
the Dumfries burghs, which lasted from December 1789 to July
1790, and the attraction of a theatrical company with whom he
had enlisted his sympathies, must often have induced him to con-
tinue for days and nights together in Dumfries. He dates a letter
to Dr. Moore, on 14th July 1790. from "Excise office, Dumfries,"
and another, addressed to Mr. Graham of Fintry, on 4th September
1790, from "Dumfries, Globe Inn." In this last letter, he tells
his patron that he had resolved "either to give up or sublet" his
farm directly. There also the fact is revealed that, through certain
perquisites and irregular additions to his salary, his excise-income
was more than doubled during his first year's practice. He says :
—"As my division consists of ten large parishes (and, I am sorry
to say, hitherto very carelessly surveyed), I had a good deal of
business for the Justices ; and my 'decreet' will amount to between
fifty and sixty pounds."
  The Globe Tavern, therefore, from an early stage of his excise
career, became his place of rendezvous in Dumfries, and continued
till the last to be his favorite "howff," when permanently located
in that town. Considerable mystery hangs over the after history
of the young woman who inspired the song in the text. Cunning-

ham says :—"She was accounted beautiful by the customers at the inn, when wine made them tolerant in matters of taste ; and, as may be surmised from the song, had other pretty ways to render herself agreeable to them than the serving of wine." Some years after the poet's death, through the benevolent exertions of Alderman Shaw of London, a sum of four hundred pounds was raised as a provision for two illegitimate daughters of Burns, the one being his "dear bought Bess," referred to at page 69, vol. I., and the other being Elizabeth, daughter of Anne Park, of the Globe Tavern, Dumfries, born 31st March 1791. Chambers, in 1852, first published the fact that the infant was not nursed by its own parent, but sent for a short while to be taken care of by the poet's mother and sisters at Mossgiel, and thence brought to Ellisland to be fostered by Mrs. Burns along with her infant *William Nicol*, who was born just ten days after the other. The girl was carefully reared in the household of the poet, and lived with his widow till her marriage to John Thomson, a soldier, who afterwards followed the trade of a hand-loom weaver at Pollockshaws, and by whom she had a large family. She bore a remarkable likeness to her father, the poet ; and her children were objects of great interest in the West country, chiefly on account of the physical resemblance to their ancestor which they possessed.* She herself died at Cross-my-loof so recently as June 1873, at the age of 82. Chambers is silent regarding the fate of "Anna of the gowden locks ;" who seems to have disappeared after the birth of the poet's child ; consequently it has been assumed that she died in child-birth. Mrs. Thomson used to say that she was born in Edinburgh, her mother having been sent there to be confined and nursed in the house of a married sister.

Burns himself thought highly of the song in the text. He recorded it in the Glenriddell collection, where it is introduced after the poem on Captain Grose's Peregrinations : it is there comprised in sixteen lines only, and the other eight lines are inserted a page or two farther on. The "Postcript" was a still later performance, having been appended to the song when he inserted it in his collection for the "Crochallan Fencibles." The author recommended the song to George Thomson in April 1793, and even took the trouble to transcribe it with several of the warmer expressions cooled down with a view to make it admissible into his collection. Currie prints only four lines to indicate the production, and adds that Mr. Thomson "did not approve of the song, even in its altered state." Burns intended the words to

---

* Mrs. Burns's forbearance on this occasion is almost without parallel. She laid the child in the same cradle with her own son ; and when her father (who had come on a visit to her) asked with astonishment if she had again had twins. she simply said :—" It's a neebor's bairn who is unweel."—J. H

be sung to a sentimental Irish air called "The Banks of Banna."
He remarks to Thomson : " It is to me a heavenly air—what
would you think of a set of Scots verses to it ? I made one a
good while ago, which I think is the best love-song I ever com-
posed in my life; but in its original state is not quite a lady's
song."]

SONG—I MURDER HATE.

(KILMARNOCK ED., 1876.)

I MURDER hate by flood or field,
 Tho' glory's name may screen us ;
In wars at home I'll spend my blood—
 Life-giving wars of Venus.
The deities that I adore
 Are social Peace and Plenty ;
I'm better pleas'd to make one more,
 Than be the death of twenty.

I would not die like Socrates,
 For all the fuss of Plato ;
Nor would I with Leonidas,
 Nor yet would I with Cato :
The zealots of the Church and State
 Shall ne'er my mortal foes be ;
But let me have bold Zimri's fate,
 Within the arms of Cozbi ! *

[The first eight lines of this song were inscribed by Burns
with his diamond pen on the window-pane of one of the bed-
rooms of the Globe Inn, and were published by Stewart in 1801.
The complete song the bard inserted in the Glenriddell MS.
Book, immediately under the kindred song which precedes this.
 The Globe Inn, situated in one of the closes of the High
Street, consists of three stories with about a dozen good apart-
ments. It has undergone little change since the days of Burns,

---

* *Vide* Numbers, Chap. xxv. verses 8-15.—*R. B.*

the windows—doors, flooring, panelling, stair-railings, &c., remaining almost unaltered. What is termed "Burns's corner" is a little snuggery on the ground-floor, which is reached by passing through the kitchen. It measures fourteen feet by twelve, is lined with painted panels, and contains an arm-chair, said to be the very one used by the poet when Stephen Clarke and he sat there together over their music and whisky-punch. Over the fire-place is a pretty fair painting representing Coila casting the inspiring mantle over her adopted son ; and the "rough burr thistle" climbs the wall on each side of the mantle-piece. One of the latest additions to the Burns-relics at "the Globe," is the poet's china punch-bowl acquired by the present landlord in 1877 for £5, at a sale by auction.] (Any one sitting down in the poet's chair requires to replenish the bowl.—J. H.)

GUDEWIFE, COUNT THE LAWIN.

(JOHNSON'S MUSEUM, 1792.)

GANE is the day, and *mirk's* the night,   dark's
But we'll ne'er stray for *faute* o' light ;   want
Gude ale and brandy's stars and moon,
And blue-red wine's the rysin sun.

Chorus.—Then gudewife, count the *lawin,* reckoning
          The lawin, the lawin,
          Then gudewife, count the lawin,
          And bring a coggie* mair.

There's wealth and ease for gentlemen,
And simple folk *maun fecht* and *fen';*   must fight }
          struggle }
But here we're a' in ae accord,
For *ilka* man that's drunk's a lord.   every
          Then gudewife, &c.

---

* A cog or coggie is properly a small wooden vessel out of which ale was commonly drank in Scotland in olden times.—J. H.

My coggie is a *haly* pool   holy
That heals the wounds o' care and *dool*;   grief
And Pleasure is a wanton trout,
An ye drink it a', ye'll find him out.
      Then gudewife, &c.

[The original MS. of this song is in the British Museum, where
the chorus and title read "Landlady, count the lawin;" but as a
song so commencing had already appeared in Johnson's collection,
it was altered to what we have in the text. There can be little
doubt that this song was produced about the same period with
the two preceding: the amatory element is excluded; but in the
second verse the philosophy of Bacchus is exhibited to perfection,
and Anacreon himself never made a better lyric hit than we have
here in stanza third. Burns appreciated its value, and inscribed
the latter, with his diamond pen, on one of the window-panes
of the Globe Inn, Dumfries. It remained long there, a special
attraction, among similar scribblings, till a high price offered for
the pane induced the owner to part with it.

The lively melody to which this song is set in the *Museum*,
was communicated to Johnson by Burns, without intimation whence
it was derived; and as it is not generally known, we here annex
it. In sending the production he remarked that the chorus is
part of an old song which concluded thus:—

        " My wife she's ay a-tellin me
          That drink will be the dead o' me;
          But if gude liquor be my dead,
          This shall be written on my head:—
          Landlady, count the lawin !" &c.]

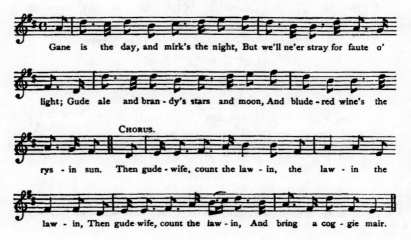

Gane is the day, and mirk's the night, But we'll ne'er stray for faute o'
light; Gude ale and bran - dy's stars and moon, And blude - red wine's the
CHORUS.
rys - in sun. Then gude - wife, count the law - in, the law - in the
law - in, Then gude wife, count the law - in, And bring a cog - gie mair.

ELECTION BALLAD,

AT CLOSE OF THE CONTEST FOR REPRESENTING THE DUMFRIES BURGHS, 1790.

ADDRESS TO R. GRAHAM, ESQ. OF FINTRY.

(CUNNINGHAM, 1834.)

FINTRY, my stay in worldly strife,
Friend o' my muse, friend o' my life,
  Are ye as idle as I am?
Come then, wi' uncouth *kintra fleg*, country leap
O'er Pegasus I'll fling my leg,
  And ye shall see me try him.

But where shall I go rin a ride,
That I may splatter nane beside?
  I wad na be uncivil:
In manhood's various paths and ways
There's ay some *doytin* body strays, stupid
  And *I* ride like the devil.

Thus I break aff wi' a' my *birr* energy
An' down yon dark, deep alley spur,
  Where Theologics *daunder:* saunter
Alas! curst wi' eternal fogs,
And damn'd in everlasting bogs,
  As sure's the creed I'll blunder!

I'll stain a band, or *jaup* a gown, splash
Or rin my reckless guilty crown
  Against the haly door:
Sair do I rue my luckless fate,
When, as the Muse an' Deil wad hae't,
  I rade that road before.

Suppose I take a spurt, and mix
Amang the wilds o' Politics—
     Elector and elected,
Where dogs at Court (sad sons of bitches!)
Septennially a madness touches,
     Till all the land's infected.

All hail! Drumlanrig's haughty Grace,*
Discarded remnant of a race
     Once godlike—great in story;
Thy *forbears'* virtues all contrasted,   ancestors
The very name of Douglas blasted,
     Thine that inverted glory!

Hate, envy, oft the Douglas bore.
But thou hast superadded more,
     And sunk them in contempt;
Follies and crimes have stain'd the name,
But, Queensberry, thine the virgin claim,
     From aught that's good exempt!

I'll sing the zeal Drumlanrig bears,
Who left the all-important cares
     Of princes, and their darlings:
And, bent on winning borough towns,
Came shaking hands wi' *wabster-loons,* weaver-scamps
     And kissing *barefit carlins.* barefooted women

Combustion thro'· our boroughs rode,
Whistling his roaring pack abroad
     Of mad unmuzzled lions;
As Queenberry blue and buff† unfurl'd,
And Westerha'‡ and Hopeton § hurl'd
     To every Whig defiance.

---

* William Duke of Queensberry, elevated to Ducal honors in 1778, died in December 1810. The poet here employs the Duke's second title for the sake of the rythm. Drumlanrig is a magnificent castle on the Nith. now owned by the Duke of Buccleuch.—J. H.

† The Fox or Whig livery.   ‡ The Tory candidate.   § Earl of Hopeton.

But cautious Queensberry left the war,
Th' unmanner'd dust might soil his star,
      Besides, he hated *bleeding :*   paying
But left behind him heroes bright,
Heroes in Cæsarean fight,
      Or Ciceronian pleading.

O for a throat like huge Mons-Meg,*
To muster o'er each ardent Whig
      Beneath Drumlanrig's banners ;
Heroes and heroines commix,
All in the field of politics,
      To win immortal honors,

M'Murdo † and his lovely spouse,
(Th' enamor'd laurels kiss her brows !)
      Led on the Loves and Graces :
She won each gaping burgess heart,
While he, *sub rosa*, played his part
      Among their wives and lasses.

Craigdarroch ‡ led a light-arm'd core,
Tropes, metaphors, and figures pour,
      Like Hecla streaming thunder:
Glenriddell,§ skill'd in rusty coins,
Blew up each Tory's dark designs,
      And bared the treason under.

In either wing two champions fought ;
Redoubted Staig,‖ who set at nought
      The wildest savage Tory ;
And Welsh ** who ne'er yet flinch'd his ground,
High-wav'd his *magnum-bonum* round
      With Cyclopean fury.

---

* A gigantic piece of ordnance at Edinburgh Castle—20 inches diameter.
† John M'Murdo, Esq., the duke's chamberlain, an intimate friend of Burns.
‡ Fergusson of Craigdarroch, champion of "The Whistle."
§ Robert Riddell, Esq. of Carse.   ‖ Provost of Dumfries.
** Sheriff of the county.

Miller * brought up th' artillery ranks,
The many-pounders of the Banks,
    Resistless desolation !
While Maxwelton,† that baron bold,
'Mid Lawson's ‡ port entrench'd his hold,
    And threaten'd worse damnation.

To these what Tory hosts oppos'd,
With these what Tory warriors clos'd,
    Surpasses my *descriving* :   describing
Squadrons, extended long and large,
With furious speed rush to the charge,
    Like furious devils driving.

What versè can sing, what prose narrate,
The butcher deeds of bloody Fate,
    Amid this mighty *tulyie !*   struggle
Grim Horror *girn'd*, pale Terror roar'd,   grinned
As Murder at his *thrapple shor'd*,   throat attempted
    And Hell mix'd in the *brulyie.*   quarrel

As Highland craigs by thunder cleft,
When lightnings fire the stormy lift,
    Hurl down with crashing rattle ;
As flames among a hundred woods,
As headlong foam a hundred floods,
    Such is the rage of Battle.

The stubborn Tories dare to die ;
And soon the rooted oaks would fly
    Before th' approaching fellers :
The Whigs come on like Ocean's roar,
When all his wintry billows pour
    Against the Buchan Bullers.§

---

* Patrick Miller, Esq., father of the Whig candidate, who had been a banker.
† Sir Robert Lawrie of Maxwelton, M.P.
‡ Lawson, an eminent wine merchant.
§ Remarkable rocky caverns, on the coast near Peterhead.

Lo, from the shades of Death's deep night,
Departed Whigs enjoy the fight,
      And think on former daring:
The muffled murtherer of Charles *
The Magna Charta flag unfurls,
      All deadly gules its bearing.

Nor wanting ghosts of Tory fame;
Bold Scrimgeour † follows gallant Graham; ‡
      Auld Covenanters shiver—
Forgive! forgive! much-wrong'd Montrose!
Now Death and Hell engulph thy foes,
      Thou liv'st on high for ever.

Still o'er the field the combat burns,
The Tories, Whigs, give way by turns;
      But Fate the word has spoken:
For woman's wit and strength o' man,
Alas! can do but what they can;
      The Tory ranks are broken.

O that my een were flowing *burns*!   rivulets
My voice, a lioness that mourns
      Her darling cubs' undoing!
That I might *greet*, that I might cry,   weep
While Tories fall, while Tories fly,
      And furious Whigs pursuing!

What Whig but melts for good Sir James,
Dear to his country, by the names, ·
      Friend, Patron, Benefactor!
Not Pulteney's wealth can Pulteney save;
And Hopeton falls, the generous, brave;
      And Stewart,§ bold as Hector.

---

* The executioner of Charles I. was masqued.
† Scrimgeour, Lord Dundee.   ‡ Graham, Marquis of Montrose.
§ Stewart of Hillside.—*R. B.*

Thou, Pitt, shalt rue this overthrow,
And Thurlow growl a curse of woe,
          And Melville melt in wailing:
Now Fox and Sheridan rejoice,
And Burke shall sing, O Prince, arise!
          Thy power is all prevailing!

For your poor friend, the Bard, afar
He only hears and sees the war,
          A cool spectator purely!
So, when the storm the forest rends,
The robin in the hedge descends,
          And, sober chirps securely.

Now, for my friends' and brethren's sakes,
And for my dear-lov'd Land o' Cakes,*
          I pray with holy fire:
Lord, send a rough-shod troop o' Hell
O'er a' wad Scotland buy or sell,†
          To grind them in the mire!

[A few pages back, the reader has seen two ballads which Burns
threw off at an early stage of this election contest. According to
Chambers—"the canvas had been proceeding with excessive vigor
all this spring, and when the election at length took place in July,
the agitation and fervor of the public mind in the district ex-
ceeded everything of the kind previously known. The influence
of the Duke of Queensberry on the Whig side, proved too much
for the merits of the 'good Sir James,' and the dismissal of his
Grace from the bed-chamber was revenged on Pitt by the return
of Captain Miller." In illustration of verse eighth of the text, the
following passage in a letter from Burns to the provost of Loch-
maben, dated 20th December 1789, will be perused with interest:—
"If at any time you expect a field-day in your town—a day when
dukes, earls, and knights, pay their court to weavers, tailors, and
cobblers—I should like to know of it two or three days before-
hand. It is not that I care three skips of a cur-dog for the
politics, but I should like to see such an exhibition of human
nature."

---

* Scotland, from oatmeal cakes being commonly eaten there.—J. H.
† Over all who would buy or sell Scotland.

Although the poet's manuscripts of this ballad are numerous, it does not seem to have found its way into print until the Edinburgh Magazine published it in 1811. Our text is enlarged by the introduction of six stanzas—from second to seventh—which appear in a holograph copy possessed by J. B. Greenshields, Esq. of Kerse, Lesmahagow. It has also been carefully collated with a fine copy in the Afton MSS. now possessed by Wm. Allason Cunningham, Esq. of Logan and Afton. From this latter source the patriotic stanza which closes the ballad has been obtained.

ELEGY ON CAPTAIN MATTHEW HENDERSON,

A GENTLEMAN WHO HELD THE PATENT FOR HIS HONORS IMMEDIATELY FROM ALMIGHTY GOD.

(EDINBURGH ED., 1793.)

"ELLISLAND, 23rd July 1790.—Do not ask me, my dear Sir, why I have neglected so long to write to you. Accuse me of indolence, my line of life of hurry, my stars of perverseness—in short, accuse anything but me of forgetfulness. You knew Matthew Henderson. At the time of his death, I composed an elegiac stanza or two, as he was a man I much regarded; but something came in my way, so that the design of an Elegy to his memory I gave up. Meeting with the fragment the other day, among some old waste papers, I tried to finish the piece, and have this moment put the last hand to it. This I am going to write you is the first fair copy of it. . . . . . Let me know how you like it. My best compliments to Mrs. Cleghorn and family.—I am, most truly, my dear sir, yours. ROBERT BURNS."—*Letter to Mr. Robert Cleghorn, Saughton Mills, near Edinburgh.*

"Should the poor be flattered?"—*Shakspeare.*

O DEATH! thou tyrant fell and bloody!
The *meikle* devil wi' a *woodie*   large   gallows-rope
Haurl thee hame to his black *smiddie*, drag smithy
    O'er *hurcheon* hides,   hedgehog
And like stock-fish come o'er his *studdie*   anvil
    Wi' thy auld sides!

He's gane, he's gane! he's frae us torn,
The ae best fellow e'er was born!
Thee, Matthew, Nature's sel' shall mourn,
   By wood and wild,
Where, haply, Pity strays forlorn,
   Frae man exil'd.[1]

Ye hills, near neibors o' the *starns*,   stars
That proudly cock your cresting cairns!
Ye cliffs the haunts of sailing *earns*,   eagles
   Where Echo slumbers!
Come join, ye Nature's sturdiest bairns,
   My wailing numbers!

Mourn, *ilka* grove the *cushat* kens! each wood-pigeon
Ye haz'ly *shaws* and briery *dens!* woods dells
Ye burnies, wimplin down your glens,
   Wi' *toddlin din*,   purling noise
Or foaming, strang, wi' hasty *stens*, leaps
   Frae *lin* to lin.[2]   fall

Mourn, little harebells o'er the lea ;
Ye stately foxgloves, fair to see ;
Ye woodbines hanging bonilie,
   In scented bow'rs ;
Ye roses on your thorny tree,
   The first o' flow'rs.

At dawn, when ev'ry grassy blade
Droops with a diamond at his head,
At ev'n, when beans their fragrance shed,
   I' th' rustling gale,
Ye *maukins*, *whiddin* thro' the glade, hares scudding
   Come join my wail.

Mourn, ye wee songsters o' the wood ;
Ye grouse that crap the heather bud ;
Ye curlews, calling thro' a *clud;*   cloud
    Ye whistling plover ;
And mourn, ye whirring *paitrick* brood ;   partridge
    He's gane for ever !

Mourn, sooty coots, and speckled teals ;
Ye fisher herons, watching eels ;
Ye duck and drake, wi' airy wheels
    Circling the lake ;
Ye bitterns, till the quagmire reels,
    Rair for his sake.   roar

Mourn, clam'ring *craiks* at close o' day,   landrails
'Mang fields o' flow'ring clover gay ;
And when ye wing your annual way
    Frae our cauld shore,*
Tell *thae* far warlds wha lies in clay,   these
    Wham we deplore.   whom

Ye *houlets*, frae your ivy bow'r   owls
In some auld tree, or *eldritch* tow'r,   haunted
What time the moon, wi' silent *glow'r,*   stare
    Sets up her horn,
Wail thro' the dreary midnight hour,
    Till *waukrife* morn !   wakeful

O' rivers, forests, hills, and plains !
Oft have ye heard my *canty* strains :   merry
But now, what else for me remains
    But tales of woe ;
And frae my een the drapping rains
    Maun ever flow.   must

---

* Landrails migrate south from Scotland before winter.—J. H.

Mourn, Spring, thou darling of the year!
Ilk cowslip cup shall *kep* a tear :   catch
Thou, Simmer, while each corny spear
        Shoots up its head,
Thy gay, green, flow'ry tresses shear,
        For him that's dead!

Thou, Autumn, wi' thy yellow hair,
In grief thy sallow mantle tear!
Thou, Winter, hurling thro' the air
        The roaring blast,
Wide o'er the naked world declare
        The worth we've lost.

Mourn him, thou Sun, great source of light!
Mourn, Empress of the silent night!
And you, ye twinkling starnies bright,
        My Matthew mourn! ·
For through your orbs he's ta'en his flight,
        Ne'er to return.

O Henderson! the man! the brother!
And art thou gone, and gone forever!
And hast thou crost that unknown river,
        Life's dreary bound!
Like thee, where shall I find another,
        The world around!

Go to your sculptur'd tombs, ye Great,
In a' the tinsel trash o' state!
But by thy honest turf I'll wait,
        Thou man of worth!
And weep the ae best fellow's fate
        E'er lay in earth.

THE EPITAPH.

Stop, passenger! my story's brief,
 And truth I shall relate, man;
I tell nae common tale of grief,
 For Matthew was a great man.

If thou uncommon merit hast,
 Yet spurn'd at Fortune's door, man;
A look of pity hither cast,
 For Matthew was a poor man.

If thou a noble sodger art,
 That passest by this grave, man;
There moulders here a gallant heart,
 For Matthew was a brave man.

If thou on men, their works and ways,
 Canst throw uncommon light, man;
Here lies wha weel had won thy praise,
 For Matthew was a bright man.

If thou, at Friendship's sacred ca',
 Wad life itself resign, man;
Thy sympathetic tear maun fa',
 For Matthew was a kind man.

If thou art staunch, without a stain,
 Like the unchanging blue, man;
This was a kinsman o' thy ain,
 For Matthew was a true man.

If thou hast wit, and fun, and fire,
 And ne'er guid wine did fear, man;
This was thy *billie*, dam, and sire,   brother
 For Matthew was a queer man.

If ony whiggish, *whingin* sot,   whining
 To blame poor Matthew dare, man;
May *dool* and sorrow be his lot,   grief
 For Matthew was a rare man.

But now, his radiant course is run,
For Matthew's was a bright one !
His soul was like the glorious sun,
A matchless, Heav'nly light, man.

[The copy of the foregoing poem, referred to in the headnote,
wants the two closing verses, and also the Epitaph, which, as
Burns intimates, were added at a later date.   On the authority
of Allan Cunningham, we have transferred the motto, as printed
in the author's editions, to its original place at the end of the
Epitaph, which seemed to close abruptly wanting it.   The poet's
manuscripts of the finished piece, have one line of motto from
Shakespeare, instead of these four lines borrowed from the Epi-
taph.   In sending a copy to his friend John M'Murdo of Drum-
lanrig, he makes reference to that motto, thus :—" You knew
Henderson—I have not flattered his memory."

Along with other pieces, he sent this poem to his correspondent,
Dr. Moore, and concerning it he remarked—" It is a tribute to
the memory of a man I much loved.   Poets have in this, the
same advantage as Roman Catholics ; they can be of service to
their friends after they have passed that bourne where all other
kindness ceases to be of avail."

It is very singular to find Burns bursting out into the sublime
eloquence of this Elegy, on a departed Edinburgh acquaintance
whose name had not hitherto been mentioned in his corre-
spondence, or in connection with any incident in his Edinburgh
life.   Chambers, after many a searching enquiry, could get no
intelligence about this highly honored citizen of Edinburgh, ex-
cept the fact that he had once existed as a very social soul.
A fragment of a contemporaneous letter fell in his way, in which
Burns is referred to, in February 1787, as the lion of the day,
and Matthew Henderson, and Mr. Hagart, the Secretary of the
Caledonian Hunt, are spoken of as fit for the office of Master
of Ceremonies at the forthcoming Assemblies.   "But," says the
writer, "Would Matthew leave his friend and bottle to go bow
at an Assembly ? " *

Chambers adds that "there is a sad want of documentary or
contemporary evidence about Matthew, and that the obituaries

* We learn from a note in Blackie's edition, that Captain Henderson was re-
membered in Edinburgh " as a gentleman of highly agreeable manners and
correct principles, who resided in Edinburgh, when Burns was there, dined reg-
ularly at Fortune's tavern, and was a member of the Cappillaire Club, much fre-
quented by the gay and witty."   Having regard to the person to whom the poem
and elegy were addressed, the Captain, namely, of the "Crochallan Fencibles,"
we cannot doubt but that Matthew was a member of this jovial club also.—J. H.

have been searched in vain for his death." A persevering en-
quirer, however, found by searching the Records at the Sasine
Office, that he was owner of a subject at the head of Carrubber's
Close, where he lived and died, and the obituary of the Scots
Magazine announces his demise on 21st November, 1788. A search
also among the Burial Registers farther certified the very spot of
earth where this "man of worth" had been interred. namely in
the venerable Greyfriars' churchyard, near the foot of the ground,
close to the west side of Duncan Ban Macintyre's monument.
That record showed more, for instead of the prefix "Captain"
being "a mere pet-name for the man among his friends, adopted
from his position in some convivial society," as Chambers sup-
posed, we there read—"Captain Matthew Henderson of Tunnoch-
side; buried 27th November 1788; Place of Interment, 6 D paces
South Pitcairlie's tomb.—Old A."—Here then it is established that
although "Matthew was a poor man," he was, nevertheless, laird
of Tunnochside: and not a mock, but a real Captain. It tells
another important fact, namely, that although he did stick to "his
friend and bottle," he succumbed to no malady but old age.

The only variations of consequence between the printed poem
and the manuscripts are the following:—

> [1] Thee, Matthew, woods and wilds shall mourn,
> 　　　Wi' a' their birth;
> For whunstane Man to grieve wad scorn—
> 　　　For poor, plain WORTH!

> [2] ————wimplin down the glens,
> 　　　At toddlin leisure,
> Or o'er the linns, wi' hasty stens,
> 　　　Flinging your treasure.]

VERSES ON CAPTAIN GROSE,

WRITTEN ON AN ENVELOPE, ENCLOSING A LETTER TO HIM.

(CURRIE, 1800.)

KEN ye ought o' Captain Grose?—Igo and ago,
If he's among his friends or foes?—Iram, coram, dago,
Is he to Abra'm's bosom gane?—Igo and ago,
Or *haudin* Sarah by the wame?—Iram, coram, holding
　　dago.

III.　　　　　　K

Is he south or is he north?—Igo and ago,
Or drownèd in the river Forth?—Iram, coram,
    dago,
Is he slain by *Hielan' bodies?*—Igo and ago,   Highland} creatures
And eaten like a wether haggis?—Iram, coram, dago.

Where'er he be, the Lord be near him!—Igo and ago,
As for the deil, he *daur na steer* him,— dare not meddle
    Iram, coram, dago,
But please transmit th' enclosèd, letter,—Igo and ago,
Which will oblige your humble debtor,—Iram, coram,
    dago.

So may ye hae auld stanes in store,—Igo and ago,
The very stanes that Adam bore—Iram, coram, dago,
So may ye get in glad possession,—Igo and ago,
The coins o' Satan's coronation!—Iram coram dago.

[A letter written by Burns to his patron, Mr. Graham of Fintry,
from the Globe Inn, Dumfries, on 4th September 1790, contains a
paragraph that shews he had recently been in correspondence with
Captain Grose. Professor Dugald Stewart had expressed to the
poet a desire to be introduced to Grose, and accordingly he wrote
to his jolly friend intimating that fact, and letting him know that
the Professor's summer residence at Catrine was situated less than
a mile from Sorn Castle, which the antiquary had proposed visit-
ing. Not knowing the Captain's address, he enclosed the letter to
Mr. Cardonnel, a brother antiquary resident in Edinburgh, and
within the envelope, the poet inscribed the verses in the text,
which are a parody of a familiar old ditty, beginning :—

    " Ken ye ought o' Sir John Malcolm?—Igo and ago,
      If he's a wise man, I mistak him,—Iram, coram, dago."

It is very probable that along with the letter of introduction to
Dugald Stewart, Burns performed a promise he had made to Grose,
to send him certain witch-stories he had heard relating to Alloway
Kirk. A few years after the death of Captain Grose. the poet's
letter to him, containing three of these stories, was published by
Sir Egerton Brydges, in the *Censura Literaria.* It was the second
of these stories that Burns chiefly had in his eye, as the ground-
work of his immortal tale, "Tam O' Shanter," which seems to
have been composed in October or November of this year.]

CORRESPONDENCE.

INTRODUCTORY NOTE TO PROSE OF THE THIRD VOLUME.

OUR Second Volume brought us down to the period of publication of the first Edinburgh edition. This volume is of his Ellisland period. Burns is now married, but we regret that we cannot add—happy. His farming venture proves a failure.

As in the two previous vols., the prose will be fitted to keep time with the Poetry both covering precisely the same Chronology.
—G. G.

(⁵) TO MR. RICHARD BROWN, GREENOCK.

(WALKER'S ED., 1811.)

GLASGOW, 26 *March* 1788.

I AM monstrously to blame, my dear Sir, in not writing to you and sending you the Directory. I have been getting my Tack extended, as I have taken a farm, and I have been racking shop accounts with Mr. Creech ; both of which, together with watching, fatigue, and a load of care almost too heavy for my shoulders, have in some degree actually fevered me. I really forgot the Directory yesterday, which vexed me ; but I was convulsed with rage a great part of the day. I have to thank you for the ingenious, friendly, and elegant epistle from your friend, Mr. Crawford.* I shall certainly write to him, but not now. This is merely a card to you, as I am posting to Dumfriesshire, where many perplexing arrangements

---

* Thomas Crawford, Esq., of Cartsburn, a friend of Brown, had written a kind letter to the poet inviting him to spend a day or two with him.

163

await me. I am vexed about the Directory ; but my dear Sir, forgive me ; these eight days I have been positively crazed. My Compliments to Mrs. B. I shall write to you at Grenada. I am ever, my dearest friend, yours, .   ROB^T. BURNS.

(²) TO MR. ROBT. CLEGHORN, SAUGHTON MILLS, EDINBURGH.

(CURRIE, 1800.)

MAUCHLINE. 31 *March* 1788.

YESTERDAY, my dear Sir, as I was riding thro' a track of melancholy, joyless muirs, between Galloway and Ayrshire ; it being Sunday, I turned my thoughts to psalms and hymns, and spiritual songs ; and your favorite air, *Capt. O' Kean*, coming at length in my head, I tried these words to it. You will see that the first part of the tune must be repeated :—

> The small birds rejoice in the green leaves returning,
>   The murmuring streamlet winds clear thro' the vale ;
> The hawthorn-trees blow in the dew of the morning,
>   And wild scatter'd cowslips bedeck the green dale :
> But what can give pleasure, or what can seem fair,
> While the lingering moments are numbered by Care ?
>   No flow'rs gaily springing, nor birds sweetly singing,
> Can soothe the sad bosom of joyless Despair.

I am tolerably pleased with these verses, but as I have only a sketch of the tune, I leave it with you to try if they suit the measure of the music.

I am so harassed with care and anxiety, about this farming project of mine, that my Muse has degenerated into the veriest prose-wench that ever picked cinders or followed a tinker. When I am fairly got into the routine of business, I shall trouble you with a longer epistle ; perhaps with some queries respecting farming : at present, the world sits such a load on my mind, that it has effaced almost every trace of the [minstrel] in me.

My very best compliments and best wishes to Mrs. Cleghorn.   R. B.

The honest, social farmer of Saughton Mills, replied to the above, expressing satisfaction with these lines as "fitting the tune to a hair," and recommending the poet to add another stanza (which was ultimately done) ; suggesting at the same time that a Jacobite turn be given to the song, which might be placed in the lips of the unfortunate Prince Charles, after the fatal issue of Culloden. He concludes his letter thus sensibly :—

"Any skill I have in country business you may truly command. Situation, soil, customs of countries, may vary from each other, but Farmer-Attention is a good farmer in every place. I beg to hear from you soon. Mrs. Cleghorn joins me in best compliments.

I am, in the most comprehensive sense of the word, your very sincere friend,   ROBERT CLEGHORN."

Mr. James Findlay, Excise Officer in Tarbolton, received formal instructions dated from the Excise Office, Edinburgh, 31 March 1788, to "instruct the bearer Mr. Robert Burns in the art of gauging, and fit him for surveying victuallers, rectifiers, chandlers, tanners, tawers, malsters, &c." The period for instruction in these arts, and in the mode of keeping Excise books, was to extend over six weeks, after which Findlay and his Supervisor were to report on Mr. Burns's qualifications, &c. Mr. Findlay, through this connexion, was introduced to the "divine Miss Markland," one of the "six proper belles of Mauchline," and in the following September they were made man and wife. The latter survived till August 1851, when she was 86 years old.

Burns's object was to have these Excise arrangements accomplished before Whitsunday 1788, when he was to enter into his Dumfriesshire farm. His brother Gilbert had been struggling with the ungrateful soil of Mossgiel, and in renewing his lease of Mossgiel, Mr. Gavin Hamilton seems to have proposed that Burns should put his name to the deed as security for his brother's rent, which involvement, however, the not incautious poet thought proper to decline. He nevertheless, in addition to former advances, put into Gilbert's hands a farther supply of money to help him on the present occasion —the sum in all thus advanced extending to £180.

(5) TO MR. GAVIN HAMILTON.

(CHAMBERS, 1851.)

MOSSGIEL, *Friday Morning.*

THE language of refusal is to me the most difficult language on earth, and you are the man in the world, excepting one of Right Honble. designation, to whom it gives me the greatest pain to hold such language. My brother has already got money, and shall want nothing in my power to enable him to fulfil his engagement with you : but to be security on so large a scale, even for a brother, is what I dare not do, except I were in such circumstances of life as that the worst that might happen could not greatly injure me.

I never wrote a letter which gave me so much pain in my life, as I know the unhappy consequences : I shall incur the displeasure of a gentleman for whom I have the highest respect, and to whom I am deeply obliged. I am ever, Sir, your obliged and very humble servant　　　　ROBERT BURNS.

(2) TO MR. WILLIAM DUNBAR, W.S., EDINBURGH.

(HOGG AND MOTHERWELL, 1835.)

MAUCHLINE, *7th April* 1788.

I HAVE not delayed so long to write you, my much respected friend, because I thought no further of my promise. I have long since given up that kind of formal correspondence, where one sits down irksomely to write a letter, because we are in duty bound to do so.

I have been roving over the country, as the farm I have taken is forty miles from this place, hiring servants and preparing matters ; but most of all, I am earnestly busy to bring about a revolution in my own mind. As, till within these eighteen months, I never was the wealthy master of ten guineas, my knowledge of business is to learn ; add to this, my late scenes of idleness and dissipation have enervated my mind to an alarming degree. Skill in the sober science of life is my most serious and hourly study. I have dropt all conversation and all reading (prose reading) but what tends in some way or other to my serious aim. Except one worthy young fellow, I have not a single correspondent in Edinburgh. You have indeed kindly made me an offer of that kind. The world of wits, and *gens comme il faut* which I lately left, and with whom I never again will intimately mix—from that port, Sir, I expect your Gazette : what *les beaux esprits* are saying, what they are doing, and what they are singing. Any sober intelligence from my sequestered walks of life ; any droll original ; any passing remark, important forsooth, because it is mine ; any little poetic effort, however embryoth ; these, my dear Sir, are all you have to expect from me. When I talk of poetic efforts, I must have it always understood, that I appeal from your wit and taste to your friendship and good nature. The first would be my favorite tribunal, where I defied censure ; but the last, where I declined justice.

I have scarcely made a single distich since I saw you. When I meet with an old Scots air that has any facetious idea in its name, I have a peculiar pleasure in following out that idea for a verse or two.

I trust that this will find you in better health than I did the last time I called for you. A few lines from you, directed to me at Mauchline, were it but to let

me know how you are, will ease my mind a good
deal. Now, never shun the idea of writing me be-
cause, perhaps, you may be out of spirits. I could
give you a hundred good consequences attending a
dull letter; one, for example, and the remaining
ninety-nine some other time — it will always serve to
keep in countenance, my much respected Sir, your
obliged friend and humble servant,   R. B.

(¹⁰) TO MISS MARGARET CHALMERS.

(CROMEK, 1808.)

MAUCHLINE, 7*th April* 1788.

I AM indebted to you and Miss Nimmo for letting
me know Miss Kennedy. Strange! how apt we are
to indulge prejudice in our judgments of one another!
Even I, who pique myself on my skill in marking
characters; because I am too proud of my character
as a man, to be dazzled in my judgment *for* glaring
wealth; and too proud of my situation as a poor man
to be biassed *against* squalid poverty; I was unac-
quainted with Miss K.'s very uncommon worth.

I am going on a good deal progressive in *mon grand
bût,* the sober science of life. I have lately made some
sacrifices, for which, were I *viva voce* with you to
paint the situation and recount the circumstances, you
would applaud me.   R. B.

The "Sacrifices" alluded to in the last sentence, appear
to refer to a resolution which, about this period, must have
been working in the poet's mind, as to the future disposal
of himself among the various claimants of his affections.
He had, as we have seen, made offer to, and been declined
by, Miss Chalmers, on the plea of her pre-engagement to Mr.
Lewis Hay. The letters addressed by that lady to Burns,
have been withheld from the world; but the reader has seen
in the Clarinda correspondence that the poet had allowed the
latter lady a perusal of them. She had formerly told him,

"I am proud to be registered in the same bosom with Peggy Chalmers," and afterwards she remarked—"Miss Chalmers' letters are charming. Why did not such a woman secure your heart?" Professor Walker in his observations regarding the poet's matrimonial views, seems to take it for granted that when Burns discovered "the interest which he had the power of creating" in accomplished women of the higher ranks of Society, he must have aspired to find a wife among them. Lockhart observes that it is "extremely doubtful that Burns, if he ever had this view, could have found any high-born maiden willing to partake such fortunes as his were likely to be, and yet possessed of such qualifications for making him a happy man, as he *had*, ready for his acceptance, in his Jean. The proud heart of the poet could never have stooped to woo for gold; and birth and high-breeding could only have been introduced into a farm-house to embitter, in the upshot, the whole existence of its inmates. It is very easy to say, that had Burns married an accomplished woman, he *might* have found domestic evenings sufficient to satisfy all the cravings of his mind—abandoned tavern haunts and jollities for ever—and settled down into a pattern character: but it is at least as possible, that consequences of an exactly opposite nature might have ensued."

One of the poet's main difficulties in making up his mind to rescue Jean Armour from further obloquy, by openly acknowledging her as his wife, instead of keeping her as his private mistress, was the mad engagement he had made with Clarinda to wait for her until her husband might happen to die (an event which did not occur till sixteen years after his own death!). "I could show," thus he wrote to that lady after his marriage, "how my precipitate, headlong, unthinking conduct, leagued with a conjuncture of unlucky events to thrust me out of a possibility of keeping the path of rectitude—to curse me by an irreconcileable war between my duty and my nearest wishes—and to damn me with a choice only of different species of error and misconduct." This was really the case with the hapless bard at the time he was roused from the Clarinda spell, and forced to examine the cold realities of his position. Under the potency of that spell he had made the unfeeling remarks regarding poor Jean which are contained in his letter of 23 Feb. to Clarinda, and had acted towards her as explained in his letter to Ainslie of 3d March (page 392, Vol. II). Lockhart, with considerate candor, observes that "so far from Burns having

all along regarded Miss Armour as his wife, it is extremely
doubtful whether *she* had ever for one moment considered
him as actually her husband, until he declared the marriage
of 1788. Burns did no more than was demanded by justice
as well as honor ; but the act was one which no human
tribunal could have compelled him to perform." It is too
probable, that even when he made up his mind to this
marriage, the poet's respect for Jean had considerably abated :
"her mercenary fawning," he had recently remarked, and,
nearly a year before, he had spoken to James Smith of his
"disgust at the mean, servile compliance of the Armours."
His letter to Johnson in May, 1788, indicates that, as the
Marquis of Montrose in relation to *his* mistress had done,
Burns now "called a synod in his heart," and put Jean to
the test of a trial thus :—"Pride and seeming Justice were
murderous King's Advocates on the one side ; yet Humanity,
Generosity, and Forgiveness were such powerful—such irre-
sistible counsel on the other side, that a Jury of all new
Endearments and Attachments brought in a unanimous ver-
dict of 'Not guilty!'" A recollection of the poet's sister
is that when he returned from Edinburgh at the end of
March, he wore a breast-pin which enclosed a miniature of
Clarinda's face ; and after he declared his marriage with Jean,
he sent his brother William, with "bonie Jean" behind him
on a horse, to Glasgow, where an artist executed a similar
likeness of her, which was substituted for the other. The
pin thus altered had the following apt motto engraved on
it :—"To err is human ; to forgive divine." As a corollary
to this anecdote we must add that in December 1791 Burns
thus wrote to Mrs. M'Lehose. "I sent some of your hair—a
part of the parcel you gave me—to Mr. Bruce the jeweller
in Princes Street, with a measure, to get a ring done for me."
Thus Clarinda was dethroned from her place in his breast, and
worn as an ornament round his little finger !

(⁵) TO MR. JAMES SMITH,

AVON PRINTFIELD, LINLITHGOW.

(CURRIE, 1800.)

MAUCHLINE, *April* 28*th* 1788.

BEWARE of your Strasburgh, my good Sir ! Look
on this as the opening of a correspondence, like the
opening of a twenty-four gun battery !

There is no understanding a man properly, without knowing sometimes of his previous ideas (that is to say, if the man has any ideas ; for I know many who, in the animal-muster, pass for men, that are the scanty masters of only one idea on any given subject, and by far the greatest part of your acquaintances and mine can barely boast of ideas, 1·25—1·5—1·75, or some such fractional matter) ; so to let you a little into the secrets of my pericranium, there is, you must know, a certain clean-limbed, handsome, bewitching young hussy of your acquaintance, to whom I have lately and privately given a matrimonial title to my corpus.

> " Bode a robe and wear it,
> Bode a pock and bear it,"

says the wise old Scots adage ! I hate to presage ill-luck ; and as my girl has been *doubly* kinder to me than even the best of women usually are to their partners of our sex, in similar circumstances, I reckon on twelve times a brace of children against I celebrate my twelfth wedding day :

* * * * * *

"Light's heartsome," quo' the wife when she was stealing sheep. You see what a lamp I have hung up to lighten your paths, when you are idle enough to explore the combinations and relations of my ideas. 'Tis now as plain as a pike staff, why a twenty-four gun battery was a metaphor I could readily employ.

Now for business. I intend to present Mrs. Burns with a printed shawl, an article of which I daresay you have variety : 'tis my first present to her since I have irrevocably called her mine ; and I have a kind of whimsical wish to get the first said present from an old and valued friend of hers and mine—a trusty Trojan, whose friendship I count myself possessed of as a liferent lease.

Look on this letter as a "beginning of sorrows;" I will write you till your eyes ache reading nonsense.

Mrs. Burns ('tis only her private designation) begs her best compliments to you. R. B.

(¹⁰) TO MRS. DUNLOP, OF DUNLOP.

(CURRIE, 1800.)

MAUCHLINE, 28*th April* 1788.

MADAM,—Your powers of reprehension must be great indeed, as I assure you they made my heart ache with penitential pangs, even though I was really not guilty. As I commence farming at Whitsunday, you will easily guess I must be pretty busy; but that is not all. As I got the offer of the excise business without solicitation, and as it costs me only six weeks' attendance for instructions, to entitle me for a commission—which commission lies by me, and at any future period, on my simple petition, can be resumed—I thought five-and-thirty pounds a-year was no bad *dernier ressort* for a poor poet, if Fortune in her jade tricks should kick him down from the little eminence to which she has lately helped him up.

For this reason, I am at present attending these instructions to have them completed before Whitsunday. Still, Madam, I prepared with the sincerest pleasure to meet you at the Mount, and came to my brother's on Saturday night, to set out on Sunday; but for some nights preceding I had slept in an apartment, where the force of the winds and rains was only mitigated by being sifted through numberless apertures in the windows, walls, &c. In consequence, I was on Sunday, Monday, and part of Tuesday, unable to stir out of bed, with all the miserable effects of a violent cold.

You see, Madam, the truth of the French maxim, *Le vrai n'est pas toujours le vrai-semblable.* Your last was so full of expostulation, and was something so like the language of an offended friend, that I began to tremble for a correspondence, which I had with grateful pleasure set down as one of the greatest enjoyments of my future life. * * * *

Your books have delighted me : Virgil, Dryden, and Tasso, were all equally strangers to me ; but of this more at large in my next.   R. B.

(¹) TO PROF. DUGALD STEWART.

(CURRIE, 1800.)

SIR,—I inclose you one or two more of my bagatelles. If the fervent wishes of honest gratitude have any influence with that Great Unknown Being, who frames the chain of causes and' events ; prosperity and happiness will attend your visit to the continent, and return you safe to your native shore.

Wherever I am, allow me, Sir, to claim it as my privilege, to acquaint you with my progress in my trade of rhymes ; as I am sure I could say it with truth, that, next to my little fame, and the having it in my power to make life more comfortable to those whom nature has made dear to me, I shall ever regard your countenance, your patronage, your friendly good offices, as the most valued consequence of my late success in life.—I have the honor to be, most truly, Sir, your much indebted humble serv'.,

ROB™. BURNS.

MAUCHLINE, *May* 3, 1788.

(^{11}) TO MRS. DUNLOP, OF DUNLOP.
(CURRIE, 1800.)

MAUCHLINE, *4th May* 1788.

MADAM,—Dryden's Virgil has delighted me.   I do not know whether the critics will agree with me, but the Georgics are to me by far the best of Virgil.   It is indeed a species of writing entirely new to me ; and has filled my head with a thousand fancies of emulation : but, alas ! when I read the Georgics, and then survey my own powers, 'tis like the idea of a Shetland pony drawn up by the side of a thorough-bred hunter, to start for the plate.   I own I am disappointed in the Æneid.   Faultless correctness may please, and does highly please, the letter critic : but to that awful character I have not the most distant pretensions.   I do not know whether I do not hazard my pretensions 'to be a critic of any kind, when · I say that I think Virgil, in many instances, a servile copier of Homer.   If I had the Odyssey by me, I could parallel many passages where Virgil has evidently copied, but by no means improved, Homer. Nor can I think there is anything of this owing to the translators ; for, from every thing I have seen of Dryden, I think him in genius and fluency of language, Pope's master.   I have not perused Tasso enough to form an opinion : in some future letter, you shall have my ideas of him ; though I am conscious my criticisms must be very inaccurate and imperfect, as there I have ever felt and lamented my want of learning most.   R. B.

(¹) TO MR. SAMUEL BROWN, KIRKOSWALD.*

(Cunningham, 1834.)

Mossciel, *4th May* 1788.

Dear Uncle,—This, I hope, will find you and your conjugal yoke-fellow in your good old way. I am impatient to know if the Ailsa fowling be commenced for this season yet, as I want three or four stones of feathers, and I hope you will bespeak them for me. It would be a vain attempt for me to enumerate the various transactions I have been engaged in since I saw you last; but this know—I engaged in a *smuggling trade*, and God knows if ever any poor man experienced better returns—two for one: but as freight and delivery have turned out so dear, I am thinking of taking out a licence, and beginning in fair trade.

I have taken a farm on the borders of the Nith, and in imitation of the old patriarchs, get men-servants and maid-servants, and flocks and herds, and beget sons and daughters. Your obedient nephew

Robᵗ. Burns.

---

* Samuel Brown was a half-brother to the poet's mother, and resided at Ballochneil, about a mile west of Kirkoswald. It was with him Burns lodged during the summer of 1775, while attending Rodger's school to learn trigonometry, &c. The following fragment of song, having for its subject the same which forms the burden of the above letter, is attributed to Burns.

AUNTIE JEANIE'S BED.

My auntie Jean held to the shore
  As Ailsa boats came back,
Aud she has *coft* a feather bed,   bought
  For twenty and a plack;
The feathers gained her fifty merk
  Before a *towmond* sped: twelve-month
O sic a noble bargain
  Was Auntie Jeanie's bed!

(²) MR. JAMES JOHNSON, ENGRAVER, EDINBURGH.

(CHAMBERS, 1851.)*

MAUCHLINE. 25*th May* 1788.

MY DEAR SIR,—I am really uneasy about that money which Mr. Creech owes me per note in your hand, and I want it much at present as I am engaging in business pretty deeply both for myself and my brother. A hundred guineas can be but a trifling affair to him, and 'tis a matter of most serious importance to me.†
To-morrow I begin my operations as a farmer, and God speed the plough !

I am so enamored of a certain girl's prolific, twin-bearing merit, that I have given her a legal title to the best blood in my body, and so farewell rakery ! To be serious, I found I had a long and much-loved fellow-creature's happiness or misery in my hands ; and though Pride and seeming Justice were murderous King's Advocates on the one side, yet Humanity, Generosity, and Forgiveness, were such powerful, such irresistible council on the other side, that a jury of all Endearments and new attachments brought in a unanimous verdict *Not Guilty!*   And the Panel, be it known unto all whom it concerns, is installed and instated into all the rights, privileges, immunities, franchises, services, and paraphernalia that at present do, or at any time coming may, belong to the name, title and designation.   [MS. *torn away here.*]
Present my best Compliments to . . . .

---

* The holograph of this letter is now in the British Museum. The reader, on comparing this version with the copy in Chambers, will find that several passages and warm expressions had been omitted by that decorous editor.

† Creech's promissory note, quoted at page 279, Vol. II., had been placed by the poet in Mr. Johnson's hands to be presented for payment six months after its date, 23d Oct. 1787. Creech paid the amount on May 30th, 1788.

(⁶) TO MR. ROBERT AINSLIE.

(CROMEK, 1808.)

MAUCHLINE, *May 26th* 1788.

MY DEAR FRIEND,—I am two kind letters in your debt, but I have been from home, and horridly busy buying and preparing for my farming business : over and above the plague of my Excise instructions, which this week will finish.

As I flatter my wishes that I foresee many future years correspondence between us, 'tis foolish to talk of excusing dull epistles : a dull letter may be a very kind one. I have the pleasure to tell you that I have been extremely fortunate in all my buyings and bargainings hitherto ; Mrs. Burns not excepted ; which title I now avow to the world. I am truly pleased with this last affair ; it has indeed added to my anxieties for futurity, but it has given a stability to my mind and my resolutions, unknown before ; and the poor girl has the most sacred enthusiasm of attachment to me, and has not a wish but to gratify my every idea of her deportment.—I am interrupted, Farewell ! my dear Sir. ROBT. BURNS.

(¹²) TO MRS. DUNLOP, OF DUNLOP.

(CURRIE, 1800.)

MAUCHLINE, 27th *May* 1788.

MADAM,—I have been torturing my philosophy to no purpose, to account for that kind partiality of yours, which unlike . . . . . has followed me, in my return to the shade of life, with assiduous benevolence. Often did I regret, in the fleeting hours of my late will-o'-wisp appearance, that "here I had no continu-

III. L

ing city;" and, but for the consolation of a few solid
guineas, could almost lament the time that a mo-
mentary acquaintance with wealth and splendor put
me so much out of conceit with the sworn companions
of my road through life — insignificance and poverty.

.   .   .

There are few circumstances relating to the unequal
distribution of the good things of this life that give
me more vexation (I mean in what I see around me)
than the importance the opulent bestow on their tri-
fling family affairs, compared with the very same
things on the contracted scale of a cottage. Last after-
noon I had the honor to spend an hour or two at a
good woman's fire-side, where the planks that com-
posed the floor were decorated with a splendid carpet,
and the gay table sparkled with silver and china.
'Tis now about term-day, and there has been a revo-
lution among those creatures, who though in appear-
ance partakers, and equally noble partakers, of the
same nature with Madame, are from time to time—
their nerves, their sinews, their health, strength, wis-
dom, experience, genius, time, nay a good part of their
very thoughts—sold for months and years, . . . not
only to the necessities, the conveniences, but, the
caprices of the important few.* We talked of the
insignificant creatures ; nay, notwithstanding their gen-
eral stupidity and rascality, did some of the poor devils
the honor to commend them. But light be the turf
upon his breast who taught "Reverence thyself!"
We looked down on the unpolished wretches, their
impertinent wives and clouterly brats, as the lordly
bull does on the little dirty ant-hill, whose puny in-
habitants he crushes in the carelessness of his ramble,
or tosses in the air in the wantonness of his pride.

R. B.

---

* Servants in Scotland are hired from term to term—Whitsunday to Martin-
mas, or Martinmas to Whitsunday.

THE ELLISLAND PERIOD.

JUNE 1788 TO NOVEMBER 1791.

([13]) TO MRS. DUNLOP,

AT MR. DUNLOP'S, HADDINGTON.

ELLISLAND, *14th June* 1788.*

" Where'er I roam, whatever realms I see,
My heart, untravell'd, fondly turns to thee:
Still to my friend it turns with ceaseless pain,
And drags at each remove a lengthened chain."

Goldsmith.

THIS is the second day, my honored friend, that I have been on my farm. A solitary inmate of an old, smoky *spence;* far from every object I love, or by whom I am beloved; nor any acquaintance older than yesterday except *Jenny Geddes*, the old mare I ride on; while uncouth cares, and novel plans, hourly insult my awkward ignorance and bashful inexperience. There is a foggy atmosphere native to my soul in the hour of care, consequently the dreary objects seem larger than life. Extreme sensibility, irritated and prejudiced on the gloomy side by a series of misfortunes and disappointments, at that period of my existence when the soul is laying in her cargo of ideas for the voyage of life, is, I believe, the principal cause of this unhappy frame of mind.

" The valiant, in himself what can he suffer?
Or what need he regard his *single* woes?" &c.

Your surmise, Madam, is just; I am indeed a husband. . . . I found a once much-loved, and still much-loved female, literally and truly cast out to the mercy of the naked elements; but as I enabled her to *pur-*

---

* In the MS. "13th June" has been set down in mistake for 14th.

chase a shelter—and there is no sporting with a fellow-creature's happiness or misery. . . . The most placid good-nature and sweetness of disposition; a warm heart, gratefully devoted with all its powers to love me; vigorous health and sprightly cheerfulness, set off to the best advantage by a more than common handsome figure—these, I think, in a woman, may make a good wife, though she should never have read a page but the "Scriptures of the Old and New Testament," nor have danced in a brighter assembly than a penny pay wedding.*   R. B.

(⁷) TO MR. ROBERT AINSLIE, EDINBURGH.

(CROMEK, 1808.)

ELLISLAND, *June* 15*th* 1788.

THIS is now the third day, my dearest Sir, that I have sojourned in these regions; and during these three days you have occupied more of my thoughts than in three weeks preceding; in Ayrshire I have several variations of friendship's compass, here it points invariably to the pole. My farm gives me a good many uncouth cares and anxieties, but I hate the language of complaint. Job, or some one of his friends, says well—"Why should a living man complain?"

I have lately been much mortified with contemplating an unlucky imperfection in the very framing and construction of my soul; namely, a blundering inaccuracy of her olfactory organs in hitting the scent of craft or design in my fellow-creatures. I do not mean any compliment to my ingenuousness, or to hint that the defect is in consequence of the un-

---

* The above letter, which we take verbatim from Currie, has been sadly garbled in all editions of the poet's correspondence, from that of Cunningham downwards. Cromek had, in the *Reliques*, page 60, printed in a foot-note an interesting passage regarding Mrs. Burns, which Dr. Currie had omitted in his version of a letter from the poet to Mrs. Dunlop, dated July 10, 1788, and Cunningham incorporated the omitted passage with the present letter, of which it never formed a part.

suspicious simplicity of conscious truth and honor : I
take it to be, in some way or other, an imperfection
in the mental sight ; or, metaphor apart, some modi-
fication of dulness.   In two or three small instances
lately, I have been most shamefully out.

I have all along hitherto, in the warfare of life,
been bred' to arms among the light-horse—the piquet-
guards of fancy ; a kind of Hussars and Highlanders
of the *Brain :* but I am firmly resolved to *sell out* of
these giddy battalions, who have no ideas of a battle
but fighting the foe, or of a siege but storming the
town.   Cost what it will, I am determined to *buy in*
among the grave squadrons of heavy-armed Thought,
or the artillery corps of plodding Contrivance.

What books are you reading, or what is the subject
of your thoughts, besides the great studies of your
profession?   You said something about Religion in
your last.   I don't exactly remember what it was, as
the letter is in Ayrshire ; but I thought it not only
prettily said, but nobly thought.   You will make a
noble fellow, if once you were married.   I make no
reservation of your being *well*-married : you have so
much sense, and knowledge of human nature, that
though you may not realise perhaps the ideas of
romance, yet you will never be " ill-married." *

Were it not for the terrors of my ticklish situation
respecting provision for a family of children, I am
decidedly of opinion that the step I have taken is
vastly for my happiness.   As it is, I look to the
Excise scheme as a certainty of maintenance.   A
maintenance! luxury to what either Mrs. Burns or I
were born to.   Adieu !   R. B.

Burns arrived at Ellisland on 13th June, but his heart was

---

* MARRIAGE.—" Edinburgh, 22 Decem. 1798. Robert Ainslie, Esq., W.S., St.
Andrew's Church parish, and Miss Jean Cunningham, parish of Colinton,
daughter of the late Lieut.-Col. James Cunningham, of the Scots Brigade."—*Par-
ish Ch. Record.*

away in "the west," and ere ten days had elapsed he was
back to Ayrshire. While his farm-house was being erected,
he had to "shelter in a wretched hovel pervious to every
blast that blew, and every shower that fell ; and was only pre-
served from being chilled to death, by being suffocated with
smoke." Social communication of any kind he seldom could
enjoy ; for nothing flourished there in any degree of perfection
except stupidity and canting, and the people about him had
as much an idea of a rhinoceros as of a poet." No wonder
therefore, that "about half of his time was spent in Ayrshire
with his darling Jean." In his graphic epistle to Hugh Parker,
printed at p. 1, Vol. III., he appoints his correspondent to
meet him at Tarbolton on 24th June, and accordingly we find
him at Mauchline on the 23rd inditing a note to Ainslie thus :—

(⁸) TO MR. ROBERT AINSLIE, EDINBURGH.

(CUNNINGHAM, 1834.)

MAUCHLINE, 23rd *June* 1788.

THIS letter, my dear Sir, is only a business scrap.
Mr. Miers, profile painter in your town, has executed
a profile of Dr. Blacklock for me : do me the favor
to call for it, and sit to him yourself for me, which
put in the same size as the doctor's. The account of
both profiles will be fifteen shillings which I have
given to James Connel, our Mauchline Carrier, to pay
you when you give him the parcel. You must not,
my friend, refuse to sit. The time is short. When I
sat to Mr. Miers, I am sure he did not exceed two
minutes. I propose hanging Lord Glencairn, the doc-
tor, and you, in trio, over my new chimney-piece that
is to be. Adieu !   R. B.

His stay in Ayrshire on that occasion was very short ; for
we find him again at Ellisland before the 28th of June which
is the date appended to one of his manuscript copies of the
verses composed in Friar's Carse Hermitage. His next neigh-
bor up the Nith, on the west side of the river, was Robert
Riddell, Esq., of Glenriddell, a gentleman of literary and anti-

quarian tastes, and of a kindly social nature. His beautiful little estate with pleasant mansion, finely situated on a rocky promontory at a bend of the river, was named Friar's Carse. Amid some shrubbery near the end of his grounds adjacent to the poet's farm, Mr. Riddell had erected a romantic little grotto or hermitage, comfortably seated and furnished with a writing table ; and he was so polite as to give Burns a key which admitted him to the grounds, and occasionally this hermitage became his favorite place of retirement.*

(⁹) TO MR. ROBERT AINSLIE, EDINBURGH.

(CROMEK, 1808.)

ELLISLAND, *June 30th* 1788.

MY DEAR SIR,—I just now received your brief epistle ; and to take vengeance on your laziness, I have, you see, taken a long sheet of writing paper, and have begun at the top of the page, intending to scribble on to the very last corner.

I am vext at that affair of the . . . but dare not enlarge on the subject until you send me your direction, as I suppose that will be altered on your late master and friend's death.† I am concerned for the old fellow's exit only as I fear it may be to your disadvantage in any respect—for an old man's dying, except he have been a very benevolent character, or

---

* We have found some confusion in our attempts to trace Mr. Riddell's pedigree, and none of the poet's annotators has pointed out where the estate of "Glenriddell" is situated and who possessed it. In the obituaries of old Magazines we find the name of (1) Robert Riddell, Esq. of Glenriddell, who died in 1770. His widow, Mrs. Jean Ferguson, only daughter of Alex. Ferguson, of Craigdarroch, M.P., by his lady, Anne Laurie, daughter of Sir Robt. Laurie of Maxwelton, surviving him 22 years, dying in Dec. 1792, aged 81. She married Mr. Riddell in 1731. Then (2) we have "Died at Dumfries, 12th April 1788. Walter Riddell, Esq. of Glenriddell, in his 70th year."
The *Robert Riddell*, Esq. of Glenriddell and Friar's Carse, with whom Burns contracted such an intimacy, was, in all likelihood, a son of the latter; his wife's surname was Elizabeth. Mr. Riddell died 21st April 1794, and the title "laird of Glenriddell" devolved on his brother Mr. Walter Riddell, husband of Burns's correspondent, Maria Riddell of Woodley Park. Finally we notice the death of her son, thus recorded :—"June 4, 1804. Died at Hampton Court, of a deep decline, Alex. Riddell, Esq. of Glenriddell."
† Mr. Samuel Mitchelson, W.S., with whom Ainslie had served his apprenticeship, died 21st June 1788.

in some particular situation of life, that the welfare
of the poor or the helpless depended on him, I think
it an event of the most trifling moment to the world.
Man is naturally a kind benevolent animal, but he is
dropt into such a needy situation here in this vexa-
tious world, and has such a whoreson, hungry, growling,
multiplying pack of necessities, appetites, passions and
desires about him, ready to devour him for want of other
food ; that in fact he must lay aside his cares for
others that he may look properly to himself. You have
been imposed upon in paying Mr. Miers for the pro-
file of a Mr. H. I did not mention it in my letter to
you, nor did I ever give Mr. Miers any such order.
I have no objection to lose the money, but I will *not*
have any such profile in my possession.

I desired the carrier to pay you, but as I mentioned
only fifteen shillings to him, I will rather enclose you
a guinea note. I have it not indeed to spare here, as
I am only a sojourner in a strange land in this place ;
but in a day or two I return to Mauchline, and there
I have the bank-notes through the house like salt
permits.

There is a great degree of folly in talking unneces-
sarily of one's private affairs. I have just now been
interrupted by one of my new neighbors, who has made
himself absolutely contemptible in my eyes, by his
silly, garrulous pruriency. I know it has been a fault
of my own too ; but from this moment I abjure it as
I would the service of hell ! Your poets, spendthrifts,
and other fools of that kidney, pretend forsooth to
crack their jokes on prudence ; but 'tis a squalid vag-
abond glorying in his rags. Still, imprudence respect-
ing money matters is much more pardonable than
imprudence respecting character. I have no objection
to prefer prodigality to avarice, in some few instances ;
but I appeal to your observation, if you have not met,
and often met, with the same disingenuousness, the

same hollow-hearted insincerity, and disintegritive depravity of principle, in the hackneyed victims of profusion, as in the unfeeling children of parsimony. I have every possible reverence for the much-talked-of world beyond the grave, and I wish that which piety believes, and virtue deserves, may be all matter of fact. But in things belonging to, and terminating in 'this present scene of existence, man has serious and interesting business on hand. Whether a man shall shake hands with welcome in the distinguished elevation of respect, or shrink from contempt in the abject corner of insignificance ; whether he shall wanton under the tropic of plenty, at least enjoy himself in the comfortable latitudes of easy convenience, or starve in the arctic circle of dreary poverty ; whether he shall rise in the manly consciousness of a self-approving mind, or sink beneath a galling load of regret and remorse—these are alternatives of the last moment.

You see how I preach. You used occasionally to sermonize too ; I wish you would, in charity, favor me with a sheet full in your own way. I admire the close of a letter Lord Bolingbroke writes to Dean Swift : "Adieu, dear Swift ! with all thy faults I love thee entirely ; make an effort to love me with all mine !" Humble servant, and all that trumpery, is now such a prostituted business, that honest Friendship, in her sincere way, must have recourse to her primitive, simple—farewell !   R. B.

(14) TO MRS. DUNLOP OF DUNLOP.

(CURRIE, 1800, AND CROMEK, 1808.)

MAUCHLINE, 10th *July* 1788.

MY MUCH HONORED FRIEND,—Yours of the 24th June is before me. I found it, as well as another valued friend—my wife, waiting to welcome me to Ayrshire : I met both with the sincerest pleasure.

When I write you, madam, I do not sit down to answer every paragraph of yours, by echoing every sentiment, like the faithful Commons of Great Britain in parliament assembled, answering a speech from the best of kings! I express myself in the fulness of my heart, and may perhaps be guilty of neglecting some of your kind inquiries; but not from your very odd reason that I do not read your letters. All your epistles for several months have cost me nothing, except a swelling throb of gratitude, or a deep-felt sentiment of veneration.

Mrs. Burns, madam, is the identical woman.

* * * * *

When she first found herself "as women wish to be who love their lords;" as I loved her nearly to distraction, we took steps for a private marriage. Her parents got the hint; and not only forbade me her company and their house, but on my rumored West Indian voyage got a warrant to put me in jail, till I should find security in my about-to-be paternal relation. You know my lucky reverse of fortune. On my eclatant return to Mauchline, I was made welcome to visit my girl. The usual consequences began to betray her; and as I was at that time laid up a cripple in Edinburgh, she was turned, literally turned, out of doors, and I wrote to a friend to shelter her till my return, when our marriage was declared. Her happiness or misery were in my hands, and who could trifle with such a deposit?

To jealousy or infidelity I am an equal stranger. My preservative against the first, is the most thorough consciousness of her sentiments of honor, and her attachment to me : my antidote against the last, is my long and deep-rooted affection for her. I can easily *fancy* a more agreeable companion for my journey of life; but, upon my honor, I have never *seen* the individual instance. In household matters,

of aptness to learn, and activity to execute, she is
eminently mistress ; and during my absence in Niths-
dale, she is regularly and constantly apprentice to my
mother and sisters in their dairy and other rural
business. The Muses must not be offended when I
tell them, the concerns of my wife and family will,
in my mind, always take the *pas ;* but I assure them
their ladyships will ever come next in place.   You
are right, that a bachelor state would have insured
me more friends ; but, from a cause you will easily
guess, conscious peace in the enjoyment of my own
mind, and unmistrusting confidence in approaching
my God, would seldom have been of the number.

Circumstanced as I am, I could never have got a
female partner for life who could have entered into
my favorite studies, relished my favorite authors, &c.,
without probably entailing on me, at the same time,
expensive living, fantastic caprice, perhaps apish af-
fection, with all the blessed, boarding school ac-
quirements, which (*pardonnez moi, Madame*) are
sometimes to be found among females of the upper
ranks, but almost universally pervade the misses of
the would-be-gentry.

I like your way in your church-yard lucubrations.
Thoughts that the spontaneous result of accidental
situations, either respecting health, place, or com-
pany, have often a strength, and always an origin-
ality, that would in vain be looked for in fancied
circumstances and studied paragraphs.   For me, I
have often thought of keeping a letter, *in progression*,
by me, to send you when the sheet was written out.
Now I talk of sheets, I must tell you my reason for
writing to you on paper of this kind, is my
pruriency of writing to you at large.   A page of
post is on such a dis-social, narrow-minded scale,
that I cannot abide it ; and double letters, at least in
my miscellaneous reverie manner, are a monstrous
tax in a close correspondence.   R. B.

The reader has already seen two notes of Burns addressed to Mr. Peter Hill, who was the principal assistant of Mr. Creech the Bookseller. Mr. Hill had, in February 1788, opened a shop on his own account, in Parliament Square; and our poet having conceived a liking for him, a high degree of intimacy was soon formed between them. Chambers remarks that "having no similar affection for Creech, Burns resolved to send to Hill for any books he might henceforth have occasion for, including, above all, that prime essential of a Scotsman's house-furniture—a Family Bible."

(³) MR. PETER HILL, BOOKSELLER, EDINBURGH.

(CROMEK, IN PART, AND HERE COMPLETED.*)

MAUCHLINE, 18th July 1788.

YOU injured me, my dear Sir, in your construction of the cause of my silence. From Ellisland in Nithsdale to Mauchline in Kyle is forty and five miles. *There*, a house a-building, and farm enclosures and improvements to tend; *here*, a new—not so much indeed a *new* as a *young* wife: good God, Sir, could my dearest brother expect a regular correspondence from me! I who am busied with the sacred pen of Nature, in the mystic volume of Creation—can I dishonor my hand with a dirty goose-feather, on a parcel of mashed old rags? I who am "called as was Aaron," to offer in the *sanctum sanctorum*, not indeed the mysterious, bloody types of future MURDER, but the thrice hallowed quintessences of future EXISTENCE—can I—but I have apologised enough. I am certain that you, my liberal-minded and much respected friend, would have acquitted me, though I had obeyed to the very letter that famous statute among the irrevocable decrees of the Medes and Per-

---

* For the privilege of collating and completing this and other letters addressed to Mr. Peter Hill, from the original manuscripts, we are indebted to George Wilson, Esq., of Dalmarnock, a grandson of the poet's correspondent.

sians, "not to ask petition for forty days of either God or man, save thee, O Queen, only!"

I am highly obliged to you, my dearest Sir, for your kind, your elegant compliments on my becoming one of that most respectable, that most truly venerable corps, they who are, without a metaphor, the fathers of posterity, the benefactors of all coming generations; the editors of Spiritual Nature, and the authors of Immortal Being. Now that I am "one of you," I shall humbly but fervently endeavor to be a conspicuous member. Now it is "called to-day" with my powers and me, and the time fast approacheth when, beholding the debilitated victim of all-subduing Time, they shall exclaim, "How are the mighty fallen, and the weapons of war perished!"

Your book came safe, and I am going to trouble you with further commissions. I call it troubling you—because I want only BOOKS; the cheapest way, the best; so you may have to hunt for them in the evening auctions. I want Smollett's works, for the sake of his incomparable humor. I have already Roderick Random, and Humphrey Clinker.—Peregrine Pickle, Launcelot Greaves, and Ferdinand Count Fathom, I still want; but as I said, the veriest ordinary copies will serve me. I am nice only in the appearance of my poets. I forget the price of Cowper's Poems, but I believe I must have them. I saw the other day, proposals for a publication, entitled, "Banks's new and complete Christian's Family Bible," printed for C. Cooke, Paternoster-row, London.—He promises at least to give in the work, I think it is three hundred and odd engravings, to which he has put the names of the first artists in London. You will know the character of the performance, as some numbers of it are published; and if it is really what it pretends to be, set me down as a subscriber, and send me the published numbers.

Let me hear from you your first leisure minute, and trust me, you shall in future have no reason to complain of my silence. The dazzling perplexity of novelty will dissipate, and leave me to pursue my course in the quiet path of methodical routine.

I might go on to fill up the page, but I dare say you are already sufficiently tired of, my dear Sir, yours sincerely   ROBᵀ. BURNS.

(¹) TO MR. GEORGE LOCKHART, MERCHANT,
AT MISS GRAY'S, GLASGOW.
(CROMEK, 1808.)

MY Dᴿ. SIR,—I am just going for Nithsdale, else I would certainly have transcribed some of my rhyming things for you.   The Miss Bailies I have seen in Edinʳ.   " Fair and lovely are Thy works, Lord God Almighty! who would not praise Thee for these Thy gifts in Thy goodness to the sons of men!!!" It needed not your fine taste to admire them.   I declare, one day I had the honor of dining at Mr. Bailies, I was almost in the predicament of the Children of Israel, when they could not look on Moses' face for the glory that shone in it when he descended from Mount Horeb.

I did once write a poetic Address from the falls of Bruar to his Grace of Athole, when I was in the Highlands.   When you return to Scotland let me know, and I will send such of my pieces as please myself best.

I return to Mauchline in about ten days.   My compᵗˢ. to Mr. Purden.—I am in truth, but at present in haste, yours sincerely,   ROBᵀ. BURNS.

MAUCHLINE, *July 18th*, 1788.

(¹) TO MR. ALEXANDER CUNNINGHAM, WRITER,

ST. JAMES' SQUARE, EDINBURGH.

(DOUGLAS, 1877.)

ELLISLAND, NITHSDALE, *July 27th* 1788.

MY GODLIKE FRIEND,—

> Nay, do not stare,
> You think the phrase is odd-like;
> But "God is Love," the saints declare,—
> Then, surely thou art god-like.
> &c., &c., see page 9, *supra.*

MY spur-galled, spavened Pegasus makes so hobbling a progress over the course of Extempore, that I must here alight and try the foot-path of plain prose. I have not met with anything this long while, my dear Sir, that has given my inward man such a fillip as your kind epistle.

For my own Biographical story, I can only say with the venerable Hebrew Patriarch—"Here am I with the children God has given me!" I have been a farmer since Whitsunday, and am just now building a house—not a Palace to attract the train-attended steps of pride-swollen Greatness, but a plain, simple domicile for Humility and Contentment. I am too a married man. This was a step of which I had no idea when you and I were together. On my return to Ayrshire, I found a much-loved female's positive happiness, or absolute misery among my hands, and I could not trifle with such a sacred deposit. I am, since, doubly pleased with my conduct. I have the consciousness of acting up to that generosity of principle which I would be thought to possess, and I am really more and more pleased with my choice. When I tell you that Mrs. Burns was once "my Jean," you will know the rest. Of four children she bore me in seventeen months, my eldest boy is only living. By the bye, I intend breeding him up for the Church ; and from an innate dexterity in secret mischief which he possesses, and a certain hypocritical gravity as he looks on the consequences, I have no small hopes of him in the sacerdotal line.

Mrs. Burns does not come from Ayrshire till my said new house be ready, so I am eight or ten days at Mauchline and this place alternately. Hitherto my direction was only "at Mauchline," but "at Ellisland near Dumfries," will now likewise find me ; though I prefer the former. I need not tell you that I shall expect to hear from you soon, Adieu !

ROB^T. BURNS.

Lowe's poem I shall transcribe in my first leisure hour.   R. B.

(¹⁵) TO MRS. DUNLOP OF DUNLOP.

(CURRIE, 1800.)

MAUCHLINE, 2d August 1788.

HONORED MADAM,—Your kind letter welcomed me, yesternight, to Ayrshire. I am indeed seriously angry with you at the *quantum* of your *luckpenny;* but vexed and hurt as I was, I could not help laughing very heartily at the noble lord's apology for the missed napkin.

I would write you from Nithsdale, and give you my direction there, but I have scarce an opportunity of calling at a post office once in a fortnight. I am six miles from Dumfries, am scarcely ever in it myself, and, as yet, have little acquaintance in the neighborhood. Besides, I am now very busy on my farm, building a dwelling-house ; as at present I am almost an evangelical man in Nithsdale, for I have scarce "where to lay my head."

There are some passages in your last that brought
tears in my eyes. "The heart knoweth its own sor-
rows, and a stranger intermeddleth not therewith."
The repository of these "sorrows of the heart," is a
kind of *sanctum sanctorum;* and 'tis only a chosen
friend, and that too at particular, sacred times, who
dares enter into them.

> 'Heav'n oft tears the bosom-chords
> 'That nature finest strung.'

You will excuse the quotation for the sake of the au-
thor. Instead of entering on this subject farther, I
shall transcribe you a few lines I wrote in a hermitage,
belonging to a gentleman in my Nithsdale neighbor-
hood. They are almost the only favors the Muses
have conferred on me in that country.

> Thou whom chance may hither lead,
> Be thou clad in russet weed,
> Be thou decked in silken stole,
> Grave these maxims on thy soul, &c.
>   See page 7, *supra.*

Since I am in the way of transcribing, the follow-
ing were the production of yesterday as I jogged
through the wild hills of New Cumnock. I intend
inserting them, or something like them, in an Epistle
I am going to write to the gentleman on whose friend-
ship my Excise hopes depend, Mr. Graham of Fintry;
one of the worthiest and most accomplished gentlemen,
not only of this country, but I will dare to say it,
of this age. The following are just the first crude
thoughts "unhousel'd, unanointed, unaneal'd."

> Pity the tuneful Muses' helpless train,
> Weak, timid landsmen on Life's stormy main!
> The world were blest, did bliss on them depend;
> Ah, that "the friendly e'er should want a friend!"
> The little Fate bestows they share as soon;
> Unlike sage proverb'd Wisdom's hard-wrung boon.

III.   M

> Let Prudence number o'er each sturdy son
> Who life and wisdom at one race begun ;
> Who feel by reason, and who give by rule ;
> (Instinct's a brute, and Sentiment a fool !)
> Who make poor " will do " wait upon " I should " ;
> We own they're prudent ; but who feels they're good !
> Ye wise ones, hence ! ye hurt the social eye ;
> God's image rudely etch'd on base alloy !
> But come, ye . . . . . .

Here the Muse left me. I am astonished at what you tell me of Anthony's writing me. I never received it. Poor fellow ! you vex me much by telling me that he is unfortunate. I shall be in Ayrshire ten days from this date. I have just room for an old Roman fare-well !   R. B.

The reader may have noted that about 7th April 1788—just a fortnight after parting with Clarinda—Burns began to show relenting symptoms of returning affection towards *his own Jean*. It required strong reasoning efforts on his part to bend his proud spirit into so condescending a mood ; and when at length he saw the necessity of adopting her as his wife, he nevertheless conceived he was making sacrifices for which the world would applaud him. Very gradually did he break the intelligence of this resolution to his friends. On 28th April he whispered the fact to James Smith, the old confidential negotiator betwixt Jean and him : he ordered a wedding shawl for her, and closed his letter in these words :— " Mrs. Burns ('tis only her private designation), begs her best compliments to you." On 4th May, so many stones of down-feathers are bespoke to provide the nuptial couch ; and finally, on 25th May, he intimated to an Edinburgh correspondent that he had lately given his Jean " a *legal title* to the best blood in his body." This last announcement gives countenance to a tradition which (curiously enough, while we are penning the present sentence), we find publicly advertised in this morning's *Scotsman* :—

" To be sold by public roup in Dowell's Rooms, George Street, on Wednesday 8th May 1878, at 2 p.m. Lot 1. Mauchline Castle, with dwelling house and grounds, extending to one acre, one rood, and seven poles, in occupation of Mrs. Hamilton. Property is held of the Crown, nominal feu-duty. The house was formerly the residence of Gavin Hamilton, the friend and patron of Robert Burns, who was married there. Upset price £1.000."

Gavin Hamilton was a Justice of the Peace, and a marriage certificate from him was law-binding enough; but it did not altogether suit the requirements of Jean and her relatives. The annal Communion season at Mauchline took place in those days on the second Sunday of August. and the Session-books evince that about the end of July and early days of the following month, a great "clearing of characters" formed the daily work of Mr. Auld and his staff of elders. Burns and his bride, among other tainted parties, humbled themselves before this conclave which he had so bitterly satirized in former days, and was, in the near future, about to do again. The following entry we copied from the veritable record in the Session-clerk's hands: be it observed, however, that Jean's signature is in the Bridegroom's handwriting; from which circumstance we infer that the Bride was either too nervous to hold a pen, or, at that period, she had not acquired so much of the art of penmanship as to enable her to sign her own name. She ultimately was taught to do so.

1788.

Aug. 5. Sess. con:—Compeared Robert Burns, with Jean Armour, his alleged Spouse. They both acknowledged their irregular marriage, and their sorrow for that irregularity, and desiring that the Session will take such steps as may seem to them proper, in order to the Solemn Confirmation of the said marriage.

The Session, taking this affair under their consideration, agree that they both be rebuked for this acknowledged irregularity, and that they be taken solemnly engaged to adhere faithfully to one another as husband and wife all the days of their life.

In regard the Session have a title in Law to some fine for behoof of the Poor, they agree to refer to Mr. Burns his own generosity.

The above Sentence was accordingly executed, and the Session absolved the said parties from any scandal on this acct.   ROBᵀ. BURNS.

WILLIAM AULD, *Modr.*   JEAN ARMOUR.

(Mr. Burns gave a guinea-note for behoof of the poor.)

On the very day of the above solemnity, which happened to be Mauchline Fair-Day, the bridegroom resolved that Jean should not want her fairing, so he dispatched the following letter to a Glasgow silk-mercer, containing an order for the materials to make a black silk dress for his bride.

(¹) TO MR. ROBERT M'INDOE,

MERCHANT, GLASGOW.

(DR. HATELY WADDELL'S ED., 1869.)*

MAUCHLINE, 5th Aug. 1788.

MY DEAR SIR,—I am vexed for nothing more, that I have not been at Glasgow, than not meeting with you. I have seldom found my friend Andrew M'Culloch wrong in his ideas of mankind; but respecting your worship he was as true as Holy Writ. This is the night of our Fair, and I, as you see, cannot keep well *in a line:* but if you will send me by the bearer, John Ronald, carrier between Glasgow and Mauchline, fifteen yards of black silk, the same kind as that of which I bought a gown and petticoat from you formerly—lutestring, I think is its name—I shall send you the money and a more coherent letter, when he goes again to your good town. To be brief, send me fifteen yds. black lutestring silk, such as they used to make gowns and petticoats of, and I shall choose, some sober morning before breakfast, and write you a sober answer, with the sober sum which will then be due from, dear Sir, fu' or fasting, yours sincerely,

ROB^T. BURNS.

---

* The original MS. is now possessed by John Reid, Esq., Kingston Place, Glasgow, a memorandum inscribed on the letter intimates that the price was 5s. 6d, or 5s. 9d. per yard.

(¹⁶) TO MRS. DUNLOP OF DUNLOP.

(CURRIE, 1800.)

ELLISLAND, 16*th August* 1788.

I AM in a fine disposition, my honored friend, to send you an elegiac epistle ; and want only genius to make it quite Shenstonian :

> "Why droops my heart with fancied woes forlorn?
> Why sinks my soul beneath each wintry sky?"

My increasing cares in this, as yet strange country —gloomy conjectures in the dark vista of futurity— consciousness of my own inability for the struggle of the world—my broadened mark to misfortune in a wife and children—I could indulge these reflections, till my humor should ferment into the most acid chagrin that would corrode the very thread of life.

To counterwork these baneful feelings, I have sat down to write to you ; as I declare upon my soul I always find *that* the most sovereign balm for my wounded spirit.

I was yesterday at Mr. Miller's to dinner for the first time. My reception was quite to my mind ; from the lady of the house quite flattering. She sometimes hits on a couplet or two, *impromptu.* She repeated one or two to the admiration of all present. My suffrage, as a professional man, was expected : I for once went agonizing over the belly of my conscience. Pardon me, ye my adored household gods, independence of spirit, and integrity of soul ! In the course of conversation, "Johnson's Musical Museum," a collection of Scottish songs with the music, was talked of. We got a song on the harpsichord, beginning,

> "Raving winds around her blowing."

The air was much admired : the lady of the house asked me whose were the words. " Mine, Madam—

they are indeed my very best verses;'' she took not the smallest notice of them! The old Scottish proverb says well, "king's caff is better than ither folks' corn.'' I was going to make a New Testament quotation about "casting pearls," but that would be too virulent, for the lady is actually a woman of sense and taste.

After all that has been said on the other side of the question, man is by no means a happy creature. I do not speak of the selected few, favored by partial heaven, whose souls are tuned to gladness amid riches and honors, and prudence and wisdom. I speak of the neglected many, whose nerves, whose sinews, whose days are sold to the minions of fortune.

If I thought you had never seen it, I would transcribe for you a stanza of an old Scottish ballad, called, "The Life and Age of Man;'' beginning thus :

> " 'Twas in the sixteen hunder year
>   Of God and fifty-three,
> Frae Christ was born, that bought us dear,
>   As writings testifie.''

I had an old grand-uncle, with whom my mother lived awhile in her girlish years : the good old man, for such he was, was long blind ere he died ; during which time his highest enjoyment was to sit down and cry, while my mother would sing the simple old song of "the Life and Age of Man.''

It is this way of thinking—it is these melancholy truths, that make religion so precious to the poor, miserable children of men. If it is a mere phantom, existing only in the heated imagination of enthusiasm,

> "What truth on earth so precious as the lie?''

My idle reasonings sometimes make me a little sceptical, but the necessities of my heart always give the cold philosophisings the lie. Who looks for the heart weaned from earth, the soul affianced to her God, the correspondence fixed with heaven, the pious supplication and devout thanksgiving, constant as the vicissitudes of even and morn—who thinks to meet with them in the court, the palace, in the glare of public life? No: to find them in their precious importance and divine efficacy, we must search among the obscure recesses of disappointment, affliction, poverty and distress.

I am sure, dear Madam, you are now *more* than pleased with the *length* of my letters. I return to Ayrshire, middle of next week; and it quickens my pace to think that there will be a letter from you waiting me there. I must be here again very soon for my harvest. R. B.

(¹⁰) TO MR. ROBᵀ. AINSLIE, WRITER,

CARE OF MR. AINSLIE, BOOKSELLER, NEW TOWN, EDINBURGH.

(DOUGLAS, 1877.)*

MAUCHLINE, 23*rd Aug.* 1788.

I RECᴰ. your last, my dear friend, but I write you just now on a vexatious business.

I don't know if ever I told you some very bad report that Mrs. M'————se once told me of Mr. Nicol. I had mentioned the affair to Mr. Cruickshank in the course of conversation about our common friend, that a lady had said so and so, which I suspected had originated from some malevolence of Dr. Adam's. He had mentioned this story to Mr. Nicol cursorily, and there it rested; till now, a prosecution has commenced between Dr. A. and Mr. N————, and Mr. N. has

---

* The original MS. of this letter was communicated to us by Mr. Robert Forrester, Bookseller, Glasgow, previous to its becoming the property of Mr. Archibald Munro, M.A., Clare Hall Academy, Newington, Edinburgh.

press'd me over and over to give up the lady's name.
I have refused this; and last post Mr. N. acquaints
me, but in very good natur'd terms, that if I persist
in my refusal, I am to be served with a summons to
compear and declare the fact.

Heaven knows how I should proceed! I have this
moment wrote Mrs. M'————se, telling her that I
have informed you of the affair; and I shall write
Mr. Nicol by Tuesday's post that I will not give up
my female friend till farther consideration; but that I
have acquainted you with the business and the name;
and that I have desired you to wait on him, which I
intreat, my dear Sir, you will do; and give up the
name or not, as your and Mrs. M'————se's prudence
shall suggest.

I am vexed to the heart that Mr. Ainslie has dis-
appointed my brother. I grasp at your kind offer,
and wish you to enquire for a place among the Sad-
dler's shops. If I get him into a first rate shop, I
will bind him a year or two, I almost do not care
on what terms. He is about eighteen; really very
clever; and in what work he has seen, not a despic-
able tradesman; but I will have him a first rate hand
if possible.

Why trouble yourself about Hamilton? let me pay
the expense, for I don't know where he is now to be
found.* Dr. Blacklock — where he lodged, which
caused me to meet with him—and Signior Dasti,
junr., one of his greatest cronies, are the only intelli-
gencers to whom I can refer you. Adieu! I am ever
most cordially yours   ROB^T. BURNS.

---

* See, on this subject, Letter to Ainslie, page 183, *supra*.

(²) TO MR. JOHN BEUGO, ENGRAVER, EDINBURGH.

(CROMEK, 1808.)

ELLISLAND, *Sep. 9th* 1788.

MY DEAR SIR,*—There is not in Edinburgh above the number of the Graces whose letters would have given me so much pleasure as yours of the 3d instant, which only reached me yesternight.

I am here on my farm, busy with my harvest; but for all that most pleasurable part of life called SOCIAL COMMUNICATION, I am here at the very elbow of existence. The only things that are to be found in this country, in any degree of perfection, are stupidity and canting. Prose, they only know in graces, prayers, &c. and the value of these they estimate as they do their plaiding webs — by the ell! As for the Muses, they have as much an idea of a rhinoceros as a poet. For my old capricious but good-natured hussy of a Muse—

> " By banks of Nith I sat and wept
> When Coila I thought on,
> In midst thereof I hung my harp
> The willow trees upon."

I am generally about half my time in Ayrshire with my "darling Jean," and then, I, at *lucid intervals*, throw my horny fist across my be-cob-webbed lyre, much in the same manner as an old wife throws her hand across the spokes of her spinning wheel.

I will send you "The Fortunate Shepherdess" as soon as I return to Ayrshire, for there I keep it by a

---

* Most readers will be aware that the gentleman here addressed was the engraver of a little head of Burns, which formed the frontispiece to his Edinburgh edition of 1787, after Nasmyth's painting. He was born in the same year with the poet, and was so intimate with him as to take private lessons in French along with him from Mr. Louis Cauvin. He died 13th December 1841, aged 82.

careful hand, as I would not for any thing it should be mislaid or lost. I do not wish to serve you from any benevolence, or other grave Christian virtue; 'tis purely a selfish gratification of my own feeling whenever I think of you.

You do not tell me if you are going to be married. Depend upon it, if you do not make some foolish choice, it will be a very great improvement upon the dish of life. I can speak from experience, though, God knows, my choice was as random as blind man's buff. . . .

If your better functions would give you leisure to write to me, I should be extremely happy; that is to say, if you neither keep nor look for a regular correspondence. I hate the idea of being obliged to write a letter. I sometimes write a friend twice a week; at other times once a quarter.

I am exceedingly pleased with your fancy in making the author you mention place a map of Iceland instead of his portrait before his works: 'twas a glorious idea. *

Could you conveniently do me one thing?—whenever you finish any head I should like to have a proof copy of it. I might tell you a long story about your fine genius; but as what everybody knows cannot have escaped you, I shall not say one syllable about it.

If you see Mr. Nasmyth, remember me to him most respectfully, as he both loves and deserves respect; though if he would pay less respect to the mere carcase of greatness, I should think him much nearer perfection. 　　　R. B.

---

* The idea which Burns refers to with so much relish, of having prefixed by way of frontispiece to a certain author's book, a map of Iceland, is a hit at Creech, and his frozen temperament. He was then about to publish his "Fugitive Pieces."

(²) TO ROBERT GRAHAM, ESQ. OF FINTRY,

ENCLOSING A POETICAL EPISTLE. (*See* p. 15, *supra*.)

(CHAMBERS, 1856.)

ELLISLAND, 10*th Sep.* 1788.

SIR,—The scrapes and premunires into which our indiscretions and follies, in the ordinary constitution of things, often bring us, are bad enough ; but it is peculiarly hard that a man's virtues should involve him in disquiet, and the very goodness of his heart cause the persecution of his peace. You, Sir, have patronized and befriended me—not by barren compliments, which merely fed my vanity, or little marks of notice, which perhaps only encumbered me more in the awkwardness of my native rusticity ; but by being my persevering friend in real life : and now, as if your continued benevolence had given me a prescriptive right, I am going again to trouble you with my importunities.

Your Honorable Board sometime ago gave me my Excise commission, which I regard as my sheet-anchor in life. My farm, now that I have tried it a little, though I think it will in time be a saving bargain, yet does by no means promise to be such a pennyworth as I was taught to expect. It is in the last stage of worn-out poverty, and it will take some time before it pays the rent. I might have had cash to supply the deficiencies of these hungry years ; but I have a younger brother and three sisters on a farm in Ayrshire, and it took all my surplus over what I thought necessary for my farming capital, to save not only the comfort, but the very existence of that fireside circle from impending destruction. This was done before I took the farm ; and rather than abstract my money from my brother—a circumstance which would ruin him—I will resign the farm, and enter immediately into the service of your Honors. But I am embarked now in the farm ; I have commenced married man ; and I am determined to stand by the lease till resistless necessity compels me to quit the ground.

There is one way by which I might be enabled to extricate myself from this embarrassment—a scheme which I hope and am certain is in your power to effectuate. I live here, Sir, in the very centre of a country Excise division ; the present officer lately lived on a farm which he rented, in my nearest neighborhood ; and as the gentleman, owing to some legacies, is quite opulent, a removal could do him no manner of injury ; and on a month's warning to give me a little time to look again over my instructions, I would not be afraid to enter on business. I do not know the name of his division, as I have not yet got acquainted with any of the Dumfries Excise people ; but his own name is Leonard Smith. It would suit me to enter on it beginning of next summer ; but I shall be in Edinburgh to wait upon you about the affair, sometime in the ensuing winter.

When I think how and on what I have written to you, Sir, I shudder at my own *hardiesse*. Forgive me, Sir, I have told you my situation. If asking anything less could possibly have done, I would not have asked so much.

If I were in the service, it would likewise favor my poetical schemes. I am thinking of something in the rural way of the drama kind. Originality of character is, I think, the most striking beauty in that species of composition, and my wanderings in the way of my business would be vastly favorable to my picking up original traits of human nature.

I again, Sir, earnestly beg your forgiveness for this letter. I have done violence to my own feelings in writing it.

　　　——" If I in aught have done amiss,
　　　Impute it not ! "——

My thoughts on this business, as usual with me when my mind is burdened, vented themselves in the enclosed verses, which I have taken the liberty to inscribe to you.

You, Sir, have the power to bless ; but the only claim I have to your friendly offices is my having already been the object of your goodness, which [indeed looks like] producing my debt instead of my discharge.

I am sure I go on Scripture grounds in this affair, for I "ask in faith, nothing doubting ; " and for the true Scripture reason too, because I have the fullest conviction that "my benefactor is good."

I have the honor to be, Sir, your deeply indebted humble servant,　　　　　　　　　　ROBT. BURNS.

(¹) TO MRS. ROBERT BURNS, MAUCHLINE.

(DR. HATELY WADDELL'S ED., 1869.) *

ELLISLAND, *Friday*, 12th Sep. 1788.

MY DEAR LOVE,—I received your kind letter with a pleasure which no letter but one from you could have given me. I dreamed of you the whole night last ; but alas ! I fear it will be three weeks yet, ere I can hope for the happiness of seeing you. My harvest is going on. I have some to cut down still, but I put in two stacks to-day, so I'm as tired as a dog.

---

* The MS. of this very interesting letter is possessed by Mr. Andrew Nicolson, shoemaker, Dumfries ; unfortunately it is considerably damaged throughout, and the latter portion is wanting. The reader will perceive the connexion between this letter and the one at page 147, *supra*, ordering the silk for Jean's dress. It is proper to explain here, that a young woman in rural districts, on *her first appearance* in a new dress in those days was subject to a "baiveridge" tax, if claimed by the young men who chanced to meet her. That is to say, she had to "give a kiss" on the occasion.

You might get one of Gilbert's sweet milk cheeses, and send it to . . . . On second thoughts, I believe you had best get the half of Gilbert's web of table linen, and make it up; tho' I think it damnable dear, but it is no outlaid money to us, you know. I have just now consulted my old landlady about table linen, and she thinks I may have the best for two shillings per yard; so after all, let it alone until I return; and some day next week I will be in Dumfries, and will ask the price there. I expect your new gowns will be very forward, or ready to make, against I be home to get the baiveridge. I have written my long-thought-on letter to Mr. Graham, the Commissioner of Excise; and have sent sheetful of Poetry besides. Now I talk of poetry, I had [a fine] strathspey among my hands to make verses to, for Johnson's Collection, which I [intend as my honeymoon song.]   *   *   *

(")MISS MARGARET CHALMERS, EDINBURGH.

(CROMEK, 1808.)

ELLISLAND, NEAR DUMFRIES, *Sept.* 16, 1788.

WHERE are you? and how are you? and is Lady Mackenzie recovering her health? for I have had but one solitary letter from you. I will not think you have forgot me, Madam; and for my part—

> " When thee, Jerusalem, I forget,
> Skill part from my right hand!"

"My heart is not of that rock, nor my soul careless as that sea." I do not make my progress among mankind as a bowl does among its fellows — rolling through the crowd without bearing away any mark or impression, except where they hit in hostile collision.

I am here, driven in with my harvest-folks by bad weather; and as you and your sister once did me the honor of interesting yourselves much à *l'égard de moi*, I sit down to beg the continuation of your goodness. —I can truly say that, all the exterior of life apart, I never saw two, whose esteem flattered the nobler feelings of my soul—I will not say, more, but, so much as Lady Mackenzie and Miss Chalmers. When I think of you—hearts the best, minds the noblest of human kind—unfortunate, even in the shades of life—when I think I have met with you, and have lived more of real life with you in eight days than I can do with almost anybody I meet with in eight years — when I think on the improbability of meeting you in this world again — I could sit down and cry like a child! —If ever you honored me with a place in your esteem, I trust I can now plead more desert. I am secure against that crushing grip of iron poverty, which, alas! is less or more fatal to the native worth and purity of, I fear, the noblest souls; and a late important step in my life has kindly taken me out of the way of those ungrateful iniquities, which, however overlooked in fashionable licence, or varnished in fashionable phrase, are indeed but lighter and deeper shades of VILLAINY.

Shortly after my last return to Ayrshire, I married "my Jean." This was not in consequence of the attachment of romance, perhaps; but I had a long and much loved fellow-creature's happiness or misery in my determination, and I durst not trifle with so important a deposit. Nor have I any cause to repent it. If I have not got polite tattle, modish manners, and fashionable dress, I am not sickened and disgusted with the multiform curse of boarding-school affectation; and I have got the handsomest figure, the sweetest temper, the soundest constitution, and the kindest heart in the county. Mrs. Burns believes, as firmly as her creed, that I am *le plus bel esprit, et le plus honnête homme* in the universe; although she scarcely ever in her life, except the Scriptures of the Old and New Testament, and the Psalms of David in metre, spent five minutes together on either prose or verse.—I must except also from this last, a certain late publication of Scots poems, which she has perused very devoutly; and all the ballads in the country, as she has (O the partial lover! you will cry) the finest "wood note wild" I ever heard.—I am the more particular in this lady's character, as I know she will henceforth have the honor of a share in your best wishes.* She is still at Mauchline, as I am building my house; for this hovel that I shelter in, while occasionally here, is pervious to every blast that blows, and every shower that falls; and I am only preserved from being chilled to death, by being suffocated with smoke. I do not find my farm that pennyworth I was taught to expect, but I believe, in time, it may be a saving bargain. You will be pleased to hear that I have laid aside *éclat*, and bind every day after my reapers.

To save me from that horrid situation of at any time going down, in a losing bargain of a farm, to misery, I have taken my Excise instructions, and have my commission in my pocket for any emergency of fortune. If I could set *all* before your view, whatever disrespect you, in common with the world, have for this business, I know you would approve of my idea. I will make no apology, dear Madam, for this

---

* This interesting letter is the last that has been preserved of the admired series of communications which the bard addressed to her. He afterwards refers to her as "Mrs. Lewis Hay." The following notices from the Scots Magazine are interesting in this connexion:—

MARRIAGE.—" Dec. 9, 1788. At Edinburgh, Lewis Hay, Esq., Banker in Edinburgh, to Miss Margaret Chalmers, youngest daughter of the late James Chalmers, Esq., of Fingland."

DEATH.—" Feb. 28, 1800. At Edinburgh, Mr. Lewis Hay, Banker." Mrs. Hay latterly resided many years at Pau, in Berne, where she died in the Spring of 1843.

egotistic detail : I know you and your sister will be interested in every circumstance of it. What signify the silly, idle gewgaws of wealth, or the ideal trumpery of greatness! When fellow-partakers of the same nature fear the same God, have the same benevolence of heart, the same nobleness of soul, the same detestation at every thing dishonest, and the same scorn at every thing unworthy—if they are not in the dependance of absolute beggary, in the name of common sense are they not EQUALS? And if the bias, the instinctive bias, of their souls run the same way, why may they not be FRIENDS?

When I may have an opportunity of sending you this, Heaven only knows. Shenstone says, "when one is confined idle within doors by bad weather, the best antidote against *ennui* is to read the letters of, or write to, one's friends ;" in that case then, if the weather continues thus, I may scrawl you half a quire.

I very lately—to wit, since harvest began—wrote a poem, not in imitation, but in the manner, of Pope's Moral Epistles. It is only a short essay, just to try the strength of my Muse's pinion in that way. I will send you a copy of it, when once I have heard from you. I have likewise been laying the foundation of some pretty large poetic works : how the superstructure will come on, I leave to that great maker and marrer of projects—TIME. Johnson's collection of Scots songs is going on in the third volume ; and, of consequence, finds me a consumpt for a great deal of idle metre. One of the most tolerable things I have done in that way is two stanzas that I made to an air, a musical gentleman * of my acquaintance composed for the anniversary of his wedding day, which happens on the seventh of November. Take it as follows :—

---

* Robert Riddell, Esq., of Glenriddell, who was no great musician, yet ventured to publish something in that line.

The day returns—my bosom burns,
The blissful day we twa did meet, &c.

See p. 18, *supra.*

I give over this letter for shame. If I should be seized with a scribbling fit, before this goes away, I shall make it another letter ; and then you may allow your patience a week's respite between the two. I have not room for more than the old, kind, hearty, FAREWELL.

To make some amends, *mes chères Mesdames*, for dragging you on to this second sheet ; and to relieve a little the tiresomeness of my unstudied and uncorrectable prose, I shall transcribe you some of my late poetic bagatelles ; though I have, these eight or ten months, done very little that way. One day, in a Hermitage on the Banks of the Nith, belonging to a gentleman in my neighborhood, who is so good as give me a key at pleasure, I wrote as follows ; supposing myself the sequestered venerable inhabitant of the lonely mansion.

Thou whom chance may hither lead, &c.—page 7, *supra.*

R. B.*

---

* As this may be the last opportunity we will have of referring to this amiable lady, we avail ourselves of the opportunity to quote from Professor Walker, who was personally acquainted with her : " At Harvieston, the poet's attention seems to have been chiefly engaged by Miss Chalmers, now Mrs. Hay, with whom he afterwards maintained a correspondence by which no reader can fail to be charmed. He might indeed have wandered far before he met with an acquaintance so well adapted to call forth all that was laudable in his character, and to check all that was reprehensible ; and by this means to draw him into the fairest light, both to others and himself. Burns required friends who at once could fascinate and restrain : and this he found in one who united the resolution of the stronger sex, without its rigor, to the tenderness of the weaker, without its errors ; and the graceful playfulness which became her age, to a discretion which is generally the gift of long experience. By a penetrating reader her character might indeed be conjectured from the letters which the poet addressed to her ; for in no others of the collection do we find the easy confidential strain, to which he was encouraged by the kindness of his correspondent, so happily tempered with a propriety imposed by the gentle control of her recollected virtues."

A relative of Mrs. Hay thus described her person to Robert Chambers :—" In early life, when her hazel eyes were large and bright, and her teeth white and regular, her face possessed a charm not always the result or the accompaniment of fine features. She was short, but her figure was faultless. Her conversation was cheerful and intelligent. She talked rarely of books, yet greatly liked reading. She spoke readily and well, but preferred listening to others."

(¹) TO MR. MORISON, WRIGHT, MAUCHLINE.
(CROMEK, 1808.)

ELLISLAND, *Sep.* 22, 1788.

MY DEAR SIR,—Necessity obliges me to go into my new house even before it be plastered. I will inhabit the one end until the other is finished. About three weeks more, I think will, at farthest, be my time beyond which I cannot stay in this present house. If ever you wished to deserve the blessing of him that was ready to perish ; if ever you were in a situation that a little kindness would have rescued you from many evils ; if ever you hope to find rest in future states of untried being ;—get these matters of mine ready.* My servant will be out in the beginning of next week for the clock. My compliments to Mrs. Morison.—I am, after all my tribulation, dear Sir, yours.　　　　　　　　　　　　　ROBᵀ. BURNS.

(³) TO ROBERT GRAHAM, ESQ., OF FINTRY.
(CHAMBERS, 1856.)

ELLISLAND, 23*rd Sept.* 1788.

SIR,—Though I am scarce able to hold up my head with this fashionable influenza, which is just now the rage hereabouts, yet with half a spark of life, I would thank you for your most generous favor of the 14th, which, owing to my infrequent calls at the post-office in the hurry of harvest, came only to hand yesternight. I assure you, my ever-honored Sir, I read it with eyes brimful of other drops than those of anguish. Oh, what means of happiness the Author of goodness has put into their hands to whom he has

---

* Cromek made reference to this passage as a fine specimen of "the bathos." The reader has already, at page 374, Vol II., seen a sample of the same style in the letter to Mr. Francis Howden. A farther instance of it will appear in a letter to Mr. Creech, dated 30th May 1795.

given the power to bless !—and what real happiness
has he given to those on whom he has likewise be-
stowed kind, generous, benevolent dispositions ! Did
you know, Sir, from how many fears and forebodings
the friendly assurance of your patronage and protec-
tion has freed me, it would be some reward for your
goodness.

I am cursed with a melancholy prescience, which
makes me the veriest coward in life. There is not
any exertion which I would not attempt, rather than
be in that horrid situation—to be ready to call on the
mountains to fall on me, and the hills to cover me
from the presence of a haughty landlord, or his still
more haughty underling, to whom I owed—what I
could not pay. My muse, too, the circumstance that
after my domestic comfort, is by far the dearest to
my soul, to have it in my power to cultivate her ac-
quaintance to advantage—in short, Sir, you have,
like the great Being whose image you so richly bear,
made a creature happy, who had no other claim to
your goodness than his necessity, and who can make
you no other return, than his grateful acknowledg-
ment.

My farm, I think I am certain, will in the long-
run be an object for me ; and as I rent it the first
three years something under [its value], I will be
able to weather by a twelvemonth, or perhaps more ;
though it would make me set fortune more at defi-
ance, if it can be in your power to grant my request,
as I mentioned, in the beginning of next summer. I
was thinking that, as I am only a little more than
five miles from Dumfries, I might perhaps officiate
there, if any of these officers could be removed with
more propriety than Mr. Smith ; but besides the
monstrous inconvenience of it to me, I could not
bear to injure a poor fellow by ousting him to make
way for myself; to a wealthy son of good-fortune like

Smith, the injury is imaginary where the propriety of your rules admits.

Had I been well, I intended to have troubled you further with a description of my soil and plan of farming; but business will call me to town about February next. I hope then to have the honor of assuring you *in propriâ personâ*, how much and how truly I am, Sir, your deeply indebted and ever-grateful, humble servant, ROBᵗ. BURNS.

(¹⁷) TO MRS. DUNLOP, OF DUNLOP,

MOREHAM MAINS, HADDINGTON.*

(CROMEK, 1808.)

MAUCHLINE, *27th Sep.* 1788.

I HAVE received twins, dear Madam, more than once ; but scarcely ever with more pleasure than when I received yours of the 12th instant. To make myself understood ; I had wrote to Mr. Graham, inclosing my Poem addressed to him, and the same post which favored me with yours, brought me an answer from him. It was dated the very day he had received mine ; and I am quite at a loss to say whether it was more polite or kind.

Your criticisms, my honored Benefactress, are truly the work of a *Friend*. They are not the blasting depredations of a canker-toothed, caterpillar critic ; nor are they the fair statement of cold impartiality, balancing with unfeeling exactitude, the *pro* and *con* of an author's merits ; they are the judicious observations of animated friendship, selecting the beauties of the piece. I have just arrived from Nithsdale, and will be here a fortnight. I was on horseback this morning (for between my wife and my farm is just

---

* The original MS. of this letter is in the Poet's Monument at Edinburgh.

46 miles) by three o'clock. As I jogged on in the
dark, I was taken with a poetic fit as follows:

Mrs. F—— of C——'s lamentation for the death of
her son; an uncommonly promising youth of 18 or
19 years of age.*

> Fate gave the word, the arrow sped,
> And pierc'd my darling's heart.—*See* p. 19, *supra*.

You will not send me your poetic rambles, but you
see I am no niggard of mine. I am sure your im-
promptus give me double pleasure; what falls from
your pen can be neither unintertaining in itself, nor
indifferent to me.

The *one* fault you found is just; but I cannot please
myself in an emendation.

What a life of solicitude is the life of a parent!
You interested me much in your young couple. I
suppose it is not any of the ladies I have seen.

I would not take my folio paper for this epistle,
and now I repent it. I am so jaded with my dirty
long journey that I was afraid to drawl into the
essence of dulness with anything larger than a quarto,
and so I must leave out another rhyme of this morn-
ing's manufacture.

I will pay the sapientipotent George most cheerfully,
to hear from you ere I leave Ayrshire.

I have the honor to be, D^r. Madam, your much
obliged, and most respectful, humble serv^t.

                                    ROB^r. BURNS.

(*) TO MR. PETER HILL, BOOKSELLER.

(CURRIE, 1800.)

MAUCHLINE, *1st October* 1788.

I HAVE been here in this country about three days,
and all that time my chief reading has been the

---

* James Fergusson, Esq., younger of Craigdarroch, died in November 1787.

"Address to Lochlomond" you were so obliging as to send to me.* Were I impanelled one of the author's jury, to determine his criminality respecting the sin of poesy, my verdict should be "Guilty! A poet of nature's making!" It is an excellent method for improvement, and what I believe every poet does, to place some favorite classic author in his own walks of study and composition before him as a model. Though your author had not mentioned the name, I could have, at half a glance, guessed his model to be Thomson. Will my brother-poet forgive me, if I venture to hint that his imitation of that immortal bard is in two or three places rather more servile than such a genius as his required, *e.g.* :—

> "To soothe the maddening passions all to peace."
> ADDRESS.

> "To soothe the throbbing passions into peace."
> THOMSON.

I think the "Address" is in simplicity, harmony, and elegance of versification, fully equal to the "Seasons." Like Thomson, too, he has looked into nature for himself; you meet with no copied description. One particular criticism I made at first reading; in no one instance has he said too much. He never flags in his progress, but, like a true poet of nature's making, kindles in his course. His beginning is simple and modest, as if distrustful of the strength of his pinion; only, I do not altogether like—

> ——————————————————"Truth,
> The soul of every song that's nobly great."

Fiction is the soul of many a song that is nobly great. Perhaps I am wrong; this may be but a prose criticism. Is not the phrase, in line 7, page 6, "Great

---

* By the Rev. Dr. Cririe, afterwards minister of Dalton in Dumfriesshire. He died in 1835.

lake," too much vulgarized by every-day language for
so sublime a poem?

> " Great mass of waters, theme for nobler song,"

is perhaps no emendation. His enumeration of a
comparison with other lakes is at once harmonious
and poetic. Every reader's ideas must sweep the

> " Winding margin of an hundred miles."

The perspective that follows, mountains blue—the im-
prisoned billows beating in vain—the wooded isles—
the digressions on the yew tree—"Ben-Lomond's lofty,
cloud-envelop'd head," &c., are beautiful. A thunder-
storm is a subject which has been often tried, yet our
poet in his grand picture has interjected a circum-
stance, so far as I know, entirely original :—

> ——————————————————"the gloom
> Deep-seam'd with frequent streaks of moving fire."

In his preface to the storm, "the glens how dark be-
tween," is noble Highland landscape! The "rain
ploughing the red mould," too, is beautifully fancied.
"Ben-Lomond's lofty, pathless top," is a good ex-
pression ; and the surrounding view from it is truly
great : the

> ——————"silver mist,
> Beneath the beaming sun,"

is well described ; and here he has contrived to en-
liven his poem with a little of that passion which
bids fair, I think, to usurp the modern Muses alto-
gether. I know not how far this episode is a beauty
upon the whole, but the swain's wish to carry "some
faint idea of the vision bright," to entertain her
"partial, listening ear," is a pretty thought. But in
my opinion the most beautiful passages in the whole
poem are the fowls crowding, in wintry frosts, to

Lochlomond's "hospitable flood;" their wheeling round, their lighting, mixing, diving, &c. ; and the glorious description of the sportsman. This last is equal to any thing in the "Seasons." The idea of "the floating tribes far distant seen, all glistering to the moon," provoking his eye as he is obliged to leave them, is a noble ray of poetic genius. "The howling winds," "the hideous roar" of the "white cascades," are all in the same style.

I forget that while I am thus holding forth with the heedless warmth of an enthusiast, I am perhaps tiring you with nonsense. I must, however, mention that the last verse of the sixteenth page is one of the most elegant compliments I have ever seen. I must likewise notice that beautiful paragraph beginning, "The gleaming lake," &c. I dare not go into the particular beauties of the last two paragraphs, but they are admirably fine, and truly Ossianic.

I must beg your pardon for this lengthened scrawl. I had no idea of it when I began — I should like to know who the author is ; but, whoever he be, please present him with my grateful thanks for the entertainment he has afforded me.

A friend of mine desired me to commission for him two books, "Letters on the Religion essential to Man," a book you sent me before ; and "The World Unmasked, or the Philosopher the Greatest Cheat." Send me them by the first opportunity. The Bible you sent me is truly elegant ; I only wish it had been in two volumes.   R. B.

On October 14th 1788, on Dalswinton Loch, within the grounds of the poet's landlord, Mr. Miller, took place the first trial of the first Steam Boat in the world. The inventor and patentee was Mr. William Symington. There is no word of Burns having been present on the occasion. The model vessel was 25 feet long, by 7 feet broad, and successfully steamed across the loch at the rate of five miles an hour.

Some sensation about this time being excited by the ap-
proach of the centenary day of the landing of King William
III. at Torbay, the General Assembly of the Scottish Kirk
was pleased to appoint Wednesday the 5th of November to
be observed as "a Day of solemn Thanksgiving for that
most glorious event, the Revolution." Burns, who did not
much sympathise in this matter, was not particularly pleased
with the sermon preached by Mr. Kirkpatrick, minister of his
parish—Dunscore, and forwarded to a London liberal paper,
the long letter on the subject which next falls in course.
His patron, the Earl of Glencairn, took a prominent part in a
secular movement which was set agoing in Edinburgh in
regard to that centenary, as the following notice from the
Scots Magazine will show:—

"At Edinburgh, 4th November, a meeting was held of the
'Independent Friends,' to celebrate the secular anniversary of
the glorious Revolution in 1688, the Earl of Glencairn in the
chair. A committee was appointed to raise subscriptions for
the erection of a Public Monument at Edinburgh, or neigh-
borhood, with suitable inscription. relating to the event. Com-
mittee—the Earls of Buchan, Glencairn, Dumfries, and Sel-
kirk. Hon. Harry Erskine, Lord Elibank, Lord Ankerville,
Sir H. Wellwood Moncreiff, Bart., Sir W. A. Cunningham,
Bart., G. Douglas, Esq., of Cavers, Robert Graham. Esq., of
Gartmore, Major-General Fletcher Campbell, Wm. Ferguson,
Esq., of Raith, Archibald Spiers, Esq., of Ellerslie."

(?) TO THE EDITOR OF "THE STAR."

(CURRIE, 1800.)

November 8th 1788.

SIR,—Notwithstanding the opprobrious epithets with
which some of our philosophers and gloomy sectarians
have branded our nature—the principle of universal
selfishness, the proneness to all evil, they have given
us ; still, the detestation in which inhumanity to the
distressed, and insolence to the fallen, are held by all
mankind, shows that they are not natives of the
human heart. Even the unhappy partner of our kind
who is undone—the bitter consequence of his follies

or his crimes—who but sympathizes with the miseries of this ruined profligate brother? We forget the injuries, and feel for the man.

I went, last Wednesday, to my parish church, most cordially to join in grateful acknowledgment to the AUTHOR OF ALL GOOD, for the consequent blessings of the glorious Revolution. To that auspicious event we owe no less than our liberties, civil and religious ; to it we are likewise indebted for the present Royal Family, the ruling features of whose administration have ever been mildness to the subject, and tenderness of his rights.

Bred and educated in revolution principles, the principles of reason and common sense, it could not be any silly political prejudice which made my heart revolt at the harsh abusive manner in which the reverend gentleman mentioned the House of Stuart, and which, I am afraid, was too much the language of the day. We may rejoice sufficiently in our deliverance from past evils, without cruelly raking up the ashes of those whose misfortune it was, perhaps as much as their crime, to be the authors of those evils ; and we may bless GOD for all his goodness to us as a nation, without at the same time cursing a few ruined, powerless exiles, who only harbored ideas, and made attempts, that most of us would have done, had we been in their situation.

The "bloody and tyrannical House of Stuart," may be said with propriety and justice, when compared with the present royal family, and the sentiments of our days ; but is there no allowance to be made for the manners of the times? Were the royal contemporaries of the Stuarts more attentive to their subjects' rights? Might not the epithets of "bloody and tyrannical" be, with at least equal justice, applied to the House of Tudor, of York, or any other of their predecessors?

The simple state of the case, Sir, seems to be this;
—At that period, the science of government, the
knowledge of the true relation between king and
subject, was like other sciences and other knowledge,
just in its infancy, emerging from dark ages of ignor-
ance and barbarity.

The Stuarts only contended for prerogatives which
they knew their predecessors enjoyed, and which they
saw their contemporaries enjoying ; but these pre-
rogatives were inimical to the happiness of a nation
and the rights of subjects.

In this contest between prince and people, the con-
sequence of that light of science which had lately
dawned over Europe, the monarch of France, for ex-
ample, was victorious over the struggling liberties of
his people ; with us, luckily, the monarch failed, and
his unwarrantable pretensions fell a sacrifice to our
rights and happiness.   Whether it was owing to the
wisdom of leading individuals, or to the justling of
parties, I cannot pretend to determine ; but, likewise
happily for us, the kingly power was shifted into
another branch of the family, who, as they owed the
throne solely to the call of a free people, could claim
nothing inconsistent with the covenanted terms which
placed them there.

The Stuarts have been condemned and laughed at
for the folly and impracticability of their attempts in
1715 and 1745.   That they failed, I bless GOD : but
cannot join in the ridicule against them.   Who does
not know that the abilities or defects of leaders and
commanders are often hidden until put to the touch-
stone of exigency ; and that there is a caprice of for-
tune, an omnipotence in particular accidents and
conjunctures of circumstances, which exalt us as he-
roes, or brand us as madmen, just as they are for or
against us ?

Man, Mr. Publisher, is a strange, weak, inconsistent

being : who would believe, Sir, that in this our Augustan age of liberality and refinement, while we seem so justly sensible and jealous of our rights and liberties, and animated with such indignation against the very memory of those who would have subverted them —that a certain people under our national protection should complain, not against our monarch and a few favorite advisers, but against our WHOLE LEGISLATIVE BODY, for similar oppression, and almost in the very same terms, as our forefathers did of the House of Stuart ! I will not, I cannot, enter into the merits of the cause ; but I dare say the American Congress, of 1776, will be allowed to have been as able and enlightened as the English Convention was in 1688 ; and that their posterity will celebrate the centenary of their deliverance from us, as duly and sincerely as we do ours from the oppressive measures of the wrong-headed House of Stuart.

To conclude, Sir ; let every man who has a tear for the many miseries incident to humanity, feel for a family, illustrious as any in Europe, and unfortunate beyond historic precedent ; and let every Briton (and particularly every Scotsman), who ever looked with reverential pity on the dotage of a parent, cast a veil over the fatal mistakes of the kings of his forefathers.

R. B.

(18) MRS. DUNLOP OF DUNLOP,

CARE OF WM. KERR, ESQ., POST OFFICE, EDINBURGH.

(CURRIE, 1800.)*

MAUCHLINE, 13th Nov. 1788.

MADAM,—I had the very great pleasure of dining at Dunlop yesterday. Men are said to flatter women

---

* We are indebted to the polite liberality of R. F. Sketchley, Esq., Assistant Keeper of South Kensington Museum, London, for supplying us with a verbatim copy of this important letter, so greatly curtailed in Currie's edition. It forms one of three letters of Burns which were bequeathed to that Museum by the late Mr. John Forster.

because they are weak ; if it is so, Poets must be weaker still ; for Misses Rachel and Keith, and Miss Georgina M'Kay, with their flattering attentions and artful compliments, absolutely turned my head. I own they did not lard me over as a Poet does his Patron, or still more his Patroness, nor did they sugar me up as a Cameronian Preacher does J—s—s C——st ; but they so intoxicated me with their sly insinuations and delicate inuendoes of Compliment that if it had not been for a lucky recollection how much additional weight and lustre your good opinion and friendship must give me in that circle, I had certainly looked on myself as a person of no small consequence. I dare not say one word how much I was charmed with the Major's friendly welcome, elegant manner, and acute remark, lest I should be thought to balance my orientalisms of applause over against the finest Quey * in Ayrshire, which he made me a present of to help and adorn my farm-stock. As it was on Hallow-day, I am determined, annually as that day returns, to decorate her horns with an Ode of gratitude to the family of Dunlop.

The Songs in the second Vol. of the Museum, marked D. are Dr. Blacklock's ; but, as I am sorry to say, they are far short of his other works. I, who only know the cyphers of them all, shall never let it be known. Those marked T. are the work of an obscure, tippling, but extraordinary body of the name of Tytler ; a mortal who, though he drudges about Edinburgh as a common Printer, with leaky shoes, a sky-lighted hat, and knee-buckles as unlike as George-by-the-grace-of God, and Solomon-the son-of-David ; yet that same unknown, drunken mortal is author and compiler of three-fourth's of Elliot's pompous *Encyclopedia Britannica*. Those marked Z. I have given to

---

* Heifer.

the world as old verses to their respective tunes ; but in fact, of a good many of them, little more than the Chorus is ancient ; tho' there is no reason for telling every body, this piece of intelligence.   Next letter I write you, I shall send one or two sets of verses I intend for Johnson's third Volume.

What you mention of the Thanksgiving day is inspiration from above.   Is it not remarkable, odiously remarkable, that tho' manners are more civilized, and the rights of mankind better understood, by an Augustan Century's improvement, yet in this very reign of heavenly Hanoverianism, and almost in this very year, an empire beyond the Atlantic has its REVOLUTION too, and for the very same maladministration and legislative misdemeanors in the illustrious and sapientipotent Family of H—— as was complained of in the "tyrannical and bloody house of Stuart."

So soon as I know of your arrival at Dunlop, I shall take the first conveniency to dedicate a day, or perhaps two, to you and Friendship, under the guarantee of the Major's hospitality.   There will soon be threescore and ten miles of permanent distance between us ; and now that your friendship and friendly correspondence is entwisted with the heartstrings of my enjoyment of life, I must indulge myself in a festive day of "The feast of reason and the flow of soul."   I have the honor to be, Madam, your grateful humble ser^t.,

ROB^T. BURNS.

(^{5}) TO MR. JAMES JOHNSON, ENGRAVER.

(CROMEK, 1808.)

MAUCHLINE, 15th Nov. 1788.

MY DEAR SIR,—I have sent you two more songs. If you have got any tunes, or anything to correct, please send them by return of the carrier.

I can easily see, my dear friend, that you will very
probably have four volumes.   Perhaps you may not
find your account lucratively in this business ; but
you are a patriot for the music of your country ; and
I am certain, posterity will look on themselves as
highly indebted to your public spirit.   Be not in a
hurry : let us go on correctly ; and your name shall
be immortal.

I am preparing a flaming preface for your third vol-
ume.   I see every day new musical publications ad-
vertised ; but what are they ? Gaudy, hunted butter-
flies of a day, and then vanish forever : but your
work will outlive the momentary neglect of idle
fashion, and defy the teeth of time.

Have you never a fair goddess that leads you a
wild-goose chase of amorous devotion?   Let me know
a few of her qualities, such as, whether she be rather
black or fair, plump or thin, short or tall, &c., and
choose your air, and I shall task my muse to cele-
brate her.*

(¹) TO DR. BLACKLOCK, EDINBURGH.

(CROMEK, 1808.)

MAUCHLINE, *November* 15*th* 1788.

REVEREND AND DEAR SIR,—As I hear nothing of
your motions, but that you are, or were, out of town,
I do not know where this may find you, or whether
it will find you at all.   I wrote you a long letter,
dated from the land of Matrimony, in June ; but
either it had not found you, or, what I dread more,
it found you or Mrs. Blacklock in too precarious a
state of health and spirits to take notice of an idle
packet.

* It is believed by some that the beautiful song—" Turn again, thou fair Eliza,"
was the outcome of this promise. Others say that the name, which was originally
Rabina, was a real person beloved by a friend of the poet, and that it was changed
to Eliza at Johnson's suggestion. The name of Johnson's wife was Charlotte
Grant. Vol. III. of Johnson's work appeared on 2nd Feb. 1790.

I have done many little things for Johnson since I had the pleasure of seeing you ; and I have finished one piece in the way of Pope's "Moral Epistles ;" but, from your silence, I have every thing to fear, so I have only sent you two melancholy things, and I tremble lest they should too well suit the tone of your present feelings.*

In a fortnight I move, bag and baggage, to Nithsdale ; till then, my direction is at this place ; after that period, it will be at Ellisland, near Dumfries. It would extremely oblige me were it but half a line, to let me know how you are, and where you are. Can I be indifferent to the fate of a man to whom I owe so much ? A man whom I not only esteem, but venerate.

My warmest good wishes and most respectful compliments to Mrs. Blacklock, and Miss Johnson, if she is with you.

I cannot conclude without telling you that I am more and more pleased with the step I took respecting "my Jean." Two things, from my happy experience, I set down as apophthegms in life—A wife's head is immaterial compared with her heart ; and—"Virtue's (for wisdom, what poet pretends to it ?) ways are ways of pleasantness, and all her paths are peace." Adieu !

R. B.

The *Edinburgh Advertiser* of 28th November 1788, contained the following paragraph regarding our poet :—"Burns, the 'Ayrshire Bard,' is now enjoying the sweets of retirement at his farm. Burns, in thus retiring has acted wisely. Stephen Duck. the 'Poetical Thresher,' by his ill-advised patrons, was made a Parson. The poor man, hurried out of his proper element, found himself quite unhappy ; became insane, and with his own hands, it is said, ended his life. Burns, with propriety, has resumed the *flail;* but we hope he has not thrown away the *quill.*"

---

* The two poetical pieces here enclosed were these :—
"Fate gave the word, the arrow sped," page 19: and "The lazy mist hangs from the brow of the hill."—page 22, *supra.*

(¹) TO JOHN M'MURDO, ESQ., DRUMLANRIG.
ENCLOSING A SONG.
(DOUGLAS, 1877.)

SANQUHAR, *26th Nov.*, 1788.

SIR,—I write you this and the enclosed, literally *en passant*, for I am just baiting on my way to Ayrshire. I have philosophy or pride enough to support me with unwounded indifference against the neglect of my more dull superiors, the merely rank and file of noblesse and gentry—nay, even to keep my vanity quite sober under the larding of their compliments ; but from those who are equally distinguished by their rank and character—those who bear the true elegant impressions of the Great Creator on the richest materials—their little notices and attentions are to me amongst the first of earthly enjoyments. The honor thou didst my fugitive pieces in requesting copies of them is so highly flattering to my feelings and poetic ambition, that I could not resist even this half opportunity of scrawling off for you the enclosed, as a small but honest testimony how truly and gratefully I have the honor to be, Sir,—Your deeply obliged humble servant, ROBᵀ. BURNS.

The original MS. of the above letter is in the possession of Mr. James Graham, Mount Vernon Cottage, Carluke, and is valuable as showing how early Burns attracted the attention of the gentry and land-owners in his neighborhood, and obtained a footing of intimacy with them. The song enclosed was, in all probability, the fine compliment to his wife, beginning—

"O were I on Parnassus hill."
See page 20, *supra.*

perhaps composed on this very journey.

At Sanquhar, the hill of Corsincon which he preferred to Parnassus, was right in front of him, and the infant Nith— henceforth to be his Heliconian font, sparkled through the intervening prospect. He was on his way to Mauchline to

bring home his Jean, and "move bag and baggage into Niths-
dale:" and only ten days before, he had written these words
to Blacklock:—I am more and more pleased with the step
I took regarding ' my Jean.' Two things from my happy
experience, I set down as apophthegms in life—A wife's head
is immaterial compared with her heart : and 'Virtue's ways
are ways of pleasantness and all her paths are peace.' "

The house which he had been erecting at Ellisland was
not yet completed, and the "smoky hovel," which for some
time had been used as a shelter, was now abandoned for
more comfortable quarters in a romantic spot called "the
Isle," down the Nith from Ellisland about one mile. To this
temporary domicile, from which his letters were dated for
nearly six months thereafter, he brought Mrs. Burns in the
first week of December, where already two servant lads and
a servant girl, with some cart-loads of furniture and other
plenishing, had already arrived from Ayrshire.

(¹⁹) TO MRS. DUNLOP OF DUNLOP.

(CURRIE, 1800.)

ELLISLAND, 17th Dec., 1788.

MY DEAR HONORED FRIEND,—Yours, dated Edin-
burgh, which I have just read, makes me very
unhappy. "Almost blind and wholly deaf," are
melancholy news of human nature : but when told of
a much-loved and honored friend, they carry misery
in the sound. Goodness on your part, and gratitude
on mine, began a tie which has gradually entwisted
itself among the dearest chords of my bosom, and I
tremble at the omens of your late and present ailing
habit and shattered health. You miscalculate matters
widely, when you forbid my waiting on you, lest it
should hurt my worldly concerns. My small scale of
farming is exceedingly more simple and easy, than
what you have lately seen at Moreham mains. But,
be that as it may, the heart of the man and the
fancy of the poet are the two grand considerations for
which I live : if miry ridges and dirty dunghills are

to engross the best part of the functions of my soul immortal, I had better been a rook or a magpie at once, and then I should not have been plagued with any ideas superior to breaking of clods and picking up grubs ; not to mention barn-door cocks or mallards, creatures with which I could almost exchange lives at any time. If you continue so deaf, I am afraid a visit will be no great pleasure to either of us ; but if I hear you are got so well again as to be able to relish conversation, look you to it, Madam, for I will make my threatening good. I am to be at the New-year-day fair of Ayr ; and, by all that is sacred in the world, friend, I *will* come and see you. . . . .

Your meeting, which you so well describe, with your old schoolfellow and friend, was truly interesting. Out upon the ways of the world !—They spoil these "social offspring of the heart." Two veterans of the "men of the world" would have met with little more heart-workings than two old hacks worn out on the road. Apropos, is not the Scotch phrase, "Auld lang syne," exceedingly expressive ? There is an old song and tune which has often thrilled through my soul. You know I am an enthusiast in old Scotch songs. I shall give you the verses on the other sheet, as I suppose Mr. Kerr* will save you this postage.

AULD LANGSYNE.

Should auld acquaintance be forgot,
　And never brought to mind?
Should auld acquaintance be forgot
　And days o' langsyne?
See page 24, *supra.*

Light be the turf on the breast of the Heaven-inspired poet who composed this glorious fragment !

---

* Mr. Kerr was postmaster in Edinburgh. This worthy man was ever ready to frank a letter for a friend : it has been said that such weighty articles as a pair of buckskin breeches have passed for a brother sportsman, in those primitive days, free through the post.

There is more of the fire of native genius in it than in half-a-dozen of modern English Bacchanalians! Now I am on my hobby-horse, I cannot help inserting two other old stanzas, which please me mightily :—

MY BONIE MARY.

Go fetch to me a pint o' wine,
And fill it in a silver tassie;
That I may drink, before I go,
A service to my bonie lassie.

See page 26, *supra*.

(³) TO MR. WM. CRUIKSHANK, EDINBURGH.

(CUNNINGHAM, 1834.)

ELLISLAND, [*December*], 1788.

I HAVE not room, my dear friend, to answer all the particulars of your last kind letter. I shall be in Edinburgh on some business very soon; and as I shall be two days, or perhaps three, in town, we shall discuss matters *vivâ voce*. My knee, I believe, will never be entirely well; and an unlucky fall this winter has made it still worse. I well remember the circumstance you allude to respecting Creech's opinion of Mr. Nicol; but, as the first gentleman owes me still about fifty pounds, I dare not meddle in the affair.

It gave me a very heavy heart to read such accounts of the consequences of your quarrel with that puritanic, rotten-hearted, hell-commissioned scoundrel, Adam. If, notwithstanding your unprecedented industry in public, and your irreproachable conduct in private life, he still has you so much in his power, what ruin may he not bring on some others I could name?

Many and happy returns of seasons to you, with your dearest and worthiest friend, and the lovely little pledge of your happy union. May the great Author of life, and of every enjoyment that can render life delightful, make her that comfortable blessing to you both, which you so ardently wish for, and which, allow me to say, you so well deserve !   Glance over the foregoing verses, and let me have your blots.*

R. B.

(¹) TO MR. JOHN TENNANT, AUCHENBEY.†

CARE OF MR. JOHN ROBB, INNKEEPER, AYR.

(CUNNINGHAM, 1834.)

December 22*nd* 1788.

MY DEAR SIR,—I yesterday tried my cask of whisky for the first time, and I assure you it does you great credit.   It will bear five waters, strong, or six, ordinary toddy.   The whisky of this country is a most rascally liquor ; and, by consequence, only drunk by the most rascally part of the inhabitants.   I am persuaded, if you once get a footing here, you might do a great deal of business, in the way of consumpt : and should you commence Distiller again, this is the native barley country.   1 am ignorant if, in your present way of dealing, you would think it worth while to extend your business so far as this country side.   I write you this on the account of an accident, which I must take the merit of having partly designed too.   A neighbor of mine, a John Currie, miller in Carse-mill —a man who is, in a word a good man, a "very"

---

* The verses here enclosed were the second version of the author's " Lines written in Friar's Carse Hermitage." The unseemly quarrel between Mr. Nicol and Rector Adam is again referred to in this letter. The coarse epithets here bestowed on the latter must be read with great modification by those who are familiar with our poet's manner of " backing his friends."

† The MS. of this letter is in the poet's Monument at Edinburgh. The person addressed was a son of " gude auld Glen," otherwise, John Tennant in Glenconner, an old friend of the poet's father. James Tennant, to whom the poetic epistle at page 55, *supra*, is addressed, was a half brother of " Auchenbey." The latter was a full brother of " Wabster Charlie," " Preacher Willie," " Singing Sannock," and of David Tennant, the " manly Tar." George Reid of Barquharrie was the kind friend who lent the pony for the poet's first journey to Edinburgh. Auchenbey is in the north border of Ochiltree parish, adjoining Mauchline parish.

good man, even for a £500 bargain,—he and his wife were in my house the time I broke open the cask. They keep a country public-house and sell a great deal of foreign spirits, but all along thought that whisky would have degraded their house. They were perfectly astonished at my whisky, both for its taste and strength ; and, by their desire, I write you to know if you could supply them with liquor of an equal quality, and at what price. Please write me by first post, and direct to me at Ellisland, near Dumfries. If you could take a jaunt this way yourself, I have a spare spoon, knife, and fork very much at your service. My comp⁵. to Mrs. Tennant, and all the good folks in Glenconner and Barquharrie.—I am, most truly, my dear Sir, yours,   ROB⁹. BURNS.

1789.

Burns, on his farm by Nithside. in a choice situation, comfortably housed at the *Isle*, his Jean by his side, with menservants, and maid servants around him to execute his orders, ought to have been a contented man. The previous six months were not devoid of enjoyment to him, but they were accompanied with perpetual motion and commotion—"eight days at Mauchline, and eight days at this place alternately." Now, at all events, his life was more uniformly calm and settled, and very pleasant is Dr. Currie's picture of the domestic felicity he experienced at this period. " He resumed at times the occupation of a laborer, and found neither his strength nor his skill impaired. Pleased with surveying the grounds he had to cultivate, and with the rearing of a building that should give shelter to his wife and children. and, as he fondly hoped. to his own grey hairs ; sentiments of independence buoyed up his mind, pictures of domestic content and peace rose on his imagination ; and a few days passed away, as he himself informs us. the most tranquil, if not the happiest, which he had ever experienced."

Alas ! that those halcyon days should have been so very few ! Already had he begun to suspect that his farm by no means promised to be such a pennyworth as he had been

led to expect. "I am cursed," he said, "with a melancholy
prescience which makes me the veriest coward in life. There
is not any exertion which I would not attempt, rather than
be in that horrid situation—to be ready to call on the moun-
tains to fall, and the hills to cover me from the presence of a
haughty landlord, or his still more haughty underling, to
whom I owed—what I could not pay." "To save me from
that horrid situation, I have taken my Excise instructions,
and have my commission in my pocket, ready for any emer-
gency of fortune." That Excise scheme was a pet one of
his own early formation, and seemed to have been "hived in
his bosom like the bag o' the bee." As Touchstone said
of his Audrey, so could Burns of his gaugership—"It is a
plain thing, but *mine own*." Very nobly he remarked :
"There is a certain stigma affixed to the character of an
Excise officer ; but I do not pretend to borrow honor from my
profession ; I would much rather have it said that my profes-
sion borrowed credit from me."

It is not surprising, that after his own and his father's
bitter experience of farming, he should from the first have
conceived misgivings about Ellisland. It might have been
better perhaps had he adhered to the promptings of his
own instinct, thus communicated to his Excise patrons :—
"I had intended to have closed my late appearance on the
stage of life in the character of a country farmer : but after
discharging some filial and fraternal claims, I find I could
only fight for existence in that miserable manner which I
have lived to see throw a venerable parent into the jaws of a
jail : when Death, the poor man's last and often best friend,
relieved him. . . . I think, by my guess, I shall have
rather better than two hundred pounds ; and instead of seek-
ing, what is almost impossible at present to find—a farm that
I can certainly live by, I shall lodge this sum in a banking
house, a sacred deposit, excepting only the calls of uncom-
mon distress or necessitous old age."

On New Year's morning, while Gilbert Burns at Mossgiel
was inditing a hearty salutation to his brother at Ellisland,
the latter was engaged in penning to his friend Mrs. Dunlop,
one of the finest letters ever written by man, and which
we now proceed to give. We collate the text with a copy
kindly furnished to us by the possessor of the author's holo-
graph—Mr. Robert Clarke. Cincinnati, Ohio, U.S ; and the
reader will perceive that Dr. Currie had suppressed some
sentences which are here restored.

(20) TO MRS. DUNLOP, OF DUNLOP.

(CURRIE, 1800.)

ELLISLAND, *Newyear-day Morning*, 1789.

THIS, dear Madam, is a morning of wishes; and would to God that I came under the Apostle James's description!—"The effectual, fervent prayer of a *righteous man* availeth much." In that case, Madam, you should "welcome in" a Year full of blessings: every thing that obstructs or disturbs tranquillity and self-enjoyment should be removed, and every Pleasure that frail Humanity can taste should be yours. I own myself so little a Presbyterian that I approve of set times and seasons of more than ordinary acts of Devotion, for breaking in on that habituated routine of life and thought, which is so apt to reduce our existence to a kind of Instinct, or even sometimes, and with some minds, to a state very little superior to mere Machinery.

This day; the first Sunday of May; a breezy, blue-skyed noon, some time about the beginning, and a hoary morning and calm sunny day about the end, of Autumn; these, time out of mind, have been with me a kind of holidays. Not like the Sacramental, Executioner-face of a Kilmarnock Communion; but to laugh or cry, be cheerful or pensive, moral or devout, according to the mood and tense of the Season and Myself. I believe I owe this to that glorious Paper in the Spectator, "The Vision of Mirza;" a Piece that struck my young fancy before I was capable of fixing an idea to a word of three syllables: "On the fifth day of the moon, which, according to the custom of my forefathers, I always *keep holy;* after having washed myself, and offered up my morning devotions, I ascended the high hill of Bagdat, in order to pass the rest of the day in meditation and prayer," &c.

We know nothing, or next to nothing, of the substance or structure of our Souls, so cannot account for those seeming caprices in them; that one should be particularly pleased with this thing, or struck with that, which, on Minds of a different cast, makes no extraordinary impression. I have some favorite flowers in Spring, among which are the mountain-daisy, the hare-bell, the foxglove, the wild brier-rose, the budding birk, and the hoary hawthorn, that I view and hang over with particular delight. I never hear the loud, solitary whistle of the curlew in a Summer noon, or the wild mixing cadence of a troop of grey-plover in an Autumnal morning, without feeling an elevation of soul like the enthusiasm of Devotion or Poetry. Tell me, my dear Friend, to what can this be owing? Are we a piece of machinery, that, like the Æolian harp, passive, takes the impression of the passing accident? Or do these workings argue something within us above the trodden clod? I own myself partial to these proofs of those awful and important realities—a God that made all things—man's immaterial and immortal nature—and a World of weal or woe beyond death and the grave—these proofs that we deduct by dint of our own powers of observation. However respectable Individuals in all ages have been, I have ever looked on Mankind in the lump to be nothing better than a foolish, head-strong, credulous, unthinking Mob; and their universal belief has ever had extremely little weight with me. Still I am a very sincere believer in the Bible; but I am drawn by the conviction of a Man, not by the halter of an Ass.

Apropos to an Ass, how do you like the following Apostrophe to Dulness, which I intend to interweave in "The Poet's Progress."

O Dulness, portion of the truly blest! &c.
(Extending to 20 lines.—*See* page 33, *supra*.)

I have sketched two or three verses to you, but as a private opportunity offers immediately, I must defer transcribing them. A servant of mine goes to Ayrshire with this, but I shall write you by post. If I am to be so happy as to have it in my power to see you when I go to Ayr Fair, which I very much doubt, I will try to dine at Dunlop in the Wednesday of that week.

If it is good weather in the Fair-week, I shall try my utmost; for if I hit my aim aright, it will not be in my power in any given time again : Farewell !

ROBᵀ. BURNS.

(¹) GILBERT BURNS TO ROBERT BURNS.

(CURRIE, 1800.)

MOSSGIEL, 1st Jan. 1789.

DEAR BROTHER,—I have just finished my New Year's day breakfast in the usual form, which naturally makes me call to mind the days of former years, and the society in which we used to begin them : and when I look at our family vicissitudes, "through the dark postern of time long elapsed," I cannot help remarking to you, my dear brother, how good the GOD OF SEASONS is to us ; and that, however some clouds may seem to lour over the portion of time before us, we have great reason to hope that all will turn out well.

Your mother and sisters, with Robert the second,* join me in the compliments of the season to you and Mrs. Burns, and beg you will remember us in the same manner to William, the first time you see him.—I am dear brother, yours

GILBERT BURNS.

---

* This proves that the child did not accompany Mrs. Burns to Dumfriesshire ; so that those biographers are inaccurate who refer to the poet's happiness during this first winter at Ellisland, as arising specially from his having "his wife and children for the first time under a roof of his own." Lockhart, in particular, was very incorrect, and gave some offence to Mrs. Burns in the following passage :—" He brought his wife home to Ellisland about the end of November ; and few housekeepers start with a larger provision of young mouths to feed than did the young couple. Mrs. Burns had lain in this autumn, for the second time, of twins, and I suppose 'sonsy, smirking, dear-bought Bess' accompanied her younger brothers and sisters from Mossgiel." Not until August 1789, when Francis Wallace was born, had Mrs. Burns more than one child to bring to Ellisland. Dr. Currie gave rise to Mr. Lockhart's misstatement by remarking in a footnote, that "Mrs. Burns was about to be confined in child-bed when the house at Ellisland was rebuilding."

(⁵) TO DR. MOORE, LONDON.
(CURRIE, 1800.)·

ELLISLAND, NEAR DUMFRIES,
4th Jan. 1789.

SIR,—As often as I think of writing to you, which
has been three or four times every week these six
months, it gives me something so like the idea of an
ordinary-sized statue offering at a conversation with
the Rhodian Colossus, that my mind misgives me, and
the affair always miscarries somewhere between pur-
pose and resolve.   I have, at last, got some business
with you, and business-letters are written by the
style-book.   I say my business is with you, Sir, for
you never had any with me, except the business that
benevolence has in the mansion of poverty.

The character and employment of a poet were for-
merly my pleasure, but are now my pride.   I know
that a very great deal of my late *éclat* was owing to
the singularity of my situation, and the honest preju-
dice of Scotsmen ; but still, as I said in the preface
of my first edition, I do look upon myself as having
some pretensions from nature to the poetic character.
I have not a doubt but the knack, the aptitude to
learn the muses' trade, is a gift bestowed by him
"who forms the secret bias of the soul ;" but I as
firmly believe, that *excellence* in the profession is the
fruit of industry, labor, attention, and pains.   At least
I am resolved to try my doctrine by the test of expe-
rience.   Another appearance from the press I put off
to a very distant day, a day that may never arrive—
but poesy I am determined to prosecute with all my
vigor.   Nature has given very few, if any, of the pro-
fession, the talents of shining in every species of com-
position.   I shall try (for until trial it is impossible to
know) whether she has qualified me to shine in any

one. The worst of it is, by the time one has finished
a piece, it has been so often viewed and reviewed
before the mental eye, that one loses, in a good mea-
sure, the powers of critical discrimination.   Here the
best criterion I know is a friend—not only of abilities
to judge, but with good nature enough, like a pru-
dent teacher with a young learner, to praise perhaps
a little more than is exactly just, lest the thin-skinned
animal fall into that most deplorable of all poetic dis-
eases — heart-breaking despondency of himself.   Dare
I, Sir, already immensely indebted to your goodness,
ask the additional obligation of your being that friend
to me ?   I enclose you an essay of mine, in a walk
of poesy to me entirely new ; I mean the epistle ad-
dressed to R. G. Esq., or Robert Graham, of Fintry,
Esq., a gentleman of uncommon worth, to whom I
lie under very great obligations.   The story of the
poem, like most of my poems, is connected with my
own story, and to give you the one, I must give you
something of the other.   I cannot boast of Mr. Creech's
ingenuous, fair dealing to me.   He kept me hanging
about Edinburgh, from 7th August 1787, until the
13th April, 1788, before he would condescend to give
me a statement of affairs ; nor had I got it even then,
but for an angry letter I wrote him, which irritated
his pride.   I could—not " a tale "—but a detail " un-
fold ; " but what am I that I should speak against
the Lord's anointed Bailie of Edinburgh ?

I believe I shall, in whole (£100 copy-right in-
cluded) clear about £400, some little odds ; and even
part of this depends upon what the gentleman has yet
to settle with me.   I give you this information, be-
cause you did me the honor to interest yourself much
in my welfare—I give you this information ; but I
give it to yourself only ; for I am still much in the
gentleman's mercy.   Perhaps I injure the man in the
idea I am sometimes tempted to have of him ; God

forbid I should! A little time will try, for in a
month I shall go to town to wind up the business,
if possible.

To give the rest of my story in brief : I have
married " my Jean," and taken a farm. With the
first step, I have every day more and more reason to
be satisfied ; with the last it is rather the reverse. I
have a younger brother who supports my aged
mother ; another still younger brother, and three
sisters in a farm. On my last return from Edin-
burgh, it cost me about £180 to save them from
ruin. Not that I have lost so much ; I only inter-
posed between my brother and his impending fate by
the loan of so much. I give myself no airs on this,
for it was mere selfishness on my part : I was con-
scious that the wrong scale of the balance was pretty
heavily charged, and I thought that throwing a little
filial piety and fraternal affection into the scale in my
favor might help to smooth matters at the "grand
reckoning." There is still one thing would make
my circumstances quite easy ; I have an Excise
officer's commission, and I live in the midst of a
country division. My request to Mr. Graham, who
is one of the Commissioners of Excise, was, if in his
power, to procure me that division. If I were very
sanguine, I might hope that some of my great
patrons' might procure me a Treasury warrant for
supervisor, surveyor-general, &c. .. . . .

Thus secure of a livelihood "to thee, sweet poetry,
delightful maid," I would consecrate my future days.

R. B.

(¹¹) TO MR. ROBERT AINSLIE.

(CROMEK, 1808.)

ELLISLAND, *Jan. 6th*, 1789.

MANY happy returns of the season to you, my dear
Sir! May you be comparatively happy up to your
comparative worth among the sons of men; which
wish would, I am sure, make you one of the most
blest of the human race.

I do not know if passing a "Writer to the signet"
be a trial of scientific merit, or a mere business of
friends and interest. However it be, let me quote
you my two favorite passages, which though I have
repeated them ten thousand times, still they rouse my
manhood and steel my resolution like inspiration.

> ———————— On Reason build resolve,
> That column of true majesty in man.—*Young*.

> Hear, Alfred, hero of the state,
> Thy genius heaven's high will declare;
> The triumph of the truly great
> Is never, never to despair!
> Is never to despair!—*Masque of Alfred*.

I grant, you enter the lists of life to struggle for
bread, business, notice, and distinction, in common
with hundreds. But who are they? Men, like your-
self, and of that aggregate body, your compeers,
seven-tenths of them come short of your advantages
natural and accidental; while two of those that re-
main either neglect their parts, as flowers blooming
in a desert, or mis-spend their strength, like a bull
goring a bramble bush.

But, to change the theme; I am still catering for
Johnson's publication, and among others, I have
brushed up the following old favorite song a little,

with a view to your worship, I have only altered a word here and there; but if you like the humor of it, we shall think of a stanza or two to add to it :—

> Robin shure in hairst, I shure wi' him;
> Fient a heuk had I, yet I stack by him.
> I gaed up to Dunse to warp a wab o' plaiden;
> At his daddy's yett, wha met me but Robin?

Chorus.—Robin shure in hairst. &c.

See page 38, *supra.**

(²) TO JOHN M'MURDO, ESQ., DRUMLANRIG.

(CHAMBERS, 1852.)

ELLISLAND, 9th *Jany*. 1789.

SIR,—A poet and a beggar are in so many points of view alike, that one might take them for the same individual under different designations; were it not that, though with a trifling poetic licence, poets may be styled beggars, yet the converse of the proposition does not hold, that every beggar is a poet. In one particular, however, they remarkably agree : if you help either the one or the other to a mug of ale or the picking of a bone, they will willingly repay you with a song. This occurs to me at present, as I have just despatched a rib of J. Kilpatrick's Highlander,† a bargain for which I am indebted to you (in the style of our ballad-printers), "Five Excellent New Songs."

---

* All the poet's editors, from Cunningham downwards, in giving the foregoing letter, omit the verses. and adhibit a note stating that the title of the song here alluded to, has not been ascertained. Mr. Ainslie, who survived to 11th April 1838, had sent both letter and song to the Scots Magazine for publication, withholding only the name of the poet's correspondent. These accordingly appeared in the October number, 1801, of that periodical.

It appears that so early as August 1787, Ainslie was father of an illegitimate son, which circumstance would furnish the subject of the above song. In June 1788, Burns in his complacency regarding his own recent marriage, wrote to Ainslie thus : "You will make a noble fellow if once you were married," but his correspondent was in no hurry about that event; for not until December 1798 did he commit himself to matrimony.

† This is explained to mean a Highland wedder, which Mr. M'Murdo had bought from Kilpatrick, and presented to Burns, as a supply to his table.

The enclosed is nearly my newest song, and one that has cost me some pains, though that is but an equivocal mark of its excellence. Two or three others which I have by me shall do themselves the honor to wait on your after leisure ; petitioners for admittance into favor must not harass the condescension of their benefactor.

You see, Sir, what it is to patronize a poet. 'Tis like being a magistrate in Petty-borough ; you do them the favor to preside in their council for one year, and your name bears the prefatory stigma of " Bailie " for life.

With—not the compliments, but—the best wishes, the sincerest prayer of the season for you, that you may see many happy years with Mrs. M'Murdo and your family—two blessings, by the by, to which your rank does not entitle you, a loving wife and fine family being almost the only good things of this life to which the farm-house and cottage have an exclusive right. I have the honor to be, Sir, your much indebted and very humble servant, R. BURNS.

The poet in his letter to Mrs. Dunlop, of 17th Dec. 1788, intimated his intention to be at the New Year's Fair at Ayr, which would be about 12th of January. 1789. He afterwards in a letter to Dr. Moore refers to that journey thus :— " In January last on my road to Ayrshire, I had to put up at Bailie Whigham's in Sanquhar, the only tolerable inn in the place." On that occasion, after being, as he supposed, comfortably housed for the night, the unexpected arrival of the funeral pageantry of the late Mrs. Oswald of Auchencruive, on its way to the place of interment in Ayrshire, put Burns out of temper, because on that account he had to take horse, and resume his journey for other twelve miles to the next inn, at New Cumnock. This incident produced his powerful Ode to the memory of that lady, which is given at page 40, *supra*. Within ten days he was back to Ellisland, inditing letters to correspondents ; and after the middle of February, he proceeded to Edinburgh to have a final reck-

oning with Creech, on which occasion he did not see "Clar-
inda," because on being informed by Ainslie that the poet
was expected in town for a few days, that lady said she
would avoid her windows to prevent her, by any chance,
catching a glimpse of him.

(²) TO PROF^R. DUGALD STEWART.

(CURRIE, 1800.)

ELLISLAND, 20th Jan. 1789.

SIR,—The enclosed sealed packet I sent to Edin-
burgh a few days after I had the happiness of meet-
ing you in Ayrshire, but you were gone for the Con-
tinent. I have added a few more of my productions,
those for which I am indebted to the Nithsdale Muses.
The piece inscribed to R. G., Esq., is a copy of
verses I sent Mr. Graham, of Fintry, accompanying
a request for his assistance in a matter, to me, of
very great moment. To that gentleman I am already
doubly indebted, for deeds of kindness of serious im-
port to my dearest interests, done in a manner grate-
ful to the delicate feelings of sensibility. This poem
is a species of composition new to me ; but I do not
intend it shall be my last essay of the kind, as you
will see by the 'Poet's Progress.'* These fragments,
if my design succeeds, are but a small part of the in-
tended whole. I propose it shall be the work of my
utmost exertions ripened by years : of course I do not
wish it much known. The fragment, beginning "A
little, upright, pert, tart," &c., I have not shewn to
man living, till now I send it you. It is the postu-
lata, the axiom, the definition of a character, which
if it appear at all, shall be placed in a variety of
lights. This particular part I send you merely as a

---

* See page 31, *supra*. The particular part in which Mr. Creech was satirised,
beginning "A little upright, pert," &c., is given at page 33. The poem in-
scribed to Mr. Graham, here referred to, is that printed at page 15, *supra*.

sample of my hand at portrait-sketching ; but lest idle conjecture should pretend to point out the original, please, let it be for your single, sole inspection.

Need I make any apology for this trouble to a gentleman who has treated me with such marked benevolence and peculiar kindness ; who has entered into my interests with so much zeal, and on whose critical decisions I can so fully depend?   A poet as I am by trade, these decisions are to me of the last consequence.   My late transient acquaintance among some of the mere rank and file of greatness I resign with ease : but to the distinguished champions of genius and learning, I shall be ever ambitious of being known.   The native genius and accurate discernment in Mr. Stewart's critical strictures, the justice, (the iron justice, for he has no bowels of compassion for a poor poetic sinner) of Dr. Gregory's remarks, and the delicacy of Professor Dalzell's taste, I shall ever revere.

I shall be in Edinburgh some time next month.   I have the honor to be, Sir, your highly obliged and very humble servant,   R. B.

The next of Burns's letters in order of date is unfortunately without the address, but Chambers with every probability supposes it was written to

(²) THE HON. HENRY ERSKINE?

(CHAMBERS, 1851.)

ELLISLAND, 22nd January 1789.

SIR,—There are two things which, I believe, the blow that terminates my existence alone can destroy— my attachment and propensity to poesy, and my sense of what I owe to your goodness.   There is nothing in the different situations of a Great and Little man that

vexes me more than the ease with which the one
practices some virtues that to the other are extremely
difficult, or perhaps wholly impracticable. A man of
consequence and fashion shall richly repay a deed of
kindness with a nod and a smile, or a hearty shake
of the hand ; while a poor fellow labors under a sense
of gratitude, which, like copper coin, though it loads
the bearer, is yet of small account in the currency
and commerce of the world. As I have the honor,
Sir, to stand in the poor fellow's predicament with
respect to you, will you accept of a device I have
thought on to acknowledge these obligations I can
never cancel? Mankind, in general, agree in testify-
ing their devotion, their gratitude, their friendship, or
their love, by presenting whatever they hold dearest.
Everybody who is in the least acquainted with the
character of a poet, knows that there is nothing in
the world on which he sets so much value as his
verses. I desire, from time to time, as she may be-
stow her favors, to present you with the productions
of my humble Muse. The enclosed are the principal
of her works on the banks of the Nith. The poem
inscribed to R. G., Esq., is some verses, accompany-
ing a request, which I sent to Mr. Graham, of Fintry
—a gentleman who has given double value to some
important favors he has bestowed on me by his
manner of doing them, and on whose future patron-
age, likewise, I must depend for matters to me of
the last consequence.

I have no great faith in the boastful pretensions to
intuitive propriety and unlabored elegance. The
rough material of Fine Writing is certainly the gift
of Genius ; but I as firmly believe that the workman-
ship is the united effort of Pains, Attention, and
repeated Trial. The piece addressed to Mr. Graham
is my first essay in that didactic, epistolary way ;
which circumstance, I hope, will bespeak your in-

dulgence. To your friend Captain Erskine's strictures*
I lay claim as a relation; not, indeed, that I have
the honor to be akin to the peerage, but because he
is a son of Parnassus.

I intend being in Edinburgh in four or five
weeks, when I shall certainly do myself the honor of
waiting on you, to testify with what respect and
gratitude, &c.   R. B.

(³) MR. JAMES JOHNSON, ENGRAVER,
BELL'S WYND, EDINBURGH.
(DOUGLAS, 1877.) †
CALEDONIA, A BALLAD.

There was once a time, but old Time was then young,
   That brave Caledonia, the chief of her line,
From some of your northern deities sprung,—
   Who knows not that brave Caledonia's divine?
            (*See* page 95.—*supra.*)

I shall be in Edinburgh, my dear Sir, in about a
month, when we shall overhaul the whole collection
and report progress.

The foregoing I hope will suit the excellent air it
is designed for. Adieu till next week,

                                    ROBᵀ. BURNS.
ELLISLAND. 23*rd Jan.* 1789.

TO ROBᵀ. CLEGHORN, FARMER, SAUGHTON
MILLS, EDINBURGH.
(DOUGLAS, 1877.)‡
ELLISLAND, NEAR DUMFRIES, 23*rd Jan.* 1789.

I must take shame and confusion to myself, my
Dear Friend and Brother Farmer, that I have not

---

* The Hon. Andrew Erskine, a poet and musical amateur residing in Edin-
burgh, brother to the Earl of Kelly.
 † From the poet's holograph in the possession of W. F. Watson, Esq., Edin-
burgh.
 ‡ From the poet's autograph in possession of A. C. Lamb, Esq., Dundee.

written you much sooner. The truth is, I have been so tossed about between Ayrshire and Nithsdale that, till now I have got my family here, I have had time to think of nothing except now and then a distich or stanza as I rode along. Were it not for our gracious Monarch's cursed tax of postage, I had sent you one or two pieces of some length that I have lately done. I have no idea of the *Press*. I am more able to support myself and family, though in a humble, yet an independent way ; and I mean, just at my leisure, to pay my court to the tuneful Sisters, in hopes that they may one day enable me to carry on a Work of some importance. The following are a few verses I wrote in a neighboring Gentleman's *Hermitage*, to which he is so good as let me have a key.

(Written in Friar's Carse Hermitage 1788. See page 7, *supra.*)

I shall be in Edinburgh for a few days, sometime about latter end of February or beginning of March, when I will shew you my other pieces. My farming scheme too—particularly the management of one, inclusive of Holming land is to be decided by your superior judgment. I find, if my farm does well with me, I shall certainly be an enthusiast in the business.

R. B.

(¹) TO MR. DAVID BLAIR,

GUN MAKER, ST. PAUL'S SQUARE, BIRMINGHAM.

(DR. WADDELL'S ED., 1869.)*

ELLISLAND, 23*rd Jany.* 1789.

MY DEAR SIR,—My honor has lain bleeding these two months almost, as 'tis near that time since I received your kind though short epistle of the 29th Oct. The defensive tools do more than half mankind

---

* From the original MS. in possession of Miss Mary S. Gladstone of Fasque. Certain markings on it shew that it had passed through Dr. Currie's hands.

do, they do honor to their maker; but I trust that with me they shall have the fate of a miser's gold—to be often admired, but never used.

Long before your letter came to hand, I sent you, by way of Mr. Nicol, a copy of the book, and a proof-copy of the print, loose among the leaves of the book. These, I hope, are safe in your possession some time ago. If I could think of any other channel of communication with you than the villanous expensive one of the Post, I could send you a parcel of my Rhymes; partly as a small return for your. kind, handsome compliment, and much more as a mark of my sincere esteem and respect for Mr. Blair. A piece I did lately I shall try to cram into this letter, as I think the turn of thought may perhaps please you.

WRITTEN IN FRIAR'S CARSE HERMITAGE. ON THE BANKS OF THE NITH, DECEMBER 1788. (*See* page 7, *supra*.)

I remember with pleasure, my dear Sir, a visit you talked of paying to Dumfries, in Spring or Summer. I shall only say I have never parted with a man, after so little acquaintance, whom I more ardently wished to see again. At your first convenience, a line to inform me of an affair in which I am much interested—just an answer to the question, How you do? will highly oblige, my dear Sir, yours very sincerely

ROBᵀ. BURNS.

The pistols which form the subject of the above letter were presented by Burns before he died, to Dr. William Maxwell, his principal medical attendant. They came, through the hands of Dr. Maxwell's daughter, into the possession of the Roman Catholic Bishop Gillis, of Edinburgh, by whom they were presented to the Society of Scottish Antiquaries on 24th January 1859.* Dr. Maxwell removed his residence from Dumfries to Edinburgh in 1834, and at a sale of his effects in May of that year, several pistols and swords were disposed

---

* Bishop Gillis died, 24th February 1864.

of. but he had too much veneration for the memory of Burns, to part with his dying gift in that manner. Allan Cunningham acquired a pair of pistols and an old Highland broadsword, which had been bought at that sale, in the belief that they had formerly been the property of Burns, and hugged himself on possessing such precious relics. In the first edition of his Biography of Burns, he refers to that brace of pistols as having been *bought* by the poet "from Johnson the gunsmith, and having tried them, he wrote 'I have proved the pistols, and can say of them what I would not do for the bulk of mankind—they are an honor to their maker.'" It thus appears that Allan had heard some floating rumor about the letter in the text; but his mis-quotation, as well as blunder in the maker's name, proves he had never seen it.

Dr. Maxwell died at Edinburgh in October 1834, and Miss Maxwell, who constituted Bishop Gillis her heir, died in September 1858. The Bishop, in an elaborate paper which he read to the Society of Antiquaries on the subject of Burns's pistols, observed that Dr. Maxwell "incurred heavy responsibilities with Blair of Birmingham, for the manufacture of fire-arms," in his enthusiastic efforts to help on the Revolution of France. It is known as a fact that Maxwell in one capacity or another, was present on the scaffold when King Louis XVI. was beheaded on 21st January 1793; and it is said that he preserved a handkerchief which, on that occasion, he had dipped in the royal blood.

(²) TO ALEXANDER CUNNINGHAM, ESQ., WRITER, EDINBURGH.

(DOUGLAS, 1877.)

ELLISLAND, 24*th Jan*ʸ. 1789.

MY DEAR CUNNINGHAM—When I saw in my last newspaper that a Surgeon in Edinburgh was married to a certain amiable and accomplished young lady, whose name begins with Ann ; a lady with whom I fancy I have the honor of being a little acquainted, *

---

* Jan 13, 1788. Married at Edinburgh, Mr. Forrest Dewar, Surgeon, to Miss Anne Stewart, daughter of John Stewart, Esq. of East Craigs. See letter to Alex. Cunningham, 27th July 1788. Page 191 *supra*.

I sincerely felt for a much esteemed friend of mine.
As you are the single, only instance that ever came
within the sphere of my observation of human nature,
of a young fellow, dissipated but not debauched, a
circumstance that has ever given me the highest idea
of the native qualities of your heart, I am certain that
a disappointment in the tender passion must, to you,
be a very serious matter.　To the hopeful youth, keen
on the badger foot of Mammon, or listed under the
gaudy banners of ambition, a love-disappointment, as
such, is an easy business ; nay, perhaps he hugs
himself on his escape ; but to your scanty tribe of
mankind, whose souls bear, on the richest materials,
the most elegant impress of the Great Creator, Love
enters deeply into their existence, and is entwined
with their very thread of life.　I can myself affirm,
both from bachelor and wedlock experience, that Love
is the Alpha and Omega of human enjoyment.　All
the pleasures, all the happiness of my humble com-
peers flow immediately and directly from this delicious
source.　It is the spark of celestial fire which lights
up the wintry hut of poverty, and makes the cheerless
mansion warm, comfortable, and gay.　It is the ema-
nation of divinity that preserves the sons and daugh-
ters of rustic labor from degenerating into the brutes
with which they daily hold converse.　Without it,
life to the poor inmates of the cottage, would be a
damning gift.*

I intended to go on with some kind of consolatory
epistle, when, unawares, I flew off in this rhapsodical
tangent.　Instead of attempting to resume a subject
for which I am so ill-qualified, I shall ask your opinion
of some verses I have lately begun on a theme of
which you are the best judge I ever saw.　It is Love

---

* Here ends, in the Glenriddell MS., all that Burns chose to transcribe of this
letter, where also it is undated.　Our text is printed from the original holograph,
now in possession of the son of Burns's correspondent.

too ; though not just warranted by the law of nations.
A married lady of my acquaintance, whose *crim. con.*
amour with a certain Captain made some noise in the
world, is supposed to write to him, now in the West
Indies, as follows :—

> By all I loved, neglected and forgot,
> No friendly· face ere lights my squalid cot :
> Shunned, hated, wrong'd, unpitied, unredrest,
> The mock'd quotation of the scorners jest.*
>
> *   *   *   *   *   *

(¹) TO ROBERT RIDDELL, ESQ., OF FRIAR'S CARSE.

(CROMEK, 1808.)

ELLISLAND, 1789.

SIR,—I wish from my inmost soul it were in my
power to give you a more substantial gratification and
return for all your goodness to the poet, than tran-
scribing a few of his idle rhymes. However, "an old
song," though, to a proverb, an instance of insignifi-
cance, is generally the only coin a poet has to pay
with.

If my poems which I have transcribed, and mean
still to transcribe into your Book, were equal to the
grateful respect and high esteem I bear for the gen-
tleman to whom I present them, they would be the
finest poems in the language. As they are, they will
at least be a testimony with what sincerity I have the
honor to be, Sir, your devoted, humble servant.

R. B.

---

* In the original letter this is the bottom of page second : the other half of the
sheet which would contain the remainder of the verses, is wanting. The second
half-sheet was long ago dishonestly appropriated by some one who obtained
temporary access to it, and appears to have found its way into the manuscript
market. *See* page 43, *supra.*

(¹) TO THE RIGHT REV. DR. JOHN GEDDES.

(CURRIE, 1800.)

ELLISLAND. 3d *Feb.* 1789.

VENERABLE FATHER,—As I am conscious that wherever I am, you do me the honor to interest yourself in my welfare, it gives me pleasure to inform you that I am here at last, stationary in the serious business of life, and have now not only the retired leisure, but the hearty inclination to attend to those great and important questions—what I am? where I am? and for what I am destined?

In that first concern, the conduct of the man, there was ever but one side on which I was habitually blameable, and there I have secured myself in the way pointed out by Nature and Nature's God.   I was sensible that, to so helpless a creature as a poor poet, a wife and a family were incumbrances, which a species of prudence would bid him shun ; but when the alternative was, being at eternal warfare with myself on account of habitual follies—to give them no worse name—which no general example, no licentious wit, no sophistical infidelity, would to me ever justify.   I must have been a fool to have hesitated, and a madman to have made another choice.   Besides I had, in "my Jean," a long and much loved fellow-creature's happiness or misery among my hands, and who could trifle with such a deposit?

In the affair of a livelihood, I think myself tolerably secure : I have good hopes of my farm, but should they fail, I have an Excise Commission, which, on my simple petition, will, at any time, procure me bread. There is a certain stigma affixed to the character of an excise officer, but I do not intend to borrow honor from my profession ; and though the salary be com-

paratively small, it is luxury to any thing that the
first twenty-five years of my life taught me to expect.

*   *   *   *   *

Thus, with a rational aim and method in life, you
may easily guess, my reverend and much-honored
friend, that my characteristical trade is not forgotten ;
I am, if possible, more than ever an enthusiast to the
Muses. I am determined to study Man and Nature,
and in that view, incessantly to try if the ripening
and corrections of years can enable me to produce
something worth preserving.

You will see in your book, which I beg your pardon
for detaining so long, that I have been tuning my
lyre on the banks of Nith. Some larger poetic plans
that are floating in my imagination, or partly put in
execution, I shall impart to you when I have the
pleasure of meeting with you ; which, if you are then
in Edinburgh, I shall have about the beginning of
.March.

That acquaintance, worthy Sir, with which you were
pleased to honor me, you must still allow me to chal-
lenge ; for with whatever unconcern I give up my
transient connection with the merely Great, (those self-
important beings whose intrinsic worthlessness is often
concealed under the accidental advantages of their
birth), I cannot lose the patronising notice of the
Learned and the Good, without the bitterest regret.

                                                R. B.

Bishop Gillis, of the Romish Church in Edinburgh, thus re-
marked in 1859, in reference to the foregoing epistle : " If any
man, after perusing this letter, will still say that the mind of
Burns was beyond the reach of religious influence, or, in other
words, that he was a scoffer at Revelation, that man need not
be reasoned with, as his own mind must be hopeless beyond
the reach of argument."

The amiable gentleman thus addressed, Burns fell acquainted
with at the house of Lord Monboddo in the winter of 1786–87.
He was a man of great learning and worth, and was one of

the first clergymen of the Romish Church in Scotland on
whom, since the Reformation era, was conferred the honorary
degree of LL.D.   He had a cousin Alexander Geddes, a priest
of the same persuasion, with whom Cunningham, Waddell,
and others of the poet's biographers have confounded him.
Bishop Gillis described the latter as " that unfortunate victim
of human vanity, the unbelieving Priest, Alexander Geddes,
who died in London in 1802." But Alexander Geddes was
nevertheless a remarkable man, and in 1777 was honored by
his Alma Mater, the University of Aberdeen, with the degree
of LL.D.   He removed to London, and devoted himself to a
new translation of the Scriptures, under the patronage of
Lord Petre.   In the course of his researches, he saw cause to
change his views with respect to Scriptural authority and
doctrine, which sufficiently accounts for the irreverence with
which Bishop Gillis spoke of him.

John Geddes, the poet's correspondent, was styled by an old
citizen of Edinburgh who remembered him, "the most fashion-
able man in this city." We have already seen with what
veneration "Clarinda" regarded him, and he must have been
no bigot, for that lady met him in the house of her minister,
Mr. Kemp, whose history the reader has been made familiar
with.   She records that she "listened with the gaze of atten-
tion to every word uttered by Dr. Geddes : I saw he observed
me, and returned that glance of cordial warmth which assured
me he was pleased with my delicate flattery.   I wished that
night he had been my father, that I might shelter me in his
bosom." Burns, from the terms used regarding him, in his
letter to Mrs. Dunlop, of 4th Nov. 1787, seems to have formed
an equally high opinion of Dr. Geddes.   It is believed that he
was the means of procuring for the list of subscribers to the
Poet's Edition of April 1787, the names of no fewer than five
foreign Romish Seminaries, beginning with the Scots College
of Valladolid, of which he had for many years been Rector.

In the second-last paragraph of the letter in the text, Burns
speaks of a Book belonging to Dr. Geddes, which he apolo-
gises for having retained so long.   That was an interleaved
copy of the author's Edinburgh edition, in which he had
undertaken to insert some notes and several unpublished
poems.   The interesting relic found its way to America, many
years after the decease of Dr. Geddes, whose death is thus
announced in the Scots Magazine,—" 11th Feb. 1799, Died at
Aberdeen, the Right Rev. Dr. Geddes." It was purchased in
1863, by Mr. James Black, Detroit, a native of Nairn, who

was long in the Town Clerk's office there. At the Burns's
Anniversary Dinner at Detroit in 1867, Mr. Black produced
the highly prized volume and detailed its succession of pos-
sessors till it fell into his hands. The order in which the
MS. additions are written, and the titles prefixed to them by
the poet, are as follows :—

1. On reading in a newspaper the death of John M'Leod,
   Esq., brother to Miss Isabella M'Leod, a particular
   friend of the Author's.
2. On the death of Sir J. Hunter Blair.
3. Written on the blank leaf of my first edition, which I
   presented to an old sweetheart then married : I was
   then on the tiptoe for Jamaica.
4. An Epitaph on a Friend.
5. The Humble Petition of Bruar Water to the noble Duke
   of Athole.
6. On the death of Robert Dundas, of Arniston, Esq., late
   Lord President of the Court of Session.
7. On seeing some Water-fowl in Loch Turrit, a wild scene
   among the hills of Oughtertyre.
8. Written at the Hermitage at Taymouth.
9. Written at the Fall of Foyers.
10. Written in Friar's Carse Hermitage, on the banks of Nith,
    June 1788.
11. The same, altered from the foregoing, Dec. 1788.
12. To Robert Graham, of Fintry, Esq., accompanying a re-
    quest.

Appended to the last-named poems are these words—" The
foregoing three pieces are the favor of the Nithsdale Muses."
After No. 6, the poet writes—" The foregoing poem has some
tolerable lines in it, but the incurable wound of my pride will
not suffer me to correct or even peruse it. I sent a copy of
it, with my best prose letter, to the son of the great man, the
theme of the piece, by the hand, too, of one of the noblest
men in God's world, Alexander Wood, Surgeon, when behold,
his Solicitorship took no more notice of my poem or me than
I had been a strolling fiddler who had made free with his
lady's name over the head of a silly new reel ! Did the
gentleman think I looked for any dirty gratuity ?"
The names left blank in the printed poems, Burns wrote out
in full for Dr. Geddes. Also at the end of " Tam Samson's

Elegy," he has written the following verse, with an asterisk
to note its proper place in the poem :—

> " Here low he lies in lasting rest ;
>   Perhaps upon his mouldering breast
>   Some spitefu' moor fowl bigs her nest.
>   To hatch an' breed.
>   Alas ! nae mair he'll them molest !
>   Tam Samson's dead !"

This last stanza was introduced in the poet's edition, in 2
Vols., 1793.

ADDRESS OF THE SCOTTISH DISTILLERS

TO THE RIGHT HON. WILLIAM PITT.

(CROMEK, 1808.)

[*Feb.* 1789.]

SIR,—While pursy burgesses crowd your gate, sweat-
ing under the weight of heavy addresses, permit us,
the quondam distillers in that part of Great Britain
called Scotland, to approach you, not with venal ap-
probation, but with fraternal condolence ; not as what
you are just now, or for some time have been ; but
as what, in all probability, you will shortly be. We
shall have the merit of not deserting our *friends* in
the day of their calamity, and you will have the sat-
isfaction of perusing at least one honest address. You
are well acquainted with the dissection of human na-
ture ; nor do you need the assistance of a fellow-
creature's bosom to inform you that man is always a
selfish, often a perfidious being. This assertion, how-
ever the hasty conclusions of superficial observation
may doubt it, or the raw inexperience of youth may
deny it, those who make the fatal experiment we have
done will feel it. You are a statesman, and conse-
quently are not ignorant of the traffic of these corpo-
ration compliments. The little great man who drives
the borough to market, and the very great man who

buys the borough in that market, they two do the whole business ; and you well know they, likewise, have their price.   With that sullen disdain which you can so well assume, rise, illustrious Sir, and spurn these hireling efforts of venal stupidity.   They are the compliments of a man's friends on the morning of his execution ; they take a decent farewell, resign you to your fate, and hurry away from your approaching hour.

If fame say true, and omens be not very much mistaken, you are about to make your exit from that world where the sun of gladness gilds the path of prosperous men : permit us, great Sir, with the sympathy of fellow-feeling to hail your passage to the realms of ruin.   Whether the sentiment proceed from the selfishness or cowardice of mankind is immaterial ; but to a child of misfortune, pointing out those who are still more unhappy, is giving him some degree of positive enjoyment.   In this light, Sir, our downfall may be *again* useful to you ; though not exactly *in the same way*, it is not perhaps the first time it has gratified your feelings.   It is true, the triumph of your evil star is exceedingly despiteful.   At an age when others are the votaries of pleasure, or underlings in business, you had attained the highest wish of a British statesman ; and with the ordinary date of human life, what a prospect was before you !   Deeply rooted in *Royal Favor*, you overshadowed the land. The birds of passage, which follow ministerial sunshine through every clime of political faith and manners, flocked to your branches ; and the beasts of the field (the lordly possessors of hills and valleys) crowded under your shade.   " But behold a watcher, a holy one, came down from heaven, and cried aloud, and said thus : Hew down the tree, and cut off his branches ; shake off his leaves, and scatter his fruit ; let the beasts get away from under it, and the fowls

from his branches!" A blow from an unthought-of
quarter, one of those terrible accidents which peculiarly
mark the hand of Omnipotence, overset your career,
and laid all your fancied honors in the dust. But
turn your eyes, Sir, to the tragic scenes of our fate :
—an ancient nation, that for many ages had gallantly
maintained the unequal struggle for independence with
her much more powerful neighbor, at last agrees to a
union which should ever after make them one people.
In consideration of certain circumstances, it was cove-
nanted that the former should enjoy a stipulated alle-
viation in her share of the public burdens, particularly
in that branch of the revenue called the Excise. This
just privilege has of late given great umbrage to some
interested, powerful individuals of the more potent
half of the empire, and they have spared no wicked
pains, under insidious pretexts, to subvert the spirit
of their ancient enemies, which they yet dreaded too
much openly to attack.

In this conspiracy we fell ; nor did we alone suffer,
our country was deeply wounded. A number of (we
will say) respectable individuals, largely engaged in
trade, where we were not only useful, but absolutely
necessary to our country in her dearest interests ; we,
with all that was near and dear to us, were sacrificed,
without remorse, to the infernal deity of political Ex-
pediency, not that sound policy, the good of the whole.
We fell to gratify the wishes of dark Envy, and the
views of unprincipled Ambition ! Your foes, Sir, were
avowed ; you fell in the face of day ; your enemies
were too brave to take an ungenerous advantage. On
the contrary, our enemies, to complete our overthrow,
contrived to make their guilt appear the villainy of a
nation. Your downfall only drags with you your pri-
vate friends and partizans : in our misery are more or
less involved the most numerous and most valuable
part of the community—all those who immediately

III.   Q

depend on the cultivation of the soil, from the land-lord of a province down to his lowest hind.

Allow us, Sir, yet further, just to hint at another rich vein of comfort in the dreary regions of adversity ; —the gratulations of an approving conscience. In a certain great assembly, of which you are a distin-guished member, panegyrics on your private virtues have so often wounded your delicacy, that we shall not distress you with anything on the subject. There is, however, one part of your public conduct which our feelings will not permit us to pass in silence : our gratitude must trespass on your modesty ; we mean, worthy Sir, your whole behaviour to the Scots Dis-tillers.—In evil hours, when obtrusive recollection presses bitterly on the sense, let that, Sir, come like a healing angel, and speak the peace to your soul which the world can neither give nor take away.— We have the honor to be, Sir, your sympathizing fellow-sufferers, and grateful humble Servants,

JOHN BARLEYCORN—Præses.

The date of the foregoing political letter in the manner of Junius, is pointed out by the writer himself in his tran-script of it in the Glenriddell volume of letters, where it is headed by the following introduction :—

"At the juncture of the King's illness, while the Regency Bill was pending, and when everybody expected the Pre-mier's downfall, addresses crowded in to him from all quar-ters, and among the rest the following appeared in a news-paper. The addressers, the late Distillers of Scotland, had just been ruined by a positive breach of the public faith in a most partial tax laid on by the House of Commons to favor a few opulent English Distillers who, it seems, were of vast electioneering consequence."

(⁹) TO MR. JAMES BURNESS, MONTROSE.

(Gilbert Burns's Ed., 1820.)*

ELLISLAND, *9th Feb.* 1789.

My DEAR SIR,—Why I did not write to you long ago is what, even on the rack, I could not answer. If you can in your mind form an idea of indolence, dissipation, hurry, cares, change of country, entering on untried scenes of life, all combined, you will save me the trouble of a blushing apology. It could not be want of regard for a man for whom I had a high esteem before I knew him—an esteem which has much increased since I did know him ; and this caveat entered, I shall plead guilty to any other indictment with which you shall please to charge me.

After I parted from you, for many months my life was one continued scene of dissipation. Here at last I am become stationary, and have taken a farm and —a wife. The farm beautifully situated on the Nith, a large river that runs by Dumfries, and falls into the Solway frith. I have gotten a lease of my farm as long as I pleased ; but how it may turn out is just a guess, and it is yet to improve and enclose, &c. ; however, I have good hopes of my bargain on the whole.

My wife is my Jean, with whose story you are partly acquainted. I found I had a much-loved fellow creature's happiness or misery among my hands, and I durst not trifle with so sacred a deposit.† Indeed I have not any reason to repent the step I have taken,

---

* The original MS. is now preserved in the Poet's Monument at Edinburgh. Chambers, who seems to have never consulted Gilbert Burns's edition, notes this and several other letters to James Burness to have appeared in "Lockhart's Life of Burns," where the reader will in vain look for them.

† This expression the poet has repeated no fewer than half-a-dozen times in his correspondence between the end of May 1788 and the present date.

as I have attached myself to a very good wife, and
have shaken myself loose of a very bad failing.

I have found my book a very profitable business,
and with the profits of it I have begun life pretty
decently.   Should fortune not favor me in farming, as
I have no great faith in her fickle ladyship, I have
provided myself in another resource, which, however
some folks may affect to despise it, is still a comfort-
able shift in the day of misfortune.   .In the hey-day
of my fame, a gentleman, whose name at least I dare
say you know, as his estate lies somewhere near
Dundee, Mr. Graham, of Fintry, one of the Commis-
sioners of Excise, offered me the commission of an
Excise officer.   I thought it prudent to accept the
offer ; and accordingly I took my instructions, and have
my commission by me.   Whether I may ever do duty,
or be a penny the better for it, is what I do not
know ; but I have the comfortable assurance, that
come whatever ill fate will, I can, on my simple
petition to the Excise-board, get into employ.

We have lost poor uncle Robert this winter.   He
had long been very weak, and with very little altera-
tion in him ; he expired Janry. 3rd.*   His son Wil-
liam has been with me this winter, and goes in May
to bind himself to be a mason with my father-in-
law, who is a pretty considerable architect in Ayrshire.
His other son, the eldest, John, comes to me I expect
in summer.   They are both remarkably stout young
fellows, and promise to do well.   His only daughter,
Fanny, has been with me ever since her father's
death, and I purpose keeping her in my family till
she be quite woman-grown, and be fit for better ser-
vice.   She is one of the cleverest girls, and has one

---

* This does not mean that Uncle Robert died at Ellisland as many annotators
have supposed.   He died in his own house at Stewarton, and the poet kindly
looked after the orphans, by securing them employment.   Fanny ultimately
was married to a brother of Mrs. Burns.

of the most amiable dispositions, that I have ever seen.

All friends in this country and Ayrshire are well. Remember me to all friends in the north. My wife joins me in compliments to your bedfellow and family. I would write your brother-in-law, but have lost his address. For goodness sake don't take example by me, but write me soon. I am ever, My dear cousin, yours most sincerely,

ROBT. BURNS.

The reader will understand that Burns paid a short visit to Edinburgh sometime in the latter half of February 1789 and returned to his home at "The Isle" on the closing day of that month. Occasional mention has been made in course of the poet's correspondence, of his younger brother William, who had served an apprenticeship to the trade of a saddler. In writing to Gilbert immediately on returning from his great Highland tour, the poet says " I have been trying for a berth for William, but am not likely to be successful. A Mr. Ainslie, Bookseller in Edinburgh, afterwards, undertook to get employment for William, and in August 1788 we have Burns expressing extreme disappointment that the offer had proved a disappointing one, and then Robert Ainslie, Writer, engaged in the same undertaking, apparently with no success ; for, about the close of that year, William remained for some weeks at Ellisland unemployed. The young man crossed the border into England and obtained some work at Longtown as the following letter shows. The chief object of the poet's visit to Edinburgh was to have a final reckoning with Creech, in which he succeeded ; indeed, he owned that Mr. Creech had at length dealt fairly with him.

(¹) WILLIAM BURNS TO ROBERT BURNS.

(CROMEK, 1808.)

LONGTOWN. *Feb.* 15, 1789.

DEAR SIR,—As I am now in a manner only entering into the world, I begin this our correspondence, with a view of being a gainer by your advice, more than ever you can be

by anything I can write you of what I see, or what I hear,
in the course of my wanderings. I know not how it hap-
pened, but you were more shy of your counsel than I could
have wished the time I staid with you : whether it was
because you thought it would disgust me to have my faults
freely told me while I was dependent on you ; or whether
it was because you saw that by my indolent disposition,
your instructions would have no effect, I cannot determine ;
but if it proceeded from any of the above causes, the reason
of withholding your admonition is now done away with, for
I now stand on my own bottom, and that indolence which
I am very conscious of, is something rubbed off by being
called to act in life whether I will or not ; and my expe-
rience, which I daily feel, makes me wish for that advice
which you are so able to give, and which I can only expect
from you or Gilbert, since the loss of the kindest and ablest
of fathers.

The morning after I went from the Isle, I left Dumfries
about five o'clock and came to Annan to breakfast, and
staid about an hour ; and I reached this place about two
o'clock. I have got work here, and I intend to stay a month
or six weeks and then go forward, as I wish to be at York
about the latter end of summer, where I propose to spend
next winter, and go on for London in the spring.

I have the promise of seven shillings a week from Mr.
Proctor while I stay here, and sixpence more if he succeeds
himself, for he has only new begun trade here. I am to
pay four shillings per week of board wages, so that my neat
income here will be much the same as in Dumfries.

The inclosed you will send to Gilbert with the first oppor-
tunity. Please send me the first Wednesday after you receive
this, by the Carlisle waggon, two of my coarse shirts, one
of my best linen ones, my velveteen vest, and a neckcloth ;
write to me along with them, and direct to me, Saddler, in
Longtown, and they will not miscarry, for I am boarded in
the waggoner's house. You may either let them be given
in to the wagon, or send them to Coulthard and Gellebourn's
shop and they will forward them. Pray write me often while
I stay here.—I wish you would send me a letter, though
never so small, every week, for they will be no expense to
me and but little trouble to you. Please to give my best
wishes to my sister-in-law, and believe me to be your affec-
tionate and obliged brother,

WILLIAM BURNS.

P.S.—The great-coat you gave me at parting did me singular service the day I came here, and merits my hearty thanks. From what has been said, the conclusion is this—that my hearty thanks and my best wishes are all that you and my sister must expect from   W. B.

(¹) TO MR. WILLIAM BURNS, LONGTOWN.

(CHAMBERS, 1852.)

ISLE, *2nd March* 1789.

MY DEAR WILLIAM,—I arrived from Edinburgh only the night before last, so could not answer your epistle sooner. I congratulate you on the prospect of employ ; and I am indebted to you for one of the best letters that has been written by any mechanic lad in Nithsdale, or Annandale, or any dale on either side of the Border, this twelvemonth. Not that I would have you always affect the stately stilts of studied composition, but surely writing a handsome letter is an accomplishment worth courting ; and, with attention and practice, I can promise you that it will soon be an accomplishment of yours. If my advice can serve you (that is to say, if you can resolve to accustom yourself not only in reviewing your own deportment, manners, &c., but also in carrying your consequent resolutions of amending the faulty parts into practice), my small knowledge and experience of the world is heartily at your service. I intended to have given you a sheetful of counsels, but some business has prevented me. In a word learn *Taciturnity ;* let that be your motto. Tho' you had the wisdom of Newton, or the wit of Swift, garrulousness would lower you in the eyes of your fellow-creatures. I'll probably write you next week. I am, your brother,

ROBERT BURNS.

(²¹) TO MRS. DUNLOP OF DUNLOP.

(CURRIE, 1800.)

ELLISLAND, *4th March* 1789.

HERE am I, my honored friend, returned safe from the capital. To a man who has a home, however humble or remote (if that home is like mine, the scene of domestic comfort), the bustle of Edinburgh will soon be a business of sickening disgust :

"Vain pomp and glory of this world, I hate you!"

When I must skulk into a corner, lest the rattling equipage of some gaping blockhead should mangle me in the mire, I am tempted to exclaim—"What merits has he had, or what demerit have I had, in some state of pre-existence, that he is ushered into this state of being with sceptre of rule, and the key of riches in his puny fist, and I am kicked into the world, the sport of folly, or the victim of pride?" I have read somewhere of a monarch (in Spain, I think it was), who was so out of humor with the Ptolemæan system of astronomy, that he said, had he been of the Creator's council, he could have saved him a great deal of labor and absurdity. I will not defend the blasphemous speech ; but often, as I have glided with humble stealth through the pomp of Princes Street, it has suggested itself to me as an improvement on the present human figure, that if a man, in proportion to his own conceit of his own consequence in the world, could have pushed out the longitude of his common size, as a snail pushes out his horns, or as we draw out a prospect-glass. This trifling alteration, not to mention the prodigious saving it would be in the tear and wear of the neck and limb-sinews of many of his Majesty's liege subjects, in the way of tossing the head and tiptoe strutting, would evidently turn out a vast advantage, in enabling us at once to adjust the ceremonials in making a bow, or making way to a great man, and that too within a second of the precise spherical angle of reverence, or an inch of the particular point of respectful distance, which the important creature itself requires ; as a measuring glance at its towering altitude would determine the affair like instinct.

You are right, Madam, in your idea of poor Mylne's poem, which he has addressed to me. The piece has a good deal of merit, but it has one great fault—it is by far too long. Besides, my success has encouraged such a shoal of ill-spawned monsters to crawl into public notice, under the title of Scottish Poets, that the very term Scottish Poetry borders on the burlesque. When I write to Mr. Carfrae, I shall advise him rather to try one of his deceased friend's English pieces. I am prodigiously hurried with my own matters, else I would have requested a perusal of all Mylne's poetic performances ; and would have offered his friends my assistance in either selecting or correcting what would be proper for the press. What it is that occupies me so much, and perhaps a little oppresses my present spirits, shall fill up a paragraph in some future letter. In the mean time allow me to close this epistle with a few lines done by a friend of mine * * * * * I give you them, that, as you have seen the original, you may guess whether one or two alterations I have ventured to make in them, be any real improvement.

> " Like the fair plant that from our touch withdraws,
> Shrink mildly fearful even from applause,
> Be all a mother's fondest hope can dream,
> And all you are, my charming Rachel, seem.
> Straight as the fox-glove, ere her bells disclose,
> Mild as the maiden-blushing hawthorn blows,

Fair as the fairest of each lovely kind,
Your form shall be the image of your mind;
Your manners shall so true your soul express,
That all shall long to know the worth they guess;
Congenial hearts shall greet with kindred love,
And even sick'ning envy must approve."

R. B.

The reader will understand that the lines which close the preceding letter, form part of a little poem that Mrs. Dunlop had addressed to her daughter Miss Rachel on her birth-day. She had sent them to Burns for his inspection, and here he transcribes them with a few suggested improvements.

The Rev. Peter Carfrae, a friend of Mrs. Dunlop, had on 2nd January 1789, written to Burns enclosing a poem by a young Lothian farmer, named Mylne, recently deceased, composed in the Scots dialect, in form of an Address to Burns on the publication of his poem.

Mr. Carfrae consulted our poet on the propriety of publishing that and others of Mr. Mylne's effusions for the advantage of his family. The following is our bard's reply:

(¹) TO THE REV. PETER CARFRAE.

(CURRIE, 1800.)

[ELLISLAND, *March* 1789.]

REV. SIR,—I do not recollect that I have ever felt a severer pang of shame, than on looking at the date of your obliging letter which accompanied Mr. Mylne's poem. . . .

I am much to blame; the honor Mr. Mylne has done me, greatly enhanced in its value by the endearing, though melancholy circumstance, of its being the last production of his muse, deserved a better return.

I have, as you hint, thought of sending a copy of the poem to some periodical publication; but, on second thoughts, I am afraid, that in the present case, it would be an improper step. My success, perhaps as much accidental as merited, has brought an inundation of nonsense under the name of Scottish poetry. Subscription bills for Scottish poems have so dunned, and daily do dun the public, that the very name is in danger of contempt. For these reasons, if publishing any of Mr. Mylne's poems in a magazine, &c., be at all prudent, in my opinion it certainly should not be a Scottish poem. The profits of the labors of a man of genius are, I hope, as honorable as any profits whatever ; and Mr. Mylne's relations are most justly entitled to that honest harvest which fate has denied himself to reap. But let the friends of Mr. Mylne's fame (among whom I crave the honor of ranking myself) always keep in eye his respectability as a man and as a poet, and take no measure that, before the world knows anything about him, would risk his name and character being classed with the fools of the times.

I have, Sir, some experience of publishing ; and the way in which I would proceed with Mr. Mylne's poems is this :—I will publish, in two or three English and Scottish public papers, any one of his English poems which should, by private judges, be thought the most excellent, and mention it at the same time as one of the productions of a Lothian farmer of respectable character, lately deceased, whose poems his friends had it in idea to publish soon by subscription, for the sake of his numerous family :—not in pity to that family, but in justice to what his friends think the poetic merits of the deceased ; and to secure in the most effectual manner, to those tender connexions, whose right it is, the pecuniary reward of those merits. *   R. B.

---

* A volume of these poems, including two tragedies, was published by Creech in 1790.

(²) TO MR. Wᴹ. BURNS, LONGTOWN.

(CHAMBERS, 1856.)

ISLE, *Tuesday even.*
[*March* 10, 1789.]

DEAR WILLIAM,—In my last, I recommended that invaluable apophthegm—learn taciturnity.*

It is absolutely certain that nobody can know our thoughts ; and yet, from a slight observation of mankind, one would not think so.   What mischiefs daily arise from silly garrulity, or foolish confidence! There is an excellent Scots saying, that " A man's mind is his kingdom."   It is certainly so ; but how few can govern that kingdom with propriety?

The serious mischiefs in business which this flux of language occasions, do not come immediately to your situation ; but in another point of view, the dignity of the man, now is the time that will either make or mar you.   Yours is the time of life for laying in habits ; you cannot avoid it, though you should choose ; and these habits will stick to your last sand. At after periods, even at so little advance as my years, 'tis true, one may still be very sharp-sighted to one's habitual failings and weaknesses ; but to eradicate, or even amend them, is quite a different matter.   Acquired at first by accident, they by and by begin to be as it were *convenient*, and in time are in a manner a *necessary* part of our existence.   I have not time for more.   Whatever you read, whatever you hear, concerning the ways and works of that strange creature, Man, look into the living world about you— look into yourself for the evidence of the fact, or the application of the doctrine.   I am, ever yours,

ROBERT BURNS.

---

* On this subject of prudent taciturnity, see also Letter to Ainslie, page 184 *supra*.

(⁶) TO DR. JOHN MOORE, LONDON.

(CURRIE. 1800.)

ELLISLAND, 23rd *March* 1789.

SIR,—The gentleman who will deliver this is a Mr. Nielson,* a worthy clergyman in my neighborhood, and a very particular acquaintance of mine. As I have troubled him with this packet, I must turn him over to your goodness, to recompense him for it in a way in which he much needs your assistance, and where you can effectually serve him :—Mr. Nielson is on his way for France, to wait on his Grace of Queensbery, on some little business of a good deal of importance to him, and he wishes for your instructions respecting the most eligible mode of travelling, &c., for him, when he has crossed the channel. I should not have dared to take this liberty with you, but that I am told, by those who have the honor of your personal acquaintance, that to be a poor honest Scotchman is a letter of recommendation to you, and that to have it in your power to serve such a character, gives you much pleasure.

The inclosed ode is a compliment to the memory of the Mrs. Oswald, of Auchencruive. You, probably, knew her personally, an honor of which I cannot boast ; but I spent my early years in her neighborhood, and among her servants and tenants. I know that she was detested with the most heartfelt cordiality. However, in the particular part of her conduct which roused my poetic wrath, she was much less blameable. In January last, on my road to Ayrshire, I had put up at Bailie Whigham's, in Sanquhar, the only tolerable inn in the place. The frost was keen, and the

---

* The Rev. Edward Nielson. minister of Kirkbean, in the Stewarty of Kirkcudbright.

grim evening and howling wind were ushering in a night of snow and drift. My horse and I were both much fatigued with the labors of the day, and just as my friend the Bailie and I were bidding defiance to the storm, over a smoking bowl, in wheels the funeral pageantry of the late great Mrs. Oswald; and poor I am forced to brave all the horrors of a tempestuous night, and jade my horse, my young favorite horse, whom I had just christened Pegasus, twelve miles farther on, through the wildest moors and hills of Ayrshire, to New Cumnock, the next inn. The powers of poesy and prose sink under me, when I would describe what I felt. Suffice it to say, that when a good fire at New Cumnock had so far recovered my frozen sinews, I sat down and wrote the inclosed ode.

I was at Edinburgh lately, and settled finally with Mr. Creech; and I must own, that, at last, he has been amicable and fair with me.   R. B.

(³) TO MR. WILLIAM BURNS, LONGTOWN.

(HOGG AND MOTHERWELL, 1835.*)

ISLE, 25*th March* 1789.

I HAVE stolen from my corn-sowing this minute to write a line to accompany your shirt and hat, for I can no more. Your sister Nannie arrived yesternight, and begs to be remembered to you. Write me every opportunity—never mind postage. My head too is as addle as an egg this morning with dining abroad yesterday. I received yours by the mason. Forgive this foolish-looking scrawl of an epistle. I am ever, my dear William, yours,   R. B.

---

* The MS. of this letter, framed and glazed, long hung in the " Traveller's Room " of the Red Lion Tavern, Shakespeare Square, Edinburgh. Our recollections of that matter date about 1839-40. The landlord's name was Fraser, and he had published a volume of short pieces in prose and verse. The whole locality, including the old Theatre Royal, is now occupied by the General Post Office.

P. S.—If you are not then gone from Longtown, I'll write you a long letter by this day se'ennight. If you shall not succeed in your tramps, don't be dejected, or take any rash step : return to us in that case, and we'll court Fortune's better humor. Remember this, I charge you.   R. B.

(⁵) MR. PETER HILL, BOOKSELLER, EDINBURGH.

(CURRIE in fragment, and completed DOUGLAS 1877.)*

ELLISLAND, *2d April* 1789.

I WILL make no excuses, my dear Bibliopolus, (God forgive me for murdering language !) that I have sat down to write you on this vile paper, stained with the sanguinary scores of "thae curs'd horse-leeches o' the Excise." It is economy, Sir ; it is that cardinal virtue, prudence : so I beg you will sit down, and either compose or borrow a panegyric : (if you are going to borrow, apply to our friend Ramsay† for the assistance of the author of those pretty little buttering paragraphs of eulogiums on your thrice-honored, and never-enough-to-be-praised, Magistracy—how they hunt down a housebreaker with the sanguinary perseverance of a blood-hound — how they out-do a terrier in a badger-hole, in unearthing a resetter of stolen goods —how they steal on a thoughtless troop of night-nymphs as a spaniel winds the unsuspecting covey— or how they riot over a ravaged bawdy-house as a cat does o'er a plundered mouse-nest—how they new-vamp old churches, aiming at appearances of piety ; plan squares and colleges, to pass for men of taste and

---

* By favor of George Wilson, Esq., a descendant of Mr. Peter Hill, we have been enabled to collate and correct the text from the original letter in his possession, and to insert here some interesting passages, hitherto suppressed.

† Mr. David Ramsay, of the "*Edinburgh Evening Courant.*"

learning, &c., &c., &c. ; while old Edinburgh, like
the doating mother of a parcel of rakehelly prodigals,
may sing "Hooly and Fairly," or cry, "Waes me that
e'er I saw ye!" but still must put her hand in her
pocket, and pay whatever scores the young dogs think
proper to contract.) I was going to say—but this
d—mn'd parenthesis has put me out of breath—that
you should get that manufacturer of the tinselled
crockery of magisterial reputations, who makes so
distinguished and distinguishing a figure in the *Ev.
Courant*, to compose, or rather to compound, some-
thing very clever on my remarkable frugality ; that I
write to one of my esteemed friends on this wretched
paper, which was originally intended for the venal fist
of some drunken exciseman, to take dirty notes in a
miserable vault of an ale-cellar.

O Frugality ! thou mother of ten thousand blessings
—thou cook of fat beef and dainty greens ! thou man-
ufacturer of warm Shetland hose, and comfortable
surtouts ! thou old housewife, darning thy decayed
stockings with thy ancient spectacles on thy aged
nose ! lead me, hand me in thy clutching palsied fist,
up those heights, and through those thickets, hitherto
inaccessible and impervious to my anxious, weary feet
—not those damn'd Parnassian crags, bleak and bar-
ren, where the hungry worshippers of fame are breath-
less, clambering, hanging between heaven and hell ;
but those glittering cliffs of Potosi, where the all-
sufficient, all-powerful deity, Wealth, holds his imme-
diate court of joys and pleasures ! where the sunny
exposure of Plenty, and the hot walls of Profusion,
produce those blissful fruits of Luxury, exotics in this
world, and natives of Paradise !—Thou withered sybil,
my sage conductress, usher me into the refulgent,
adored Presence !—The Power, splendid and potent as
he now is, was once the puling nursling of thy faith-
ful care, and tender arms ! Call me thy son, thy

cousin, thy kinsman, or favorite, and adjure the god
by the scenes of his infant years, no longer to repulse
me as a stranger or an alien, but to favor me with
his peculiar countenance and protection! He daily
bestows his greatest kindnesses on the undeserving
and the worthless—assure him, that I bring ample
documents of meritorious demerits! Pledge yourself
for me that for the glorious cause of LUCRE, I will do
any thing, be any thing—but the horse-leech of private
oppression, or the vulture of public robbery! ! ! !

But, to descend from heroics—what, in the name
of all the devils at once, have you done with my
trunk? Please let me have it by the first carrier,
except his name be Niven; he is a rascal who im-
posed, or would have imposed on me the other day
most infamously.

I want a Shakespeare: let me know what plays your
used copy of Bell's Shakespeare wants. I want like-
wise an English dictionary—Johnson's, I suppose, is
best. In these and all my *prose* commissions, the
cheapest is always the best for me. There is a small
debt of honor that I owe Mr. Robert Cleghorn, in
Saughton Mills, my worthy friend, and your well-
wisher: please give him, and urge him to take it,
the first time you see him, ten shillings' worth of any-
thing you have to sell, and place it to my account.

The library scheme that I mentioned to you is
already begun under the direction of Captⁿ. Riddell
and ME! There is another in emulation of it going
on at Closeburn, under the auspices of Mr. Menteith
of Closeburn, which will be on a greater scale than
ours. I have likewise secured it for you. Captⁿ. R.
gave his infant Society a great many of his old
books, else I had written you on that subject; but,
one of these days, I shall trouble you with a com-
mission for "The Monkland Friendly Society." A
copy of the *Spectator*, *Mirror*, *Lounger*; *Man of*

III.   R

Feeling, *Man of the World*, *Guthrie's Geographical Grammar*, with some religious pieces, will likely be our first order.

Write me first post, and send me the address of Stuart, publisher of the Star newspaper : this I beg particularly, but do not speak of it.* I'll expect along with the trunk, my Ainslie's map of Scotland ; and if you could send your boy to Mr. Beugo, Engraver; he has a picture of mine a-framing, which will be ready by this time. You see the freedom I take with you. Please direct any parcels to me to the care of Walter Auld, Saddler, Dumfries. When I grow richer, I will write to you on gilt-post, to make amends for this sheet. At present, every guinea has a five-guinea errand with, my dear Sir, your faithful, poor, but honest friend,   ROBᵀ. BURNS.

(By Stuart, I mean the famous Stuart who differed with the rest of the proprietors and set up by himself.)

(⁴) TO MR. WILLIAM BURNS, SADDLER,

CARE OF MR. WRIGHT, CARRIER, LONGTOWN.

(DR. WADDELL'S ED., 1849.)

ISLE, 15*th April* 1789.

MY DEAR WILLIAM,—I am extremely sorry at the misfortune of your legs ; I beg you will never let any worldly concern interfere with the more serious matter, the safety of your life and limbs. I have not time in these hurried days to write you anything other than a mere how d'ye letter. I will only repeat my favorite quotation :—

> "What proves the hero truly great
> Is never, never to despair."

---

* The poet's reason for wanting this address will presently appear in his next letter to Mrs. Dunlop.

My house shall be your welcome home ; and as I know your prudence (would to God you had *resolution* equal to your *prudence!*) if, anywhere at a distance from friends, you should need money, you know my direction by post.

The enclosed is from Gilbert, brought by your sister Nanny. It was unluckily forgot. Yours to Gilbert goes by post.—I heard from them yesterday, they are all well. Adieu,   R. B.

(5) TO MR. JAMES JOHNSON, BELL'S WYND, EDINBURGH.

(DOUGLAS, 1877.)*

ELLISLAND, 24*th April* 1789.

DEAR SIR,—My trunk was unaccountably delayed in Edin^r., and did not reach me till about ten days ago ; so I had not much time of your music. I have sent you a list that I approve of, but I beg and insist that you will never allow my opinion to overrule yours. I will write you more at large next post, as I, at present, have scarce time to subscribe myself, dear Sir, yours sincerely,   ROB^T. BURNS.

(1) TO MRS. M'MURDO, DRUMLANRIG.

(CUNNINGHAM, 1834.) †

ELLISLAND, 2*nd May*, 1789.

MADAM,—I have finished the piece which had the happy fortune to be honored with your approbation ; and never did little Miss, with more sparkling pleas-

---

* From the original MS. in the British Museum.
† The original MS. of this letter is now in the Collection of John Adams. Esq., Town Chamberlain, Greenock.

ure, show her applauded sampler to partial Mamma, than I now send my Poem to you and Mr. M'Murdo, if he is returned to Drumlanrig. You cannot easily imagine what thin-skinned animals—what sensitive plants poor Poets are. How do we shrink into the embittered corner of self-abasement, when neglected or contemned by those to whom we look up! and how do we, in erect importance, add another cubit to our stature on being noticed and applauded by those whom we honor and respect! My late visit to Drumlanrig has, I can tell you, Madam, given me a balloon waft up Parnassus, where on my fancied elevation I regard my poetic self with no small degree of complacency.*

Surely with all their sins, the rhyming tribe are not ungrateful creatures. I recollect your goodness to your humble guest—I see Mr. M'Murdo adding, to the politeness of the Gentleman, the kindness of a Friend, and my heart swells as it would burst, with warm emotions and ardent wishes! It may be it is not gratitude, at least it may be a mixed sensation. That strange, shifting, doubling animal MAN is so generally, at best but a negative, often a worthless creature, that one cannot see real Goodness and native Worth, without feeling the bosom glow with sympathetic approbation.—With every sentiment of grateful respect, I have the honor to be, Madam, your obliged and grateful, humble servant,

ROBT. BURNS.

---

* Mrs. M'Murdo was originally Jane Blair, a daughter of Provost Blair, of Dumfries. She died in 1836, at the age of 87. Her sister was the wife of Colonel De Peyster, who commanded the Dumfries Volunteers, while Burns was a member of that corps.

(²²) MRS. DUNLOP OF DUNLOP.

(CURRIE, 1800, and Dr. WADDELL, 1870.)

ELLISLAND, *4th May*,* 1789.

YOU see, Madam, that I am returned to my folio epistles again. I no sooner hit on any poetic plan or fancy, but I wish to send it to you ; and if knowing and reading them gives half the pleasure to you, that communicating them to you gives to me, I am satisfied.

As I am not devoutly attached to a certain monarch, I cannot say that my heart ran any risk of bursting, on Thursday was se'ennight, with the struggling emotions of gratitude. God forgive me for speaking evil of dignities ! but I must say that I look on the whole business as a solemn farce of fragrant mummery. The following are a few stanzas of new Psalmody for that "joyful solemnity," which I sent to a London newspaper with the date and preface following :—

(KILMARNOCK, 25 *April.*

MR. PRINTER,—In a certain chapel not fifty leagues from the market cross of this good town, the following Stanzas of Psalmody, it is said, were composed for, and devoutly sung on—the late joyful solemnity of the 23rd.

> O sing a new song to the L——,
> 　Make, all and every one.
> A joyful noise, even for the King
> 　His restoration, &c.—*See* page 59, *supra.*)

So much for Psalmody—You must know that the publisher of one of the most blasphemous party Lon-

---

* We have at page 60, *supra*, given our reason for holding that the month " April " in the MS is a mistake for *May.*

don newspapers is an acquaintance of mine, and as I am a little tinctured with Buff and Blue myself, I now and then help him to a stanza.

I have another poetic whim in my head, which I at present dedicate, or rather inscribe, to the Rt. Honble. Ch. J. Fox ; but how long that fancy may hold, I can't say. A few of the first lines I have just rough-sketched as follows :—

SKETCH.

How Wisdom and Folly meet, mix, and unite ;
How Virtue and Vice blend their black and their white, &c.
See page 61, *supra.*

I beg your pardon for troubling you with the enclosed to the Major's tenant before the gate ; it is to request him to look me out two milk cows ; one for myself, and another for Captain Riddell of Glenriddell, a very obliging neighbor of mine. John very obligingly offered to do so for me ; and I will either serve myself that way, or at Mauchline fair. It happens on the 20th curt., and the Sunday preceding it I hope to have the honor of assuring you in person how sincerely I am, Madam, your highly obliged and most obedient, humble servt.,   ROBT. BURNS.

(³) TO ALEXANDER CUNNINGHAM, ESQ.

(CURRIE, 1800.)

ELLISLAND, 4*th May* 1789.

YOUR *duty-free* favor of the 26th April I received two days ago ; I will not say I perused it with pleasure ; that is the cold compliment of ceremony ; I perused it, Sir, with delicious satisfaction. In short it is such a letter, that not you, nor your friend, but the legislature, by express proviso in their postage

laws, should frank.   A letter informed with the soul
of friendship is such an honor to human nature, that
they should order it free ingress and egress to and
from their bags and mails, as an encouragement and
mark of distinction to super-eminent virtue.

I have just put the last hand to a little poem which
I think will be something to your taste :—One morn-
ing lately, as I was out pretty early in the fields
sowing some grass seeds, I heard the burst of a shot
from a neighboring plantation, and presently a poor
little wounded hare came crippling by me.   You will
guess my indignation at the inhuman fellow who could
shoot a hare at this season, when they all of them
have young ones.   Indeed there is something in that
business of destroying for our sport individuals in the
animal creation that do not injure us materially, which
I could never reconcile to my ideas of virtue.

> Inhuman man! curse on thy barb'rous art,
>   And blasted be thy murder-aiming eye! &c.
> *See* page 64, *supra*.

Let me know how you like my poem.   I am doubtful
whether it would not be an improvement to keep out
the last stanza but one altogether.

Cruickshank is a glorious production of the Author
of man.   You, he, and the noble Colonel of the
Crochallan Fencibles are, to me

> "Dear as the ruddy drops that warm my breast." *

I have a good mind to make verses on you all, to the
tune of "Three gude fellows ayont the glen."

R. B.

---

* " As dear to me as are the ruddy drops
  That visit my sad heart."—*Julius Cæsar.*

(⁵) TO MR. WILLIAM BURNS,

SADDLER, NEWCASTLE-ON-TYNE.

(DR. WADDELL'S ED., 1869.)

ELLISLAND, 5th May, 1789.

MY DEAR WILLM.,—I am happy to hear by yours from Newcastle, that you are getting some employ. Remember,

"On Reason build Resolve,
That column of true majesty in man."

I had a visit of your old landlord. In the midst of a drunken frolic in Dumfries, he took it into his head to come and see me ; and I took all the pains in my power to please and entertain the old veteran. He is high in your praises, and I would advise you to cultivate his friendship, as he is, in his way, a worthy, and to you may be, a useful man.

Anderson I hope will have your shoes ready to send by the waggon to-morrow. I forgot to mention the circumstance of making them pumps ; but I suppose good calf shoes will be no great mistake. Wattie has paid me for the thongs.

What would you think of making a little inquiry how husbandry matters go, as you travel, and if one thing fail, you might try another ?

Your falling in love is indeed a phenomenon. To a fellow of your turn it cannot be hurtful. I am, you know, a veteran in these campaigns, so let me advise you always to pay your particular assiduities and try for intimacy as soon as you feel the first symptoms of passion ; this is not only best, as making the most of the little entertainment which the sportabilities of distant addresses always give, but is the best preservative for one's place. I need not caution

you against guilty amours—they are bad everywhere,
but in England they are the devil. I shall be in
Ayrshire about a fortnight. ·Your sisters send their
compliments. God bless you !

ROBERT BURNS.

(⁴) TO ROBERT GRAHAM, ESQ.

(CHAMBERS, 1856.)

ELLISLAND, 13th May 1789.

SIR,—Though I intend making a little manuscript-
book of my unpublished poems for Mrs. Graham, yet
I cannot forbear in the meantime sending her the
enclosed, which was the production of the other day.
In the plea of humanity, the ladies, to their honor be
it spoken, are ever warmly interested. That is *one*
reason of my troubling you with this ; another motive
I have is a hackneyed subject in my letters to you—
God help a poor devil who carries about with him a
load of gratitude, of which he can never hope to ease
his shoulders but at the expense of his heart ! I
waited on Collector Mitchell with your letter. It
happened to be collection-day, so he was very busy ;
but he received me with the utmost politeness, and
made me promise to call on him soon. As I don't
wish to degrade myself to a hungry rook, gaping for
a morsel, I shall just give him a hint of my wishes.
I am going on with a bold hand in my farm, and am
certain of holding it with safety for three or four
years ; and I think, if some cursed malevolent star
have not taken irremovable possession of my zenith,
that your patronage and my own priority then as an
expectant, should run a fair chance for the division I
want. By the bye, the Excise instructions you men-
tioned were not in the bundle ; but 'tis no matter ;
Marshall in his *Yorkshire*, and particularly that extra-

ordinary man, Smith, in his *Wealth of Nations*, find
me leisure employment enough. I could not have
given any mere *man* credit for half the intelligence
Mr. Smith discovers in his book. I would covet much
to have his ideas respecting the present state of some
quarters of the world that are, or have been, the scenes
of considerable revolutions since his book was written.
Though I take the advantage of your goodness, and
presume to send you any new poetic thing of mine, I
must not tax you with answers to each of my idle
letters. I remember you talked of being this way
with my honored friend, Sir William Murray, in the
course of this summer. You cannot imagine, Sir,
how happy it would make me, should you, too, illu-
minate my humble domicile. You will certainly do
me the honor to partake of a farmer's dinner with
me. I shall promise you a piece of good old beef, a
chicken, or perhaps a Nith salmon, fresh from the
wear, and a glass of good punch, on the shortest no-
tice ; and allow me to say that Cincinnatus or Fabri-
cius, who presided in the august Roman senate, and
led their invincible armies, would have jumped at
such a dinner. I expect your honors with a kind
of enthusiasm. I shall mark the year, and mark the
day, and hand it down to my children's children, as
one of the most distinguished honors of their an-
cestor.

I have the honor to be, with sincerest gratitude,
your obliged and very humble servant,

ROBT. BURNS.

(⁶) TO MR. RICHARD BROWN, PORT GLASGOW.

(DR. WALKER'S ED., 1811.)

MAUCHLINE, 21st *May* 1789

MY DEAR FRIEND,—I was in the country by acci-
dent, and hearing of your safe arrival, I could not
resist the temptation of wishing you joy on your
return — wishing you would write to me before you
sail again — wishing you would always set me down
as your bosom-friend—wishing you long life and pros-
perity, and that every good thing may attend you—
wishing Mrs. Brown and your little ones as free of
the evils of this world, as is consistent with humanity
—wishing you and she were to make two at the en-
suing lying-in, with which Mrs. B. threatens very
soon to favor me—wishing I had longer time to write
to you at present ; and, finally, wishing that, if there
is to be another state of existence, Mrs. Brown, Mrs.
Burns, our little ones of both families, and you and
I, in some snug retreat, may make a jovial party to
all eternity !

My direction is at Ellisland, near Dumfries.—Yours,

R. B.

(¹) MR. JAMES HAMILTON, GROCER, GLASGOW.

(CROMEK, 1808.)

ELLISLAND, 26th *May* 1789.

DEAR SIR,—I send you by John Glover, carrier,
the above account for Mr. Turnbull, as I suppose
you know his address.

I would fain offer, my dear Sir, a word of sympathy
with your misfortunes ; but it is a tender string, and

I know not how to touch it.   It is easy to flourish a
set of high-flown sentiments on the subject that would
give great satisfaction to—a breast quite at ease ; but
as ONE observes who was very seldom mistaken in
the theory of life, "The heart knoweth its own sor-
rows, and a stranger intermeddleth not therewith."

Among some distressful emergencies that I have
experienced in life, I have ever laid this down as my
foundation of comfort—That he who has lived the
life of an honest man has by no means lived in vain.

With every wish for your welfare and future suc-
cess.—I am, my dear Sir, sincerely yours,

ROB^T. BURNS.

(⁴) TO MR. WILLIAM CREECH, ESQ.*

(CURRIE, 1800.)

† ELLISLAND, 30*th May*, 1789.

SIR, I had intended to have troubled you with a
long letter, but at present the delightful sensations
of an omnipotent toothache so engross all my inner
man, as to put it out of my power even to write non-
sense.   However, as in duty bound, I approach my
bookseller with an offering in my hand—a few poetic
clinches, and a song.   To expect any other kind of offer-
ing from the Rhyming Tribe would be to know them
much less than you do.   I do not pretend that there is
much merit in these *morceaux*, but I have two reasons
for sending them : *primo*, they are mostly ill-natured,
so are in unison with my present feelings, while fifty
troops of infernal spirits are driving post from ear to
ear along my jaw bones ; and *secondly*, they are so
short, that you cannot leave off in the middle, and so
hurt my pride in the idea that you found any work
of mine too heavy to get through.

---

* Inclosing some poetry.
† See 30th May 1795. This letter repeated.

I have a request to beg of you, and I not only beg of you, but conjure you, by all your wishes and by all your hopes, that the muse will spare the satiric wink in the moment of your foibles : that she will warble the song of rapture round your hymeneal couch ; and that she will shed on your turf the honest tear of elegiac gratitude ! Grant my request as speedily as possible — send me by the very first fly or coach for this place three copies of the last edition of my poems, which place to my account.

Now may the good things of prose, and the good things of verse, come among thy hands, until they be filled with the *good things of this life*, prayeth

R. B.

(⁷) TO GAVIN HAMILTON, ESQ.

(CROMEK, 1808.)

[ELLISLAND, June 1789.*]

MY DEAR SIR,—It is indeed with the highest pleasure that I congratulate you on the return of days of ease, and nights of pleasure, after the horrid hours of misery in which I saw you suffering exist-ence when last in Ayrshire ; I seldom pray for any-body, "I'm baith dead-swear and wretched ill o't ;" but most fervently do I beseech the Power that

---

* This is the last letter that has been preserved of the series addressed to our author's early friend and patron. Cromek introduced it without date, excepting that he heads it "Dumfries," suggesting an improbable date, seeing the text alludes to Hamilton's "habits of intimacy with Father Auld." That "Boanerges of the gospel" died on 13th December 1791, before the Dumfries period of the poet's career had well begun ; so that an earlier date must be found for this letter. Cunningham coolly dates it "Edinburgh, December 1787," and marks it as "now published for the first time in the correspondence of Burns." Chambers has adopted Cunningham's date without remark, and it fits very awkwardly at that period. We have little hesitation in assigning this as the time it was written, shortly after the poet's return to Ellisland from a visit to Ayrshire. In a few weeks thereafter, Burns composed "The Kirk's Alarm," some stanzas of which he sent to Hamilton, as we learn from the poet's letter to John Logan, 7th August 1789.

directs the world, that you may live long and be happy, but live no longer than you are happy. It is needless for me to advise you to have a reverend care of your health. I know you will make it a point never at one time to drink more than a pint of wine (I mean an English pint), and that you will never be witness to more than one bowl of punch at a time, and that cold drams you will never more taste ; and above all things, I am convinced that after drinking perhaps boiling punch, you will never mount your horse and gallop home in a chill, late hour.

Above all things, as I understand you are in the habit of intimacy with that Boanerges of Gospel powers, Father Auld, be earnest with him that he will wrestle in prayer for you, that you may see the vanity of vanities in trusting to, even practising the carnal moral works of charity, humanity, generosity, and forgiveness of things, which you practised so flagrantly that it was evident you delighted in them, neglecting, or perhaps profanely despising the wholesome doctrine of *faith without works*, the only means of salvation. A hymn of thanksgiving would, in my opinion be highly becoming from you at present, and in my zeal for your well-being, I earnestly press on you to be diligent in chaunting over the two enclosed pieces of sacred poesy.

My best compliments to Mrs. Hamilton and Miss Kennedy.—Yours in the Lord.   ROBT. BURNS.

(¹) TO MR. JOHN M'AULEY, DUMBARTON.

(CURRIE, 1800.)

ELLISLAND, *4th June*, 1789.

DEAR SIR,—Though I am not without my fears respecting my fate at that grand, universal inquest of right and wrong, commonly called *The Last Day*, yet

I trust there is one sin which that arch-vagabond, Satan, who I understand is to be king's evidence, cannot throw in my teeth—I mean ingratitude. There is a certain pretty large quantum of kindness for which I remain, and from inability, I fear must still remain, your debtor ; but though unable to repay the debt, I assure you, Sir, I shall ever warmly remember the obligation. It gives me the sincerest pleasure to hear by my old acquaintance, Mr. Kennedy,* that you are, in immortal Allan's language, " Hale, and weel, and living ;" and that your charming family are well, and promising to be an amiable and respectable addition to the company of performers, whom the Great Mana-ger of the Drama of Man is bringing into action for the succeeding age.

With respect to my welfare, a subject in which you once warmly and effectively interested yourself, I am here in my old way, holding my plough, marking the growth of my corn, or the health of my dairy ; and at times sauntering by the delightful windings of the Nith, on the margin of which I have built my humble domicile, praying for seasonable weather, or holding an intrigue with the Muses ; the only gypseys with whom I have now any intercourse. As I am entered into the holy state of matrimony, I trust my face is turned completely Zion-ward ; and as it is a rule with all honest fellows to repeat no grievances, I hope that the little poetic licences of former days will, of course, fall under the oblivious influence of some good-natured statute of celestial prescription. In my family devo-tion, which, like a good Presbyterian, I occasionally

---

* This was, in all likelihood, Mr. John Kennedy, the poet's correspondent of 1786, who seems about this period to have removed from his employment at Dumfries House, to a similar occupation on the estate of the Earl of Breadal-bane, where he continued for 18 years. His headstone in the Old Calton at Edinburgh, records that he died 19th June 1812, aged 55. Mr. John M'Auley was a writer in Dumbarton, who would appear to have entertained Burns while returning from his Inverary tour.

give to my household folks, I am extremely fond of
the psalm, "Let not the errors of my youth," &c., and
that other, "Lo, children are God's heritage;" &c.,
in which last, Mrs. Burns—who by the by, has a
glorious "wood-note wild," at either old song or
psalmody—joins me with the pathos of Handel's Mes-
siah.   R. B.

(12) TO MR. ROBERT AINSLIE, EDINBURGH.

(CROMEK, 1808.)

ELLISLAND, 8th June 1789.

MY DEAR FRIEND,—I am perfectly ashamed of my-
self when I look at the date of your last. It is not
that I forget the friend of my heart and the companion
of my peregrinations; but I have been condemned to
drudgery beyond sufferance, though not, thank God,
beyond redemption. I have had a collection of poems
by a lady put into my hands to prepare them for the
press; * which horrid task, with sowing corn with my
own hand, a parcel of masons, wrights, plasterers, &c.,
to attend to, roaming on business through Ayrshire—
all this was against me, and the very first dreadful
article was of itself too much for me.

13th. I have not had a moment to spare from in-
cessant toil since the 8th. Life, my dear Sir, is a
serious matter. You know by experience that a
man's individual self is a good deal; but believe me,
a wife and family of children, whenever you have
the honor to be a husband and a father, will show
you that your present and most anxious hours of soli-
tude are spent on trifles. The welfare of those who

---

* We suspect that the reference here is to a parcel of poems, and particularly
a very long one by Helen Maria Williams, on "The Slave Trade," which were
sent to him from London, to peruse and criticise. He performed his task and
sent his remarks to that lady about the end of July: his letter and review will
be given in course.

are very dear to us, whose only support, hope and
stay we are—this, to a generous mind, is another sort
of more important object of care than any concerns
whatever which centre merely in the individual.   On
the other hand, let no young, unmarried, rakehelly
dog among you, make a song of his pretended liberty
and freedom from care.   If the relations we stand in
to king, country, kindred, and friends, be anything
but the visionary fancies of dreaming metaphysicians ;
if religion, virtue, magnanimity, generosity, humanity,
and justice, be aught but empty sounds ; then the
man who may be said to live only for others, for the
beloved, honorable female whose tender faithful em-
brace endears life, and for the helpless little innocents
who are to be the men and women, the worshippers
of his God, the subjects of his king, and the support,
nay the very vital existence of his COUNTRY, in the
ensuing age ;—compare such a man with any fellow
whatever, who, whether he bustle and push in busi-
ness among laborers, clerks, statesmen ; or whether
he roar and rant, and drink and sing in taverns—a
fellow over whose grave no one will breathe a single
heigh-ho, except from the cobweb tie of what is called
good-fellowship—who has no view nor aim but what
terminates in himself—if there be any grovelling
earthborn wretch of our species, a renegado to com-
mon sense, who would fain believe that the noble
creature Man is no better than a sort of fungus, gen-
erated out of nothing, nobody knows how, and soon
dissipating in nothing, nobody knows where ; such a
stupid beast, such a crawling reptile, might balance
the foregoing exaggerated comparison, but no one else
would have the patience.

Forgive me, my dear Sir, for this long silence. *To
make you amends*, I shall send you soon, and (more
encouraging still, without any postage) one or two
rhymes of my later manufacture.   R. B.

III.   S

(²³) TO MRS. DUNLOP, OF DUNLOP.

(CURRIE, 1800.)

ELLISLAND, 21st June 1789.

DEAR MADAM,—Will you take the effusions, the miserable effusions of low spirits, just as they flow from their bitter spring. I know not of any particular cause for this worst of all my foes besetting me, but for some time my soul has been beclouded with a thickening atmosphere of evil imaginations and gloomy presages. . . . .

Monday Evening.

I have just heard Mr. Kilpatrick give a sermon. He is a man famous for his benevolence, and I revere him ; but from such ideas of my Creator, good Lord deliver me ! Religion, my honored friend, is surely a simple business, as it equally concerns the ignorant and the learned, the poor and the rich. That there is an incomprehensible Great Being, to whom I owe my existence, and that he must be intimately acquainted with the operations and progress of the internal machinery, and consequent outward deportment of this creature which he has made ; these are, I think, self-evident propositions. That there is a real and eternal distinction between virtue and vice, and consequently, that I am an accountable creature ; that from the seeming nature of the human mind, as well as from the evident imperfection, nay, positive injustice, in the administration of affairs, both in the natural and moral worlds, there must be a retributive scene of existence beyond the grave ; must, I think, be allowed by every one who will give himself a moment's reflection. I will go farther, and affirm, that from the sublimity, excellence, and purity of his doctrine and precepts, unparalleled by all the aggregated wisdom and learning of many preceding ages, though, *to appearance*, he himself was the obscurest and most illiterate of our species ; therefore, Jesus Christ was from God.   *   *   *   *

Whatever mitigates the woes, or increases the happiness of others, this is my criterion of goodness ; and whatever injures society at large, or any individual in it, this is my measure of iniquity.

What think you, Madam, of my creed ?   I trust that I have said nothing that will lessen me in the eye of one, whose good opinion I value almost next to the approbation of my own mind.   R. B.

(¹) TO MISS H. M. WILLIAMS, LONDON.

(CURRIE, 1801.)*

ELLISLAND, [*July*] 1789.

MADAM,—Of the many problems in the nature of that wonderful creature, Man, this is one of the most extraordinary, that he shall go on from day to day, from week to week, from month to month, or perhaps from year to year, suffering a hundred times more in an hour from the impotent consciousness of neglecting what he ought to do, than the very doing of it would cost him.   I am deeply indebted to you first for a most elegant poetic compliment ;† then for a polite, obliging letter ; and, lastly, for your excellent poem on the Slave-Trade ; and yet, wretch that I am ! though the debts were debts of honor, and the creditor a lady, I have put off and put off even the

---

* Dr. Currie did not include this letter in his first edition, nor at all publish the poet's long critical observations on the Poem.   We first notice these in Chambers's edition 1852, and he does not say he copied them from the original MS., which is now or lately was in the possession of Mr. Francis Harvey, 4 St. James's Street, London.   It is thus endorsed :—"A few Strictures on Miss Williams's Poem on the Slave Trade."

† See Miss Williams' Sonnet on Burns, page 248, Vol. II.

very acknowledgment of the obligation, until you must indeed be the very angel I take you for, if you can forgive me.

Your poem I have read with the highest pleasure. I have a way, whenever I read a book, I mean a book in our own trade, Madam, a poetic one, and when it is my own property, that I take a pencil and mark at the end of verses, or note on margins and odd paper, little criticisms of approbation, or disapprobation as I peruse along. I will make no apology for presenting you with a few, unconnected thoughts that occurred to me in my repeated perusals of your poem. I want to show you that I have honesty enough to tell you what I take to be truths, even when they are not quite on the side of approbation ; and I do it in the firm faith, that you have equal greatness of mind to hear them with pleasure.

I know very little of scientific criticism ; so all I can pretend to in that intricate art, is merely to note as I read along, what passages strike me as being uncommonly beautiful, and where the expression seems to be perplexed or faulty.

The poem opens finely. There are none of those idle prefatory lines which one may skip over before one comes to the subject ; verses 9th and 10th in particular :—

——— "where ocean's unseen bound,
Leaves a drear world of waters round,"

are truly beautiful. The simile of the hurricane is likewise fine ; and, indeed, beautiful as the poem is, almost all the similes rise decidedly above it. From verse 31st to verse 50th is a pretty eulogy on Britain. Verse 36th, "That foul drama deep with wrong," is nobly expressive. Verse 46th, I am afraid, is rather unworthy of the rest ; "to dare to feel" is an idea that I do not altogether like. The contrast of valor and mercy, from the 46th verse to the 50th, is admirable.

Either my apprehension is dull, or there is something a little confused in the apostrophe to Mr. Pitt. Verse 55th is the antecedent to verses 57th and 58th, but in verse 58th the connexion seems ungrammatical :—

> " Powers   .   .   .   .
>
>   .   .   .   .   .
>   With no gradations mark'd their flight,
>   But rose at once to glory's height "—

ris'n should be the word instead of rose. Try it in prose, Powers,—their flight marked by no gradations, but (the same powers) risen at once to the height of glory. Likewise, verse 53d, "For this," is evidently meant to lead on the sense of the verses 59th, 60th, 61st, and 62nd : but let us try how the thread of connexion runs,—

> " For this   .   .   .   .
>
>   .   .   .   .
>   The deeds of mercy, that embrace
>   A distant sphere, an alien race,
>   Shall virtue's lips record and claim
>   The fairest honors of thy name."

I beg pardon if I misapprehend the matter, but this appears to me the only imperfect passage in the poem. The comparison of the sunbeam is fine.

The compliment to the Duke of Richmond is, I hope, as just as it is certainly elegant. The thought,

> " Virtue .   .   .   .   .
>
>   .   .   .   .
>   Sends, from her unsullied source,
>   The gems of thought in purest force,

is exceedingly beautiful. The idea, from verse 81st to the 85th, that the "blest decree" is like the beams of morning ushering in the glorious day of liberty, ought not to pass unnoticed or unapplauded. From verse 85th to verse 108th, is an animated contrast between the unfeeling selfishness of the oppressor on the one hand, and the misery of the captive on the other. Verse 88th might perhaps be amended thus : "Nor ever *quit* her narrow maze." We are said to *pass* a bound, but we *quit* a maze. Verse 100th is exquisitely beautiful :—

"They, whom wasted blessings tire."

Verse 110th is, I doubt, a clashing of metaphors; "to load a span" is, I am afraid, an unwarrantable expression. In verse 114th, "Cast the universe in shade," is a fine idea. From the 115th verse to the 142nd is a striking description of the wrongs of the poor African. Verse 120th, "The load of unremitted pain," is a remarkable, strong expression. The address to the advocates for abolishing the slave-trade, from verse 143rd to verse 208th is animated with the true life of genius. The picture of oppression,—

"While she links her impious chain,
And calculates the price of pain;
Weighs agony in sordid scales,
And marks if life or death prevails,"—

is nobly executed.

What a tender idea is in verse 180th ! Indeed, that whole description of home may vie with Thomson's description of home, somewhere in the beginning of his "Autumn." I do not remember to have seen a stronger expression of misery than is contained in these verses :—

"Condemned, severe extreme, to live
When all is fled that life can give:"

the comparison of our distant joys to distant objects is equally original and striking.

The character and manners of the dealer in the

infernal traffic is a well done, though a horrid picture.
I am not sure how far introducing the Sailor was
right ; for though the sailor's common characteristic is
generosity, yet in this case he is certainly not only an
unconcerned witness, but in some degree an efficient
agent in the business. Verse 224th is a nervous
. . . . expression—"The heart convulsive anguish
breaks." The description of the captive wretch when
he arrives in the West Indies is carried on with equal
spirit. The thought that the oppressor's sorrow on
seeing the slave pine, like the butcher's regret when
his lamb dies a natural death is exceedingly fine.

I am got so much into the cant of criticism, that I
begin to be afraid lest I have nothing except the cant
of it ; and instead of elucidating my author, am only
benighting myself. For this reason, I will not pretend
to go through the whole poem. Some few remaining
beautiful lines, however, I cannot pass over. Verse
280th is the strongest description of selfishness I ever
saw. The comparison in verse 285th and 286th is
new and fine ; and the line, "Your arms to penury
you lend" is excellent.

In verse 317th, "like" should certainly be "as"
or "so ;" for instance :—

> "His sway the harden'd bosom leads
> To cruelty's remorseless deeds ;
> As (or so) the blue lightning when it springs,
> With fury on its livid wings,
> Darts on the goal with rapid force,
> Nor heeds that ruin marks its course."

If you insert the word "*like*" where I have placed
"as," you must alter "darts" to *darting*, and "heeds"
to *heeding*, in order to make it grammar. A tempest
is a favorite subject with the poets, but I do not
remember anything, even in Thomson's "Winter,"
superior to your verses from the 347th to the 351st.
Indeed, the last simile, beginning with "Fancy may

dress," &c., and ending with the 350th verse, is, in my opinion, the most beautiful passage in the poem : it would do honor to the greatest names that ever graced our profession.

I will not beg your pardon, Madam, for these strictures, as my conscience tells me that for once in my life I have acted up to the duties of a Christian, in doing as I would be done by.

I had lately the honor of a letter from Dr. Moore, where he tells me that he has sent me some books : they are not yet come to hand, but I hear they are on the way.

Wishing you all success in your progress in the path of fame, and that you may equally escape the danger of stumbling through incautious speed, or losing ground through loitering neglect, I have the honor to be, &c.   R. B.

Miss Williams, in a short letter dated 7th August 1789, acknowledged Burns's communication, admitting that his criticism is a very flattering proof that her poem had been read with attention. She added thus :—"A much less portion of applause from *you* would have been gratifying to me, since I think its value depends entirely upon the source from whence it proceeds—the incense of praise, like other incense, is more grateful from the quality than the quantity of the odor."

This authoress first attracted public notice by her "Ode on the Peace," namely the Peace that was brought about by the Earl of Shelburne, afterwards Marquis of Lansdowne.

She afterwards wrote in favor of the savage anarchy which prevailed in France, from the summer of 1789, onwards till the Republic merged into a military Empire. She walked without horror over the ground at the Tuilleries when it was strewed with the naked bodies of the Swiss Guards.

Miss Williams, like many other early enthusiastic approvers of the French Revolution, afterwards altered her opinions very considerably. She died in 1828, aged 65.

(⁵) TO ROBERT GRAHAM, ESQ., OF FINTRY.

(CHAMBERS, 1856.)

ELLISLAND, 31st July 1789.

SIR,—The language of gratitude has been so prostituted by servile adulation and designing flattery, that I know not how to express myself when I would acknowledge the receipt of your last letter.   I beg and hope, ever-honored

"Friend of my life! *true patron of my rhymes,*"

that you will always give me credit for the sincerest, chastest gratitude !   The callous hypocrite may be louder than I in his grateful professions—professions which he never felt ; or the selfish heart of the covetous may pocket the bounties of beneficence with more rejoicing exultation ; but for the brimful eye, springing from the ardent throbbings of an honest bosom, at the goodness of a kindly active benefactor and politely generous friend, I dare call the Searcher of hearts and Author of all goodness to witness how truly these are mine to you.

Mr. Mitchell * did not wait my calling on him, but sent me a kind letter, giving me a hint of the business, and on my waiting on him yesterday, he entered with the most friendly ardor into my views and interests.   He seems to think, and from my own private knowledge I am certain he is right, that removing the officer who now does, and for these many years has done, duty in the division in the middle of which I live, will be productive of at least no disadvantage to the revenue, and may likewise be done without any detriment to him.   Should the Honorable Board

---

* Collector Mitchell, to whom the poet addressed a poetic epistle in December 1795.

think so, and should they deem it eligible to appoint
me to officiate in his present place, I am then at the
top of my wishes. The emoluments of my office will
enable me to carry on and enjoy these improvements
in my farm, which, but for this additional assistance,
I might in a year or two have abandoned. Should it
be judged improper to place me in this division, I
am deliberating whether I had not better give up my
farming altogether, and go into the Excise whenever
I can find employment. Now that the salary is £50
per annum, the Excise is surely a much superior ob-
ject to a farm, which, without some foreign assistance,
must, for half a lease, be a losing bargain. The
worst of it is I know there are some respectable char-
acters who do me the honor to interest themselves in
my welfare and behavior, and as leaving the farm so
soon may have an unsteady, giddy-headed appearance,
I had perhaps better lose a little money than hazard
such people's esteem.

You see, Sir, with what freedom I lay before you
all my little matters—little indeed to the world, but
of the most important magnitude to me. You are so
good, that I trust I am not troublesome. [I have
heard and read a good deal of Philanthropy, Benevo-
lence, and Greatness of soul, and when rounded with
the flourish of declamatory periods, or poured in the
mellifluence of Parnassian measure, they have a toler-
able effect on a musical ear; but when these high-
sounding professions are compared with the very act
and deed as it is usually performed, I do not think
there is any thing in or belonging to Human Nature
so badly disproportionate. In fact, were it not for a
very few of our kind (among whom an honored friend
of mine, that to you Sir, I will not name, is a dis-
tinguished instance), the very existence of Magna-
nimity, Generosity, and all their kindred virtues,
would be as much a question with metaphysicians as

the existence of Witchcraft.]* Perhaps the nature of man is not so much to blame for all this, as the situation in which, by some miscarriage or other, he is placed in this world. The poor, naked, helpless wretch, with such voracious appetites and such a famine of provision for them, is under a cursed necessity of turning selfish in his own defence. Except here and there a *scelerat* who seems to be a scoundrel from the womb of original Sin, thorough-paced selfishness is always the work of time. Indeed, in a little time, we generally grow so attentive to ourselves, and so regardless of others, that I have often in poetic frenzy looked on this world as one vast ocean, occupied and commoved by innumerable vortices, each whirling round its centre, which vortices are the children of men ; and that the great design and merit, if I may say so, of every particular vortex consists in how wide it can extend the influence of its circle, and how much floating trash it can suck in and absorb.†

I know not why I have got into this preaching vein, except it be to show you, Sir, that it is not any ignorance, but my knowledge of mankind which makes me so much admire your goodness to your humble servant.

I hope this will find my amiable young acquaintance, John, recovered from his indisposition, and all the members of your charming fireside circle well and happy. I am sure I am anxiously interested in all your welfares ; I wish it with all my soul ; nay, I believe I sometimes catch myself praying for it. I am not impatient of my own impotence under that

---

* The portion within square brackets is found in the poet's autograph in the British Museum, transcribed on the back of a copy of " The Kirk's Alarm," and catalogued as "a fragment of some severe reflections on human kind." That " fragment " appears in Cromek's *Reliques*, page 370, first edition.

† On this subject of human selfishness, see letter to Ainslie, page 184, *supra :* also letter to Peter Hill, 2d March 1790.

immense debt which I owe to your goodness, but I
wish and beseech that BEING who has all good things
in His hands, to bless and reward you with all those
comforts and pleasures which He knows I would be-
stow on you, were they mine to give.

I shall return your books very soon. I only wish
to give Dr. Smith one other perusal, which I will do
in two or three days. I do not think that I must
trouble you for another cargo, at least for some time,
as I am going to apply to Leadbetter and Symons on
Gauging, and to study my sliding rule, Brannan's
rule, &c., with all possible attention.

An apology for the impertinent length of this epistle
would only add to the evil.—I have the honor to be,
Sir, your deeply indebted, humble serv^t.

ROB^r. BURNS.

(¹) TO MR. DAVID SILLAR, MERCHANT, IRVINE.

(DOUGLAS, 1877.*)

ELLISLAND, NEAR DUMFRIES, 5th Aug. 1789.

MY DEAR SIR,—I was half in thoughts not to have
written to you at all, by way of revenge for the two
d—d business letters you sent me. I wanted to know

---

* The above interesting letter we happened to stumble on, in course of turning
over the leaves of the early minute-book of the Irvine Burns Club, instituted in
1827. David Sillar, who was a member of the club, produced at one of its meet-
ings the original letter addressed to him, and by order of the meeting, it was
engrossed by their clerk in the records of the club. Had it not been for that
circumstance the letter in all likelihood, had been lost, for the autograph seems
not to have been preserved by Sillar's representatives. He died at Irvine in
1830, aged 70, having been born just one year after Burns. He had engaged in
the trade of a Grocer, which he changed for the profession of a Teacher; and
between his own savings and a windfall that came to him on the death of two
brothers who had been in a lucrative trade on the African coast, he amassed
considerable means. He was much sought after in consequence of his early
connexion with Burns; but so penurious had he grown that he refused to sub-
scribe to the fund for the bard's Doon Monument in 1820. His son Zachary
Sillar. M.D.. removed to Liverpool and long survived him.

The original Members of the Irvine Burns Club numbered twenty. and in-
cluded Dr. John Mackenzie, *Chairman;* David Sillar, *Croupier;* James Dobie,

all and about your Publication—what were your views, your hopes, fears, etc., etc., in commencing poet in print. In short, I wanted you to write to *Robin* like his old acquaintance *Davie;* and not in the style of Mr. Tare to Mr. Tret:—"Mr. Tret—Sir, This comes to advise you that fifteen barrels of herrings were, by the blessing of God, shipped safe on board the 'Lovely Janet,' Q. D. C., Duncan M'Leerie, master, etc., etc.''

I hear you have commenced married man—so much the better for it. I know not whether the Nine Gypsies are jealous of my Lucky; but they are a good deal shyer since I could boast the important relation of Husband.

I have got, I think, about eleven subscribers for your book. When you send Mr. Auld, in Dumfries, his copies, you may with them pack me eleven; should I need more, I can write you; should they be too many, they can be returned. My best compliments to Mrs. Sillar, and believe me to be, dear David, ever yours,   ROBᵀ. BURNS.

(⁵) TO [ROBERT AIKEN, ESQ., AYR.]

(CROMEK, 1808.)

[*Aug.* 1789.]

DEAR SIR,—Whether in the way of my trade, I can be of any service to the Rev. Doctor,* is I fear very

---

Writer, Beith; Dr. Zachary Sillar, Irvine; Patrick Blair, Writer; James Johnstone, Town Clerk; John Fletcher, Surgeon; Daniel Stewart, Rector of Irvine Academy; James Dick, Artist; &c., &c. Lieuᵗ. Charles Gray, R.N., joined the club in 1829. About ten years ago the club purchased the old tenement in which James Montgomery the poet, is said to have been born; we were shown a handsome silver drinking-cup, with two handles, which had been presented to the club, bearing this inscription, "M.DCCC.LXIX.—To the IRVINE BURNS CLUB, Mr. John Rhodes of Sheffield, presents this Drinking-Cup, to commemorate the purchasing by the club of the House in which James Montgomery, the Christian Poet, was born."

* The indignant execrations in this letter were immediately followed by production of "The Kirk's Alarm." in favor of Dr. Wm. M'Gill of Ayr, then under a charge of Heresy. The letter, unaddressed, was forwarded to Cromek by Pro-

doubtful. Ajax's shield consisted, I think, of seven bull hides and a plate of brass, which altogether set Hector's utmost force at defiance. Alas! I am not a Hector, and the worthy Doctor's foes are as securely armed as Ajax was. Ignorance, superstition, bigotry, stupidity, malevolence, self-conceit, envy—all strongly bound in a massy frame of brazen impudence. Good God, Sir! to such a shield, humor is the peck of a sparrow, and satire the pop-gun of a school-boy. Creation-disgracing *scelerats* such as they, God only can mend, and the Devil only can punish. In the comprehending way of Caligula, I wish they had all but one neck. I feel impotent as a child to the ardor of my wishes! O for a withering curse, to blast the germins of their wicked machinations. O for a poisonous Tornado, winged from the Torrid Zone of Tartarus, to sweep the spreading crop of their villainous contrivances to the lowest hell! R. B.

(²) TO JOHN LOGAN, ESQ., OF KNOCK-SHINNOCH.

(CUNNINGHAM, 1834.)

ELLISLAND, NEAR DUMFRIES,
7th August 1789.

DEAR SIR,—I intended to have written you long ere now, and, as I told you, I had gotten three stanzas and a half on my way in a poetic Epistle to you; but that old enemy of all "good works," the devil,

---

fessor Walker, who had been on intimate terms with Mr. Aiken, the legal defender of M'Gill in the church courts. Its style incurred the censure of Jeffrey in his review of Cromek's *Reliques*, regarding which Walker observed (in 1811) that " the critic's censure would perhaps have been softened, had he been aware that the 'tumidity' which he blames, was no serious attempt at fine writing, but merely a playful effusion in mock-heroic, to divert a friend whom he had formerly succeeded in diverting with similar sallies."

This letter must have been written to either Mr. Aiken or Gavin Hamilton. Chambers has misplaced it, and fastidiously suppressed the closing sentences.

threw me into a prosaic mire, and for the soul of me, I cannot get out of it. I dare not write you a long letter, as I am going to intrude on your time with a long ballad. I have, as you will shortly see, finished "The Kirk's Alarm;" but, now that it is done, and that I have laughed once or twice at the conceits in some of the stanzas, I am determined not to let it get into the public; so I send you this copy, the first that I have sent to Ayrshire (except some few of the stanzas which I wrote off in embryo for Gavin Hamilton), under the express provision and request that you will only read it to *a few of us*, and do not on any account give or permit to be taken, any copy of the ballad.

If I could be of any service to Dr. M'Gill, I would do it, though it should be at a much greater expense than irritating a few bigoted priests; but I am afraid serving him in his present *embarras* is a task too hard for me. I have enemies enow, God knows, though I do not wantonly add to the number. Still, as I think there is some merit in two or three of the thoughts, I send it you as a small, but sincere testimony how much, and with what respectful esteem, I am, dear Sir, your obliged, humble servant,

ROBᵀ. BURNS.

Mr. John Logan, of Knockshinnoch, as we find from a newspaper obituary, died at Ayr, on 9th March 1816. Dr. Wm. M'Gill died, 30th March 1807. In addition to our notes appended to the ballad called "The Kirk's Alarm," p. 85, *supra*, we here add from the notes of an Ayrshire clergyman who, although "in holy orders" at the close of last century, personally communicated the notes to Chambers in 1831. "Dr. M'Gill was a Socinian in principle, although not a disciple of Socinus, whose works he never read. In his personal and domestic character, he was a strange mixture of simplicity and stoicism. He seldom smiled, but often set the table in a roar by his quaint remarks. He was inflexibly regular in the distribution of his time: he studied so much every day, and took his exercise in the open air

at the same hour in all kinds of weather. His views of the
ordinary dispensations of Providence were widely different
from those of the bulk of society. On being told that an old
clergyman, an early companion of his own, had suddenly
expired on entering his pulpit to commence service, he clapped
his hands and said—'That was very desirable; he lived all
the days of his life.' The morning after a domestic calamity
in his own house, of the most harrowing kind, the devout
old pastor, to the surprise of his flock, officiated in church
with his usual serenity. He used to converse on self-murder
with the coolness of a Roman philosopher."

SONNET TO ROBT. GRAHAM, ESQ., OF FINTRY.

On receiving a Favor, 10th Aug. 1789.

> I call no goddess to inspire my strains;
> A fabled Muse may suit a Bard that feigns, &c.
> *See* page 93, *supra*.

This was an Impromptu on receiving intimation from Mr.
Graham that the Board of Excise had agreed to appoint
him Exciseman in the district of which his farm formed
nearly the centre. On 18th of same month his Jean presented
him with her first child born in wedlock, a boy, named
FRANCIS WALLACE, in compliment to Mrs. Dunlop, who bore
the same name. Not long before that event the new farm-
house was ready for occupancy, and the poet's household had
been transferred to it from the temporary residence at The Isle.
Betty Smith who was in service with Burns at the time used
to tell that she was desired by him to take the great Family
Bible, with a bowl of salt placed thereon in her arms, and
make sure that she was the first of the household to enter
the new house at the time of this flitting. Chambers says—
"this was the old *freit* appropriate to taking possession of
a new house, the object being to secure good-luck for the
inmates. The poet, like a man of imagination, delighted in
such ancient observances, albeit his understanding, on a rigid
tasking, would have denied the conclusions."
[In the Scots Magazine for August 1789, there is a notice
of the erection in Canongate Kirkyard of the tombstone pro-
vided by Burns, with its Inscription, executed 2 years and

a half after it had been ordered. The London newspapers had copied the notice, as may be inferred from the following letter from the poet to his friend Mr. Stuart, editor of *The Star*.]

(²) TO MR. PETER STUART, LONDON.

(CURRIE, 1800.)

August 1789.

My DEAR SIR,—The hurry of a farmer in this particular season, and the indolence of a poet at all times and seasons, will, I hope, plead my excuse for neglecting so long to answer your obliging letter of the 5th of August.

That you have done well in quitting your laborious concern in * * * * I do not doubt; the weighty reasons you mention were, I hope, very, and deservedly indeed, weighty ones, and your health is a matter of the last importance; but whether the remaining proprietors of the paper have also done well, is what I much doubt. The * * * * so far as I was a reader, exhibited such a brilliancy of point, such an elegance of paragraph, and such a variety of intelligence, that I can hardly conceive it possible to continue a daily paper in the same degree of excellence: but if there was a man who had abilities equal to the task, that man's assistance the proprietors have lost. * * *

When I received your letter I was transcribing for [the *Star*] my letter to the magistrates of the Canongate, Edinburgh, begging their permission to place a tomb-stone over poor Fergusson, and their edict in consequence of my petition; but now I shall send them to . . . Poor Fergusson! If there be a life beyond the grave, which I trust there is; and if there be a good God presiding over all nature, which I am sure there is — thou art now enjoying existence in a glorious world, where worth of the heart alone is distinction in the man; where riches, deprived of all

III.   T

their pleasure-purchasing powers, return to their native sordid matter ; where titles and honors are the disregarded reveries of an idle dream ; and where that heavy virtue, which is the negative consequence of steady dulness, and those thoughtless, though often destructive follies, which are the unavoidable aberrations of frail human nature, will be thrown into equal oblivion as if they had never been !

Adieu, my dear Sir ! So soon as your present views and schemes are concentrated in an aim, I shall be glad to hear from you ; as your welfare and happiness is by no means a subject indifferent to, yours,

R. B.

Mr Stuart's letter to Burns in 1789, contained some anecdotes of Fergusson the poet which Currie withheld. That biographer in a footnote, says, "These interesting anecdotes we should have been happy to insert, if they could have been authenticated." In the letter of 5th August 1789, Mr. Stuart thus refers to that poet—"I cannot express my happiness sufficiently at the instance of your attachment to my late inestimable friend, Bob Fergusson, who was particularly intimate with myself and relations. That Mr. Burns has surpassed him in the art of poetry, must readily be admitted; but notwithstanding many favorable representations, I am yet to learn that he inherits his convivial powers.

"There was such a richness of conversation, such a plenitude of fancy and attraction in him, that when I call the happy period of our intercourse to my memory. I feel myself in a state of delirium. I was younger than him by eight or ten years ; but his manner was so felicitous, that he enraptured every person around him, and infused into the hearts of young and old, the spirit and animation which operated in his own mind."

(⁶) TO MR. WILLIAM BURNS,

SADDLER, NEWCASTLE-ON-TYNE.

(DR. WADDELL'S ED., 1869.)

ELLISLAND, *14th Aug.* 1789.

MY DEAR WILLIAM,—I received your letter, and am very happy to hear that you have got settled for the winter. I enclose you the two guinea-notes of the Bank of Scotland, which I hope will serve your need. It is indeed not quite so convenient for me to spare money as it once was, but I know your situation, and, I will say it, in some respects your worth. I have no time to write at present, but I beg you will endeavor to pluck up a *little* more of the Man than you used to have. Remember my favorite quotation—

> "On reason build resolve,
> That column of true majesty in Man;"

> "What proves the Hero truly great
> Is never, never to despair."

Your mother and sisters * desire their compliments. —*A Dieu je vous commende,*   ROBᵗ BURNS. †

(²⁴) TO MRS. DUNLOP, OF DUNLOP.

(CURRIE, 1800.)

ELLISLAND, *6th Sep.* 1789.

DEAR MADAM,—I have mentioned in my last my appointment to the Excise, and the birth of the little Frank; who, by the bye, I trust will be no discredit

---

* The poet's mother had a double errand in coming to Ellisland at this period. She brought young *Robert* home, now about three years old, and she waited on Mrs. Burns during her confinement with Francis Wallace (born 18th August.)

† The original MS. was parted with by Mrs. Begg to a Mr. Forrest in Tranent, and after passing through various hands, it came into the possession of the widow of Dr. Burns, Toronto.

to the honorable name of Wallace, as he has a fine manly countenance, and a figure that might do credit to a little fellow two months older ; and likewise an excellent good temper, though when he pleases he has a pipe, only not quite so loud as the horn that his immortal namesake blew as a signal to take out the pin of Stirling bridge.

I had some time ago an epistle, part poetic, and part prosaic, from your poetess, Miss J. Little, a very ingenious, but modest composition. * I should have written her as she requested, but for the hurry of this new business. I have heard of her and her compositions in this country ; and I am happy to add, always to the honor of her character. The fact is, I know not well how to write to her : I should sit down to a sheet of paper that I knew not how to stain. I am no dab at fine-drawn letter-writing ; and, except when prompted by friendship or gratitude, or, which happens extremely rarely, inspired by the Muse (I know not her name) that presides over epistolary writing, I sit down, when necessitated to write, as I would sit down to beat hemp.

Some parts of your letter of the 20th August, struck me with the most melancholy concern for the state of your mind at present. * * *

Would I could write you a letter of comfort ! I

---

* Janet Little was a dairymaid then employed at Loudon Castle, at that time rented by Mrs. Henrie, a daughter of Mrs. Dunlop. She had read and appreciated the poems of Burns, and in a letter dated 12th July 1789, appended some complimentary stanzas, ten in number, of which we shall give one as a sample. In 1792, she was induced to publish a volume of her rhymes. She was a tall, masculine looking nymph with dark hair and coarse features. Eventually she married a widower, one John Richmond, who was a laborer on the Loudon property. She died in 1813, aged 54, and a tablet is placed over her remains, in the burial-ground at Loudon Kirk. The following is the verse on Burns :—

> Did Addison or Pope but hear,
> Or Sam, that critic most severe,
> A ploughboy sing with throat sae clear,
>   They in a rage
> Their Works would a' in pieces tear,
>   And curse their page.

would sit down to it with as much pleasure, as I would to write an epic poem of my own composition that should equal "The Iliad." Religion, my dear friend, is the true comfort! A strong persuasion in a future state of existence; a proposition so obviously probable, that, setting revelation aside, every nation and people, so far as investigation has reached, for at least near four thousand years, have, in some mode or other, firmly believed it. In vain would we reason and pretend to doubt. I have myself done so to a very daring pitch; but, when I reflected, that I was opposing the most ardent wishes, and the most darling hopes of good men, and flying in the face of all human belief, in all ages, I was shocked at my own conduct.

I know not whether I have ever sent you the following lines, or if you have ever seen them; but it is one of my favorite quotations, which I keep constantly by me in my progress through life, in the language of the book of Job,

"Against the day of battle and of war"—

spoken of religion:

"'Tis *this*, my friend, that streaks our morning bright,
'Tis *this* that gilds the horror of our night:
When wealth forsakes us, and when friends are few,
When friends are faithless, or when foes pursue;
'Tis this that wards the blow, or stills the smart,
Disarms affliction, or repels his dart;
Within the breast bids purest raptures rise,
Bids smiling conscience spread her cloudless skies."

I have been very busy with "Zeluco." * The Doctor is so obliging as to request my opinion on it;

---

* "Zeluco" was a novel by Dr. Moore, of some note in its day. It appeared in June 1789, and was reviewed in the Scots Magazine for August. It is a moral tale, designed to show the inevitable misery of Vice.
Burns's copy with pencil notes on its margins was presented to Mrs. Dunlop with an inscription, and was long preserved by her descendants. Unfortunately

and I have been revolving in my mind some kind of criticisms on novel-writing, but it is a depth beyond my research. I shall however digest my thoughts on the subject as well as I can. "Zeluco" is a most sterling performance.

Farewell! *A Dieu, le bon Dieu, je vous commende.*

R. B.

During the Summer and Autumn of this year, Burns had occasional meetings with Captain Grose at the convivial board of his friend, Mr. Robert Riddell, at Friars Carse. Some account of them will be found in connexion with the Poems at pp. 81 and 82, *supra*.

An equally notable event of the same season was that William Nicol and Allan Masterton, both of the High School, Edinburgh, came to reside in the poet's neighborhood, the former being in country quarters near Moffat to enjoy his vacations in angling excursions, and the latter was employed to give lessons in penmanship and music to the young ladies at Dalswinton. The three companions, Willie, Rab, and Allan, met over a "peck o' maut," well brewed and as well distilled, in Nicol's lodgings, and the result was the unmatched Bacchanalian Song, "O, Willie brew'd a peck o' maut," which is printed at page 97, *supra*.

Evidence exists to show that the song which celebrated the sederunt of those "three merry boys" near Moffat, immediately became popular at Friars Carse; the squire and his associates must often have made the rafters of his sitting parlor ring to the chorus—

> " We are na fou, we're na that fou,
>   But just a drappie in our e'e ;
> The cock may craw, the day may daw,
>   But ay we'll taste the barley bree."

That song indeed seems to have suggested a similar symposium in which the trio consisted of three gentlemen of quality, the main variation being that old claret was substituted for the "barley bree." of the humbler three merry boys. At the mansion of Squire Johnston of Cowhill, there met,

---

the 2nd volume was destroyed by ants in India ; the companion volume, the first, is still possessed by her great-grandson, Wallace Dunlop, C.B. The poet's notes are very scant. The inscription on fly-leaf, reads—" To my much esteemed Friend, Mrs. Dunlop, of Dunlop.   ROBT. BURNS."

probably as a small dinner-party, on 10th October 1789, six brethren in the same degree, who, under the inspiration of after-dinner libations (and perhaps after joining in the above chorus), resolved on a betting scheme to the following effect: —Sir Robert Laurie of Maxwelton, one of the company, possessed a noted ebony whistle, which an ancestor of his had won at a drinking-bout with a drunken Dane. It was now proposed that the present holder of the whistle, with Alexander Ferguson of Craigdarroch, should at Friars Carse join their relative, Robert Riddell of Glenriddell, six days thereafter; and there in presence of two chosen witnesses and an umpire, contend for the championship of the whistle. The terms laid down were, that the combatants must drink bottle for bottle of claret with each other, until victory should declare itself by two of their number becoming incapable of sounding the whistle, while the third continued able to do so. A memorandum of the Bet was drawn up on the spot, and signed by the three proposed contenders, and by Mr. John M'Murdo of Drumlanrig, the stipulated umpire, together with Messrs. Patrick Miller of Dalswinton and George Johnston of Cowhill as the witnesses. This premised, the following letter of Burns will explain itself.

(²) TO CAPTAIN RIDDELL, OF FRIARS CARSE.

(CROMEK, 1808.)

ELLISLAND, 16th Oct. 1789.

SIR,—Big with the idea of this important day at Friars Carse, I have watched the elements and skies, in the full persuasion that they would announce it to the astonished world by some phenomena of terrific portent. Yesternight until a very late hour did I wait with anxious horror, for the appearance of some Comet firing half the sky; or aerial armies of sanguinary Scandinavians, darting athwart the startled heavens, rapid as the ragged lightning, and horrid as those convulsions of nature that bury nations.

The elements, however, seem to take the matter very quietly: they did not even usher in this morning

with triple suns and a shower of blood, symbolical of
the three potent heroes, and the mighty claret-shed
of the day. For me, as Thomson, in his *Winter* says
of the storm—I shall "hear astonish'd, and astonish'd
sing"

> "The whistle and the man I sing;
> The man that won the whistle," &c.

> Here are we met, three merry boys,
> Three merry boys I trow are we;
> And mony a night we've merry been,
> And mony mae we hope to be.

> Wha first shall rise to gang awa,
> A cuckold coward loon is he;
> Wha *last* beside his chair shall fa'
> He is the king amang us three.

To leave the heights of Parnassus and come to the
humble vale of prose. I have some misgivings that I
take too much upon me, when I request you to get
your guest, Sir Robert Lawrie, to frank the two
enclosed covers for me, the one of them to Sir William
Cunningham, of Robertland, Bart., at Auchenskeith,
Kilmarnock—the other to Mr. Allan Masterton, Writing-
Master, Edinburgh. The first has a kindred claim on
Sir Robert, as being a brother Baronet, and likewise
a keen Foxite; the other is one of the worthiest men
in the world, and a man of real genius; so, allow me
to say, he has a fraternal claim on you. I want them
franked for to-morrow, as I cannot get them to the
post to-night. I shall send a servant again for them in
the evening. Wishing that your head may be crowned
with laurels to-night, and free from aches to-morrow,
I have the honor to be, Sir, your deeply indebted
humble servant,   R. B.

[We have said enough of the silly controversy about "real
presence" and "real absence" of the poet on that occasion, in
our notes to the ballad of "The Whistle," at page 114, *supra*.]

The precise date when Burns entered on actual practice as an officer of Excise can only be inferred from his correspondence. The first letter which notes the circumstance is that to Ainslie of 1st November 1789; and there he does not distinctly admit that he had commenced the duties, but says "I am now appointed to an Excise division," adding however these words: "you need not doubt that I find several very unpleasant and disagreeable circumstances in my business." Writing to Blacklock on 21st October, he says:—

> " I'm turned a Gauger—Peace be here !
> Parnassian queans, I fear, I fear,
> Ye'll now disdain me !
> And then my fifty pounds a year
> Will little gain me."

The Muses, however, did not disdain him when he composed his sublime address to " Mary in Heaven " about this very period. We are willing to adopt the popular belief that on the night before that anniversary of Mary's death, he wandered solitary on the banks of the Nith in the vicinity of his farm, " in the extremest agitation of mind nearly the whole night." As the approaching dawn wiped out the stars one by one, his eyes followed a particular planet which seemed to " linger with lessening ray " till it also disappeared. More than this we cannot know, and it is all plainly told in the lyric itself: the picture is sensational enough, and requires not to have anything added to it. We do not believe that Mrs. Burns ever divined the cause of his sadness, or knew any more of the history of that secret passion—probably she knew less—than is now patent to the world. There was, no doubt, good reason for the poet's mystifications regarding that passion: perhaps chiefly on Mrs. Burns's account he was willing to throw back into a visionary distance, what he could not well acknowledge as belonging to his mature life.

(13) TO MR. ROBERT AINSLIE, EDINBURGH.

(CROMEK, 1808.)

ELLISLAND, 1st Nov. 1789.

MY DEAR FRIEND,—I had written you long ere now, could I have guessed where to find you, for I am sure you have more good sense than to waste precious days of vacation-time in the dirt of business in Edinburgh. Wherever you are God bless you, and lead you not into temptation, but deliver you from evil !

I do not know if I have informed you that I am now appointed to an Excise division, in the middle of which my house and farm lie. In this I was extremely lucky. Without ever having been an expectant, as they call their journeymen excisemen, I was directly planted down to all intents and purposes an officer of Excise, there to flourish and bring forth fruits—worthy of repentance.

I know how the word "exciseman," or still more opprobrious "gauger," will sound in your ears. I too have seen the day when my auditory nerves would have felt very delicately on this subject : but a wife and children are things which have a wonderful power in blunting these kind of sensations. Fifty pounds a year for life, and a provision for widows and orphans, you will allow is no bad settlement for a *poet*. For the ignominy of the profession, I have the encouragement which I once heard a recruiting serjeant give to a numerous, if not a respectable audience, in the streets of Kilmarnock,—"Gentlemen, for your further and better encouragement, I can assure you that our regiment is the most blackguard corps under the crown, and consequently, with us an honest fellow has the surest chance for preferment." *

You need not doubt that I find several very unpleasant and disagreeable circumstances in my business ; but I am tired with and disgusted at the language of complaint against the evils of life. Human existence in the most favorable situations does not abound with pleasures, and has its incon-

---

* Burns elsewhere observes that he would have "some wayward feelings about appearing, simply as a gauger, in a part of the country where he is only known to fame as a poet."

veniences and ills; capricious foolish man mistakes
these inconveniences and ills, as if they were the
peculiar property of his particular situation; and
hence that eternal fickleness, that love of change,
which has ruined, and daily does ruin many a fine
fellow, as well as many a blockhead; and is almost,
without exception, a constant source of disappoint-
ment and misery. So far from being dissatisfied with
my present lot, I earnestly pray the Great Disposer
of events that it may never be worse, and I think I
can lay my hand on my heart and say " I shall be
content?"

I long to hear from you how you go on — not so
much in business as in life. Are you pretty well
satisfied with your own exertions, and tolerably at
ease in your internal reflections? 'Tis much to be a
great character as a lawyer, but beyond comparison
more to be a great character as a man.

That you may be both the one and the other is
the earnest wish — and that you will be both, is the
firm persuasion of, my dear Sir, &c.　　　R. B.

(⁷) TO MR. RICHARD BROWN, PORT GLASGOW.

(DR. WALKER'S ED., 1811.)

ELLISLAND, *4th November*, 1789.

I HAVE been so hurried, my ever-dear friend, that
though I got both your letters, I have not been able
to command an hour to answer them as I wished;
and even now, you are to look on this as merely con-
fessing debt, and craving days. Few things could
have given me so much pleasure as the news that
you were once more safe and sound on terra firma,
and happy in that place where happiness is alone to
be found—in the fireside circle. May the benevolent

Director of all things peculiarly bless you in all those
endearing connexions consequent on the tender and
venerable names of husband and father! I have in-
deed been extremely lucky in getting an additional
income of £50 a year, while, at the same time, the
appointment will not cost me above £10 or £12 per
annum of expenses more than I must have inevitably
incurred. The worst circumstance is, that the Excise
division which I have got is so extensive—no less
than ten parishes to ride over; and it abounds besides
with so much business, that I can scarcely steal a
spare moment. However, labor endears rest, and both
together are absolutely necessary for the proper enjoy-
ment of human existence. I cannot meet you any
where. No less than an order from the Board of Ex-
cise, at Edinburgh, is necessary before I can have so
much time as to meet you in Ayrshire. But do you
come, and see me. We must have a social day, and
perhaps lengthen it out half the night, before you go
again to sea. You are the earliest friend I now have
on earth, my brothers excepted : and is not that an
endearing circumstance? When you and I first met,
we were at the green period of human life. The
twig would easily take a bent, but would as easily
return to its former state. You and I not only took
a mutual bent, but, by the melancholy, though strong
influence of being both of the family of the unfortu-
nate, we were entwined with one another in our
growth towards advanced age ; and blasted be the
sacrilegious hand that shall attempt to undo the
union !* You and I must have one bumper to my

---

* This is the last of the poet's letters to Richard Brown that have been pre-
served. We are indebted to Professor Walker for having recovered the whole
series—seven in number, through the medium of Mr. David Sillar of Irvine, and
he remarks that, "written as they were at a period when the Poet was in the
meridian of his reputation, they show that he was at no time so dazzled with
success as to forget the friends who had anticipated the public by discovering
his merit.

favorite toast : " May the companions of our youth be
the friends of our old age ! " Come and see me one
year ; I shall see you at Port Glasgow the next ; and
if we can contrive to have a gossiping between our
two bedfellows, it will be so much additional pleasure.
Mrs. Burns joins me in kind compliments to you and
Mrs. Brown.

Adieu ! I am ever, my dear Sir, yours.　　R. B.

(7) TO MR. WILLIAM BURNS, SADDLER, MORPETH.

(CHAMBERS', 1852.)

ELLISLAND, 10th Nov. 1789.

DEAR WILLIAM,—I would have written you sooner,
but I am so hurried and fatigued with my Excise
business, that I can scarcely pluck up resolution to
go through the effort of a letter to anybody. Indeed
you hardly deserve a letter from me, considering that
you have spare hours in which you have nothing to
do at all, and yet it was near three months between
your two last letters.

I know not if you heard lately from Gilbert. I
expect him here with me about the latter end of this
week. * * * My mother is returned, now that she
has seen my little boy Francis fairly set to the world.
I suppose Gilbert has informed you that you have got
a new nephew. He is a fine thriving fellow, and
promises to do honor to the name he bears. I have
named him Francis Wallace, after my worthy friend,
Mrs. Dunlop, of Dunlop.

The only Ayrshire news that I remember in which
I think you will be interested, is that Mr. Ronald is
bankrupt.* You will easily guess, that from his inso-

---

* Oct. 23, 1789. Sequestration, Mr. Wm. Ronald, Tobacconist, Mauchline.

lent vanity in his sunshine of life, he will now feel a
little retaliation from those who thought themselves
eclipsed by him ; for, poor fellow, I do not think he
ever intentionally injured any one.   I might indeed,
perhaps, except his wife, whom he certainly has used
very ill ; but she is still fond of him to distraction,
and bears up wonderfully—much superior to him—
under this severe shock of fortune.   Women have a
kind of sturdy sufferance, which qualifies them to
endure beyond, much beyond, the common run of
men ; but perhaps part of that fortitude is owing to
their short-sightedness, for they are by no means famous
for seeing remote consequences in all their real impor-
tance.

I am very glad at your resolution to live within
your income, be that what it will.   Had poor Ronald
done so, he had not this day been a prey to the
dreadful miseries of insolvency.

You are at the time of life when those habitudes
are begun which are to mark the character of the
future man.   Go on and persevere, and depend on less
or more success, I am, dear William, your brother,

R. B.

(⁶) TO ROBERT GRAHAM, ESQ., OF FINTRY.

(CURRIE, 1800—CHAMBERS', 1856.)

9th December 1789.

SIR,—I have a good while had a wish to trouble
you with a letter, and had certainly done it long ere
now—but for a humiliating something that throws
cold water on the resolution ; as if one should say,
"You have found Mr. Graham a very powerful and
kind friend indeed, and that interest he is so kindly
taking in your concerns, you ought by every thing in
your power to keep alive and cherish."—Now, though

since God has thought proper to make one powerful and another helpless, the connection of obliger and obliged is all fair ; and though my being under your patronage is to me highly honorable, yet, Sir, allow me to flatter myself, that, as a poet and an honest man, you first interested yourself in my welfare, and principally as such still, you permit me to approach you.

I have found the Excise business go on a great deal smoother with me than I expected ; owing a good deal to the generous friendship of Mr. Mitchell, my collector, and the kind assistance of Mr. Findlater, my supervisor. I dare to be honest, and I fear no labor. Nor do I find my hurried life greatly inimical to my correspondence with the Muses. Their visits to me, indeed, and I believe to most of their acquaintance, like the visits of good angels, are "short and far between ;" * but I meet them now and then as I jog through the hills of Nithsdale, just as I used to do on the banks of Ayr. I take the liberty to enclose you a few bagatelles, all of them the productions of my leisure thoughts in my excise rides.

If you know or have ever seen Captain Grose, the antiquarian, you will enter into any humor that is in the verses on him. Perhaps you have seen them before, as I sent them to a London newspaper. † Though, I daresay, you have none of the Solemn-League-and-Covenant fire, which shone so conspicuous in Lord

---

* The quotation here is from Blair's "Grave "—

"Visits, like those of angels, short and far between."

Thomas Campbell, with a fine ear for alliteration, thus improved on Blair :—

"Like angels' visits, few and far between."

However, the germ of the favorite line proceeded from John Norris, an old English versifier who has—

"Like angels' visits, short and bright."

† From the London newspaper the poem was reprinted in the "Kelso Chronicle" of 4th September 1789, with the signature "Thomas A. Linn," appended. Probably Grose was busy with his drawing of Kelso Abbey at the time ; and some of his associates there would cause the insertion.

George Gordon, and the Kilmarnock weavers, yet I think you must have heard of Dr. M'Gill, one of the Clergymen of Ayr, and his heretical book. God help him, poor man! Though he is one of the worthiest, as well as one of the ablest of the whole priesthood of the Kirk of Scotland, in every sense of that ambiguous term, yet the poor Doctor and his numerous family are in imminent danger of being thrown out to the mercy of the winter winds. The enclosed ballad on that business is, I confess, too local, but I laughed myself at some conceits in it, though I am convinced in my conscience that there are a good many heavy stanzas in it too.*

The Election Ballad, as you will see, alludes to the present canvass in our string of burghs.† I do not believe there will be a harder-run match in the whole general election. The *Great Man* here, like all renegadoes, is a flaming zealot kicked out before the astonished indignation of his deserted master, and despised, I suppose, by the party who took him in to be a mustering faggot at the mysterious orgies of their midnight iniquities, and a useful drudge in the dirty work of their country elections ; he would fain persuade this part of the world that he is turned Patriot, and, where he knows his men, has the impudence to aim away at the unmistrusting manner of a man of conscience and principle. Nay, to such an intemperate height has his zeal carried him that, in convulsive violence to every feeling in his bosom, he has made some desperate attempts at the hopeless business of getting himself a character for Benevolence ; and, in one or two late terrible strides in pursuit of partyinterest, has actually stumbled on something like meaning the Welfare of his Fellow-Creatures.‡ ˙ I beg

---

* "The Kirk of Scotland's Alarm," p. 85, *supra*.
† "The Five Carlines." p. 127, *supra*.
‡ The reference here is to the Duke of Queensberry.

your pardon, Sir, if I differ from you in my idea of
this *great man;* but were you to know his sins, as
well of omission as commission, to this outraged land,
you would club your curse with the execrating voice
of the country. I am too little a man to have any
political attachments ; I am deeply indebted to, and
have the warmest veneration for, individuals of both
parties ; but a man who has it in his power to be the
Father of a country, and who is only known to that
country by the mischiefs he does in it, is a character
of which one cannot speak with patience.

Sir James Johnston does "what man can do," but
yet I doubt his fate. Of the burgh of Annan he is
secure ; Kirkcudbright is dubious. He has the pro-
vost ; but Lord Daer, who does the honors of "great
man" to the place, makes every effort in his power
for the opposite interest. Luckily for Sir James, his
Lordship, though a very good Lord, is a very poor
politician. Dumfries and Sanquhar are decidedly the
Duke's "to sell or let ;" so Lochmaben, a city con-
taining upwards of fourscore living souls that cannot
discern between their right hand and their left — for
drunkenness—has at present the balance of power in
her hands. The honorable council of that ancient
burgh are fifteen in number ; but alas ! their fifteen
names endorsing a bill of fifteen pounds, would not
discount the said bill in any banking office. My lord
provost, who is one of the soundest-headed, best-
hearted, whisky-drinking fellows in the south of Scot-
land, is devoted to Sir James ; but his Grace thinks
he has a majority of the council, though I, who have
the honor to be a burgess of the town, and know
somewhat behind the curtain, could tell him a dif-
ferent story.

The worst of it for the buff and blue folks is, that
their candidate, Captain Miller, my landlord's son, is,
entre nous, a youth by no means above mediocrity in

III.   U

his abilities, and is said to have a huckster-lust for shillings, pence, and farthings. This is the more remarkable, as his father's abilities and benevolence are so justly celebrated.

The song beginning "Thou lingering star," &c., is the last, and, in my own opinion, by much the best of the enclosed compositions. I beg leave to present it with my most respectful compliments to Mrs. Graham.

I return you by the carrier, the bearer of this, Smith's *Wealth of Nations*, Marshall's *Yorkshire*, and *Angola*. *Les Contes de Fontaine* is in the way of my trade, and I must give it another reading or two. *Chansons Joyeuses*, and another little French book, I keep for the same reason. I think you will not be reading them, and I will not keep them long.

Forgive me, Sir, for the stupid length of this epistle. I pray Heaven it may find you in the humor to read *The Belfast New Almanac*, or *The Bachelor's Garland*, containing five excellent new songs, or the Paisley poet's version of the Psalms of David, and then my impertinence may disgust the less.

I have the honor to be, Sir, your ever-grateful, humble servant,   ROBT. BURNS.

(25) TO MRS. DUNLOP, OF DUNLOP.

(CURRIE, 1800.)

ELLISLAND, 13*th December*, 1789.

MANY thanks, dear Madam, for your sheet-full of rhymes. Though at present I am below the veriest prose, yet from you every thing pleases. I am groaning under the miseries of a diseased nervous system; a system, the state of which is most conducive to our happiness, or the most productive of our misery. For now near three weeks I have been so ill with a nerv-

ous head-ache, that I have been obliged to give up
for a time my Excise-books, being scarce able to lift
my head, much less to ride once a week over ten
muir parishes.   What is Man !—To-day in the luxu-
riance of health, exulting in the enjoyment of exist-
ence ; in a few days, perhaps in a few hours, loaded
with conscious painful being, counting the tardy pace
of the lingering moments by the repercussions of an-
guish, and refusing or denied a comforter.   Day fol-
lows night, and night comes after day, only to curse
him with life which gives him no pleasure ; and yet
the awful, dark termination of that life is a something
at which he recoils.

> "————— Tell us, ye dead ;
> Will none of you in pity disclose the secret
> What 'tis you are, and we must shortly be?
> 'Tis no matter —— a little time
> Will make us learn'd as you are, and as close."

Can it be possible, that when I resign this frail, fever-
ish being, I shall still find myself in conscious exis-
tence !   When the last gasp of agony has announced
that I am no more to those that knew me, and the
few who loved me ; when the cold, stiffened, uncon-
scious, ghastly corse is resigned into the earth, to be
the prey of unsightly reptiles, and to become in time
a trodden clod, shall I yet be warm in life, seeing and
seen, enjoying and enjoyed?   Ye venerable Sages and
holy Flamens, is there probability in your conjectures,
truth in your stories, of another world beyond death ;
or are they all alike, baseless visions, and fabricated
fables?   If there is another life, it must only be for
the just, the benevolent, the amiable, and the humane ;
what a flattering idea, then, is a world to come !
Would to God I as firmly believed it, as I ardently
wish it?   There I should meet an aged parent, now
at rest from the many buffetings of an evil world,
against which he so long and so bravely struggled.

There should I meet the friend, the disinterested friend of my early life; the man who rejoiced to see me, because he loved me and could serve me.—Muir!* thy weaknesses were the aberrations of human nature, but thy heart glowed with every thing generous, manly and noble; and if ever emanation from the All-Good Being animated a human form, it was thine! There should I, with speechless agony of rapture, again recognize my lost, my ever dear Mary! whose bosom was fraught with truth, honor, constancy, and love.†

> My Mary, dear departed shade!
> Where is thy place of heavenly rest?
> Seest thou thy lover lowly laid?
> Hear'st thou the groans that rend his breast?

Jesus Christ, thou amiablest of characters! I trust thou art no impostor, and that thy revelation of blissful scenes of existence beyond death and the grave, is not one of the many impositions which time after time have been palmed on credulous mankind. I trust that in thee "shall all the families of the earth be blessed," by being yet connected together in a better world, where every tie that bound heart to heart, in this state of existence, shall be, far beyond our present conceptions, more endearing.

I am a good deal inclined to think with those who maintain, that what are called nervous affections are in fact diseases of the mind. I cannot reason, I cannot think; and but to you I would not venture to write any thing above an order to a cobbler. You have felt too much of the ills of life not to sympathize with a diseased wretch, who is impaired in more than half of any faculties he possessed. Your good-

---

* Mr. Robert Muir, of Kilmarnock, who died, April 23rd, 1788.

† This is the earliest mention of "Highland Mary," in the poet's correspondence. We suspect that Burns had shortly before this date forwarded "Thou lingering star," to Mrs. Dunlop, and informed her that she was a juvenile sweetheart; otherwise she would be at a loss to understand this allusion.

ness will excuse this distracted scrawl, which the writer dare scarcely read, and which he would throw into the fire, were he able to write any thing better, or indeed any thing at all.

Rumor told me something of a son of yours who was returned from the East or West Indies. If you have gotten news of James or Anthony, it was cruel in you not to let me know ; as I promise you on the sincerity of a man, who is weary of one world, and anxious about another, that scarce any thing could give me so much pleasure as to hear of any good thing befalling my honored friend.

If you have a minute's leisure, take up your pen in pity to *le pauvre miserable*.   R. B.

(¹) TO LADY GLENCAIRN.*

(CROMEK, 1808.)

ELLISLAND, [*Dec.* 1789.]

MY LADY,—The honor you have done your poor poet, in writing him so very obliging a letter, and the pleasure the inclosed beautiful verses have given him, came very seasonably to his aid amid the cheerless gloom and sinking despondency of diseased nerves and December weather. As to forgetting the family of Glencairn, heaven is my witness with what sincerity I could use those old verses, which please me more in their rude simplicity than the most elegant lines I ever saw.

> If thee, Jerusalem, I forget,
>   Skill part from my right hand.
>
> My tongue to my mouth's roof let cleave,
>   If I do thee forget,
> Jerusalem ! and thee above
>   My chief joy do not set.

* This was the Countess Dowager Glencairn, mother of Earl James, the patron of Burns.

When I am tempted to do anything improper, I dare not, because I look on myself as accountable to your ladyship and family. Now and then, when I have the honor to be called to the tables of the great, if I happen to meet with any mortification from the stately stupidity of self-sufficient squires, or the luxuriant insolence of upstart nabobs, I get above the creatures by calling to remembrance that I am patronized by the noble House of Glencairn ; and at gala-times, such as New-year's day, a christening, or the kirn-night, when my punch bowl is brought from its dusty corner, and filled up in honor of the occasion, I begin with,—*The Countess of Glencairn!* My good woman, with the enthusiasm of a grateful heart, next cries, *My Lord!* and so the toast goes on, until I end with *Lady Harriet's** little angel!* whose epithalamium I have pledged myself to write.

When I received your Ladyship's letter, I was just in the act of transcribing for you some verses I have lately composed ; and meant to have sent them my first leisure hour, and acquainted you with my late change of life. I mentioned to my Lord, my fears concerning my farm. Those fears were indeed too true ; it is a bargain would have ruined me, but for the lucky circumstance of my having an Excise commission.

People may talk as they please, of the ignominy of the Excise : £50 a year will support my wife and children and keep me independent of the world ; and I would much rather have it said that my profession borrowed credit from me, than that I borrowed credit from my profession. Another advantage I have in this business, is the knowledge it gives me of the various shades of human character, consequently as-

---

* Lady Harriet Don, sister of the poet's patron Her "little angel" is understood to have been the late accomplished Sir Alexander Don, of Newton-Don, Bart.

sisting me vastly in my poetic pursuits. I had the most ardent enthusiasm for the Muses when nobody knew me, but myself, and that ardor is by no means cooled now that my Lord Glencairn's goodness has introduced me to all the world. Not that I am in haste for the press. I have no idea of publishing, else I certainly had consulted my generous noble patron ; but after acting the part of an honest man, and supporting my family, my whole wishes and views are directed to poetic pursuits. I am aware that though I were to give performances to the world superior to my former works, still if they were of the same kind with those, the comparative reception they would meet with would mortify me. I have turned my thoughts on the Drama. I do not mean the stately buskin of the Tragic Muse. Does not your Ladyship think that an Edinburgh theatre would be more amused with affectation, folly, and whim of true Scottish growth, than manners, which by far the greatest part of the audience can only know at second-hand? I have the honor to be your Ladyship's ever devoted and grateful, humble servant,

ROBᵗ. BURNS.

(¹) TO LADY WINIFRED MAXWELL CONSTABLE.

(LOCKHART, 1828.)

ELLISLAND, 16*th Dec.* 1789.

MY LADY,—In vain have I from day to day expected to hear from Mrs. Young, as she promised me at Dalswinton that she would do me the honor to introduce me at Tinwald ; and it was impossible not from your Ladyship's accessibility, but from my own feelings, that I could go alone. Lately, indeed, Mr. Maxwell, of Currachan, in his usual goodness offered

to accompany me, when an unlucky indisposition on
my part hindered my embracing the opportunity. To
court the notice, or the tables, of the great, except
where I sometimes have had a little matter to ask of
them, or more often the pleasanter task of witness-
ing my gratitude to them, is what I never have done,
and I trust never shall do. But with your Ladyship
I have the honor to be connected by one of the
strongest and most endearing ties in the whole world.
Common sufferers, in a cause where even to be un-
fortunate is glorious, the cause of heroic loyalty!
Though my fathers had not illustrious honors and
vast properties to hazard in the contest, though they
left their humble cottages only to add so many units
more to the unnoted crowd that followed their
leaders, yet what they could they did, and what they
had they lost : with unshaken firmness and uncon-
cealed political attachments, they shook hands with
ruin for what they esteemed the cause of their king
and their country.*   This language and the enclosed
verses are for your Ladyship's eye alone.†   Poets are
not very famous for their prudence ; but as I can do
nothing for a cause which is now nearly no more, I
do not wish to hurt myself.

I have the honor to be, my lady, your ladyship's
obliged and obedient humble servant,

ROBᵀ. BURNS.

---

* This passage is what Sir Walter Scott referred to in sending the letter to
Mr. Lockhart to assist him in his Biography of Burns :—" Here Burns plays high
Jacobite to that singular old curmudgeon, Lady Winifred Constable, and on that
account the letter is curious; though I imagine his Jacobitism, like my own,
belonged to the fancy rather than the reason."

† This was the address to Wm. Tytler, Esq., of Woodhouselee, Defender of
Mary Queen of Scots, given at page 89, vol. II.

(¹) TO PROVOST MAXWELL, OF LOCHMABEN.

(CUNNINGHAM. 1834.)

ELLISLAND, *20th Dec.* 1789.

DEAR PROVOST,—As my friend Mr. Graham goes for your good town to-morrow, I cannot resist the temptation to send you a few lines ; and as I have nothing to say, I have chosen this sheet of foolscap, and begun, as you see, at the top of the first page, because I have ever observed that when once people have fairly set out, they know not where to stop. Now that my first sentence is concluded, I have nothing to do but to pray Heaven to help me on to another. Shall I write you on politics, or religion ?— two master-subjects for your sayers of nothing. Of the first, I dare say by this time you are nearly surfeited ; and for the last, whatever they may talk of it who make it a kind of company concern, I never could endure it beyond a soliloquy. I might write you on farming, on building, on marketing ; but my poor distracted mind is so torn, so jaded, so racked and bedeviled with the task of the superlatively damned, to make *one guinea do the business of three,* that I detest, abhor, and swoon at the very word "business," though no less than four letters of my very short surname are in it.

Well, to make a matter short, I shall betake myself to a subject ever fruitful of themes—a subject, the turtle feast of the sons of Satan, and the delicious sugar-plum of the babes of grace—a subject sparkling with all the jewels that it can find in the mines of Genius, and pregnant with all the stores of learning, from Moses and Confucius to Franklin and Priestley— in short, may it please your Lordship, I intend to write [*Here, according to Cunningham, who first published the letter, the poet inserted an indecent ballad.*]

If at any time you expect a field-day, in your town
—a day when Dukes, Earls, and Knights pay their
court to weavers, tailors, and cobblers,* I should like
to know of it two or three days beforehand. It is not
that I care three skips of a cur-dog for the politics,
but I should like to see such an exhibition of human
nature. If you meet with that worthy old veteran in
Religion and good-fellowship, Mr. Jeffrey, or any of
his amiable family,† I beg you will give them my
best compliments.   R. B.

(¹) TO MR. GEORGE S. SUTHERLAND.

(DOUGLAS, 1877.) ‡

ELLISLAND, *Thursday Morning*, [*Dec.* 31, 1789.]

SIR,—Jogging home yesternight, it occurred to me
that as your next night is the first night of the New
Year, a few lines allusive to the Season by way of
Prologue, Interlude, or what you please, might take
pretty well. The enclosed verses are very incorrect,
because they are almost the first crude suggestions of my
Muse, by way of bearing me company in my darkling
journey. I am sensible it is too late to send you them :
but if they can any way serve you, use, alter, or, if
you please, neglect them. I shall not be in the least
mortified though they are never heard of; but if they

---

* See the Election Ballad, addressed to Mr. Graham, of Fintry,—p. 149, *supra*,
stanza 8 :—

> " And bent on winning borough towns,
>   Came shaking hands wi' wabster loons,
>   And kissing barefit carlins."

† The Rev. Mr. Jeffrey was father of the young lady whom the poet celebrated
in the song "I gaed a waefu' gate yestreen." She became the wife of a gentle-
man named Renwick, of Liverpool, who latterly removed to New York in the
United States. She took great offence at Cunningham's note to the above letter,
and affected to doubt the authenticity of some portions of the latter, which she
fancied to display a "want of reverence for her father." Unprejudiced readers
will scarcely detect any disrespect on Burns's part, in the epithet applied to Mr.
Jeffrey.

‡ From the poet's holograph, possessed by J. B. Greenshields, Esq., of Kerse,
Lesmahagow.

can be of any service to Mr. Sutherland and his friends, I shall kiss my hands to my lady Muse, and own myself much her debtor.—I am Sir, your very humble servant,   ROBᵀ. BURNS.

MR. GEORGE S. SUTHERLAND,
      Playwright, near Dumfries,
  at J. Hutchison's, the Post Office.

The piece enclosed was the Prologue, spoken at the theatre, Dumfries, on New-Year's-Day evening 1790, beginning—

> " No song nor dance I bring from yon great city,
> That queens it o'er our taste—the more's the pity."
>
> *See* p. 134, *supra.*

1790.

(²) TO MR. GILBERT BURNS, MOSSGIEL.

(CURRIE, 1800.)

ELLISLAND, 11*th January* 1790.

DEAR BROTHER,—I mean to take advantage of the frank, though I have not, in my present frame of mind, much appetite for exertion in writing. My nerves are in a cursed state. I feel that horrid hypochondria pervading every atom of both body and soul. This farm has undone my enjoyment of myself. It is a ruinous affair on all hands. But let it go to hell! I'll fight it out and be off with it.

We have got a set of very decent players here just now. I have seen them an evening or two. David Campbell, in Ayr, wrote to me by the manager of the company, a Mr. Sutherland, who is a man of apparent worth. On New-Year's-day evening I gave him the following prologue, which he spouted to his audience with applause.

> No song nor dance I bring from yon great city
> That queens it o'er our taste—the more's the pity:
> Tho', by the bye, abroad why will you roam?
> Good sense and taste are natives here at home, &c.

I can no more.—If once I was clear of this cursed farm, I should respire more at ease.   R. B.

(³) TO MR. WILLIAM DUNBAR, W.S., EDINBURGH.

(HOGG AND MOTHERWELL, 1835.)

ELLISLAND, 14th January 1790.

SINCE we are here creatures of a day—since "a few summer days and a few winter nights, and the life of man is at an end," why, my dear much esteemed Sir, should you and I let negligent indolence—for I know it is nothing worse—step in between us and bar the enjoyment of a mutual correspondence? We are not shapen out of the common, heavy, methodical clod, the elemental stuff of the plodding selfish race, the sons of Arithmetic and Prudence ; our feelings and hearts are not benumbed and poisoned by the cursed influence of riches, which, whatever blessing they may be in other prospects, are no friends to the nobler qualities of the heart : in the name of random Sensibility, then, let never the moon change on our silence any more. I have had a tract of bad health most part of this winter, else you had heard from me long ere now. Thank Heaven, I am now got so much better as to be able to partake a little in the enjoyments of life.

Our friend Cunningham will perhaps have told you of my going into the Excise. The truth is, I found it a very convenient business to have £50 per annum, nor have I yet felt any of those mortifying circumstances in it that I was led to fear.

Feb. 2.

I have not, for sheer hurry of business, been able to spare five minutes to finish my letter. Besides my farm-business, I ride on my Excise matter at least two hundred miles every week. I have not by any means given up the Muses. You will see in the 3rd vol. of Johnson's Scots Songs that I have contributed my mite there.

But, my dear Sir, little ones that look up to you for paternal protection are an important charge. I have already two fine, healthy, stout little fellows, and I wish to throw some light upon them. I have a thousand reveries and schemes about them, and their future destiny—not that I am a Utopian projector in these things ; but I am resolved never to breed up a son of mine to any of the learned professions. I know the value of independence ; and since I cannot give my sons an independent fortune, I shall give them an independent line of life. What a chaos of hurry, chance, and changes is this world, when one sits soberly down to reflect on it ! To a father, who himself knows the world, the thought that he shall have sons to usher into it must fill him with dread ; but if he have daughters, the prospect in a thoughtful moment is apt to shock him.

I hope Mrs. Fordyce and the two young ladies are well. Do let me forget that they are nieces of yours, and let me say that I never saw a more interesting, sweeter pair of sisters in my life. I am the fool of my feelings and attachments. I often take up a volume of my Spenser to realise you to my imagination, and think over the social scenes we have had together. God grant that there may be another world more congenial to honest fellows beyond this—a world where these rubs and plagues of absence, distance, misfortunes, ill-health, &c., shall no more damp hilarity and divide friendship. This I know is your throng season, but half a page will much oblige, my dear Sir, yours sincerely,

R. B.

(²⁶) TO MRS. DUNLOP, OF DUNLOP.

(CURRIE, 1800.)

ELLISLAND, 25*th January*, 1790.

IT has been owing to unremitting hurry of business that I have not written to you, Madam, long ere now. My health is greatly better, and I now begin once more to share in satisfaction and enjoyment with the rest of my fellow-creatures.

Many thanks, my much esteemed friend, for your kind letters : but why will you make me run the risk of being contemptible and mercenary in my own eyes? When I pique myself on my independent spirit, I hope it is neither poetic license, nor poetic rant ; and I am so flattered with the honor you have done me, in making me your compeer in friendship and friendly correspondence, that I cannot without pain, and a degree of mortification, be reminded of the real inequality between our situations.

Most sincerely do I rejoice with you, dear Madam, in the good news of Anthony. Not only your anxiety about his fate, but my own esteem for such a noble, warm-hearted, manly young fellow, in the little I had of his acquaintance, has interested me deeply in his fortunes.

Falconer, the unfortunate author of the *Shipwreck*, which you so much admire, is no more. After weathering the dreadful catastrophe he so feelingly describes in his poem, and after weathering many hard gales of fortune, he went to the bottom with the Aurora frigate ! I forget what part of Scotland had the honor of giving him birth, but he was the son of obscurity and misfortune.* He was one of those daring

---

* Falconer was the son of a tradesman near John Knox's Corner, Netherbow, Edinburgh.

adventurous spirits, which Scotland beyond any other country is remarkable for producing. Little does the fond mother think, as she hangs delighted over the sweet little leech at her bosom, where the poor fellow may hereafter wander, and what may be his fate. I remember a stanza in an old Scottish ballad, which, notwithstanding its rude simplicity, speaks feelingly to the heart :

> " Little did my mother think,
>   That day she cradled me,
> What land I was to travel in,
>   Or what death I should die ! " *

Old Scottish songs are, you know, a favorite study and pursuit of mine : and now I am on that subject, allow me to give you two stanzas of another old simple ballad, which I am sure will please you. The catastrophe of the piece is a poor ruined female, lamenting her fate. She concludes with this pathetic wish :

> "O that my father had ne'er on me smil'd ;
>   O that my mother had ne'er to me sung !
> O that my cradle had never been rock'd ;
>   But that I had died when I was young !

> "O that the grave it were my bed,
>   My blankets were my winding sheet ;
> The clocks and the worms my bedfellows a' ;
>   And O sae sound as I should sleep !"

I do not remember in all my reading to have met with anything more truly the language of misery than the exclamation in the last line. Misery is like love ; to speak its language truly, the author must have felt it.

I am every day expecting the doctor to give your little god-son the small-pox. They are *rife* in the country, and I tremble for his fate. By the way, I cannot help congratulating you on his looks and spirit.

---

* This is one of the stanzas in the ballad, called "The Queen's Maries."

Every person who sees him, acknowledges him to be the finest, handsomest child he has ever seen. I am myself delighted with the manly swell of his little chest, and a certain miniature dignity in the carriage of the head, and the glance of his fine black eye, which promise the undaunted gallantry of an independent mind.

I thought to have sent you some rhymes, but time forbids. I promise you poetry until you are tired of it next time I have the honor of assuring you how truly I am, &c.   R. B.

PREFACE TO JOHNSON'S MUSEUM, VOL. III.

Now that the editor gives this third Volume of The Scots Musical Museum to the public, he hopes it will not be found unworthy of the Volumes already published. As this is not one of those many Publications which are hourly ushered into the world merely to catch the eye of Fashion in her frenzy of a day, the Editor has little to hope or fear from the herd of readers.

Consciousness of the well-known merit of our Scottish Music, and the national fondness of a Scotchman for the productions of his own country, are at once the Editor's motive and apology for this undertaking; and where any of the pieces in the collection may perhaps be found wanting at the Critical Bar of the *first*, he appeals to the honest prejudices of the *last*.

EDINR., *February 2nd*, 1790.

In the above volume, besides the favorite songs "Of a' the airts the wind can blaw," "O were I on Parnassus hill," "Tam Glen," "John Anderson my Jo," and "O Willie brew'd a peck o' maut," appeared the recently composed address "To Mary in Heaven."

(²) TO MR. G. S. SUTHERLAND, DUMFRIES THEATRE.

(STEWART, 1801.)

I WAS much disappointed, my dear Sir, in wanting your most agreeable company yesterday. However, I heartily pray for good weather next Sunday ; and, whatever ærial Being has the guidance of the elements, that he may take any other half dozen Sundays he pleases, and clothe them with

> " Vapors and clouds and storms,
> Until he terrify himself,
> At combustion of his own raising."

I shall see you on Wednesday forenoon. In the greatest hurry, &c.   R. B.

Monday Morning, [1st Feb. 1790.]

(⁶) TO MR. PETER HILL, BOOKSELLER.

(CROMEK, in part, completed in DOUGLAS 1877.)*

ELLISLAND, *2nd Feb.* 1790.

No ! I will not say one word about apologies and excuses for not writing you. I am a poor damn'd, rascally gauger, condemned to gallop at least 200 miles every week to inspect dirty ponds and yeasty barrels, and where can I find time to write to, or importance to interest, anybody ? The upbraidings of my conscience, nay, the upbraidings of my wife, have persecuted me on your account these two or three months past. I wish to God I was a great man, that my

---

* Our thanks are due to George Wilson, Esq., a grandson of Mr. Peter Hill, for access to the original letter in his possession, whereby we are enabled to add so considerably to its interesting contents.

III.   V

correspondence might throw light upon you to let the world see what you really are ; and then I would make your fortune without putting my hand in my pocket for you, which, like all other great men, I suppose I would avoid as much as possible. What are you doing, and how are you doing? Have you lately seen any of my few friends? What has become of the BOROUGH REFORM? or, how is the fate of my poor namesake, Mademoiselle Burns, decided?* Which of their grave lordships can lay his hand on his heart, and say that he has not taken advantage of such frailty? Nay, if we may judge by near 6,000 years' experience, can the world do without such frailty? O Man! but for thee and thy selfish appetites and dishonest artifices, that beauteous form, and that once innocent and still ingenuous mind, might have shone conspicuous and lovely in the faithful wife and the affectionate mother ; and shall the unfortunate sacrifice to thy pleasures have no claim on thy humanity? As for those flinty-bosomed, puritanical prosecutors of female frailty, and persecutors of female charms—I am quite sober — I am dispassionate — to show that I am so, I shall mend my pen ere I proceed. It is written, "Thou shalt not take the name of the L—d thy G—d in vain ;" so I neither say "G— curse them!" nor "G— blast them!" nor "G— damn them!" but, may Woman curse them! may Woman blast them! may Woman damn them! . . . And when many years and much port, and great business, have delivered them over to vulture gouts and aspen palsies, then may they be tantalised with the impotent desires, which like ghosts haunt their bosoms, when all their powers to give or receive enjoyment are for ever asleep in the sepulchre of their fathers ! ! !

---

* See the Poet's "Lines written under the picture of the celebrated Miss Burns "—page 86, Vol. II. The note contains some account of the Mademoiselle alluded to. See also the letter to Peter Hill, dated 2nd April 1789, page 271, *supra*.

Now for business. Our book society owe you still £1 4s. : a friend of mine will, I suppose, have given you some money for me (It is about £3, 10s., or so), from which pay yourself the Monkland Friendly Society's account, and likewise Mr. Neilson's account, and send me a copy of it. The gentleman that will have given you the money will be Mr. Allan Masterton, writing master in Carrubber's Close. I saw lately in a Review some extracts from a new poem called "The Village Curate," I think ; send it me. I want likewise a cheap copy of "The World." Mr. Armstrong, the young poet, who does me the honor to mention me so kindly in his works, please give him my best thanks for the copy of his book. I shall write him my first leisure hour. I like his poetry much, but I think his style in prose quite astonishing.

What is become of that veteran in Genius, Wit, and Baudry, Smellie, and his book? Give him my compliments. Does Mr. Graham of Gartmore ever enter your shop now? He is the noblest instance of great talents, great fortune, and great worth, that ever I saw in conjunction.

Remember me to Mrs. Hill ; and believe me to be, my dear Sir, ever yours,　　ROBᵀ. BURNS.

The Scots Magazine of the period has the following notice in reference to the subject so largely dwelt on in the foregoing letter: "To rid the city of a part of those unfortunate females, and if possible to introduce them again into the world with habits of honest industry, one of the magistrates (Creech) in harvest time 1789, ordered all those who were in confinement for openly exercising their pernicious calling to be brought before him in the Council Chambers, and after addressing them, handed each one shilling, and a reaper's sickle, and liberated the whole (about 30), under their promise to apply for harvest work. But in three days the greater part of them were again apprehended for offences similar to those for which they had been previously convicted."

Miss Margaret Burns, *alias* Matthews, after some years' absence in England, returned to Edinburgh in 1789, accompanied by a Miss Sanderson, with whom she set up a fine house in Rose Street. The back windows of Lord Swinton's house looked into this establishment, and he soon became so annoyed with midnight brawls and other disturbances that he brought a complaint against the frail sisters before the magistrates. The special protector of Miss Burns was Mr. Robert Anderson of St. Germains, and the late Henry Guthrie befriended the other, who thereafter in gratitude adopted the name of "Mrs. Guthrie." Notwithstanding a stout defence, the Bench, presided over by Creech, convicted them of the offences with which they were charged, and condemned them to be "banished furth of this city and liberties forever." A bill of suspension, followed by a reclaiming petition, was brought before the Court of Session, who after various proceedings, passed the bill on 22nd December, giving the cause in favor of the petitioners.

The case created considerable excitement and some amusement among those who felt interested in such actions. The Hon. Henry Erskine was counsel for Miss Burns, and Lord Braxfield on one occasion interrupted him while pleading, by asking the question—"Mr. Erskine, can you tell me the reason that in the record whenever Mr. Creech's name is mentioned, it is printed in *italics?*" Mr. Erskine replied, "Indeed, my Lord, I can hardly tell you, unless it is done to show that none but an *Italian* would have used Miss Burns as Mr. Creech has done." This was a sly reference to Mr. Creech's very effeminate voice and smooth face.

The closing chapter in the history of poor Mademoiselle is very affecting. She fell into a deep decline and was removed to lodgings in Roslin for change of air, where she died in 1792, and was interred in the common burial ground there, which is, or was then, unenclosed. An aged friend in 1843 wrote to Dr. Carruthers of the Inverness Courier, regarding her fate thus:—"I never saw Miss Burns in the *flesh*, but I did in the *bones*. I remember when a stripling, popping into Elliot's Auction Room to witness the sale of her skeleton, which had been catalogued among other articles of *virtu*. The auctioneer encouraged the lagging bidders with this assurance —'Gentlemen, I can vouch for it, Miss Burns did *not* die of small pox, as some allege. No risk here, I assure you!' The *lovely Burns* was sold for about seven guineas!"

From "Kay's portraits" we quote "Miss Burns came to Edinburgh about 1789, at which period she had scarcely com-

pleted her twentieth year. Her youth, beauty, and handsome
figure—decked out in the highest style of fashion—attracted
very general notice as she appeared on the "Evening Prom-
enades;" and the fame of her charms having at length
brought her before the Magistrates, on a complaint at the
instance of some of her neighbors, the case excited an un-
usual sensation. Banishment 'forth of the city,' under the
penalty, in case of return, of being drummed through the
streets, beside confinement for six months in the house of
correction, was the severe decision of Bailie Creech.

"Bailie Creech was greatly annoyed in consequence of this
decision ; and as his antipathy to the 'fair but frail' victim
of his magisterial indignation was well known, various squibs
were circulated at his expense. Among others, it was an-
nounced in a London journal that 'Bailie Creech, of literary
celebrity in Edinburgh, was about to lead the beautiful and
accomplished Miss Burns to the hymeneal altar.'

"The Bailie was exceedingly wroth, and only abandoned
his threatened action against the editor, on the promise of
a counter-statement being given in next publication. The
per contra accordingly appeared, but in a way by no means
calculated to allay the irritation of the civic functionary.
It was to the following effect :—' In a former number we
noticed the intended marriage between Bailie Creech of Edin-
burgh, and the beautiful Miss Burns of the same place. We
have now the authority of that gentleman to say that the
proposed marriage is not to take place, matters having been
otherwise arranged to the mutual satisfaction of both parties
and their respective friends !' "—See Kay's celebrated portrait,
page 86, Vol. II.

(¹) TO MR. WILLIAM NICOL, EDINBURGH.

(CROMEK, 1808.)

ELLISLAND, *9th Feb.* 1790.

MY DEAR SIR,—That d–mned mare of yours is dead.
I would freely have given her price to have saved her ;
she has vexed me beyond description. Indebted as I
was to your goodness beyond what I can ever repay, I
eagerly grasped at your offer to have the mare with me.
That I might at least show my readiness in wishing

to be grateful, I took every care of her in my power.
She was never crossed for riding above half a score
of times by me, or in my keeping. I drew her in
the plough, one of three, for one poor week. I refused
55 shillings for her, which was the highest bode I
could squeeze for her. I fed her up and had her in
fine order for Dumfries fair; when four or five days
before the fair, she was seized with an unaccountable
disorder in the sinews, or somewhere in the bones of
the neck; with a weakness or total want of power in
her fillets; and in short the whole vertebræ of her
spine seemed to be diseased and unhinged, and in
eight-and-forty hours, in spite of the two best farriers
in the country, she died, and be d—mned to her! The
farriers said that she had been quite strained in the
fillets beyond cure before you had bought her; and
that she poor devil, though she might keep a little
flesh, had been jaded and quite worn out with fatigue
and oppression. While she was with me, she was
under my own eye; and I assure you, my much
valued friend, everything was done for her that could
be done; and the accident has vexed me to the heart.
In fact, I could not pluck up spirits to write you, on
account of the unfortunate business.

There is little new in this country. Our theatrical
company, of which you must have heard, leave us in
a week. Their merit and character are indeed very
great, both on the stage and in private life; not a
worthless creature among them; and their encourage-
ment has been accordingly. Their usual run is from
eighteen to twenty-five pounds a night; seldom less
than the one, and the house will hold no more than
the other. There have been repeated instances of
sending away six, and eight, and ten pounds in a
night, for want of room. A new theatre is to be
built by subscription; the first stone is to be laid on
Friday first to come. 300 guineas have been raised

by 30 subscribers, and 30 more might have been got
if wanted. The manager, Mr. Sutherland, was intro-
duced to me by a friend from Ayr; and a worthier
or cleverer fellow I have rarely met with. Some of
our clergy have slipt in by stealth now and then;
but they have got up a farce of their own. You
must have heard how the Rev^d. Mr. Lawson of Kirk-
mahoe,* seconded by the Rev^d. Mr. Kirkpatrick of
Dunscore, and the rest of that faction, have accused,
in formal process, the unfortunate and Rev. Mr. Heron
of Kirkgunyeon, that in ordaining Mr. Neilson to the
cure of souls in Kirkbean, he, the said Heron, feloni-
ously and treasonably bound the said Neilson to the
Confession of Faith, "*so far as it is agreeable to reason
and the word of God!*"

Mrs. B. begs to be remembered most gratefully to
you. Little Bobby and Frank are charmingly well
and healthy. I am jaded to death with fatigue. For
these two or three months, on an average, I have not
ridden less than 200 miles per week. I have done
little in the poetic way. I have given Mr. Suther-
land two prologues : one of which was delivered last
week. I have likewise strung four or five barbarous
stanzas, to the tune of Chevy Chase, by way of elegy
on your poor unfortunate mare, beginning (the name
she got here was Peg Nicholson),

'Peg Nicholson was a good bay mare.'—*See* page 142, *supra*.

My best compl^t. to Mrs. Nicol, and little Neddy,
and all the family. I hope Ned is a good scholar,
and will come out to gather nuts and apples with me
next harvest. I am ever, my dearest Friend, yours,

ROB^T. BURNS.

---

* Obit.—"Dec. 14, 1796. At the manse of Kirkmahoe, the Rev. Archibald
Lawson, minister of that parish."

(²) WILLIAM BURNS TO ROBERT BURNS.

(CROMEK, 1808.)

NEWCASTLE, 24th Jan. 1790.

DEAR BROTHER,—I wrote you about six weeks ago,* and I have expected to hear from you every post since, but I suppose your Excise business, which you hinted at in your last, has prevented you from writing. By the bye, when and how have you got into the Excise; and what division have you got about Dumfries? These questions please answer in your next, if more important matter do not occur. But in the meantime let me have the letter to John Murdoch (which Gilbert wrote me you meant to send): inclose it in your's to me, and let me have them as soon as possible, for I intend to sail for London in a fortnight, or three weeks at farthest.

You promised me when I was intending to go to Edinburgh, to write me some instructions about behavior in companies rather above my station, to which I might be eventually introduced. As I may be introduced into such companies at Murdoch's, or on his account, when I go to London, I wish you would write me some such instructions now; I never had more need of them, for having spent little of my time in company of any sort since I came to Newcastle, I have almost forgot the common civilities of life. To these instructions pray add some of a moral kind, for though (either through the strength of early impressions, or the frigidity of my constitution) I have hitherto withstood the temptation to those vices to which young fellows of my station and time of life are so much addicted, yet, I do not know if my virtue will be able to withstand the more powerful temptations of the metropolis; yet, through God's assistance and your instructions, I hope to weather the storm.

Give the compliments of the season and my love to my sisters, and all the rest of your family. Tell Gilbert the

* Chambers informs his readers that William Burns's letter to the poet, dated "Morpeth, 29th Nov. 1789," was in his possession, and he thus indicates its contents: he hopes that "young Wallace bids fair to rival his great predecessor in strength and wisdom," and apologises for not writing oftener, pleading in excuse that all his leisure is devoted to devouring the contents of a circulating library—"I have read Kames's 'Sketches of the History of Man,' Boswell's 'Tour to the Hebrides,' Burns's Poems, and 'Beattie's Dissertations,' and will be glad if you would name a few other books which I should enquire for."

first time you write him, that I am well, and that I will
write him either when I sail or when I arrive at London.
I am, &c.　　　　　　　　　　　　　　　　　　W. B.

(8) TO MR. WILLIAM BURNS, SADDLER, NEWCASTLE-ON-TYNE.

(CHAMBERS, 1852.)*

MY DEAR WILLIAM,—I would have written you
sooner, but I have mislaid Mr. Murdoch's letter, and
cannot for my life lay my hand on it ; so I cannot
write him for want of a direction.　If I find it after-
wards, I will write him and inclose it to you in Lon-
don.　Now that you are setting out for that place,
put on manly resolve, and determine to persevere ;
and in that case you will less or more be sure of suc-
cess.　One or two things allow me to particularise to
you.　London swarms with worthless wretches, who
prey on their fellow-creatures' thoughtlessness or in-
experience.　Be cautious in forming connections with
comrades and companions.　You can be pretty good
company to yourself, and you cannot be too shy of
letting anybody know you further than to know you
as a Saddler.　Another caution : I give you great
credit for your sobriety with respect to that universal
vice, bad women.　It is an impulse the hardest to be
restrained ; for if once a man accustoms himself to
gratifications of that impulse, it is then nearly, or
altogether impossible to restrain it.　W——g is a most
ruinous, expensive species of dissipation.　Is spending
a poor fellow's money, with which he ought to clothe
and support himself, nothing?　W——g has ninety-
nine chances in a hundred to bring on a man the
most nauseous and excruciating diseases to which

---

* We are indebted to Mr. Robert Burns Begg, Solicitor, Kinross, for enabling
us to supply some hitherto suppressed passages of this letter.

human nature is liable. Are disease and an impaired constitution trifling considerations? all this independent of the criminality of it.

I have gotten the Excise division, in the middle of which I live. Poor little Frank is this morning at the height in the small-pox. I got him inoculated, and I hope he is in a good way.

Write me before you leave Newcastle, and as soon as you reach London. In a word, if ever you be, as perhaps you may be, in a strait for a little ready cash, you know my direction. I shall not see you beat, while you fight like a man. Farewell! God bless you ! ROB⊤. BURNS.

ELLISLAND, 10*th Feb.* 1790.

(¹)TO DR. MUNDELL, DUMFRIES.

(DR. WADDELL'S ED.. 1869.) *

ELLISLAND, *Tuesday Morning.*

DEAR DOCTOR,—The bearer, Janet Nievison, is a neighbor, and occasionally a laborer of mine. She has got some complaint in her shoulder, and wants me to find her out a Doctor that will cure her, so I have sent her to you. You will remember that she is just in the jaws of matrimony, so for heaven's sake, get her "hale and sound" as soon as possible. We are all pretty well; only the little boy's sore mouth has again inflamed Mrs. B.'s nipples.—I am, yours,

ROB⊤. BURNS.

[*Feb.* 1790.]

---

* Printed from a fac-simile of the original MS.

(¹) TO ALEX. CUNNINGHAM, ESQ., WRITER, EDINBURGH.

(CURRIE, 1800.)

ELLISLAND, 13th February 1790.

I BEG your pardon, my dear and much valued friend, for writing to you on this very unfashionable, unsightly sheet—

"My poverty but not my will consents."

But to make amends, since modish post I have none except one poor widowed half-sheet of gilt, which lies in my drawer among my plebeian foolscap pages, like the widow of a man of fashion, whom that unpolite scoundrel, Necessity, has driven from Burgundy and Pine-apple, to a dish of Bohea with the scandal-bearing help-mate of a village priest; or a glass of whisky-toddy with a ruby-nosed yoke-fellow of a foot-padding exciseman—I make a vow to enclose this sheetful of epistolary fragments in that my only scrap of gilt paper.

I am indeed your unworthy debtor for three friendly letters.* I ought to have written to you long ere now, but it is a literal fact, I have not almost a spare moment. It is not that I *will not* write to you; Miss Burnet is not more dear to her guardian angel, nor his grace of Queensberry to the powers of darkness, than my friend Cunningham to me. It is not that I *cannot* write you; should you doubt it, take the following fragment, which was intended for you some time ago, and be convinced that I can *antithesize*

---

* The present letter was specially in reply to one from Cunningham dated 28th January, 1790, printed by Currie. He writes, "In these days of merriment, I have frequently heard your name proclaimed at the jovial board. under the roof of our hospitable friend at Stenhouse Mills, where there were no 'lingering moments numbered wi' care.'" (The words in inverted commas are quoted from *The Chevalier's Lament*, which the reader will recollect was written for Cleghorn.)

sentiment, and *circumvolute* periods, as well as any coiner of phrase in the regions of philology.

[December, 1789.

MY DEAR CUNNINGHAM,—Where are you? And what are you doing? Can you be that son of levity who takes up a friendship as he takes up a fashion ; or are you, like some other of the worthiest fellows in the world, the victim of indolence, laden with fettters of ever-increasing weight?

What strange beings we are! Since we have a portion of conscious existence, equally capable of enjoying pleasure, happiness, and rapture, or of suffering pain, wretchedness, and misery, it is surely worthy of inquiry, whether there be not such a thing as a science of life ; whether method, economy, and fertility of expedients be not applicable to enjoyment, and whether there be not a want of dexterity in pleasure, which renders our little scantling of happiness still less ; and a profuseness, an intoxication in bliss, which leads to satiety, disgust, and self-abhorrence. There is not a doubt but that health, talents, character, decent competency, respectable friends, are real and substantial blessings ; and yet do we not daily see those who enjoy many or all of these good things, and *notwithstanding* contrive to be as unhappy as others to whose lot few of them have fallen? I believe one great source of this mistake or misconduct is owing to a certain stimulus, with us called ambition, which goads us up the hill of life—not as we ascend other eminences, for the laudable curiosity of viewing an extended landscape, but rather for the dishonest pride of looking down on others of our fellow-creatures, seemingly diminutive in humbler stations, &c., &c.]

Sunday, 14th February 1790.

GOD help me! I am now obliged to

"Join night to-day, and Sunday to the week."

If there be any truth in the orthodox faith of these churches, I am d-mned past redemption, and what is worse, d-mned to all eternity. I am deeply read in Boston's "Fourfold State," Marshall "on Sanctification," Guthrie's "Trial of a Saving Interest," &c., &c.; but, "there is no balm in Gilead, there is no physician there" for me; so I shall e'en turn Arminian, and trust to "sincere though imperfect obedience."

Tuesday 16th.

Luckily for me I was prevented from the discussion of the knotty point at which I had just made a full stop. All my fears and cares are of this world : if there is another, an honest man has nothing to fear from it. I hate a man that wishes to be a Deist; but I fear, every fair, unprejudiced inquirer must in some degree be a Sceptic. It is not that there are any very staggering arguments against the immortality of man; but like electricity, phlogiston, &c. the subject is so involved in darkness, that we want data to go upon. One thing frightens me much; that we are to live for ever, seems *too good news to be true.* That we are to enter into a new scene of existence, where, exempt from want and pain, we shall enjoy ourselves and our friends without satiety or separation—how much should I be indebted to any one who could fully assure me that this was certain!

"Tell us, ye dead! will none of you in pity
To those you left behind, reveal the secret,
What 'tis you are, and we must shortly be!"

My time is once more expired. I will write to Mr. Cleghorn soon. God bless him and all his concerns!

And may all the powers that preside over conviviality and friendship be present with all their kindest influence, when the bearer of this, Mr. Syme, and you meet! I wish I could also make one. I think we should be Trinity in Unity.

Finally, brethren, farewell! Whatsoever things are lovely, whatsoever things are gentle, whatsoever things are charitable, whatsoever things are kind, think on these things, and think on me. ROBERT BURNS.

(⁷) TO MR. PETER HILL, BOOKSELLER.

(CURRIE, 1800.)*

ELLISLAND, 2nd March 1790.

MY DEAR SIR,—At a late meeting of the Monkland Friendly Society, it was resolved to augment the Library by the following books which you are to send us as soon as possible :—The Mirror, The Lounger, Man of Feeling, Man of the World (these, for my own sake, I wish to have by the first carrier); Knox's History of the Reformation ; Rae's History of the Rebellion in 1715 ; any good History of the Rebellion 1745 ; A Display of the Secession Act and Testimony, by Mr. Gib ; Hervey's Meditations ; Beveridge's Thoughts ; and another copy of Watson's Body of Divinity. This last heavy performance is so much admired by many of our members, that they will not be content with one copy ; so Capⁿ. Riddell our president and patron agreed with me to give you private instructions not to send *Watson*, but to say that you could not procure a copy of the book so cheap as the one you sent formerly, and therefore, you wait further orders.

---

* By favor of George Wilson, Esq., of Dalmarnock, we are enabled to supply here some portions of this letter that were omitted by Dr. Currie.

I wrote to Mr. A. Masterton three or four months ago, to pay some money he owed me into your hands, and lately I wrote to you to the same purpose, but I have heard from neither one nor other of you.

In addition to the books I commissioned in my last, I want very much, "An Index to the Excise Laws, or an Abridgement of all the Statutes now in force, relative to the Excise," by Zellinger Symons. I want three copies of this book ; if the book is now to be had, cheap or dear, get it for me. An honest country neighbor of mine wants too a Family Bible, the larger the better ; but second-handed, for he does not chuse to give above ten shillings for the book. I want likewise for myself, as you can pick them up, second-handed or anything cheap, copies of Otway's Dramatic Works, Ben Jonson's Do. ; Dryden's, Congreve's, Wycherley's, Vanbrugh's, Cibber's ; or any dramatic works of the more modern Macklin, Garrick, Foot, Colman, or Sheridan. A good copy, too, of Molière in French I much want. Any other good French dramatic authors in their native language, I want these : I mean comic authors chiefly, though I should wish Racine, Corneille, and Voltaire too. I am in no hurry for all, or any of these, but if you accidentally meet with them very cheap, get them for me.

And now, to quit the dry walk of business, how do you do, my dear friend ! and how is Mrs. Hill ? I trust, if now and then not so *elegantly* handsome, at least as amiable, and sings as divinely as ever. My Goodwife too has a charming "wood-note wild ;" now, could we four get anyway snugly together in a corner, in the New Jerusalem (remember, I bespeak your company there), you and I, though Heaven knows we are no singers ; yet, as we are all to have harps, you know, we shall continue to support the ladies' pipes, as we have oft done before, with all the powers of our instruments.

I am out of all patience with this vile world for one thing. Mankind. are by nature benevolent creatures, except in a few scoundrelly instances. I do not think that avarice of the good things we chance to have is born with us ; but we .are placed here amid so much nakedness and hunger, and poverty and want, that we are under a damning necessity of studying selfishness, in order that we may EXIST ! Still there are, in every age, a few souls that all the wants and woes of life cannot debase to selfishness, or even give the necessary alloy of caution and prudence. If ever I am in danger of vanity, it is when I contemplate myself on this side of my disposition and character. God knows I am no saint ; I have a whole host of follies and sins to answer for ; but if I could, (and I believe I do it as far as I can), I would " wipe away all tears from all eyes." Even the knaves who have injured me, I would oblige them ; though, to tell the truth, it would be more out of vengeance, to shew them that I was independent of and above them, than out of the overflowings of my benevolence. Adieu !

ROBT. BURNS.

(³) WILLIAM BURNS TO ROBERT BURNS.

(CROMEK, 1808.)

LONDON, 21st March 1790.

DEAR BROTHER,—I have been here three weeks come Tuesday, and would have written you sooner but was not settled in a place of work :—We were ten days on our passage from Shields ; the weather being calm I was not sick, except one day when it blew pretty hard. I got into work the Friday after I came to town ; I wrought there only eight days, their job being done. I got work again in a shop in the Strand, the next day after I left my former master. It is only a temporary place, but I expect to be settled soon in a shop to my mind, although it will be a harder task than I at first imagined, for there are such swarms of fresh hands just come from the country, that the town is quite overstocked, and except one is a particularly good workman (which you know I am not, nor I am afraid ever will be), it is hard to get a place: However, I don't yet despair to bring up my lee-way, and shall endeavor if possible to sail within three or four points of the wind. The encouragement here is not what I expected, wages being very low in proportion to the expense of living, but yet, if I can only lay by the money that is spent by others in my situation in dissipation and riot, I expect soon to return you the money I borrowed of you and live comfortably besides.

In the mean time I wish you would send up all my best linen shirts to London, which you may easily do by sending them to some of your Edinburgh friends, to be shipped from Leith. Some of them are too little; don't send any but what are good, and I wish one of my sisters could find as much time as to trim my shirts at the breast, for there is no such thing to be seen here as a plain shirt, even for wearing, which is what I want these for. I mean to get one or two new shirts here for Sundays, but I assure you that linen here is a very expensive article. I am going to write to Gilbert to send me an Ayrshire cheese; if he can spare it he will send it to you, and you may send it with the shirts, but I expect to hear from you before that time. The cheese I could get here; but I will have a pride in eating Ayrshire cheese in London, and the expense of sending it will be little, as you are sending the shirts any how.

I write this by J. Stevenson, in his lodgings, while he is writing to Gilbert. He is well and hearty, which is a blessing to me as well as to him: We were at Covent Garden chapel this forenoon, to hear the *Calf* preach; he is grown very fat, and is as boisterous as ever.* There is a whole colony of Kilmarnock people here, so we don't want for acquaintance.

Remember me to my sisters and all the family. I shall give you all the observations I have made on London in my next, when I shall have seen more of it.—I am, Dear Brother, yours, &c.,   W. B.

The foregoing is the last which has been preserved of the interesting series of letters that passed between Burns and his brother William. Unfortunately, for want of John Murdoch's

---

* The Rev. James Steven : " The Calf."

address, the latter had been nearly four months in London before he fell in with the old tutor, who then had a little shop in Bloomsbury Square, for selling stationery, &c. Within a fortnight after his first and only meeting with Murdoch, poor William was seized with a malignant fever, and died on 24th July, before his friend Murdoch was apprised of his illness. See onward for Burns's letter to Murdoch, 16th July 1790.

(²⁷) TO MRS. DUNLOP OF DUNLOP.

ELLISLAND, 10*th April* 1790.

I HAVE just now, my ever honored friend, enjoyed a very high luxury, in reading a paper of the *Lounger.* You know my national prejudices. I had often read and admired the *Spectator*, *Adventurer*, *Rambler*, and *World;* but still with a certain regret, that they were so thoroughly and entirely English. Alas! have I often said to myself, what are all the boasted advantages which my country reaps from the Union, that can counterbalance the annihilation of her independence, and even her very name! I often repeat that couplet of my favorite poet, Goldsmith—

" ——— States of native liberty possest,
Tho' very poor, may yet be very blest."

Nothing can reconcile me to the common terms, "English ambassador, English court," &c. And I am out of all patience to see that equivocal character, Hastings, impeached by "the Commons of England." Tell me, my friend, is this weak prejudice? I believe, in my conscience, such ideas as, "my country; her independence; her honor; the illustrious names that mark the history of my native land;" &c.—I believe these, among your *men of the world;* men who in fact guide, for the most part, and govern our world, are looked on as so many modifications of wrong-headedness. They know the use of bawling out such terms, to rouse or lead THE RABBLE: but for their own private use, with almost all the *able statesmen* that ever existed, or now exist, when they talk of right and wrong, they only mean proper and improper; and their measure of conduct is not, what they ought, but *what they dare.* For the truth of this, I shall not ransack the history of nations, but appeal to one of the ablest judges of men, and himself one of the ablest men that ever lived—the celebrated earl. of Chesterfield. In fact, a man who could thoroughly control his vices whenever they interfered with his interest, and who could completely put on the appearance of every virtue as often as it suited his purposes, is, on the Stanhopian plan, the *perfect man;* a man to lead nations.* But are great abilities, complete without a flaw, and polished without a blemish, the standard of human excellence? This is certainly the staunch opinion of *men of the world;* but I call on honor, virtue, and worth, to give the Stygian doctrine a loud negative! However, this must be allowed, that, if you abstract from man the idea of an existence beyond the grave, *then*, the true measure of human conduct is *proper* and *improper:* virtue and vice, as dispositions of the heart, are, in that case, of scarcely the same import and value to the world at large, as harmony and discord in the modifications of sound; and a delicate sense of honor, like a nice ear for music, though it may sometimes give the possessor an ecstacy unknown to the coarser organs of the herd, yet, considering the harsh gratings, and inharmonic jars, in this ill-tuned state of being, it is odds but the individual would be as happy, and certainly would be as much respected by the true judges of society, as it would then stand, without either a good ear or a good heart.

---

* Lord Chesterfield died in 1773. In the year following were published his celebrated letters to his bastard son, Mr. Stanhope, who was for some time British envoy at Dresden.

You must know I have just met with the "Mirror" and "Lounger" for the first time, and I am quite in raptures with them ; I should be glad to have your opinion of some of the papers. The one I've just read (*Lounger*, No. 61), has cost me more honest tears than anything I have read for a long time.* Mackenzie has been called "the Addison of the Scots," and in my opinion, Addison would not be hurt at the comparison. If he has not Addison's exquisite humor, he as certainly outdoes him in the tender and the pathetic. His "Man of Feeling"—but I am not counsel-learned in the laws of criticism—I estimate as the first performance of the kind I ever saw. From what book, moral or even pious, will the susceptible young mind receive impressions more congenial to humanity and kindness, generosity and benevolence— in short, more of all that ennobles the soul to herself, or endears her to others, than from the simple, affecting tale of poor Harley?

Still, with all my admiration of Mackenzie's writings, I do not know if they are the fittest reading for a young man who is about to set out, as the phrase is, to make his way into life. Do not you think, Madam, that among the few favored of heaven in the structure of their minds (for such there certainly are), there may be a purity, a tenderness, a dignity, an elegance of soul, which are of no use, nay, in some degree, absolutely disqualifying for the truly important business of making a man's way into life? If I am not much mistaken, my gallant young friend Anthony, is very much under these disqualifications ; and for the young females of a family I could mention, well may they excite parental solicitude, for I, a common acquaintance, or as my vanity will have it, an humble friend, have often trembled for a turn of mind which may

---

* This paper relates to the attachments between servants and masters, and concludes with the story of "Albert Bane."

render them eminently happy—or peculiarly miserable.

I have been manufacturing some verses lately ; but as I have got the most hurried season of excise business over, I hope to have more leisure to transcribe any thing that may show how much I have the honor to be, Madam, yours, &c.   R. B.

(¹) TO MR. ALEX. FINDLATER, DUMFRIES.

(DOUGLAS, 1877.)

DEAR SIR,—Mrs. B., like a true good wife, looking on my taste as a standard, and knowing that she cannot give me anything eatable more agreeable than a new-laid egg, she begs your acceptance of a few. They are all of them *couch*, not thirty hours out.

I am, dear Sir, your obliged, humble servᵗ.

ROBᵀ. BURNS.

ELLISLAND, *Saturday Morning*.

The poet's holograph of this note is now preserved in his monument at Edinburgh. Originally were appended to it five verses of extempore poetry, beginning thus.

> "Dear Sir—our Lucky humbly begs
> Ye'll prie her caller, new-laid eggs;
> Lord grant the cock may keep her legs
> Aboon the chuckies," &c., &c.

but the verses have long been detached from the prose note. They were sold among a lot of the Pickering manuscripts that were reckoned too gross for publication, and are doubtless yet in existence. In sentiment they remind us of a passage in one of the poet's letters to Mrs. Dunlop :—" If miry ridges and dirty dung-hills are to engross the best part of my soul immortal, 1 had better been a rook or a magpie at once, and then I should not have been plagued with any ideas superior to the breaking of clods and picking up grubs ; not to mention barn-door cocks and mallards—creatures with which I could

almost exchange lives at any time." The two closing stanzas
are the only ones fully quotable :

> " Nae cursed, clerical excise
> On honest Nature's laws and ties :
> Free as the vernal breeze that flies
>   At early day,
> We'd tasted Nature's richest joys,
>   But stint or stay.
>
> " But as this subject's something kittle,
> Our wisest way's to say but little,
> Yet, while my Muse is at her mettle,
>   I am most fervent,
> Or, may I die upon a whittle,
>   Your friend and servant,
>   ROBERT BURNS."

(?) TO DR. JOHN MOORE, LONDON.

(CURRIE, 1800.)

DUMFRIES, EXCISE-OFFICE, 14th July 1790.

SIR,—Coming into town this morning to attend my
duty in this office, it being collection-day, I met with
a gentleman who tells me he is on his way to Lon-
don ; so I take the opportunity of writing to you, as
franking is at present under a temporary death.   I
still have some snatches of leisure through the day,
amid our horrid business and bustle, and I shall im-
prove them as well as I can ; but let my letter be as
stupid as * * * * * *, as miscellaneous as a
newspaper, as short as a hungry grace-before-meat, or
as long as a law-paper in the Douglas cause ; as ill-
spelt as country John's billet-doux, or as unsightly a
scrawl as Betty Byre-mucker's answer to it ; I hope,
considering circumstances, you will forgive it ; and as
it will put you to no expense of postage, I shall have
the less reflection about it.

I am sadly ungrateful in not returning you my
thanks for your most valuable present, "Zeluco."   In
fact, you are in some degree blameable for my neglect.
You were pleased to express a wish for my opinion

of the work, which so flattered me that nothing less would serve my overweening fancy, than a formal criticism on the book. In fact, I have gravely planned a comparative view of you, Fielding, Richardson, and Smollet, in your different qualities and merits as novel-writers. This, I own, betrays my ridiculous vanity, and I may probably never bring the business to bear; but I am fond of the spirit young Elihu shews in the book of Job—"And I said, I will also declare my opinion." I have quite disfigured my copy of the book with my annotations. I never take it up without at the same time taking my pencil and marking with asterisms, parentheses, &c., wherever I meet with an original thought, a nervous remark on life and manners, a remarkably well-turned period, or a character sketched with uncommon precision.

Though I shall hardly think of fairly writing out my "Comparative View," I shall certainly trouble you with my remarks, such as they are.

I have just received from my gentleman that horrid summons in the book of Revelation, that "time shall be no more!"

The little collection of sonnets have some charming poetry in them. If *indeed* I am indebted to the fair author for the book, and not, as I rather suspect, to a celebrated author of the other sex, I should certainly have written to the lady, with my grateful acknowledgments, and my own ideas of the comparative excellence of her pieces.* I would do this last, not from any vanity of thinking that my remarks could be of much consequence to Mrs. Smith, but merely from my own feelings as an author, doing as I would be done by.   R. B.

---

* This book was the Sonnets of Charlotte Smith.

(?) TO MR. MURDOCH, TEACHER OF FRENCH, LONDON.

(CROMEK, 1808.)

ELLISLAND, 16th July 1790.

MY DEAR SIR,—I received a letter from you a long time ago, but unfortunately, as it was in the time of my peregrinations and journeyings through Scotland, I mislaid or lost it, and by consequence your direction along with it. Luckily my good star brought me acquainted with Mr. Kennedy,* who, I understand, is an acquaintance of yours : and by his means and mediation I hope to replace that link which my unfortunate negligence had so unluckily broke in the chain of our correspondence. I was the more vexed at the vile accident, as my brother William, a journeyman saddler, has been for some time in London ; and wished above all things for your direction, that he might have paid his respects to his father's friend.

His last address he sent to me was, "Wm. Burns, at Mr. Barber's, saddler, No. 181 Strand." I writ him by Mr. Kennedy, but neglected to ask him for your address ; so, if you find a spare half-minute, please let my brother know by a card where and when he will find you, and the poor fellow will joyfully wait on you, as one of the few surviving friends of the man whose name, and Christian name too, he has the honor to bear.

The next letter I write you shall be a long one. I have much to tell you of "hair-breadth 'scapes in th' imminent deadly breach," with all the eventful history of a life, the early years of which owed so much

---

* This was probably Thomas Kennedy, whose epitaph under the title of "Tam the Chapman" was an early production of Burns, (see p. 76, Vol. I.). Wm. Cobbett, in whose Magazine the lines first appeared, described him as "an aged person resident in London."

to your kind tutorage ; but this at an hour of leisure. My kindest compliments to Mrs. Murdoch and family. I am ever, my dear Sir, your obliged friend,

Robt. Burns.

FROM MR. MURDOCH TO THE BARD.

GIVING HIM AN ACCOUNT OF HIS BROTHER WILLIAM'S DEATH.

(Cromek, 1808.)

Hart Street, Bloomsbury Square, London.
September 14th 1790.

My dear Friend,—Yours of the 16th of July I received on the 26th, in the afternoon, per favor of my friend Mr. Kennedy, and at the same time was informed that your brother was ill. Being engaged in business till late that evening, I set out next morning to see him, and had thought of three or four medical gentlemen of my acquaintance, to one or other of whom I might apply for advice, provided it should be necessary. But when I went to Mr. Barber's, to my great astonishment and heartfelt grief, I found that my young friend had, on Saturday, bid an everlasting farewell to all sublunary things.* It was about a fortnight before that he had found me out. by Mr. Stevenson's accidentally calling at my shop to buy something. We had only one interview, and that was highly entertaining to me in several respects. He mentioned some instruction I had given him when very young, to which he said he owed, in a great measure, the philanthropy he possessed.—He also took notice of my exhorting you all, when I wrote, about eight years ago, to the man who. of all mankind that I ever knew, stood highest in my esteem, "not to let go your integrity."— You may easily conceive that such conversation was both

---

* The 26th July 1790, was a Monday, and when Mr. Murdoch called for Wm. Burns at his lodgings on Tuesday morning, he found that his poor young friend had died on the previous Saturday of a putrid fever. Consequently Wm. Burns's death happened on 24th July, and a few days thereafter he was buried in St. Paul's Churchyard, Mr. Murdoch attending in the capacity of chief-mourner.· It seems odd that Murdoch should have so long delayed to send intelligence of this calamity to Burns.

The poet remitted to Mr. Barber, his brother's landlord, the expense of the funeral, on 5th October thereafter.

pleasing and encouraging to me : I anticipated a deal of rational happiness from future conversations.—Vain are our expectations and hopes.—They are so almost always—perhaps, (nay, certainly) for our good. Were it not for disappointed hopes we could hardly spend a thought on another state of existence, or be in any degree reconciled to the quitting of this.

I know of no one source of consolation to those who have lost young relatives equal to that of their being of a good disposition, and of a promising character. . . .

******

Your letter to Dr. Moore, I delivered at his house, and shall most likely know your opinion of "Zeluco" the first time I meet with him. I wish and hope for a long letter. Be particular about your mother's health. I hope she is too much a Christian to be afflicted above measure, or to sorrow as those who have no hope.

One of the most pleasing hopes I have is to visit you all ; but I am commonly disappointed in what I most ardently wish for. I am, dear Sir, yours sincerely,

JOHN MURDOCH.

(⁴) TO MR. ROBERT CLEGHORN,

SAUGHTON MILLS, NEAR EDINBURGH.

(DOUGLAS, 1877.)*

ELLISLAND, 23rd July 1790.

Do not ask me, my dear Sir, why I have neglected so long to write to you. Accuse me of indolence, my line of life, of hurry, my stars of perverseness — in short, accuse anything but me of forgetfulness. You knew Matthew Henderson. At the time of his death† I composed an elegiac stanza or two, as he was a man I much regarded ; but something came in my way, so that the design of an Elegy to his memory I gave up. Meeting with the fragment the other day among some

---

* We are indebted to the kindness of A. C. Lamb, Esq., Dundee, for the use of the manuscript of this letter and the precious first draft of the " Elegy on Captain Matthew Henderson," which accompanied it. See p. 155, *supra*.

† "Nov. 21, 1788, died at Edinburgh, Matthew Henderson, Esq."—*Scots Magazine*.

old waste papers, I tried to finish the piece, and have this moment put the last hand to it. This I am going to write you is the first fair copy of it :—

> O Death! thou tyrant fell and bloody!
> The mickle devil wi' a woodie,
> Haurl thee hame to his black smiddie, &c.

Let me know how you like the foregoing. My best compliments to Mrs. Cleghorn and family. I am, most truly, my dear Sir, yours, ROBERT BURNS.

(³) TO JOHN M'MURDO, ESQ., DRUMLANRIG.

(CUNNINGHAM, 1834.)

ELLISLAND, *2nd Aug.* 1790.

SIR,—Now that you are over with the Sirens of Flattery, the Harpies of Corruption, and the Furies of Ambition — those infernal deities that on all sides, and in all parties, preside over the villanous business of Politics—permit a rustic Muse of your acquaintance to do her best to soothe you with a song.

You knew Henderson — I have not flattered his memory, I have the honor to be, Sir, your obliged humble servant, ROBᵀ. BURNS.

The "soothing song" which accompanied the above brief note was, of course, the "Elegy on Captain Matthew Henderson," and the opening reference in the note is to the close of the great election contest for the parliamentary representation of the Dumfries Burghs, that had been agitating the county for nearly ten months.

(^{28}) TO MRS. DUNLOP, OF DUNLOP.

(CURRIE, 1800.)

ELLISLAND, 8*th Aug.* 1790.

DEAR MADAM,—After a long day's toil, plague, and care, I sit down to write to you. Ask me not why I have delayed it so long? It was owing to hurry, indolence, and fifty other things; in short, to anything but forgetfulness of *la plus aimable de son sexe.* By the bye, you are indebted your best curtsey to me for this last compliment as I pay it from my sincere conviction of its truth—a quality rather rare in compliments of these grinning, bowing, scraping times.

Well, I hope writing to *you* will ease a little my troubled soul. Sorely has it been bruised to-day! A *ci-devant* friend of mine, and an intimate acquaintance of yours, has given my feelings a wound that I perceive will gangrene dangerously ere it cure. He has wounded my pride !* R. B.

(^{5}) TO ALEX. CUNNINGHAM, ESQ., WRITER, EDINBURGH.

(CURRIE, 1800.)

ELLISLAND, 8*th August* 1790.

FORGIVE me, my once dear, and ever dear friend, my seeming negligence. You cannot sit down and fancy the busy life I lead.

I laid down my goose feather to beat my brains for an apt simile, and had some thoughts of a country

---

* Who this personage was, no one of the poet's editors has ventured to say, or even suggest. In the letter to Cunningham which follows (dated on the same Sunday, 8th August), he writes in a like strain of bitterness ; but Currie has suppressed the most indignant passages of invective.

grannum at a family christening ; a bride on the
market-day before her marriage ; an orthodox clergy-
man at a Paisley sacrament ; an Edinburgh bawd on
a Sunday evening ; or a tavern-keeper at an election-
dinner ; &c. &c.—but the resemblance that hits my
fancy best, is that blackguard miscreant, Satan, who,
as Holy Writ tells us, roams about like a roaring
lion, seeking, *searching* whom he may devour. How-
ever, tossed about as I am, if I chuse (and who would
not chuse) to bind down with the crampets of atten-
tion, the brazen foundation of integrity, I may rear
up the superstructure of Independence, and from its
daring turrets, bid defiance to the storms of fate. And
is this not a "consummation devoutly to be wished?"

> "Thy spirit, Independence, let me share ;
> Lord of the lion-heart and eagle eye!
> Thy steps I follow with my bosom bare,
> Nor heed the storm that howls along the sky!"

Are not these noble verses? They are the introduc-
tion of Smollet's "Ode to Independence" : if you
have not seen the poem, I will send it to you. How
wretched is the man that hangs on by the favors of
the great ! To shrink from every dignity of man, at
the approach of a lordly piece of self-consequence,
who, amid all his tinsel glitter and stately hauteur, is
but a creature formed as thou art, and perhaps not so
well formed as thou art—came into the world a
puling infant as thou didst, and must go out of it,
as all men must, a naked corse ; * * *   R. B.

On 1st Sept. 1790.—Dr. Blacklock addressed a rhyming letter
to Burns along with the prospectus of a new periodical called
"The Bee," which was projected by Dr. James Anderson. He
introduced Dr. Anderson to his notice and requested the poet
to be an occasional contributor to that work, which commenced
in Dec. following, and kept itself afloat during three years.
Burns thus addressed Dr. Anderson on the subject :—

(¹) TO DR. JAMES ANDERSON, EDINBURGH.

(CROMEK. 1808.)

SIR,—I am much indebted to my worthy friend,
Dr. Blacklock, for introducing me to a gentleman of
Dr. Anderson's celebrity ; but when you do me the
honor to ask my assistance in your proposed publica-
tion, alas ! Sir, you might as well think to cheapen
a little honesty at the sign of an Advocate's wig, or
humility under the Geneva band.   I am a miserable
hurried devil, worn to the marrow in the friction of
holding the noses of the poor publicans to the grind-
stone of the Excise ! and like Milton's Satan, for
private reasons, am forced "to do what yet tho'
damn'd 1 would abhor;" and, except a couplet or
two of honest execration,   * * *   R. B.

(¹) TO MISS H. CRAIK, ARBIEGLAND.

(CURRIE, 1800.)

ELLISLAND, *Aug.* 1790.*

MADAM,—Some rather unlooked-for accidents have
prevented me from doing myself the honor of a second
visit to Arbiegland, as I was so hospitably invited,
and so positively meant to have done.   However, I
still hope to have that pleasure before the busy
months of harvest begin.

I inclose you two of my late pieces, as some kind
of return for the pleasure I have received in perusing

---

* In Dr. Currie's edition this letter is dated " August 1793," upon what author-
ity we know not. Burns transcribed it into Capt. Riddell's collection of his let-
ters, where most distinctly the poet has dated it " 1789 or 90." The poet's refer-
ence to harvest occupations seems to identify this letter with the Ellisland
period. Currie has also taken liberties with the structure of some of the sen-
tences, which we here restore. Arbiegland is in the stewartry of Kirkcudbright.

a certain MS. volume of poems in the possession of Captain Riddell. To repay one' with an *old song* is a proverb, whose force you, Madam, I know will not allow. What is said of illustrious descent is, I believe, equally true of a talent for poesy ; none ever despised it who had any pretensions to it. It is often a train of thought of mine when I am disposed to be melancholy—the fates and characters of the rhyming tribe. There is not among all the martyrologies ever penned, so rueful a narrative as the lives of the poets. In the comparative view of wretches, the criterion is not what they are doomed to suffer, but how they are formed to bear. Take a being of our kind, give him a stronger imagination and a more delicate sensibility, which between them will ever engender a more ungovernable set of passions than are the usual lot of man ; implant in him an irresistible impulse to some idle vagary, such as arranging wild flowers in fantastical nosegays, tracing the grasshopper to his haunt by his chirping song, watching the frisks of the little minnows in the sunny pool, or hunting after the intrigues of wanton butterflies—in short, send him adrift after some pursuit which shall eternally mislead him from the paths of lucre, and yet curse him with a keener relish than any man living for the pleasures that lucre can purchase ; lastly, fill up the measure of his woes by bestowing on him a spurning sense of his own dignity, and you have created a wight nearly as miserable as a poet. To you, Madam, I need not recount the fairy pleasures the muse bestows to counterbalance this catalogue of evils. Bewitching poesy is like bewitching woman ; she has in all ages been accused of misleading mankind from the counsels of wisdom and the paths of prudence, involving them in difficulties, baiting them with poverty, branding them with infamy, and plunging them in the whirling vortex of ruin ; yet, where is

the man but must own that all our happiness on
earth is not worth the name—that even the holy her-
mit's solitary prospect of paradisaical bliss is but the
glitter of a northern sun rising over a frozen region,
compared with the many pleasures, the nameless rap-
tures that we owe to the lovely Queen of the heart
of Man !   R. B.

(¹) TO MR. DAVID NEWALL, WRITER, DUMFRIES.

(CHAMBERS, 1852.)

[*Sep.* 1790.]

Dᴿ. Sɪʀ,—Enclosed is a state of the account be-
tween you and me and James Halliday respecting the
drain.   I have stated it at 20*d*. per rood, as, in fact
even at that, they have not the wages they ought to
have had, and I cannot for the soul of me see a poor
devil a loser at my hand.

Humanity, I hope, as well as Charity, will cover a
multitude of sins, a mantle, of which — between you
and me—I have some little need.   I am, Sir, yours
                                    R. B.

(⁷) TO ROBT. GRAHAM, ESQ., OF FINTRY.

(CHAMBERS, 1856.)

Dᴜᴍꜰʀɪᴇꜱ. Gʟᴏʙᴇ Iɴɴ, 4*th Sep.* 1790.

Sɪʀ,—The very kind letter you did me the honor
to write me reached me just as I was setting in to
the whirlpool of an Excise-fraud court, from the vor-
tex of which I am just emerged — Heaven knows, in
a very unfit situation to do justice to the workings
of my bosom when I sit down to write to the

' Friend of my life, true patron of my rhymes.'

As my division consists of ten large parishes, and I am sorry to say, hitherto very carelessly surveyed, I had a good deal of business for the Justices; and I believe my decreet* will amount to between fifty and sixty pounds. I took, I fancy, rather a new way with my frauds; I recorded every defaulter, but at the court I myself begged off every poor body that was unable to pay, which seeming candor gave me so much implicit credit with the honorable Bench, that, with high compliments, they gave me such ample vengeance on the rest, that my *decreet* is double the amount of any Division in the district.

I am going either to give up or subset my farm directly. I have not liberty to subset; but if my master will grant it me, I propose giving it, just as I have it myself, to an industrious fellow, a near relation of mine. Farming, in this place in which I live, would just be a livelihood to a man who would be the greatest drudge in his own family, so is no object; and living here hinders me from that knowledge in the Excise which it is absolutely necessary for me to attain.

I did not like to be an incessant beggar from you. A port-division I wish if possible, to get; my kind, my funny friend, Captain Grose, offered to interest Mr. Brown, and perhaps Mr. Wharton for me : a very handsome opportunity offered of getting Mr. Corbet, supervisor-general, to pledge every service in his power; and then I was just going to acquaint you with what I had done, or rather, what was done for me; that as all have their own particular friends to serve, you might find less obstacle in what, I assure you, Sir, I constantly count on—your wishes and endeavors to be of service to me. As I had an eye to

---

* This "decreet" was the amount adjudicated to him, in shape of reward as informer against convicted offenders, in course of a given time. No bad perquisite for one year.

III.   X

getting on the examiner's list, if attainable by me, I was going to ask you if it would be of any service to try the interest of some great, and some *very* great folks, to whom I have the honor to be known—I mean in the way of a Treasury warrant. But much as early impressions have given me of the horrors of spectres, &c., still I would face the arch-fiend, in Miltonic pomp, at the head of all his legions, and hear that infernal shout which blind John says "tore hell's concave," rather than crawl in, a dust-licking petitioner, before the lofty presence of a mighty man, and bear, amid all the mortifying pangs of self-annihilation, the swelling consequence of his d——d state, and the cold monosyllables of his hollow heart!

It was in view of trying for a port, that I asked Collector Mitchell to get me appointed, which he has done, to a vacant foot-walk in Dumfries. If ever I am so fortunate as to be called out to do business as a supervisor, I would then choose the north of Scotland; but until that Utopian period, I own I have some wayward feelings of appearing as a simple gauger in a country where I am only known by fame. Port-Glasgow, Greenock, or Dumfries ports would, in the meantime, be my ultimatum.

I enclose you a tribute I have just been paying to the memory of my friend, Matthew Henderson, whom I daresay you must have known! I had acknowledged your goodness sooner, but for want of time to transcribe the poem. Poor Matthew? I can forgive Poverty for hiding virtue and piety. They are not only plants that flourish best in the shade, but they also produce their sacred fruits, more especially for another world; but when the haggard beldam throws her invidious veil over wit, spirit, &c.,—but I trust another world will cast light on the subject.

I have the honor to be, Sir, your deeply obliged and very humble serv'.   ROBᵀ. BURNS.

(¹) TO ALEX. FERGUSSON, ESQ., J. P.

(CHAMBERS, 1856.)

GLOBE INN, Noon, Wednesday, [Sep. 1790.]

Blessed be he that kindly doth
The poor man's case consider.

I HAVE sought you all over the town, good Sir, to learn what you have done, or what can be done, for poor Robie Gordon. The hour is at hand when I must assume the execrable office of whipper-in to the blood-hounds of Justice, and must let loose the carrion sons of * * * on poor Robie. I think you can do something to save the unfortunate man, and am sure, if you can, you will. I know that Benevolence is supreme in your bosom, and has the first voice in, and last check on, all you do; but that insidious * * * Politics, may * * * the honest cully Attention, until the practicable moment of doing good is no more. I have the honor to be, Sir, your obliged, humble servant.   ROBᵀ. BURNS.

The foregoing letter forms an apt illustration of "the business before the Justices," which the poet refers to in his long letter to Mr. Graham. In the Burns Monument at Edinburgh is preserved another illustration of the same: but displaying the poet's conscientious fidelity in the interests of the Excise, by refusing to cover real offenders or to connive at fraud. Thomas Johnston, a farmer at Mirecleugh, had been convicted and fined £5 by the Justices for making fifty-four bushels of malt, "without entry, notice, or licence." The convicted party lodged a reclaiming appeal to the Quarter Sessions, and Burns, as the informing officer, was requested to state in writing his answers to Johnston's exculpatory allegations, and this he did as follows. The letter to Collector Mitchell is on the same subject.

ANSWER TO THE PETITION OF THOMAS JOHNSTON.

(CHAMBERS, 1852.)

[*Sep.* 1790.]

1. Whether the Petitioner has been in use formerly to malt all his grain at one operation, is foreign to the purpose : this last season he certainly malted his crop at four or five operations ; but be that as it may, Mr. J. ought to have known that by express act of parliament no malt, however small the quantity, can be legally manufactured until previous entry be made in writing of all the ponds, barns, floors, &c., so as to be used before the grain can be put to steep.   In the Excise entry-books for the division, there is not a syllable of T. J.'s name for a number of years bygone.

2. True it is that Mr. Burns, on his first ride, in answer to Mr. J.'s question anent the conveying of the notices, among other ways pointed out the sending it by post as the most eligible method, but at the same time added this express clause, and to which Mr. Burns is willing to make faith : "At the same time, remember, Mr. J., that the notice is at your risk until it reach me!"   Further, when Mr. Burns came to the Petitioner's kiln, there was a servant belonging to Mr. J. ploughing at a very considerable distance from the kiln, who left his plough and three horses without a driver, and came into the kiln, which Mr. B. thought was rather a suspicious circumstance, as there was nothing so extraordinary in an Excise-officer going into a legal malt-floor as to make him leave three horses yoked to a plough in the distant middle of a moor.   This servant, on being repeatedly questioned by Mr. Burns, could not tell when the malt was put to steep, when it was taken out, &c.—in short, was

determined to be entirely ignorant of the affair. By and by, Mr. J.'s son came in ; and on being questioned as to the steeping, taking out of the grain, &c., Mr. J., junior, referred me to this said servant, this ploughman, who, he said, must remember it best, as having been the principal actor in the business. The lad *then*, having gotten his cue, circumstantially recollected all about it.

All this time, though I was telling the son and servant the nature of the premunire they had incurred, though they pleaded for mercy keenly, the affair of the notice having been sent never once occurred to them, not even the son, who is said to have been the bearer. This was a stroke reserved for, and worthy of the gentleman himself. As to Mrs. Kelloch's oath, it proves nothing. She did, indeed, depone to a line being left for me at her house, which said line miscarried. It was a sealed letter ; she could not tell whether it was a malt-notice or not ; she could not even condescend on the month, nor so much as the season of the year. The truth is, T. J. and his family being Seceders, and consequently coming every Sunday to Thornhill Meeting-house, they were a good conveyance for the several malsters and traders in their neighborhood to transmit to post their notices, permits, &c.

But why all this tergiversation? It was put to the Petitioner in open court, after a full investigation of the cause : "Was he willing to swear that he meant no fraud in the matter?" And the Justices told him, that if he swore, he would be assoilzied, otherwise he should be fined ; still the Petitioner, after ten minutes' consideration, found his conscience unequal to the task, and declined the oath.

Now, indeed, he says he is willing to swear ; he has been exercising his conscience in private, and will perhaps stretch a point. But the fact to which he is

to swear was equally and in all parts known to him
on that day when he refused to swear as to-day :
nothing can give him further light as to the inten-
tion of his mind, respecting his meaning or not mean-
ing a fraud in the affair.   No time can cast further
light on the present resolves of the mind ; but time
will reconcile, and has reconciled many a man to that
iniquity which he at first abhorred.

(¹) TO COLLECTOR MITCHELL, DUMFRIES.

(CUNNINGHAM, 1834.)

ELLISLAND, [*Sep.* 1790.]

SIR,—I shall not fail to wait on Captain Riddell
to-night—I wish and pray that the goddess of Justice
herself would appear to-morrow among our hon. gen-
tlemen, merely to give them a word in their ear that
mercy to the thief is injustice to the honest man.
For my part I have galloped over my ten parishes
these four days, until this moment that I am just
alighted, or rather, that my poor jackass-skeleton of a
horse has let me down ; for the miserable devil has
been on his knees half a score of times within the last
twenty miles, telling me in his own way, "Behold,
am not I thy faithful jade of a horse, on which thou
hast ridden these many years ! "

In short, Sir, I have broke my horse's wind, and
almost broke my own neck, besides some injuries in
a part that shall be nameless, owing to a hard-hearted
stone of a saddle.   I find that every offender has so
many great men to espouse his cause, that I shall not
be surprised if I am committed to the stronghold of
the law to-morrow for insolence to the dear friends
of the gentlemen of the country.   I have the honor
to be, Sir, your obliged and obedient humble

ROBᵗ. BURNS.

Mr. Ramsay of Auchtertyre on Teith, communicated to Dr. Currie an incident of this autumn which falls to be reproduced here. We gave it in the writer's own words :—

"I had an adventure with Burns in the year 1790, when passing through Dumfriesshire, on a tour to the South, with Dr. Stewart of Luss. Seeing him pass quickly near Closeburn, I said to my companion, 'that is Burns.' On coming to the inn, the ostler told us he would be back in a few hours to grant permits : that where he met with anything seizable, he was no better than any other gauger ; in everything else, that he was perfectly a gentleman. After leaving a note to be delivered to him on his return, I proceeded to his house, being curious to see his Jean, &c. I was much pleased with his *uxor Sabina qualis*,* and the poet's modest mansion, so unlike the habitation of ordinary rustics. In the evening he suddenly bounced in upon us. and said, as he entered, 'I come (to use the words of Shakespeare) stewed in haste.' In fact, he had ridden incredibly fast after receiving my note. We fell into conversation directly, and soon got into the *mare magnum* of poetry. He told me that he had now gotten a story for a Drama, which he was to call 'Rob Macquechan's Elshon,' from a popular story of Robert Bruce being defeated on the water of Caern, when the heel of his boot having loosened in his flight, he applied to Robert Macquechan to fix it ; who, to make sure, ran his awl two inches up the King's heel. We were now going on at a great rate. when Mr. Stewart popped in his head, which put a stop to our discourse that had become very interesting. Yet in a little while it was resumed, and such was the force and versatility of the bard's genius, that he made the tears run down Mr. Stewart's cheeks, albeit unused to the poetic strain.

"From that time we met no more, and I was grieved at the reports of him afterwards. Poor Burns ! we shall hardly ever see his like again. He was in truth, a sort of comet in literature, irregular in its motions, which did not do good proportioned to the blaze of light it displayed."

---

* Horace V. Ode 2.

EXCISE ANECDOTES.

[As we have already given one or two anecdotes, illustrative of Burns as a practical Exciseman, we are reminded of a few more illustrative of the man.]

In consequence of official information, Burns was ordered to make some investigation into the doings of a certain canny old woman called "Janet," in the parish of Holywood, who was charged with serving thirsty souls on Sundays with a stronger beverage than treacle-beer, under pretence of selling some home-brewed article that was in great request among her customers. When Burns arrived one day, she, not knowing him, asked if it was a glass of home-brewed he wanted. To her surprise, he answered that he could not drink such wishy-washy stuff, and would prefer something with more smeddum in it. She instantly suspected his errand, and in her trepidation cried out "Mercy on us! are ye an Exciseman! God help me, man, ye'll surely no inform on a puir auld body like me, as I hae nae other means o' leevin than sellin my drap o' home-brew'd to decent folk that come to Holywood Kirk." Burns at once put her fears to rest (concludes our respected authority) by patting her on the shoulder while he made the almost heavenly reply—"Janet, Janet, sin awa there, and I'll protect ye!"

Cunningham assures us that against the regular smugglers, the looks of Burns were stern, and his hand was heavy, while to the poor country dealer he was mild and lenient. As an instance of the latter he tells that "the poet and a brother exciseman one day suddenly entered a widow woman's shop in Dunscore, and made a seizure of smuggled tobacco. 'Jenny,' said Burns, 'I expected this would be the upshot; here, Lewars, take a note of the number of rolls as I count them. Now Jock, did ye ever hear an auld wife numbering her threads before check-reels were invented? Thou's ane, an' thou's ane, an' thou's ane, a' out—listen!' As he handed out the rolls, he went on with his enumeration, but dropping every second roll into Janet's lap. Lewars took the desired note with much gravity, and saw, as if he saw not, the merciful conduct of his companion.

The late Professor Gillespie of St. Andrews remembered seeing Burns one August Fair-day, in the village of Thornhill, where a poor woman (Kate Watson) had, for one day, taken up the public-house trade without licence; "I saw the poet enter her door and anticipated nothing short of an immediate seizure of a certain greybeard* and barrel, which to my personal knowledge, contained the contraband commodities our bard was in search of. A nod, accompanied by a significant movement of the forefinger, brought Kate to the doorway or trance, and I was near enough to hear the following words distinctly uttered: "Kate, are you mad? Don't you know that the Supervisor and I will be in upon you in the course of forty minutes? Good-by t'ye at present." Burns was in the street and in the midst of the crowd in an instant, and I had access to know that the friendly hint was not neglected. It saved a poor widow from a fine of several pounds, for committing a quarterly offence by which the Revenue was probably subject to an annual loss of five shillings." †

The late Joseph Train also communicated an anecdote of the same nature as those above recorded, complimentary enough to an exciseman's humanity, but not quite compatible with his fidelity as a revenue officer: "Jean Dunn, a suspected contraband trader in Kirkpatrick-Durham observing Burns and Robertson (another exciseman) approaching her house on the morning of a Fair-day, slipped out at the back door, apparently to avoid scrutiny, leaving in the house only a hired assistant, and her own child, a daughter. 'Has there been any brewing for the Fair here to-day?' demanded one of the officers. 'O no, sir,' was the reply of the servant, 'we hae nae license for that.' 'That's no true,' exclaimed the child, 'the muckle kist is fu' o' the bottles o' yill that my mother sat up brewing for the Fair.' 'Does that bird speak?' said Robertson, pointing to one hanging in a cage. 'There's no use for another speaking-bird here,' said Burns, 'while that little lassie is so good at it. We are in a hurry just now; but as we return from the Fair, we'll examine the muckle kist.' Of course when they returned the kist did not correspond with the lassie's account of it."

The foregoing wreath of anecdotes is crowned with the allegation that the poet's dog, "Thurlow," was trained to go before him into the premises of revenue defaulters and apprise the inmates of his approach. This he did by shaking his head and rattling his loose brass collar, on which was engraved the legend—"Robert Burns, Poet and Exciseman."

---

* Greybeard is a large bottle or demijohn.
† Edinburgh Literary Journal, 1829.

(¹) TO CRAUFORD TAIT, ESQ., W.S., EDINBURGH.

(CROMEK, 1808.)

ELLISLAND, 15*th* *Oct.* 1790.

DEAR SIR,—Allow me to introduce to your acquaintance the bearer, Mr. William Duncan, a friend of mine, whom I have long known, and long loved. His father, whose only son he is, has a decent little property in Ayrshire, and has bred the young man to the law, in which department he comes up an adventurer to your good town. I shall give you my friend's character in two words : as to his head, he has talents enough, and more than enough, for common life ; as to his heart, when Nature had kneaded the kindly clay that composes it, she said—"I can no more."

You, my good Sir, were born under kinder stars ; but your fraternal sympathy, I well know, can enter into the feelings of the young man who goes into life with the laudable ambition to *do* something, and to *be* something among his fellow-creatures ; but whom the consciousness of friendless obscurity presses to the earth, and wounds to the soul !

Even the fairest of his virtues are against him. That independent spirit, and that ingenuous modesty —qualities inseparable from a noble mind—are, with the million, circumstances not a little disqualifying. What pleasure is in the power of the fortunate and the happy, by their notice and patronage, to brighten the countenance and glad the heart of such depressed youth ! I am not so angry with mankind for their deaf economy of the purse—the goods of this world cannot be divided without being lessened—but why be a niggard of that which bestows bliss on a fellow-creature, yet takes nothing from our own means of enjoyment? We wrap ourselves up in the cloak of our own better-fortune, and turn away our eyes, lest the wants and woes of our brother-mortals should disturb the selfish apathy of our souls!

I am the worst hand in the world at asking a favor. That indirect address, that insinuating implication, which, without any positive request, plainly expresses your wish, is a talent not to be acquired at a plough-tail. Tell me then, for you can, in what periphrasis of language, in what circumvolution of phrase, I shall envelope, yet not conceal, this plain story.—"My dear Mr. Tait, my friend Mr. Duncan, whom I have the pleasure of introducing to you, is a young lad of your own profession, and a gentleman of much modesty and great worth. Perhaps it may be in your power to assist him in the, to him, important consideration of getting a place; but at all events, your notice and acquaintance will be a very great acquisition to him; and I dare pledge myself that he will never disgrace your favor."

You may possibly be surprised, Sir, at such a letter from me; 'tis, I own, in the usual way of calculating these matters, more than our acquaintance entitles me to; but my answer is short; Of all the men at your time of life whom I knew in Edinburgh, you are the most accessible on the side on which I have assailed you. You are very much altered indeed from what you were when I knew you, if generosity point the path you will not tread, or humanity call to you in vain.

As to myself, a being to whose interest I believe you are still a well-wisher; I am here, breathing at all times, thinking sometimes, and rhyming now and then. Every situation has its share of the cares and pains of life, and my situation I am persuaded has a full ordinary allowance of its pleasures and enjoyments.

My best compliments to your father and Miss Tait. If you have an opportunity, please remember me in the solemn league and covenant of friendship to Mrs. Lewis Hay. I am a wretch for not writing to her ; but I am so hackneyed with self-accusation in that way, that my conscience lies in my bosom with scarce the sensibility of an oyster in its shell. Where is Lady M'Kenzie? wherever she is, God bless her! I likewise beg leave to trouble you with compliments to Mr. Wm. Hamilton, Mrs. Hamilton and family, and Mrs. Chalmers, when you are in that country. Should you meet with Miss Nimmo, please remember me to her.   R. B.*

(³) TO PROF. DUGALD STEWART, EDINBURGH.

PER FAVOR OF CAPTAIN GROSE.

(DOUGLAS, 1877.)

[ELLISLAND, *Oct.* 1790.]

SIR,—I will be extremely happy if this letter shall have the honor of introducing you to Captain Grose, a gentleman whose acquaintance you told me you so much coveted. I inclose this to him, and should his pursuits lead him again to Ayrshire, and should his time, and (what I am sorry to say is more precarious) his health permit, I have no doubt but you will have the mutual pleasure of being acquainted. I am, &c.

R. B.

---

* The gentleman to whom the above letter is addressed was a son of Mr. John Tait of Harvieston, at whose abode, by the banks of the Devon, Burns spent several happy days in the autumn of 1787. Mr. Crauford Tait succeeded to the family estate at his father's death in 1800, and his sister, Miss Elizabeth Tait, noticed in the letter, died at Aberdona in 1802. On 17th June 1795, the poet's correspondent was married to Susan, the fourth daughter of Lord President, Sir Islay Campbell. She died in 1814, leaving a large family, of whom the eldest was the late John Tait, Sheriff of Perthshire, who died in 1877; and the fifth and youngest son was Archbishop of Canterbury, Archbibald Tait, D.D. (1877).

(¹) TO FRANCIS GROSE, ESQ., F.S.A.

(CROMEK, 1808.)

[*Oct.* 1790.]

SIR,—I believe among all our Scots literati you have not met with Professor Dugald Stewart, who fills the moral philosophy chair in the University of Edinburgh. To say that he is a man of the first parts, and, what is more, a man of the first worth, to a gentleman of your general acquaintance, and who so much enjoys the luxury of unencumbered freedom and undisturbed privacy, is not perhaps recommendation enough ; but when I inform you that Mr. Stewart's principal characteristic is your favorite feature — *that* sterling independence of mind which, though every man's right, so few men have the courage to claim, and fewer still the magnanimity to support ; when I tell you that, unseduced by splendor, and undisgusted by wretchedness, he appreciates the merits of the various actors in the great drama of life merely as they perform their parts—in short, he is a man after your own heart, and I comply with his earnest request in letting you know that he wishes above all things to meet with you. His house, Catrine, is within less than a mile of Sorn Castle, which you proposed visiting ; or if you could transmit him the enclosed, he would, with the greatest pleasure, meet you anywhere in the neighborhood. I write to Ayrshire to inform Mr. Stewart that I have acquitted myself of my promise. Should your time and spirits permit your meeting with Mr. Stewart, 'tis well ; if not, I hope you will forgive this liberty, and I have at least an opportunity of assuring you with what truth and respect, I am, Sir, your great admirer, and very humble servant,   R. B.

The previous editors of Burns's works have given an insufficient history of Captain Grose, and an altogether erroneous idea of the importance of the works with which he was connected. We, therefore, record a full list of the publications with which Captain Grose's name was associated. It will be seen from this list that a good many of them partake of the character of broad humor, and as we are undoubtedly indebted to the chance meeting of Burns with Grose, for his immortal "Tam O'Shanter," it will be seen that in more respects than in his girth of waist was he like Falstaff, who, as Jack has it, "was not only witty himself, but the cause of wit in others." We can easily conceive the effect of such a congenial soul on the impressible Poet ; it was like flint meeting steel.

The following list of publications will give a key to the prominent characteristics of the man :—

The Antiquities of England and Wales, 4 volumes. With a supplement, 2 volumes. London, 1773-1787. Super royal 4to, 6 volumes. This, the first edition, is the one most prized by collectors. The supplemental volumes are frequently wanting.

The Antiquities of England and Wales. London, Hooper, 1783. Imperial 8vo, 8 volumes.

The Antiquities of Scotland. London, 1789-1791. Imperial 8vo, 2 vols. Published at £6, 6s., large paper, in super royal 4to. Some copies have proof-plates, which are distinguishable by having the inscriptions in a hair-letter. Published at £8, 15s.

A Treatise on Ancient Armor and Weapons, illustrated by plates taken from the original armor in the Tower of London, and other Arsenals, Museums and Cabinets. London, 1786, 4to.

Military Antiquities respecting a History of the English Army, from the Conquest to the present time. London, 1786-1788, 4to, 2 volumes.

Military Antiquities, including the Ancient Armor. A new edition, with material additions and improvements. London, 1801, 4to, 2 volumes [published posthumously].

The Olio: being a collection of Humorous Essays, Dialogues, Letters, etc. London, 1792, 8vo [published posthumously].

The Grumbler: containing 16 Essays by the late Francis Grose, Esq., F.A.S. London, 1791, 12mo, pp. 71. This production was originally published in the English Chronicle. An improved edition will be found in the Olio.

Rules for drawing Caricatures, with an Essay on Comic Painting. London, 1788.

A Provincial Glossary, with a collection of local Proverbs and popular Superstitions. London, 1787, 8vo.

A Classical Dictionary of the Vulgar Tongue. London, 1785, 8vo. In this first edition are some words and explanations pointed out as rather indecent or indelicate, which in the later editions have been either omitted or softened.

A Guide to Health, Beauty, Riches and Honor. London, 1783, 8vo. 10s. 6d. A collection of the most remarkable advertisements of quacks, money-lenders, borough brokers, men for wives, women for husbands, conjurors, etc., with a humorous preface by Grose.

[WHILE printing this third volume, we have had sent us the fac-simile of an unpublished letter of Burns, the original of which is now in the possession of Mr. James Noble, 424 West 25th Street, New York ; the fly-leaf, on which the post address would appear, is lost, and the words which follow in brackets are torn from the edge which connected the fly-leaf.   *

Instead of being last in this volume, it should have been in its chronological place, and, on the receipt of the copy, we were inclined to altogether omit it, as unimportant ; but, after a careful study as to whom the letter could have been origin-ally addressed, we come to the conclusion that it must have been to Gavin Hamilton.   And it is curious for the following reason :

There is a restraint manifest throughout which can only be explained by the *feeling* which Burns no doubt carried forward against the precaution which Hamilton sought to secure in having Robert insure or guarantee the back indebtedness of Gilbert Burns on the Mossgiel lease (see letter to Hamilton 7th April 1788, page 166, *supra*).   The poet was a man of shrewd discernment, and would certainly resent Hamilton's sinking the friend in the lawyer, seeking in the flush of the Edinburgh success to exact a security which Robert Burns was under no obligation to give.   Two months only had elapsed since that episode, and though Burns no doubt, in settling at Ellisland, deemed it his duty to write to his old friend, it is so unlike the spontaneous manner of the Bard, that had it not been vouched for by his undoubted hand-writing, we would have rejected it as bogus.

That Burns subsequently got over his sore feeling against Gavin Hamilton is evident from his next letter to him, eleven months after, June 1789.   See page 285, *supra.*—G. G.]

(⁶) [TO GAVIN HAMILTON (?).]

(Here first published.)

ELLISLAND,* 14*th June* 1788.

THIS is now the third day, my dearest Sir, th[at I have] sojourned in these regions, and during these

---

* On pp. 179 and 180, *supra*, will be found two letters—one to Mrs. Dunlop and one to Robert Ainslie—the former dated 14th June, the latter 15th June. In the opening sentence of each he says, respectively: "This is my second," and "This is my third day." We would surmise that 15th June should have been the date of the above.—G. G.

th[ree days] you have occupied more of my thoughts than i[*n many*] weeks preceding : in Ayrshire I have several, [varia]tions of Friendship's Compass, here it points in[variab]ly to the Pole.—My Farm gives me a good man[y] uncouth Cares & Anxieties, but I hate the language [of] Complaint—Job or some one of his friends, says, "Why should a living man complain?"

What books are you reading or what is the subject of your thoughts, beside the great studies of your Profession? You said something about Religion in your last letter : I don't exactly remember what it was, as the letter is in Ayrshire, but I thought it not only prettily said but nobly thought.

Keep my old Direction, at Mauchline, till I inform myself of another.—Adieu,   ROBT. BURNS.

END OF VOL. III.

CPSIA information can be obtained at www.ICGtesting.com
Printed in the USA
LVOW071847280313

326546LV00009B/432/A

4/22   £10.